Believing God for the I...

BREAKTHROUGH
TO YOUR
MIRACLE

STUDY GUIDE

JASON
NOBLE

Breakthrough to Your Miracle:
Believing God for the Impossible—Study Guide
by Jason Noble

copyright © 2019, Jason Noble
ISBN: 9781950718009

CONTENTS

INTRODUCTION

Reflect and Discuss

Before you begin reading *Breakthrough to Your Miracle,* take a few minutes to reflect on what you want to get out of this book. Pray and ask the Holy Spirit to reveal to you any areas of your faith walk you'd like to strengthen or heal. Write your reflections below.

_____

_____

_____

_____

_____

Reflect and Discuss

We see miracles throughout the Old and New Testaments, pointing people to God so that they believe in and glorify Him. Miracles happen because we have a God of compassion and power. God is still in the miracle business today.

Respond

What do you truly believe about God's ability and will when it comes to doing miracles? Do you believe He does them today? Why or why not?

_____

_____

_____

_____

_____

If you could ask God for any miracle right now, what would it be?

_____

_____

_____

_____

_____

What is keeping you from fully believing that God can do the miracle you seek?

_____

_____

_____

_____

_____

What do you hope to get out of this book for your faith journey?

_____

_____

_____

_____

_____

Our walk with God is directly impacted by the friends and family sur-rounding us. Take a few moments to think about your current support system. Is there anyone you could go through this book together with, who could encourage you in your journey? Or maybe there's some-one you could ask to pray for and with you as explore God's miracu-lous works?

_____

_____

_____

_____

Perhaps you've already thought about and studied God's miracles. Do you have any reservations, questions, or concerns going into this study? What comes to mind as you consider asking God for a miracle?

Take a moment to write your unanswered questions below—those you hope to answer and address when you conclude this study.

_____

_____

_____

_____

_____

CHAPTER 1

GOD STILL BREAKS THROUGH

💡 Big Idea

A miracle is when God does something only God can do…when God chooses to reach down and intervene in the world He created.

▶️ Watch: Video Episode #1

📖 Read: Chapter 1 in *Breakthrough*

🎤 Reflect and Discuss

Many believers don't think that God still does miracles. This is due to the way we think about God, the way we think about life, or the way we want others to think about us. Pastor Jason writes, "Whether or not you believe God can do a miracle may well be the difference between whether or not you receive one."

📝 Respond

Which of the three reasons above is holding you back from believing in God's power to do miracles? Explain.

_____

_____

_____

_____

_____

Have you experienced a cultural pressure to act like you have it all together? What would it look like to give up maintaining this image?

_____

_____

_____

_____

_____

As believers, should we seem "normal" to the world? Why or why not?

_____

_____

_____

_____

_____

Reflect and Discuss

Many times, we don't see potential for a miracle—and miss out on the opportunity to see God move—because we aren't properly positioned for God to move on our behalf.

Respond

Look at the miracle that you wrote down earlier. Would you consider yourself positioned to receive this miracle? Why or why not (or are you unsure)?

_____

_____

_____

_____

_____

Pastor Jason writes, "Your problem is not your problem. Your problem is also not God." Have you been tempted to point the finger at God or at circumstances when things go awry? How can we shift this way of thinking?

_____

_____

_____

_____

_____

_____

How does it make you feel to know that God feels our pain, and at the same time, has the power to do something about it?

_____

_____

_____

_____

_____

CHAPTER 2

PLAY YOUR PART

💡 Big Idea

"Jesus not only asked for, or perhaps even required, faith; He also often asked people to participate in the needed miracle in some way."

▶ Watch: Video Episode #2

📖 Read: Chapter 2 in *Breakthrough*

🎙 Reflect and Discuss

Jesus chose to do miracles through people. God doesn't do miracles without human partnership. Because of this, it's paramount that we submit and cooperate with Him in the process.

_____

_____

_____

_____

Recall a time you've witnessed or heard about something miraculous. Who was it who told you about the miracle? Who were the people involved? Why do you think God chooses to do miracles through people?

_____

_____

_____

_____

Reread the passage in Mark 6 where Jesus was in his hometown. In your own words, how can our lack of belief or cooperation keep the power of God from operating in our lives?

_____

_____

_____

_____

Pastor Jason likens our part in the miraculous process to that of a catcher in baseball: we can't make the batter hit the ball our way; we can only position ourselves to be ready, in case he does. How does this analogy make you feel? Do you agree with it?

_____

_____

_____

_____

_____

🎙 Reflect and Discuss

Our part in the miraculous process is to believe and obey God. When crisis hits, we go to Jesus. Then, trusting Him for the outcome, we ask what He would have us do.

📄 Respond

Do you find it difficult to go to Jesus first during a crisis? Why or why not?

_____

_____

_____

_____

_____

Can you think of a time that you were obedient and saw God make an impact through you in someone else's life? Who has made a spiritual impact in your life?

_____

_____

_____

_____

_____

Is there a situation where you prayed and believed God for a miracle, but the result was not what you expected? How did that affect you?

_____

_____

_____

_____

_____

Jesus said, "Anyone who believes in me will do the same works I have done, and even greater works, because I am going to be with the Father" (John 14:12—14). Pastor Jason writes that every miracle begins with a crisis. What do these two insights imply for the life of the believer?

_____

_____

_____

_____

_____

GET CLOSE TO JESUS

💡 Big Idea

Jesus wants us to be honest about where we truly are. Only when we acknowledge the truth can we reach towards Him, demonstrating our faith in Him.

📺 Watch: Video Episode #3

📖 Read: Chapter 3 in *Breakthrough*

🎙️ Reflect and Discuss

In the story of the healed woman, we see that Jesus requires us to be honest about where we are. He gives us a miracle only after we've brought him the whole truth.

📝 Respond

Does being honest with God about where you are come naturally to you? Why or why not?

_____

_____

_____

_____

_____

_____

_____

_____

Jesus wants more than to simply perform miracles for us; He wants relationship with us. How does this make trusting Him easier? How does it make trusting Him harder?

_____

_____

_____

_____

_____

🎙️ Reflect and Discuss

The woman didn't simply walk up and touch Jesus; she had to fight her way through crowds, pushing and reaching for him. Her belief drove her to pursue Jesus relentlessly, despite what others would think about her.

📄 Respond

What situation in your life has been bad for so long that it's easy to believe it will always be that way? Ask Him to give you faith to know He can still bring change.

_____

_____

_____

_____

_____

How close do you feel to Jesus right now? Reflect on why that may be.

_____

_____

_____

_____

_____

What's holding you back right now from pursuing Jesus with all that you have? Is it the opinions of others? Insecurity? Fear? The loss of comfort?

_____

_____

_____

_____

_____

How can you get closer to Jesus this week? What does "reaching" for Him look like practically for you?

_____

_____

_____

_____

_____

CHAPTER 4

OVERCOMING FEAR

💡 Big Idea

We cannot live in both fear and faith at the same time. We will choose to believe God's Word, or we will give in to the lies of the enemy. That decision will determine whether or not we receive a miracle.

▶️ Watch: Video Episode #4

📖 Read: Chapter 4 in *Breakthrough*

🎙️ Reflect and Discuss

Pastor Jason writes that "desperation is a good thing." Though this may not be our natural perspective, there are some positive aspects of being desperately dependent on God.

📝 Respond

Have you found yourself in a desperate situation recently? How does this affect if, or in what way, you come to God?

_____

_____

_____

_____

_____

_____

_____

_____

What is your greatest fear, and why?

_____

_____

_____

_____

_____

How can you begin to make God your go-to when you feel desperate or afraid?

_____

_____

_____

_____

_____

⚑ Reflect and Discuss

Fear will hold back the healing power of Jesus; faith will release the healing power of Jesus. We are always operating in one of these two modes. Often, when we're living in faith, there will be those around us who are operating out of a place of fear. Whom we surround ourselves with can make all the difference.

📄 Respond

Sometimes, operating in faith means ignoring what other people say. Is there anyone you need to 'put out of the room' right now?

_____

_____

_____

_____

_____

What fearful thoughts creep into your mind naturally? Write them down, and make a prayerful commitment not to entertain a single one of them.

_____

_____

_____

_____

_____

Look at the thoughts you've written above. Surrender them to God and ask Him to reveal His truth—what He wants to give you to replace the fear. Write those truths down.

_____

_____

_____

_____

_____

What's a good strategy to help you begin choosing faith over fear when crisis arises? Is it memorizing a certain verse? Surrounding yourself with more faith-filled people?

_____

_____

_____

_____

_____

LIVE DESPERATE

💡 Big Idea

When we live desperately dependent on God, we position ourselves for a miracle. When we cry out to God, our focus remains on Him instead of our storm.

▶ Watch: Video Episode #5

📖 Read: Chapter 5 in *Breakthrough*

🎙 Reflect and Discuss

"When the righteous cry for help, the LORD hears and delivers them out of all their troubles. The LORD is near to the brokenhearted and saves the crushed in spirit."—Psalm 34:17-18

📝 Respond

What area of your life has felt desperate lately? Have you been ignoring any desperation?

_____

_____

_____

_____

_____

_____

_____

_____

How do you think you might call out to and experience God in the midst of that storm?

_____

_____

_____

_____

What you do when a storm comes says a lot about you. What's your default response to desperation?

_____

_____

_____

_____

⏺ Reflect and Discuss

Storms often take us beyond our ability, training, and experience. The disciples were experienced sailors, but felt desperately out of their league during the storm in Matthew 8. Their faith gave way to fear in the face of something bigger than they could handle.

📝 Respond

In what ways has your storm taken you beyond the depth of your experience or ability?

_____

_____

_____

_____

Pastor Jason writes, "We must cry out to God. Often we need to be desperate to do that." Do you see any positive aspects of your desperation? How can God use them?

_____

_____

_____

_____

_____

How can you prepare for future storms in your life?

_____

_____

_____

_____

_____

Storms come and go, but our desperation for God should not cease. How can you live a life desperate for God in both the good times and the bad?

_____

_____

_____

_____

_____

CHAPTER 6

BELIEVE BIG, PRAY BIG

💡 Big Idea

We must know God's promises, and the stories of His faithfulness, to know His heart. While we can't control the outcome of our prayers, we trust in His ability to do BIG things!

▶️ Watch: Video Episode #6

📖 Read: Chapter 6 in *Breakthrough*

🎙️ Reflect and Discuss

Sometimes God chooses to give us what we ask for in prayer. Sometimes, He chooses not to give it to us. Regardless of the outcome, we can trust His goodness and His will.

📝 Respond

How does your prayer life currently reflect your view of God? Do you pray big prayers? Or have you found yourself holding back? What does this say about your view of God?

_____

_____

_____

_____

_____

_____

_____

Have you found yourself trying to control the outcome of your prayers? How does it make you feel to know that we don't have control over what God does?

_____

_____

_____

_____

_____

In your own words, describe the difference between faith and belief, according to Pastor Jason.

_____

_____

_____

_____

_____

🎙 Reflect and Discuss

Our prayer life needs to be proactive, not reactive. When we prioritize prayer, we build our trust in God before the storm hits, and are ready to act in faith automatically when the time comes.

📝 Respond

Is your current prayer life more proactive or reactive? Explain.

_____

_____

_____

_____

_____

What is the Lord saying to you when it comes to building your belief? Are there areas in which you currently have strong belief? What about unbelief?

_____

_____

_____

_____

_____

List the big prayers you are praying right now. Write them down, and
track when and how God answers these prayers.

_____

_____

_____

_____

_____

Pastor Jason encourages believers to pray for specific outcomes, and
leave the details of HOW up to God. Taking the big prayers you listed
above, write specific outcomes you want to pray for. Then, lift up those
outcomes to God, and trust His good, pleasing, and perfect will.

_____

_____

_____

_____

_____

CHAPTER 7

SPEAK LIFE

💡 Big Idea

There is immense spiritual power in speaking life. When we speak God's Word, proclaimingHis promises, we position ourselves for a miracle.

▶️ Watch: Video Episode #7

📖 Read: Chapter 7 in *Breakthrough*

🎙️ Reflect and Discuss

We absorb and reflect whatever we are most exposed to in our day-to-day lives. We can't entertain praise and negative thinking at the same time. We need to fill our hearts with God's Word, so that it overflows into every area of our lives.

📝 Respond

Luke 6:45 says, "A good man brings good things out of the good stored up in his heart, and an evil man brings evil things out of the evil stored up in his heart. For the mouth speaks what the heart is full of." Based on what comes out of your mouth most often, are you meditating on God's truth more, or on negative thinking?

_____

_____

_____

_____

_____

What are you listening to that is bolstering your faith in God and His promises? What positive voices are present in your life?

_____

_____

_____

_____

_____

The first step to having a heart overflowing with truth is filling, or preparing, your heart. How can you practically go about filling your heart with God's truth this week?

_____

_____

_____

_____

_____

🎙 Reflect and Discuss

Feelings are not a good barometer of reality. Often, what we see, feel, and hear become what we believe. Ezekiel saw dry bones, and chose to speak life over them. The centurion saw a hopeless situation, but chose to place his faith in Jesus' ability to bring life. When we shift our focus from our feelings to God's power, our faith grows exponentially, positioning us for a miracle.

📑 Respond

The second step to having a heart overflowing with truth is guarding your heart. What feelings, or voices, are contradicting God's truth in your life?

_____

_____

_____

_____

_____

Perhaps what we ask God for isn't necessarily in line with His Word. Praying for a miracle isn't a "blab-it-and-grab-it" affair. Reflect on your prayer life lately. What have you asked for that directly aligns with God's Word?

_____

_____

_____

_____

_____

Have you asked for anything, or asked with motives, that doesn't line up with God's Word?

_____

_____

_____

_____

_____

Feelings will lie to us, but God's Word is a true foundation for assessing life's events. How can you prioritize His truth over your feelings moving forward? Take a few minutes to pray that God will reorient your heart to believe Him above everything else.

_____

_____

_____

_____

_____

CHAPTER 8

SURROUND YOURSELF

💡 Big Idea

To position ourselves for a miracle, we need to surround ourselves with faith-filled friends. Who is carrying you to Jesus? Who are you carrying to Him? The answers to these questions will greatly affect your faith.

⏯️ Watch: Video Episode #8

📖 Read: Chapter 8 in *Breakthrough*

🎤 Reflect and Discuss

The friends of the paralyzed man enabled him to get to Jesus. Their faith led them to overcome setbacks, obstacles, and a literal ceiling. They didn't stop when things seemed impossible, but held out hope.

📝 Respond

Who do you have in your life who displays this kind of faith? How have they demonstrated their trust in God during setbacks and challenges?

_____

_____

_____

_____

_____

_____

_____

Can you recall a time recently that you carried a friend during a rough time? If so, what got you through that time? If not, what can you do to carry someone else who's struggling right now?

_____

_____

_____

_____

As Pastor Jason writes, we live in a Do-It-Yourself culture that glorifies self-reliance. What does the Bible say about this? What does the story of the paralyzed man teach us?

_____

_____

_____

_____

_____

🎙 Reflect and Discuss

The paralyzed man and his friends hoped for a physical healing. Jesus did this, but he also addressed the more important issue of the man's spiritual condition. By attending to both needs, Jesus healed him holistically.

📄 Respond

Are your prayers more centered on physical healing, or spiritual healing? How can you incorporate the other kind of healing into your prayer life?

_____

_____

_____

_____

_____

Jesus deeply cares about our physical needs. Read Matthew 6:26-34. How does this knowledge make you feel? What physical needs can you lift up to Him in faith today?

_____

_____

_____

_____

_____

Jesus wants to heal us spiritually, so that we can be with Him and have freedom from sin. This is what he did for the paralyzed man. Have you accepted Jesus's spiritual salvation? If you have what areas of spiritual healing do you still need to ask for? If you haven't, what's holding you back?

_____

_____

_____

_____

_____

How can you friends support you in praying for your physical and spiritual needs? How can you support others?

_____

_____

_____

_____

_____

CHAPTER 9

KEEP YOUR EYES OPEN

Big Idea

We have the propensity to be both physically and spiritually blind. God's miracles aren't one-size-fits-all. We must keep our eyes open to see how He's moving, and what He's up to, even if it defies our expectations.

Watch: Video Episode #9

Read: Chapter 9 in *Breakthrough*

Reflect and Discuss

God is a creative miracle-worker. His sovereign ways are higher than ours, and so He often doesn't do things how or when we would like. Sometimes, this causes us to miss what God is doing, and we assume He isn't doing anything at all. But God is always at work in the lives of believers.

Respond

Have you been tempted to try to reproduce a formula in the Bible to get a miracle? If so, explain.

_____

_____

_____

_____

_____

How has God defied your expectations in the last year? How has this stretched your faith? What good things have come from it?

_____

_____

_____

_____

_____

Is it possible that God won't give you what you're asking for right now? What would happen if He didn't? Could this be better for His glory and your good?

_____

_____

_____

_____

_____

✒ Reflect and Discuss

God often does His best work in stages. This is why keeping a prayer journal is so important. When we reflect back on what God has done in our past, it builds our faith to trust Him with our present and our future.

🗎 Respond

Recall a time that God came through for you in a big way. What were the odds stacked against you? Did He surprise you with how He answered your prayers and got you through it?

_____

_____

_____

_____

_____

Is it possible God has been answering your current prayers in stages? Have you overlooked answered prayer because of this?

_____

_____

_____

_____

_____

Why is it important to remember that God's timing might be different from your timing?

_____

_____

_____

_____

What is the most important thing you can do while waiting for a miracle?

_____

_____

_____

_____

If you haven't already, start a prayer journal. Jot down a few requests you will add, and commit to surrendering the results to the Lord to answer, in His timing.

_____

_____

_____

_____

_____

CHAPTER 10

DO BATTLE

💡 Big Idea

Following Jesus means we agree to go to the battlefront and face the spiritual forces of darkness. There's a war raging around us that we do not see. Only through our connection to God can we be victorious against the evil one.

📺 Watch: Video Episode #10

📖 Read: Chapter 10 in *Breakthrough*

🎤 Reflect and Discuss

We tend to view our problems as primarily physical in nature. However, there is an unseen side to things—the spiritual side. The way we see our problems will determine how well we are able to do battle in the spiritual realm.

📝 Respond

Do you tend to view your problems as physical, or spiritual? Why do you think that is?

_____

_____

_____

_____

_____

_____

Pastor Jason writes, "When you start praying for a miracle, you are entering dangerous territory." How does this perspective affect the way we come to God with requests for a miracle?

_____

_____

_____

_____

_____

2 Corinthians 10:3-4 says, "For though we live in the world, we do not wage war as the world does. The weapons we fight with are not the weapons of the world. On the contrary, they have divine power to demolish strongholds." What fear needs to be demolished in your life? How will you take hold of this divine power to get rid of fear?

_____

_____

_____

_____

_____

🎙 Reflect and Discuss

By putting on the spiritual armor of God, we proactively strategize to defeat the enemy. We also become more aware of the enemy's strategy to pull us away from God. This has to be a daily practice, so we can walk confidently and protected into the day's spiritual battles.

📑 Respond

Read Ephesians 6:10-18. List the parts of the armor of God, and in your own words, describe what each one does for the believer.

_____

_____

_____

_____

_____

Do you intentionally put on the armor of God regularly? How could you make this part of your routine?

_____

_____

_____

_____

_____

Satan has a strategy to take you out. Rather than being reactive, we must be proactive. Keeping the armor of God in mind, reflect on what the devil's strategy might include.

_____

_____

_____

_____

_____

Ask God to reveal His strategy to give you the victory over the enemy. What does it include?

_____

_____

_____

_____

_____

CHAPTER 11

KNOW JESUS AND MAKE HIM KNOWN

○ Big Idea

The reasons we ask for miracles are sometimes more important than the miracles themselves. We can't ask from selfish motives; we must ask for miracles that bring us closer to Jesus and make Him known to others. God's presence must mean more to us than God's presents.

▶ Watch: Video Episode #11

📖 Read: Chapter 11 in *Breakthrough*

🎙 Reflect and Discuss

Too many people know about Jesus, but don't have a relationship with Him. It's easy to confuse the two, and assume that these people are true believers. But Jesus knows the difference. He doesn't want someone who can recite facts about Him, but someone who has a personal love relationship with Him.

📝 Respond

Have you settled for simply knowing about Jesus in some areas, instead of inviting Him into those areas? If so, when?

_____

_____

_____

_____

How can you practically commit to getting closer to Jesus this week?

_____

_____

_____

_____

_____

When we spend time with Jesus, we find that His presence is even better than His blessings. In your own words, describe the difference between seeking God's face and seeking God's hand.

_____

_____

_____

_____

_____

The world will tell you that what you truly want can be found outside of God. Sometimes, we have a hard time remembering that He is what our hearts truly long for. How can you remind yourself of this truth on a daily basis?

_____

_____

_____

_____

_____

♀ Reflect and Discuss

Pastor Jason writes, "Miracles are signs that point people to Jesus that they might believe, and that, by believing, find life in Him." The miracles Jesus performed revealed Himself to people, and drew them in closer. We must ensure that this is our purpose when asking for a miracle, as well.

📝 Respond

How did the miracles of Jesus help people know Him more?

_____

_____

_____

_____

_____

Be honest with yourself: why do you want the miracle you seek? What's your motivation? Pray and ask the Holy Spirit to reveal your heart, and purify your motives.

_____

_____

_____

_____

_____

"In eternity, the miracles will not really matter. How you knew and loved God will." In light of this thought, what would you do if you didn't get the miracle you are asking for?

_____

_____

_____

_____

_____

CHAPTER 12

WHEN GOD DOESN'T GIVE YOU WHAT YOU WANT

💡 Big Idea

We don't always get the miracles we ask for. We often want to know why this is. The more important question, though, is how we will respond when this happens. In the end, we must trust that He knows best, and keeping walking with Him.

▶️ Watch: Video Episode #12

📖 Read: Chapter 12 in *Breakthrough*

🎙️ Reflect and Discuss

Getting your miracle isn't always God's plan. He has always been capable of doing miracles, but has not always done what people expect Him to do. Sometimes, the best miracle is not getting the miracle that we prayed for in the first place.

📄 Respond

Have you ever prayed for a miracle that God didn't give to you? How did that make you feel?

_____

_____

_____

_____

_____

If you answered "yes" above, have you seen any good things come out of that situation?

_____

_____

_____

_____

If you answered "no" above, when was the last time that you prayed for a miracle? How long did it take to see it come to pass?

_____

_____

_____

_____

_____

Based on the story of Christ's death and resurrection, in your own words, explain why not getting the miracle we want is sometimes in God's best plan.

_____

_____

_____

_____

_____

🎙️ Reflect and Discuss

When we don't get the miracle we asked for, it's imperative that we keep hanging onto God. The temptation can be to embrace disappointment or frustration with Him. However, He is our only lifeline during this time, and hardship is a unique place to experience His love in new ways.

📖 Respond

"We can be disappointed with God or we can be disappointed without God?" Which of these do you tend to choose automatically when you feel hurt or disappointed?

_____

_____

_____

_____

_____

_____

Do you see disappointments as a grace disguised? Why or why not?

_____

_____

_____

_____

_____

_____

How can you practically hang onto God during times of hardship and trial? How can you demonstrate that trust to others?

_____

_____

_____

_____

_____

_____

℘ Reflect and Discuss

When we don't get the miracle we ask for, we also must choose to give God the benefit of the doubt. When we're not with Him for his gifts, but for Himself, we can trust Him even when we don't get what we want.

🖹 Respond

How can you decide, before crisis hits, what you believe about God? How can you prepare yourself to stand firm in your faith when disappointment and desperation hit?

_____

_____

_____

_____

_____

Take some time to pray and read Scriptures that tell what God says about Himself. Write down the characteristics of God you want to remember during the hard times.

_____

_____

_____

_____

We are in the middle of a story, and we don't have all the information yet. In the end, there will always be a great ending. For now, we go through trials and hardships as part of the Christian life. Have you found that you grow more during hard times, or during good times? Is it possible that the hard times have, in some ways, been the good times?

_____

_____

_____

_____

What strategy have you developed while reading this book for positioning yourself for a miracle? How will you go about practically implementing that strategy on a daily basis?

_____

_____

_____

_____

"We are invited to name our hopelessness and to let ourselves be soaked, enfolded, immersed in the counter-story of Jesus' life, death and resurrection, because they are the basis for hope."

—John Goldingday

APPENDIX

🎙 Reflect and Discuss

The biggest miracle we can ask for, and the one that was granted before we asked for it, is a way of taking our sin away so we can have life with God. Jesus dying on the cross and rising from the dead was the greatest miracle of all.

📝 Respond

How does this truth alter your perspective on God doing the miraculous?

_____

_____

_____

_____

_____

Read the Breakthrough Prayer below. Take a few moments and pray that God would align your heart with His truth and His will. Make this prayer your declaration of faith and trust in God to do the best thing for His glory and your good. Surrender the results of your prayers to Him, and know that, whether or not He does the miraculous, He can be fully trusted with every aspect of your life!

The Breakthrough Prayer

Holy Spirit, breathe life back into my home.
Holy Spirit, breathe life back into my relationships.
Holy Spirit, breathe life back into my dreams.
Holy Spirit, breathe life back into my finances.
Holy Spirit, breathe life back into my family.
Holy Spirit, breathe life back into my church.
Holy Spirit, breathe life back into my life.
In the mighty name of Jesus, Amen!

M000266777

Global Bollywood

Global Bollywood

EDITED BY

*Anandam P. Kavoori and
Aswin Punathambekar*

New York University Press

NEW YORK AND LONDON

NEW YORK UNIVERSITY PRESS
New York and London
www.nyupress.org

© 2008 by New York University
All rights reserved

Library of Congress Cataloging-in-Publication Data
Global Bollywood / edited by Anandam P. Kavoori and
Aswin Punathambekar.
p.   cm.
Includes bibliographical references and index.
ISBN-13: 978-0-8147-4799-5 (pb : alk. paper)
ISBN-10: 0-8147-4799-X (pb : alk. paper)
ISBN-13: 978-0-8147-4798-8 (cl : alk. paper)
ISBN-10: 0-8147-4798-1 (cl : alk. paper)
1. Motion picture industry—India. 2. Motion pictures—India.
I. Kavoori, Anandam P. II. Punathambekar, Aswin.
PN1993.5.I8G53 2008
302.23'430954—dc22   2008010219

New York University Press books are printed on acid-free paper,
and their binding materials are chosen for strength and durability.
We strive to use environmentally responsible suppliers and materials
to the greatest extent possible in publishing our books.

Manufactured in the United States of America

c 10 9 8 7 6 5 4 3 2 1
p 10 9 8 7 6 5 4 3 2 1

Contents

Introduction

Global Bollywood

Aswin Punathambekar and
Anandam Kavoori

Aishwarya Rai made it to the cover of *Time* magazine, and even taught Oprah Winfrey and her viewers to wear a sari; The Simpsons ended their trip to India with a dance set to a Hindi film song; Bollywood films sold more tickets in the United Kingdom than English-language films; the Indian government granted "industry" status to cinema, and instructed Bollywood to set its house in order and speak the language of "corporatization"; Bollywood stars, no longer obliged to entertain the mafia, partied at Cannes instead; urban India mourned the decline of single-screen theaters but quickly grew accustomed to glitzy multiplexes; young men and women, many non–South Asian, wrote and shared erotic fan-fiction featuring Bollywood's hottest stars; and Shekhar Kapur, acclaimed director of *Elizabeth* and *Bandit Queen*, declared that Bollywood would define and dominate global entertainment in the twenty-first century.

Such fragments are interesting not only because they serve as useful entry points for thinking about Bollywood's intersections with the "global" over the past decade. More important, they signal that the emergence of Bollywood as a space of cultural production and expression that is now decidedly global spells trouble for categories such as "Indian cinema," "nation," "public," "culture," "modernity," "identity," and "politics," and our assumptions and understandings of relationships among these categories. These fragments of a larger and more complicated narrative of Bollywood's arrival on the global stage also point to rapidly changing, complex, and often surprising connections within and among industry practices, state policy, new media technologies, sites and modes of consumption, and networks and forms of sociality that criss-cross regional, national, and transnational boundaries and affiliations.

In this anthology, we bring together a set of essays that critically examine the complex ways in which the transnational and transmedia terrain of "Global Bollywood" has reframed relationships between geography, cultural production, and cultural identities. When and how did Bollywood emerge as an arena of public culture distinct from Hindi-language Bombay cinema? In what ways do diasporic imaginations of "India" shape Bollywood's encounters with the global? How can we rethink the state's relationship to cinema given varied state institutions' defining role in the corporatization and globalization of Bollywood? What new modes of distribution, exhibition, and reception have emerged in different sociocultural contexts, and how do we study them? How are "stars" constructed in Bollywood? Can Bollywood's convergence with new media, and fan practices that emerge therein, be historicized? In what ways has Mumbai's emergence as a center of transnational cultural production changed its relationship with other "media capitals" such as Chennai, Hyderabad, Hong Kong, and Los Angeles?[1]

The essays collected here tackle these and other questions, and highlight many other themes and issues for further inquiry. In doing so, these essays participate in ongoing scholarly efforts to map a vast and complex mediascape that is not only worthy of investigation on its own terms, but one whose study is critical for advancing our understandings of the social, cultural, and political dimensions of media globalization. Authors here employ a range of methodological approaches including institutional, cultural, textual, and ethnographic analyses and together, offer an inclusive approach that marks a departure from studies of the cinema in India that until recently have focused on questions of representation and the formal properties of film (Liang 2005; Singh 2003). We do not wish to suggest that this anthology offers a major paradigm shift—essays here amply demonstrate that the study of cinema in India has a long, rich history, and that the insights and vocabulary developed over the past two decades continue to influence our inquiries today.

Cinema in India has been studied as a profoundly important "national-popular" domain that has negotiated various transitions and conflicts in the sociocultural and political fabric of India for over a century now. In essays published in the *Journal of Arts and Ideas* and *Economic and Political Weekly*, and in several book-length studies and collections, scholars have written extensively on the politics of representation in Indian cinema. Juxtaposing readings of films' narrative and representational strategies with the sociocultural and political context within which they were produced, circulated, and debated, these studies help us understand how cinema mediates ideas regarding nation, gender, caste, class, community, and sexuality. Over the past decade, others have built on this work and focused attention on a range of filmic and extra-filmic sites with varied theoretical lenses: Indian cinema and the question of national identity (Chakravarty 1993), as a "site of ideological production . . . as the (re)production of the state form" (Prasad 1998: 9), popular films as social history (Virdi 2003), relationship between spectatorship and democracy (Rajadhyaksha 2000; Srinivas 2000), fan practices and cinema's links to political mobilization (Dickey 1993; Srinivas 2000), state policy and censorship (Mehta 2001), stardom (Majumdar 2001; Mazumdar 2000), style and visual culture (Dwyer and Patel 2002), urban experience (Mazumdar 2007; Liang 2005; Kaarsholm 2004), and as a site for the articulation of queer desire (Gopinath 2005; Desai 2004). These studies grapple with the idea of how cinema (Bombay-based Hindi cinema, for the most part) relates in complex ways to the civic and the political, and offer us several vantage points to tackle what Rajadhyaksha has termed the "Bollywoodization" of Indian cinema (Rajadhyaksha, in this volume). In dialogue with this established body of scholarship, the essays in this anthology seek to broaden the study of cinema by approaching Bollywood not just as a textual form, but, as Singh suggests, as a "socially embedded set of practices . . . as a technology, as a commodity, and lastly, as implicated within diverse modes of sociality" (Singh 2003: n.p.).

We also wish to position this anthology as one that approaches Bollywood as a distinct zone of cultural production, and not as the latest phase in Bombay cinema's global travels that extend back several decades. Films from India have always traveled to different parts of the world and, as Gopinath notes, they have been an "important form of pan–Third Worldist cultural exchange between India and East and South Africa, the Middle East, and Eastern Europe" (Gopinath 2005: 94). Tracing these networks certainly constitutes an important and much needed corrective to accounts which suggest that it is only recently, with the gradual institutionalization of the overseas, diasporic box office, that Bollywood has acquired international dimensions. As Eleftheriotis and Iordanova point out, such narratives are "misleading as they overlook historically significant processes, periods and cultural exchanges" (2006: 79). However, we would argue that fixing Bollywood within a narrative that seeks to claim that the cultural geography of Indian cinema has always been global will be equally misleading. While remaining attuned to the history of Indian cinema's flows worldwide, we situate "Global Bollywood" in relation to the specific historical conjuncture of India's entry into a transnational economy over the past 10–15 years, the centrality of the NRI (Non-resident Indian) figure to India's navigation of this space, reorientation of state policy toward cinema, and the challenges of operating in a de-regulated and global electronic mediascape defined by the phenomenal growth of the television and advertising industries during the 1990s (Rajadhyaksha, Prasad, both in this volume; Thussu, in this volume). In other words, we can approach Bollywood as marking something new, as providing a window into the dynamics of public culture in contemporary, post-liberalization India, while remaining attentive to historical continuities. Let us, then, sketch the contours of this space before providing an overview of the essays in this anthology.

In 1998, at a conference on "Challenges Before Indian Cinema," the Union Information and Broadcasting Minister Sushma Swaraj announced that the government had decided to accord "industry" status to the business of filmmaking in India.[2] Among a series of financial and regulatory concessions that accompanied this major shift in state policy—such as reduction in import duties on cinematographic film and equipment, exemption on export profits, and other tax incentives—the most significant one was a declaration made in October 2000. The Industrial Development Bank Act of 2000 made it possible for filmmakers to operate in "clean" and "legitimate" fashion, instead of using the mix of personal funds, money borrowed from individuals at exorbitant interest rates (in some cases, from the mafia), and minimum guarantee payments advanced by distributors which characterized film financing in India (Ganti 2004).[3]

Further, this state intervention came with a rider: filmmakers would have to "corporatize" their businesses since money would only be lent to companies and not individuals. Over the past five to six years, "corporatization" has become a catchall buzzword that alludes not only to new modes of film financing and the attenuation of the mafia's hold over the film industry, but to a series of changes including preparing a bound script, developing and working with schedules, getting stars to sign and honor contracts instead of proceeding with verbal assurances, in-film branding through corporate tie-ins, aggressive marketing and promotions that reflected processes of market segmentation under way in India, the emergence of the multiplex mode of exhibition, and the entry of large industrial houses, corporations, and television companies into the business of film production and distribution.

These transitions in the film industry, and the re-articulation of state-cinema ties, occurred during the same time period as another key development: the emergence of the diaspora as a strategic site in both economic and cultural terms. Over the last decade, films such as *Dilwale Dulhania Le Jayenge* (DDLJ, 1995, Aditya Chopra), *Taal* (1998, Subhash Ghai), *Kuch Kuch Hota Hai* (1998, Karan Johar), and *Kabhi Khushi Kabhie Gham* (K3G, 2001, Karan Johar) established diasporic markets as a vital source of revenue, which, in turn, led to the reconfiguration of what was an undifferentiated "overseas" distribution territory into North America, United Kingdom, Gulf States, South Africa, and so on (Ganti 2004).

In addition to theatrical releases in cities with sizeable South Asian populations, Bollywood's entrance into overseas markets has been enabled by satellite television and online delivery systems. For example, B4U (Bollywood for You), a 24/7 digital Hindi movie channel launched in 1999 in the United Kingdom, is now available on eight satellites in more than 100 countries in North America, Europe, the Middle East, Africa, and South Asia. Other major players, such as Zee Network, Star Plus, and Sony Entertainment Television, are increasingly using Hindi film-based programming to reach an international market. More recently, Eros International, the world's largest distributor of Hindi films, has collaborated with Intel to deliver its content over broadband to consumers around the globe, and announced plans to launch its content on Movielink, a leading broadband movie download service (see Thussu, in this volume).

Several scholars have analyzed these developments, focusing particularly on the centrality of the diaspora in the cultural imagery of Hindi films in post-liberalization India. Through close readings of the narrative and representational strategies of films, particularly *DDLJ*, they have shown how NRI-centric films have played a pivotal role in constituting the figure of the global and cosmopolitan NRI as critical to India's navigation of a transnational economy (Mankekar 1999; Mishra 2002; Virdi 2003). When seen in relation to state-sponsored rituals such as *Pravasi Bharatiya Divas* (Non-resident Indian Day), where several film personalities were called upon to perform the role of cultural ambassadors, Bollywood's role in mediating ties between the state and the diaspora becomes particularly clear.[4]

To these analyses of NRI-centric films and ethnographic accounts of film viewing in diasporic spaces, Rajadhyaksha adds the necessary historical and political dimensions. Partly a response to celebratory accounts of the globalization of the Bombay film industry, Rajadhyaksha argues that "while cinema has been in existence as a national industry of sorts for the past 50 years, *Bollywood* has been around for only a decade now" (page 22, this volume, original emphasis). Revisiting the period between 1945 and 1951, when the Bombay film industry managed to establish itself as a "national" film industry in the absence of state support, he goes on to argue that the most recent attempt by the state to redefine its relationship with cinema is, quite simply, a response to the problem of defining "national culture" in globalized modernity. In other words, Bollywood (not "Indian" cinema as a whole), as a (corporatized) culture industry, serves as a mediating institution par excellence for a state that seeks to reproduce itself under the sign of globalization (Rajadhyaksha, in this volume; Mehta 2005).

We see this anthology as a critical response to these and other transitions in cinema's place in Indian public culture. The goal is not so much to make claims about the *extent* of Bollywood's globalization or to speculate on the possibility that Bollywood will challenge and ultimately subvert Hollywood's hegemony (Curtin 2007). Rather, it is to acknowledge the fact that ongoing changes in the imaginations and practices of a range of stakeholders are ensuring that Bollywood films and film music will constitute an important circuit of global flows during the twenty-first century. Essays here offer one possible mapping of this terrain, and invite readers to think about Bollywood as a compelling site of mediation not just for the reproduction of the state form or diasporic imaginations, but also as one where films and film music draw on and articulate our experiences, desires, and anxieties of dwelling in (global) modernity (Martin-Barbero 1993; Chakrabarty 2002). Divided into three thematic sections, these essays focus on a range of questions dealing with the industry, film and star texts, social contexts, reception, and participatory culture.

Framing "Bollywood"

Essays in the first section provide a critical overview of material and discursive dimensions of "Bollywood," and locate the emergence of Bollywood in relation to broader social, cultural, political, and economic contexts. Taken together, they provide a useful conceptual grid for readers to use as they go through essays in the next two sections. It is only appropriate, then, that we begin with Ashish Rajadhyaksha's "Bollywoodization of the Indian Cinema." Rajadhyaksha argues that it is not enough to say that cinema, as *the* most dominant culture industry in India, naturally emerged as the site where transitions related to globalization were negotiated and made intelligible. "Bollywoodization," he suggests, is best understood in relation to the more complex issue of cinema's ability to "maneuver itself into a certain position that made it indispensable to the State" (page 34 in this volume). "Bollywoodization," then, is related to the articulation of a "freer form of civilizational belonging explicitly delinked from the political rights of citizenship" and the neoliberal state's attempts at re-defining the sociocultural boundaries of "India" and "Indianness," exemplified by rituals such as the *Pravasi Bharatiya Divas* (Day of the Diaspora) (32).

Following this, Madhava Prasad interrogates the history of the term Bollywood, and its current usage, and argues that the term is neither suggestive of Indian popular cinema's derivativeness nor is it a way of signaling and maintaining difference in the world. For Prasad, Bollywood carries the weight it does because of its pivotal role in articulating definitions of national identity to the figure of the Non-resident Indian, given that the "NRI is increasingly beginning to look like the sole guarantor of Indian identity" in a global arena. Prasad goes on to argue that the "idea of India" being essentially a global idea, sustained by the efforts of European Indology and the nationalist desire for the desire of the Other, India's identity was always anchored in some kind of external locus. The discourse of "Bollywood" then allows us to see how this locus has been redefined for our times.

In the next essay, Tejaswini Ganti adds another dimension to contestations over "Bollywood" by focusing on commemorations of the hundredth year of the arrival of cinema in India (staged by the Government of Maharashtra). She demonstrates how the history of cinema becomes an arena for the regional government to proclaim its distinct cultural identity (in regional terms) and how public rituals are appropriated by the state government to assert a particular claim over the city of Bombay and the institution of cinema.

Shanti Kumar further complicates Bollywood's transnational status by shifting our attention to the emergence of Hyderabad as a center of global cultural production. Focusing on Ramoji Film City, the largest, most comprehensive, and professionally planned film production center in the world, he argues that we need to pay attention to the "rise of a new transnational vernacular" in Indian cinema (particularly Telugu and Tamil cinema) that challenges easy distinctions between global/local and national/regional and forces a more careful consideration of Bollywood's claims on the global.

Finally, Daya Kishan Thussu's essay tracks Bollywood films' global flows, and provides an important account of changing industry dynamics over the past decade, particularly in the domains of production and distribution. He details the "corporatization" of the film industry and pays close attention to television's role in enabling and shaping Bollywood films' circulation worldwide. Thussu's essay underscores the importance of rethinking studies of media globalization that continue to position Hollywood as the pre-eminent center of transnational media production (Curtin 2003). Careful examination of how a range of stakeholders in Bollywood develop and sustain relationships with other "media capitals" will also help us develop better accounts of how Bollywood films and film music are gradually moving out of the "south-Asian" diasporic market into American or British public culture more broadly.

Texts and Audiences

Chapters in this section focus on the representational politics of key Bollywood films and star texts, and how these texts circulate in diverse sociocultural contexts and get hinged to varied meanings. The first essay by Vamsee Juluri explores the ideology of violence as a relatively autonomous concern in itself, particularly since popular Indian films frequently espouse contradictory ethical positions on the instrumentality of violence. Using perspectives drawn from the Gandhian philosophy of non-violence and post-colonial critiques of modernity and the epistemic politics of cultural reception in India, Juluri argues that the emotional and relational framework of Indian cinema must be recognized if we are to understand the nature of violence in Indian cinema. Through a close examination of violence in movies like *Mission: Kashmir* and *Khadgam*, he highlights the possibilities for an alternative epistemic location in the reception of violence in Indian cinema.

Chadha and Kavoori's essay problematizes a key contradiction in Bollywood cinema—the placement of Muslim actors in key roles. Even as communal differences and violence have increasingly come to mark Hindu-Muslim relations in India, Hindi cinema, one of India's central mediating institutions, has traditionally appeared to be a "cultural-industrial structure that has resisted Hindu-Muslim separatism" (Masud 1997: n.p.). However, although the presence of Muslim artists in the Hindi film industry has been widely invoked as evidence of its diversity, the representation of Muslims in Hindi films has received comparatively little attention. Focusing on this issue, this chapter traces the portrayal of Muslims within mainstream Hindi films from the 1950s to the current period, and finds that Muslims have been variously "Othered," and attempts to link such portrayals to changing discourses of interreligious harmony/discord in India.

Parmesh Shahani extends the question of identity politics and Bollywood into the realm of male same-sex desire. Drawing on his own experiences navigating the world of gay Bombay, he examines two key texts —BOMgAY (1996) and *Gulabi Aaina* (2003, *The Pink Mirror*)—to interrogate the structures on which gay identities in Bombay cinema are constructed. Shahani's insights into the lived realities of gay Bombay also underscore how class, caste, and gender shape urban gay culture. Situating the problematic of sexuality in mainstream media in relation to commodity culture in post-1990s Mumbai, this essay pays close attention to the ways in which gay identity, as read through these two important films, intrudes upon the life-worlds of Bollywood actors, producers, and festival participants. In doing so, Shahani also seeks to defamiliarize received (Western) notions of "authentic" gay identity/culture by foregrounding issues of language, class, and performativity in the Indian context.

Atticus Narain explores the complex ethnic and cultural configurations that comprise the East Indian Bollywood experience in Guyana, stressing how the reception of Bollywood cinema reflects historical and contemporary class/caste movements in Guyana. Hindi films are a cultural form produced by a dominant (India), but nevertheless are one of many other cultural intermediaries that provide Indo-Guyanese with the resources to construct new subjectivities. Focusing on issues of gender and the construction of femininity, Narain draws on his fieldwork experiences in Guyana to argue that in the context of persistent ethnic hostility between Afro-Guyanese and Indo-Guyanese, Indian films denote a cultural "intactness" in a diasporic context. This essay makes an important contribution to understanding Bollywood's flows into diasporas with historical trajectories that are radically different compared to those in the United Kingdom or the United States.

Govindan and Dutta explore the multifaceted creation of messages of femininity by elite producers of "new" Indian media, and the hybrid reconstitutions of those messages by elite female youths who consume them. In the wake of privatization of media in the late 1980s, Hindi films and television shows have become vehicles for celebrating not only global consumerism, but also the transnational and hybridized life experiences of the wealthy in India. Embedded within this is a contradictory body of imagery regarding womanhood and sexuality, as crafted by transnational media elites. The male *and* female producers of media images—who themselves participate in "Westernized" sexual relationships—reconstitute in their works their own ambivalence regarding "liberated" female sexuality, the exhilaration of sexual conquest, and the contradiction between Western sexuality and so-called Indian values that exalt feminine modesty. They argue that the intersection of ongoing narratives about the nature of "Indianness," and the simultaneous *fear of* and *fascination with* the expanding boundaries of female sexuality among Indian elites, has led to a narrative schizophrenia. Women in popular Hindi films and television are simultaneously marketed and condemned for overt expressions of sexuality.

Natalie Sarazzin's essay fills an important gap in scholarship on Bollywood by focusing on aural constructions of transnational identity. Despite the popularity of songs and non-diegetic music in Indian films, there has been little scholarly analysis explaining music's existence or function within every Bollywood text. She argues that music is not only of primary importance, but is a crucial component in the development of an array of narrative genres and the propagation of "Indianness" in national and especially diaspora-destined films. Identifying basic emotional, cultural, and dramatic musical codes, Sarazzin demonstrates how music generates relationships between music and the filmic image in engendering an Indian romantic narrative. Specifically, she examines the construction of aural illustrations of "heart" which reemerge as a critical concept and narrative theme in the romantic genre. Sarazzin also explores the ways in which aesthetics and sentiments based on accepted traditional tropes are selected and musically "modernized" by subverting popular global sounds, to create new meanings easily identified and consumed by a diasporic audience.

Beyond Film: Stars, Fans, and Participatory Culture

Essays in this section shift attention away from film and the space of the cinema hall to grapple with questions of stars, fans, and film journalism. First, Jyotika Virdi examines the success of *Deewar/The Wall* (1975, Yash Chopra) in terms of its narrative and the construction of Amitabh Bachchan as the "angry young man." Virdi shows how the film reworks a narrative structure that assumes mythic proportion in Indian culture, the mother-son bond, and deftly meshes this with contemporary events occurring on the eve of Indira Gandhi's notorious political Emergency that suspended citizens' fundamental rights for 19 months in 1975.

Virdi argues that the manner in which the film interlocks strains of a melodramatic family saga, the action genre, and the musical with oblique social and political commentary is the hallmark of Hindi cinema and what makes *Deewar/Wall* stand out as its classic prototype. In doing so, Virdi also offers crucial insights into how the established and emerging star power of the on-screen performers, Shashi Kapoor and Amitabh Bachchan respectively, off-screen credits, notably the director, Yash Chopra, and the screenwriter duo, Javed Akhtar and Saleem Khan (credited for Bachchan's super-stardom), shape the film's circulation and its status as a classic.

Following this, Rachel Dwyer focuses attention on film magazines, a highly visible site of cultural production that shapes stardom and "star texts" in important ways. Dwyer argues that magazines such as *Filmfare* and *Stardust* deserve serious study not only for their coverage of stars and other aspects of the film industry, but also because they are central to the history of print culture in India. Drawing on interviews with editors and writers, Dwyer discusses *Stardust's* major concerns and examines how it has constituted an "imagined," interpretive community of readers in India. While the terrain that Dwyer maps has changed considerably over the past decade, with television channels and dot-com companies covering Bollywood stars and their lifestyles, her essay creates a space for further research on film journalism.

In the next essay, Ananda Mitra examines the production of Bollywood content on the World Wide Web. He discusses how the polysemic nature of the Web, and its openness to noninstitutional voices, has led to the emergence of different modes of content production. Demonstrating how this space is occupied by people who are able to create a novel communal

connection around the overarching commonality of an interest in Bollywood with subgroups interested in specific aspects of Bollywood such as
its music and its stars, he argues that this collection of voices about Bollywood could eventually become the digital memory about Bollywood that
records the way in which the film industry of India moves into a global
arena.

The final essay in this section seeks to rework received notions of fan
culture surrounding cinema in India. Focusing on a fan collective that has
cohered around the renowned music director A. R. Rahman, Punathambekar argues against framing fan activity in Indian film culture in terms
of devotional excess or in relation to political mobilization in south India. He argues that developing fan activity surrounding film music as an
entry point entails rethinking the history of cinema's publicness as a history of media convergence, that is, a history of cinema's intersections with
various "new" media (radio, TV, Internet). Such a reconceptualization of
cinema's publicness, he suggests, will also help us steer away from treating fan activity as mere epiphenomena of politics and transitions in the
political sphere proper.

As with any such collection, there are other ways of grouping these essays and we hope that readers will notice the thematic and methodological concerns that several essays here share and go on to explore further
what is already an international field of "Indian" film and media studies.
Furthermore, as Arvind Rajagopal points out in the Afterword, even as we
move from the question of "national cinema" to map "Global Bollywood,"
we need to remain attuned to several other circuits of cultural production
—"a growing folk culture of VCD and DVD production, not only of pirated copies of big city cinema, but also produced by new entrepreneurs,
morality tales as well as news events set to voiceover and folksongs, in regional languages like Bhojpuri and Haryanvi"—that shape public culture
in contemporary India.

NOTES

1. See Curtin (2003).

2. "Film Accorded Industry Status," *Business Line,* October 19, 2000, http://
www. indiaserver.com/businessline/2000/10/19/stories/141918re.htm.

3. "IDBI Outlines Norms for Film-Financing," *Financial Express,* March 31,
2001, http://www.financialexpress.com/fe/daily/20010331/fc031005.html.

4. For a more detailed account, see A. Punathambekar (2005), "Bollywood in the Indian-American Diaspora: Mediating a Transitive Logic of Cultural Citizenship," *International Journal of Cultural Studies* 8 (2): 151–73; and M. Mehta (2005), "Globalizing Bombay Cinema: Reproducing the Indian State and Family," *Cultural Dynamics* 17 (2): 135–54.

BIBLIOGRAPHY

Appadurai, A. 1996. *Modernity at Large: Cultural Dimensions of Globalization.* Minneapolis: University of Minnesota Press.

Chakrabarty, D. 2000. *Provincializing Europe: Postcolonial Thought and Historical Difference.* Princeton, N.J.: Princeton University Press.

———. 2002. *Habitations of Modernity: Essays in the Wake of Subaltern Studies.* New Delhi: Permanent Black.

Chakravarty, S. 1993. *National Identity in Indian Popular Cinema 1947–1987.* Austin: University of Texas Press.

Curtin, M. 2003. "Media Capital: Towards the Study of Spatial Flows." *International Journal of Cultural Studies* 6 (2): 202–28.

———. 2007. *Playing to the World's Biggest Audience: The Globalization of Chinese Film and TV.* Berkeley: University of California Press.

Desai, J. 2004. *Beyond Bollywood: The Cultural Politics of South Asian Diasporic Film.* New York: Routledge.

Dickey, S. 1993. *Cinema and the Urban Poor in South India.* Cambridge: Cambridge University Press.

Dwyer, R., and D. Patel. 2002. *Cinema India: The Visual Culture of Hindi Film.* New Delhi: Oxford University Press.

Eleftheriotis, D., and D. Iordanova. 2006. "Introduction: Indian Cinema in the World." *South Asian Popular Culture* 4 (2): 79–82.

Ganti, T. 2004. *Bollywood: A Guidebook to Popular Hindi Cinema.* New York: Routledge.

Gopinath, G. 2005. *Impossible Desires: Queer Diasporas and South Asian Public Cultures.* Durham, N.C.: Duke University Press.

Kaarsholm, P. 2004. *City Flicks: Indian Cinema and the Urban Experience.* Calcutta: Seagull Books.

Kaur, R., and S. J. Ajay. 2005. *Bollyworld: Popular Indian Cinema through a Transnational Lens.* New Delhi: Sage.

Kumar, S. 2006. Gandhi Meets Primetime: Globalization and Nationalism in Indian Television. Urbana: University of Illinois Press.

Liang, L. 2005. "Cinematic Citizenship and the Illegal City." *Inter-Asia Cultural Studies* 6 (3): 366–85.

Majumdar, N. 2001. "The Embodied Voice: Song Sequences and Stardom in

Popular Hindi Cinema." In *Soundtrack Available: Essays on Film and Popular Music*, ed. P. R. Wojcik and A. Knight, 161–85. Durham, N.C.: Duke University Press.

Mankekar, P. 1999. "Brides Who Travel: Gender, Transnationalism, and Nationalism in Hindi Film." *Positions* 7 (3): 731–61.

Martin-Barbero, J. 1993. *Communication, Culture and Hegemony: From the Media to Mediations*. Trans. Elizabeth Fox and Robert A. White. Newbury Park, N.J.: Sage.

Masud, I. 1997. "Muslim Ethos in India Cinema." Retrieved on September 5, 2006, from http://www.screenindia.com/fullstory.php?content id=9980.

Mazumdar, R. 2000. "From Subjectification to Schizophrenia: The 'Angry Man' and the 'Psychotic' Hero of Bombay Cinema." In *Making Meaning in Indian Cinema*, ed. R. Vasudevan, 238–66. New Delhi: Oxford University Press.

———. 2007. *Bombay Cinema: An Archive of the City*. Minneapolis: University of Minnesota Press.

Mazzarella, W. 2003. *Shoveling Smoke: Advertising and Globalization in Contemporary India*. New Delhi: Oxford University Press.

Mehta, M. 2001. "Selections: Cutting, Classifying and Certifying in Bombay Cinema." Ph.D. diss., University of Minnesota.

———. 2005. "Globalizing Bombay Cinema: Reproducing the Indian State and Family." *Cultural Dynamics* 17: 135–54.

Mishra, V. 2002. *Bollywood Cinema Temples of Desire*. New York: Routledge.

Prasad, M. 1998. *Ideology of the Hindi Film: A Historical Construction*. New Delhi: Oxford University Press.

Rajadhyaksha, A. 2000. "Viewership and Democracy in the Cinema." In *Making Meaning in Indian Cinema*, ed. Ravi Vasudevan, 267–96. New Delhi: Oxford University Press.

———. 2003. "The Bollywoodization of Indian Cinema: Cultural Nationalism in a Global Arena." *Inter-Asia Cultural Studies* 4 (1): 25–39.

Sharma, A. 2003. "India's Experience with the Multiplex." *Seminar* 525, New Delhi.

Singh, B. 2003. "The Problem." *Seminar* 525, New Delhi.

Srinivas, S. V. 2000. "Devotion and Defiance in Fan Activity." In *Making Meaning in Indian Cinema*, ed. Ravi Vasudevan, 297–317. New Delhi: Oxford University Press.

———. 2003. "Film Culture: Politics and Industry." *Seminar* 525. Retrieved on August, 18, 2004, http://www.india-seminar.com/2003/525.htm.

Virdi, J. 2003. *The Cinematic Imagination: Indian Popular Films as Social History*. New Brunswick, N.J.: Rutgers University Press.

Part I

||||||||||||||||||||||||||||||||||||||||||||||||||||||

Framing Bollywood

Chapter 1

IIIIIIIIIIIIIIIIIIIIIIIIIIIIIIIIIIIIIIIIIIIIIIIIIIIIIII

The "Bollywoodization" of the Indian Cinema
Cultural Nationalism in a Global Arena

Ashish Rajadhyaksha

Rajnikant in Japan

The West may have the biggest stalls in the world's media bazaar, but it is not the only player. Globalization isn't merely another word for Americanization—and the recent expansion of the Indian entertainment industry proves it. For hundreds of millions of fans around the world, it is Bollywood—India's film industry—not Hollywood, that spins their screen fantasies. Bollywood, based in Mumbai, has become a global industry. India's entertainment moguls don't merely target the billion South Asians, or desis, at home: they make slick movies, songs, and TV shows for export. Attracted by a growing middle class and a more welcoming investment environment, foreign companies are flocking to Bollywood, funding films and musicians. The foreign money is already helping India's pop culture to reach even greater audiences. And it may have a benign side effect in cleaning up an Indian movie industry business long haunted by links to the underworld ("Bollywood Goes International," *Newsweek International*, February 28, 2000).

Let us keep aside for a moment the gross misrepresentations in *Newsweek*: that the Indian film industry is not solely based in Mumbai, that "foreign money" is still hardly available for film *productions* even though it would like to cream off nonlocal *distribution* profits; that such money is not necessarily distinguishable from the "underworld" and is, therefore, not exactly what you would describe as "benign"; that *Newsweek*'s assumptions about good and bad money are unsustainable and pernicious.

Let us concentrate instead on just what this literature claims is happening. For something like the past decade, leading up to *Newsweek*'s final consecration, a range of print and television media have been claiming the occurrence of some rather dramatic developments in the Indian cinema. Practically every newspaper has commented, usually in the same breathless prose as *Newsweek*, on the phenomenon: there is a craze for "Bollywood" masala that quite exceeds anything we've ever seen before; from Tokyo to Timbuktu people are dancing to Indipop, names such as Shah Rukh Khan are circulating in places where people may never have heard of Indira Gandhi, and there seems to be an opportunity, there is apparently money to be made. Everyone, it seems, is scrambling—new Bollywood websites continue to emerge, new distributors and intermediaries rise with new ideas of how to exploit this development, new television channels are available, satellite technology is projected with an unprecedented ability to overcome distribution inefficiencies—and every one of these is powered by entrepreneurs and their venture-capitalist backers, and their unique idea about what will earn money.

On what is this hype based? Interestingly, in the past year, the box office of an Indian cinema made indigenously was itself less central to the phenomenon than a range of ancillary industries, mostly based in London, including theater (the much-hyped London stage musical *Bombay Dreams*, a collaboration between Indian composer A. R. Rehman and Andrew Lloyd Webber), the music industry, advertising, and even fashion (the month-long "Bollywood" festival of food, furniture, and fashion marketing in Selfridges, London), all of which culminated in the extraordinary marketing exercise known as *Indian Summer*, in July 2002.[1]

All of this began, it is usually said, with the four films that *Newsweek* also mentions as having made distribution history, three of them directly or indirectly Yash Chopra productions: *Dilwale Dulhania Le Jayenge* (*DDLJ*, 1995), the film which in some ways started it all; *Dil To Pagal Hai* (*DTPH*, 1997); Karan Johar's *Kuch Kuch Hota Hai* (*KKHH*, 1998); and Subhash Ghai's *Taal* (1998). Before all these, there is of course the original box office hit *Hum Aapke Hain Kaun?* (1994). Of *Taal*, for example, producer and noted "showman" of Hindi cinema Ghai said,

> There'll be 125 prints of *Taal* only for the foreign market. This is almost a three-fold increase since *Pardes*, for which I'd made 45 prints, and five times that of *Khalnayak*. Hindi films now have a significant market in the

US, Canada, UK and the Middle East. It is making inroads into South Africa and Australia. And it is also popular in Japan, Hong Kong, South East Asia and, of course, Mauritius. In most if not all these countries, Hindi films are no longer weekend events, they are showing three shows everyday wherever they're released. Now, beginning with *Taal*, there will be vinyl banner hoardings advertising the films on the roads of the Western cities. Everybody, including the Westerners, will now see what films are on! The whole world will take note, because we will also be on the net. (Sengupta 1999)

How much did these films collectively earn? That's difficult to say, but *The Economic Times* reported that "The first big success of the new Bollywood is *Who Am I to You?* (*Hum Aapke Hain Koun?* dubbed), a musical that focuses on two weddings. Thanks to its untraditional [sic] plot and effective marketing, it's India's biggest hit ever. Playing for nearly a year, the film grossed more than $30 million, a phenomenal amount in a country where the average moviegoer pays 65 per cent admission and the average movie makes about $3 million—barely what an arthouse film makes in the U.S." (Moshavi 1995). Of *Taal*, the same paper reports that it was released around the world on August 13 and grossed the highest average collection per cinema hall (per screen average) for movies "released in North America on the August 13–15 weekend. According to Weekend Box-Office figures, the first three-day collections were $591,280. Released simultaneously on 44 theatres in North America, *Taal* has set a record for Bollywood releases abroad by notching the highest first three-day collections with $13,438 per screen. Though there is no independent verification, a press release by Eros Entertainment Inc, the distributor of the film abroad, claimed that *Taal*'s initial collections have even surpassed that of Hollywood blockbusters like *Haunting, The Blair Witch Project* and *Eyes Wide Shut*."

All of these are undoubtedly marketing successes, and the releases—in particular of *Kuch Kuch* in South Africa, *Dil to Pagal Hai* in Israel, and the brief weekend when *Taal* made it to the top 10 in the U.S. domestic market—are now the stuff of marketing legend. On the other hand, here is a salutary fact: *Newsweek* claims that "India's movie exports jumped from $10 million a decade ago to $100 million last year, and may top $250 million in 2000."

Contrast these figures with the brief dot-com boom when every Indian

Internet portal, such as satyam online, rediff-on-the-net, and planetasia, marketed itself with Bollywood paraphernalia. Following the unprecedented sale of just one portal, indiainfo.com, for Rs 500 crore (or over $100 million), it would have been a safe argument that just ten of the top websites of the time (as computed by a *Businessworld* issue, "Hot New Dot.coms," January 24, 2000) were, in that period, collectively worth more than the total box office earnings of the Indian film industry.

There was, and continues to be, a real discrepancy. Contrary to *Newsweek*'s statement that Bollywood is "India's film industry . . . based in Mumbai," perhaps we could argue instead precisely that, at least in one sense, this is not so: that Bollywood is *not* the Indian film industry, or at least not the film industry alone.

Bollywood admittedly occupies a space analogous to the film industry, but might best be seen as a more diffuse cultural conglomeration involving a range of distribution and consumption activities from websites to music cassettes, from cable to radio. If so, the film industry itself—determined here solely in terms of its box office turnover and sales of print and music rights, all that actually comes back to the producer—can by definition constitute only a part, and perhaps even an *alarmingly small* part, of the overall culture industry that is currently being created and marketed.

If this is so, then at the back of it all is a real difficulty, one that, for all its unprecedentedness, has a disarmingly familiar tone. The fact is that nobody responsible for the production of the film narrative, if we include in this the producers, directors, and stars responsible for the nuts-and-bolts assembly of the cinematic product that goes into these markets, actually knows what is going on. How do they make sense of these developments? Why is *Dil To Pagal Hai* popular in Tel Aviv, and why now? How would they convert all this hoopla into a stable market that would guarantee their next product an audience? Nobody quite knows the overall picture, and it is worth exploring some of the literature that has emerged on these developments to speculate on just why that is so.

Amitabh Bachchan, for example, was one of the iconic stars of the 1970s and early 1980s, before his career nosedived following the "first-ever" effort to corporatize the film industry with the lame-duck ABCL, which most critics say was "an idea before its time." Despite not having a substantial hit for over a decade, Bachchan is India's most famous "film personality," mainly through a Bollywoodized makeover that owes itself to television (he hosted the Hindi version of *Who Wants to Be a Millionaire?* for Star TV), and he has this to say:

Evidently, our film personalities have begun to matter in world fora. Hindi cinema is gaining worldwide recognition and I don't mean only those films which make it to Berlin or Cannes. Once, I was walking down London's Piccadilly Circus and I saw this group of Kurds running towards me. (Laughs) I thought they wanted to assassinate me. But they stopped right there and started singing songs from *Amar Akbar Anthony* and *Muqaddar Ka Sikandar*. Rajnikant is tremendously popular in Japan. And I'm told that our stars are known even in Fiji, Bali and Chile. Amazing! But we're not marketing ourselves properly. Someone out there is making pots of money at our expense. (Interview, '*Netvamsham!*' *The Times of India*, July 18, 1999)

Who is this mysterious "someone" making money and how come Bachchan doesn't know? Let us explore this further with the instance that Bachchan himself provides, perhaps the most bizarre instance in this whole new development: the sudden, inexplicable, popularity of Rajnikant in Japan.

Rajnikant is, of course, well known as perhaps the biggest Tamil film star ever, after the legendary M. G. Ramachandran, but it is also important to say that his career has largely been restricted to that language, despite several efforts to get into Hindi film, where he has often played subsidiary parts in Bachchan films (*Andha Kanoon*, 1983; *Giraftaar*, 1985; *Hum*, 1991) and one marginal effort in a Hollywood production (*Bloodstone*, 1989). Within Tamil Nadu, where he reigns supreme, on the other hand, he has demonstrated all the hallmarks of a major star who knows his audience and his market: he has carefully constructed his screen persona, built a team around him that understands how to work it, has even tested out his popularity politically when he campaigned on behalf of the DMK and was at least partially responsible for its victory in the 1996 elections. And then came his Japanese success. Here is the *New Indian Express* on this phenomenon:

An entire generation of recession-hit Japanese have discovered a new hero: Rajnikant. Jayalalitha's bete noire and the man with that unflagging swagger and oh-so-cool wrist flicks has emerged there as the hippest craze after Leonardo DiCaprio and *Muthu*, his 150th film, is the biggest grosser in Japan after *Titanic*. So far the film has been seen by over 1,27,000 Japanese in a 23-week run at Tokyo's Cinema Rise alone, netting as much as $1.7 million and premieres on satellite television in

June. ("Rajnikant Bowls over Japanese Youth," *The New Indian Express*, June 10, 1999)

So how does one explain this success? B. Kandaswamy Bharathan, executive producer at Kavithalaya, credited with having masterminded the Japanese marketing of this film, offers a typically "Bollywoodist-culturalist" explanation:

> The movie carries an important message—that money is not everything in life. Instead, it propagates human values, highlighted in the first song itself—and this philosophy appealed to the Japanese audience. This is especially significant for a youth that's been talked down about for not being as hardworking as the post-war generation. ("Rajnikant Bowls over Japanese Youth," *The New Indian Express*, June 10, 1999)

Indeed. Keeping aside the distortions by which the producer of *Muthu* represents his own production, in fact a violent feudal drama addressing caste differences, I am reasonably sure that if one were to ask Bharathan why only this film proved a hit and no other, and how he suggests that Rajnikant capitalize on this sudden popularity to stabilize a Japanese market for his next film and his future career, we may perhaps get an honest answer, that he has no idea why *Muthu* did well in Tokyo.

Cinema versus the Bollywood Culture Industry

> Says Fort Lauderdale housewife Sameera Biswas, "We go to the movies to keep our culture alive."
> "Kids in Bombay go to night clubs to become Western. Here (i.e. in Brisbane) we go to assert our Eastern identity. The basic difference lies there."
> —Fiji Indian enthusiast of Indipop (Ray 2000)

The main contention of this chapter seeks to separate out the Bollywood industry from the Indian cinema. It suggests that while the cinema has been in existence as a national industry of sorts for the past 50 years (the Indian cinema, of course, has celebrated its centenary, but the industry, in the current sense of the term, might be most usefully traced to the post–Second World War boom in production), *Bollywood* has been around for only about a decade now. The term today refers to a reasonably specific narrative and a mode of presentation: the *Newsweek* essay, for example, quotes Plus Channel's Amit Khanna as saying that "Indian movies are feel-good, all-happy-in-the-end, tender love stories with lots of songs and dances. . . . That's what attracts non-Indian audiences across the world." To this we could add "family values" and their palpable, if not entirely self-evident, investment in "our culture." To such content we would need also to add a distinctive mode of presentation, couched in the post–Information Technology claims that Indian enterprise has been making in the past few years of global competitiveness, and in language such as the following:

> Spurred by competition from dubbed versions of such flashy Western hits as *Jurassic Park* and *Speed*, Bollywood is rushing to enter the era of high tech films. Producers are founding new companies, boosting their marketing, and seeking new sources of financing. . . . [C]ameras are rolling for the first Bollywood high-tech films. CMM Ltd, an 18-month-old special-effects company backed by such stalwarts as State Bank of India, has bought more than $1 million worth of software and hardware from Silicon Graphics Inc, the Mountain View (California) computer company whose special-effects equipment is used by nearly every Hollywood studio. The technology is key to a still untitled film featuring Indian megastar Shah Rukh Khan in a double role, allowing him to appear with himself in the same scene. Silicon Graphics is lining up other clients in India as well. (Moshavi 1995)

There are further distinctions to be made: while Bollywood exists for, and prominently caters to, a diasporic audience of Indians, and sometimes (as, for example, with Bhangra-rap) exports *into* India, the Indian cinema —much as it would wish to tap this "non-resident" audience—is only occasionally successful in doing so, and is in almost every instance able to do so only when it, so to speak, *Bollywoodizes* itself, a transition that very few films in Hindi, and hardly any in other languages, are actually able to do.

Speaking historically, ever since the film industry in India assumed something like its current form—the period roughly between 1946 and 1975—the export market of films has been a relatively minor, disorganized and chaotic, but at the same time familiar, field. Few films were made with a non-Indian audience in mind, and the "foreign market" (usually a single territory) remained small, and entirely controlled by the government of India's Indian Motion Picture Export Corporation, which in its initial years was accountable to the Reserve Bank of India and later merged with the National Film Development Corporation. Film was dominated by State policy on export and remained, until 1992 when the area was decontrolled and opened to private enterprise, subsidiary to the policy of exporting "art" films within the film festival circuit. It was generally assumed in this time that Indian mainstream films, to the extent to which they had an offshore audience at all, addressed émigré Indians or their descendants. In 1975–77, for example, statistics show that Indian films were exported to Africa, the Arab states, Trinidad, Guyana and Barbados, Burma, Hong Kong, Indonesia, Iran, Malaysia, Singapore, Sri Lanka, and Thailand.[2] Perhaps the most visible form of export in this time was the "gulf boom," of workers (domestic, industrial, white-collar) exported to the Middle East becoming an audience for Malayalam films through the 1970s. Apart from this kind of market, the only other that existed was the one related to bilateral trade arrangements with the Socialist bloc, as part of what came to be called Nehruite internationalism, but which nevertheless did yield some spectacular marketing successes, such as Raj Kapoor's films, and later Mithun Chakraborty's, in the former USSR.

Such audiences, and such modes of marketing, could hardly resemble what we are trying here to identify as the Bollywood culture industry of the 1990s. The term itself, Bollywood, has been around most notably in film trade journals—it was probably invented in a slightly jokey self-deprecating way by the journal *Screen* in Bombay and by its page "Bollywood Beat," with the companion words Tollywood for the Calcutta film industry based in Tollygunge and even, for a while, Mollywood for the Madras industry, neither of which are of course used these days. It is probable that its current usage is a British one, associated with Channel-4's ethnic programming as we see in Kabir (2001), and came into circulation via literary speculations on film as mass culture by writers such as Shashi Tharoor or Farrukh Dhondy on Indian film to mean what it does today: an expression of the outsider's fascination with a slightly surreal practice that nevertheless appears to possess the claim to be a genuine popular art form. So Tharoor, for example, says:

The way in which different communities have come together for simply secular ends whether in ecological movements like the Himalayan agitations against deforestation, or in the social work of Baba Amte, or in the cinema industry of Bollywood—points to the potential for co-operative rather than divisive mobilisation. It is when groups have stayed apart, and failed to interact in secular activities, that their communal identities prevail; the lack of brotherhood guarantees their "other" hood. And then conflict, hatred and violence can erupt. Not surprisingly, this idea of India is one that is sustained by our popular culture. Some readers might think my reference to Bollywood out of place. One of my novels deals with the trashy world of commercial cinema—because to me, Indian films, with all their limitations and outright idiocies, represent part of the hope for India's future. In a country that is still 50 per cent illiterate, films represent the prime vehicle for the transmission of popular culture and values. ("Make Bollywood's India a Reality," *The Indian Express*, April 19, 1998)

Today, as Tharoor shows (or rather unwittingly demonstrates), the term comes with its own narrative, one that we could perhaps call techno-nostalgia, and is clearly no longer restricted solely to the cinema but informs a range of products and practices. It would certainly have informed the displays around the Swaminarayan Sanstha's Cultural Festival of India in Edison, New Jersey, in 1991, when one apparently entered through large gates signifying traditional temple entrances which were named Mayur Dwar (Peacock Gate) and Gaja Dwar (Elephant Gate), and saw traditional artisans making handicrafts sharing their space with entrepreneurs from Jackson Heights, New York, selling electronic products, with sponsorship from AT&T. Of this form, most directly demonstrated in recent cinematic memory by the foreign-returned Rani Mukherjee in *KKHH* suddenly bursting into the bhajan *Om jai jagdish hare*, Sandhya Shukla has this to say:

> Emerging as it did out of a constellation of interests—Indian, Indian-American and otherwise American—the Cultural Festival generated questions about common ground: where was it and how did it function? [T]he Cultural Festival deliberately intertwined culture, nation and identity in its production of metaphors and myths. *With the synchronous developments of international capital and diasporic nationalism, we see infinitely complex realms of cultural production.* (Shukla 1997)

The "our culture" argument, of which Bollywood forms an admittedly prime exemplar, clearly then also informs a range of productions, all combining the insatiable taste for nostalgia with the felt need to keep "our (national) culture alive": from websites to chat shows, from Ismail Merchant and Madhur Jaffrey cookery programs to advertising, soap operas to music video, niche marketing of various products, satellite channels, journalism, the Indipop "remix" audio cassette and CD industry.

If, then, we see Bollywood as a culture industry, and see the Indian cinema as only a part, even if culturally a significant one, of that industry, then it is also likely that we are speaking of an industry whose financial turnover could be many times larger than what the cinema itself can claim. This would almost certainly be true of the export market, but —if we include the extraordinary dot-com boom being witnessed in India right now—it may even be true already within India itself.

The transition, or crossover in marketing terms, from a domestic film product that has comparatively fewer options for merchandising its products to one that more successfully gears itself for exploiting the new marketing opportunities that Bollywood now presents, are now palpably evident, certainly to any savvy filmgoer. The difference between the "Bollywood" movie and the rest of the Hindi and other language films being made would be, say, the difference between Karan Johar and David Dhawan, between Shah Rukh Khan and Govinda, between *Phir Bhi Dil Hai Hindustani* and *Anari Number 1* (see, for example, Banker 2001). While *Hum Aapke Hain Koun?* was perhaps the first Indian film to recognize and then systematically exploit a marketing opportunity here, it has since been most visibly Shah Rukh Khan who has been committed to the Bollywood mode, mainly as an actor (*DDLJ, Pardes, DTPH, KKHH*) but this year with *Phir Bhi Dil Hai Hindustani* having personally taken charge of its global marketing.

I want to drive a further wedge into the difference, by pointing to two crucial consequences of making this a distinction between the cinema and the more generalized Bollywood culture industry. In one obvious sense, Bollywood is of course identical to the Hindi (if not Indian) cinema: film continues to remain the most prominent presence figure-heading the global "Indian" culture industry. However, in ironic contrast, whereas practically every other ancillary industry seems to have by now defined an audience, a market, and a means of sustained production for that market, the cinema continues to suffer from its old difficulties of defining a generic production line and thus of defining a stable channel of capital inflow.

Let us see the problem as one of *defining culture economically*. If one were to extrapolate a larger theoretical question from all this, it would be: what are the circumstances under which cultural self-definitions *resist* economic or (we could now add) political resolution? And why does the cinema suffer from this problem in India, when other forms from television to radio to the music industry and, of course these days the Internet, seem to have no problem here?

To ask the question in these terms is, I suggest, to get to the very basis of why the Indian cinema exists at all. It is the further contention of this chapter that since the Second World War, when the Indian cinema first defined itself as a mass-culture industry, the very reason it occupied so crucial and prominent a space in the emerging postwar and—more crucially, post-Partition—public sphere has actively forced it to resist capitalist organization. The globalization of this duality in the past decade under the aegis of Bollywood, I finally suggest, leads us to important insights into the phenomenon that I shall argue is also, and among other things, the globalization of a crucial set of conflicts bred into Indian *nationalism*.

The Resistance to Industrialization

On May 10, 1998, the former Information & Broadcasting Minister, Sushma Swaraj, declared, at a national conference on "Challenges before Indian Cinema," that she would shortly pass a Government Order declaring "industry status" to the film industry in India. This was a direct response to perhaps the most intense lobbying the film industry had yet done to achieve what Hollywood, for instance, achieved in the 1930s and what the Indian cinema has been denied since its inception. K. D. Shorey, the General Secretary of the Film Federation of India, had already, in 1996, sought to include this declaration into the Ninth Five-Year Economic Plan, saying that

> the situation in the film industry is very alarming. While the cost of production is on the increase, the revenue at the box-office is dwindling because of the rampant piracy of feature films on the cable and satellite networks. India should have more than a lakh of theatres, considering its population and according to an UNESCO report. But unfortunately, there is a declining trend in cinema houses from 13,000 and odd to 12,000. . . . What is worrying us, producers, is that the entertainment tax, which was started by the British as a war-time measure, has been increased to such large proportions by various state governments that it is eating into the

revenue of films. Nowhere in the world is entertainment tax levied, barring in countries like India, Pakistan and Sri Lanka. . . . What is Rs800 crore to the Government? The Planning Commission can ask state govts to abolish the entertainment tax and the Central Govt can easily allocate that much of reimbursement. As far as the other central duties are concerned, they hardly work out to Rs35 crore. . . . If only financial institutions lend money for the construction of theatres and institutional finance for film production (is made available) as it is prevalent in western countries . . . the film industry can survive in a healthy atmosphere.

Shorey was of course not talking about Bollywood here: the problems to which *he* refers are the old ones, the ones that the film industry still continues to face on the ground, problems we have heard since at least the 1960s. However, for independent and more contemporary reasons, this seemed an appropriate time for the government to make the move of declaring film as an industry capable of attracting institutional finance.

By the early 1990s, the growing economic power of the non-resident Indian, or NRI, people of Indian origin who were domiciled abroad—whom the Indian government was actively wooing with attractive investment schemes that already formed a substantial part of the Reserve Bank of India's foreign exchange reserves—had already announced the arrival of a new culture industry that we have here named Bollywood. The failure of the Broadcast Bill by the previous government had placed growing pressure upon the Bharatiya Janata Party (BJP)-led coalition to come up with some kind of consolidated media bill that would address in an integrated fashion the merger of satellite communications with cable, television, and the Internet, all of which featured film prominently in their output, and all of which stood at the threshold of attracting serious financial investment from a range of international investors. Already, Rupert Murdoch's entry into the satellite television market with his STAR-TV had transformed the field, and it appeared as though film production would be the next target as Murdoch's 20th Century-Fox acquired a majority stake in the Bombay-based UTI-TV production house.

This was then not merely a matter of abolishing entertainment tax or making local institutional finance available for production alone, as Shorey seemed to think. The reform of the film industry through corporatization—signaled most directly by the formation of the Amitabh Bachchan Corporation and indirectly by a range of films, from Shekhar Kapur's *Mr. India* (1987), Mani Rathnam's *Roja* (1992), or Vinod Chopra's *1942 A Love*

Story (1994), all addressing the theme of techno-nationalism that was on its way to being incarnated as *the* Bollywood thematic—had made it a prime candidate for international, including NRI, investor support.[3]

At the back of it all there was also the more complex political issue involved, of the Indian state itself negotiating a transition from an earlier era of decolonization and "high nationalism" and into the newer times of globalization and finance capital. The BJP's own investment into the concept of a "cultural nationalism"—a rather freer form of civilizational belonging explicitly delinked from the political rights of citizenship, indeed delinked even from the State itself, replaced by the rampant proliferation of phrases like "Phir Bhi Dil Hai Hindustani" and "Yeh mera India/I love my India"—has clearly taken the lead in resuscitating the concept of nation from the very real threats that the State faces as an institution of legitimation, particularly following its policy of widespread disinvestment in a range of functions. The significance of the cultural turn has been well documented, as has the unexpected support that such a brand of cultural definition—and the ensuing industry that, to quote the Fort Lauderdale housewife mentioned earlier, functions to keep "our culture" alive—extended to the form of 1990s Hindutva governance in which Sushma Swaraj has been, of course, a prominent presence.

It was for both economic as well as political reasons that the cinema had to feature prominently in all this, if for no other reason than simply by virtue of its presence as *the* most prominent culture industry in modern India. There are, however, deeper issues involved, as well as a few problems, which involve an investigation into just why the cinema occupies such a prominent location in India in the first place. We may need to digress here slightly, to revisit a situation in the late 1940s, which I want to suggest bears direct relevance to, and helps illuminate, the "Indian cinema versus Bollywood" divide that I am trying to map.

The period to which I refer is between 1945 and 1951, when film production in India suddenly more than doubled (from 99 films in 1945 to 221 in 1951). This is usually seen as a low moment in Indian film history, when a whole range of independent financiers and producers jumped into the fray, effectively ending the more stable studio systems of the prewar period, whom the Film Enquiry Committee Report of 1951—the most elaborate and authentic record of this crucial time—castigates in no uncertain language as "leading stars, exacting financiers and calculating distributors" who "forged ahead" at the "cost of the industry and the taste of the public."[4]

It was nevertheless an extraordinary achievement, perhaps unparalleled in the history of world cinema, that in this period the film industry set itself up as a national industry in the sense of assembling a national market, even devising a narrative mode that has since been extensively analyzed as nationalist melodrama in ways that actually *precede* and even anticipate institutionalized State functioning in this field.[5] Film theory has repeatedly demonstrated the crucial role that nationalist-political constructions play in determining narrative and spectatorial practices. Even in the instance of American film, it has been demonstrated that it was only around 1939 when the notion of "American unity," informed by the prewar situation that "both necessitated and enabled national cohesion," and that saw the "unified, national subject—the paradigmatic American viewer"—being put in place, did Hollywood actually deploy several of the technical and narrative conventions for which it is today renowned (Cormack 1994: 140–42) and for which *Gone with the Wind* (1939) remains so crucial an event in American film history.

This departure from the more usual condition of a decolonizing nation-state was a source of some embarrassment to the Nehru government, as the Film Enquiry Committee report consistently shows. Unlike any other comparable instance—where, much more conventionally, newly formed "third world" nations established national film industries from scratch, usually by reducing or eliminating their financial and infrastructural dependence on the erstwhile colonial power, and where, from North Africa to Latin America to large parts of East Asia, the founding of a local film industry has almost always been a culturally prominent part of national reconstruction—India in contrast inherited an already established, even if chaotic, production and exhibition infrastructure for a cinema industry that was poised, even then, to become the largest in the world.

The Enquiry Committee Report's main thrust is in startling contrast to the stand taken by film organizations in other countries with whom India, in fact, had exchange links, like FEPACI (the Federation of Pan-African Cineastes, affiliated with the Organization of African Unity, OAU), who believed their "prophetic mission was to unite and to use film as a tool for the liberation of the colonized countries" (Diawara 1992: 39). The Indian government wanted to keep the film industry in check, to regulate it in some way, to reform its dubious credentials as a national form and also thereby to address cultural nationalism's discomfort at having to depend on such inauthentic resources; eventually to replace it with something better, something that more authentically represented the modernist aspirations of India's newly enfranchised civil society (Rajadhyaksha 1993).

Some of these perceptions of the industry would seem quaint today, and even then were controversial. Critic Chidananda Das Gupta, India's leading theorist of precisely the kind of cinema that the government of India tried to launch after the 1950s with the direct involvement of State agencies, for instance tried to re-integrate the difficulties posed by the typically modernist divide between "good" and "bad" culture. He attributed to the mainstream cinema a specifically, even consciously, nationalist function. Coining the term "All India film," he suggested that India had evolved an idiom, and industry, that appropriated aspects both from indigenous popular film and theater genres and from Hollywood, subordinating them to an all-encompassing entertainment formula designed to overcome regional and linguistic boundaries, providing in the process "cultural leadership [that reinforces] some of the unifying tendencies in our social and economic changes [a]nd provides an inferior alternative [to a leadership that] has not emerged because of the hiatus between the intelligentsia, to which the leaders belong, and the masses" (Das Gupta 1968). The contention that the All India film performed by default an integrating nationalist function similar to the consciously stated aim of, say, All India Radio (whose name Das Gupta clearly evokes in his term All India Film) and, more recently, Doordarshan, went on to have an important influence on India's national film industry policies after the Enquiry Committee Report. The industry's inability to be financially self-sustaining thereafter often came to be counterbalanced by its alleged ability to foster a unified contemporary "indigenous" culture.

The claim of the mainstream cinema as a repository of national-cultural value in one sense has its origin in these times. The claim by itself does not, however, explain how the cinema industry pulled together a national market or national audience even before national independence, and consequently without state support. How, to return to our earlier question, did the cinema pull this off and how did it come to occupy its crucial presence as a "cultural unifier" and a keeper of the flame in the sense in which that Fort Lauderdale housewife sees the ritual of cultural bonding involved in going to the movies?

I suggest that the answer would need to be sought in the very categories of national culture that India invoked in the 1940s and early 1950s, and identify something of a zone, a domain of some sort, a blind spot, in the role that this *national culture* had to play *politically*, a zone into which the cinema came to ensconce itself. Partha Chatterjee offers here a larger argument around the "hiatus" that contextualizes Das Gupta's move, for what was going on at the time.

> [W]hereas the legal-bureaucratic apparatus of the state had been able, by the late colonial and certainly in the post-colonial period, to reach as the target of many of its activities virtually all of the population that inhabits its territory, the domain of civil social institutions as conceived above is still restricted to a fairly small section of "citizens." The hiatus is extremely significant because it is the mark of non-Western modernity as an always-incomplete project of modernisation. (Chatterjee 1997)

Given a corresponding analytical problem posed by the usual ways of working through this hiatus—that we either "regard the domain of the civil as a depoliticized domain in contrast with the political domain of the state" or blur all distinctions by claiming that everything is political, neither of which helps us get very far—Chatterjee posits the existence of an intermediary domain of some kind: a "domain of *mediating institutions between civil society and the state*" (emphasis added). He names this "political society."

It is not the purpose of this chapter to go into the complex nature of the political maneuvers that ensued within State functioning and within the domain of private capital at this time (the late 1940s–1950s) in India. Suffice it to say that if part of Indian nationalism defined itself in terms of a modern "national" culture, and instituted a whole paraphernalia of activities defining the identity of the "modern citizen," then there was another part of the national State functioning at another level altogether, the level for example of population control, welfarism, democracy, and finally, there was a "domain" of something in between, something that enabled the protagonists of national culture, its civil society, to talk to, negotiate with, the State, something that we more commonly refer to as the sphere of "politics."

It is mainly the concept of "mediating institutions" that I shall briefly explore here, and their relevance to the cinema of this time. Let me trace back into this era yet another familiar characteristic of the 1990s Bollywood movie, one incarnated by its first big manifestation *Hum Aapke Hai Kaun?* that this cinema addresses a "family" audience and deals with "family values," as against another kind of film, the non-Bollywood variety, that did not and maybe still does not know how to do this. In this time, says Chatterjee, there was a move by the dominant State to name its people as "citizens" of some kind, and this move was a displacement away "from the idea of society as constituted by the elementary units of homogeneous families to that of a population, differentiated but classifiable, describable and enumerable."

It is possible to see the cinema as the suturing agency par excellence of such displacement and mediation. The cultural role of the neighborhood movie theater as a prominent institution of the new public sphere in this time is crucially accounted for by the fact that a ticket-buying spectator automatically assumed certain rights that were symbolically pretty crucial to the emerging State of the 1940s–1950s. (In some ways the contentious aspect of "entertainment tax"—effectively equating the spectator with the price of his ticket, extended into equating the film solely with its box office income, all the problems to which K. D. Shorey refers above—is a legacy of these times.) These rights—the right to enter a movie theater, to act as its privileged addressee, to further assert that right through, for example, various kinds of fan activity both inside and outside the movie theater (Srinivas 1996), went alongside a host of political rights that defined the "describable and enumerable" aspects of the population, like, for example, the right to vote, the right to receive welfare, the right to have a postal address and a bank account. Film historians through this period repeatedly assert how, for example, in many parts of India the cinema was perhaps the first instance in Indian civilization where the "national public" could gather in one place that was not divided along caste difference (Sivathamby 1981).

It is not important that these rights were not necessarily enforced on the ground. It is important instead to recognize that spectators were, and continue to be, *symbolically* and *narratively* aware of these rights, aware of their political underpinnings, and do various things—things that constitute the famous "active" and vocal Indian film spectator—that we must understand as a further assertion of these rights in the movie theater. I am suggesting here that, first, the many characteristics of film viewing in India—as well known as its masala and songs—of vocal audiences, throwing money at the screen, going into trances during devotional films and so forth, were in turn characteristic of *spectators identifying themselves* through identifying the film's address. And second, that this entire process of identification and counteridentification narratively spans precisely the divide that Chatterjee's "domain of mediating institutions" would play in the world outside the movie theater. It now appears that the aspect of "identification" that film theorist Christian Metz, for instance, once defined when he answered the question, who does the film spectator "identify" with? by suggesting that the spectator identifies with "*himself* . . . as a pure act of perception" (Metz 1982), developed a distinctly political meaning in the India of the 1940s and early 1950s.

There now developed a serious contradiction, from which the Indian cinema never really recovered: one as glaring today in the Bollywood versus film industry divide as it has ever been. In one sense, the film industry was able to maneuver itself into a certain position that made it indispensable to the State. As, in many ways, the most prominent independent cultural exemplar of the national market and the provider of leisure activity to the "people" in the larger populational sense to which Chatterjee gestures in his more encompassing definition of the citizen, the cinema demanded the right to exist and receive some kind of industrial sustenance. It did, for example, win certain regulatory concessions in the form of the various State Film Chambers of Commerce, a certain limited amount of infrastructural support, such as a subsidy for imported film stock (via the public sector Hindustan Photo Film); and in turn it also chose to view disciplinary institutions such as the Censor Board as not merely capable of punitive action, but also, and more positively, as agencies underscoring and validating the objects of its spectatorial address.

On the other hand, the very space that the film industry came to occupy disqualified it by definition from the range of *new* concessions and supports that the Film Enquiry Committee recommended, including, most crucially, institutional finance. Indeed, all these concessions, then and ever since, were meant for precisely a kind of cinema that the film industry was *not*. They were meant for a different cinema that the State hoped to encourage, one that would fit better into what Chatterjee calls the "pedagogical mission" of civil society and its agendas of modernization: a "different" cinema that we could today see as the direct ancestor of the Bollywood mode.

Indeed, in the barely concealed claims to some sort of reformism that Bollywood so often presents these days in its biggest successes—the claims of commitment to family values, to the "feel-good-happy-ending" romance that carries the tag of "our culture"—one can see the ghosts of past trends going pretty far back in time. The problem of the cinema's legitimacy has, since the prewar years, consistently produced version after version of what was claimed as culturally authentic cinema: authentic because it was *authenticated* by the national culture. One long-distance ancestor to, say *HAHK*, would be the prewar "Swadeshi" movie: the devotionals and socials emphasizing *indigenism* of story and production. Post-war and in the early years of Independence, there appeared the first descendant of this indigenism: the cinema that the State repeatedly anointed as "authentically national." The process of authentication in this time was more palpable than the films that benefited by various declarations of recommended viewing—and continues to be so, if we see, for example, the extraordinary premium that the film industry continues to place upon the government's national film awards and its tax exemption criteria. One could safely say, however, that among the candidates vying for this kind of accreditation were Devika Rani and Ashok Kumar socials from the Bombay Talkies studios, reformist musicals such as some of Raj Kapoor's work or some of Dev Anand's Navketan production house (both of which often hired ex-practitioners from the Indian People's Theatre Association movements of the 1940s), and realist-internationalist films by directors from Satyajit Ray to Bimal Roy to the early Merchant-Ivory (Rajadhyaksha 1993).

This then was the situation. The film industry had won for itself a distinct, even unique, space of spectatorial address and spectatorial attention that is even today not shared by any of its other ancillary industries —not, for example, by television, despite the many programs seeking to evoke the excitement of the filmgoing experience with its coverage of the industry, its "behind-the-scenes" programs and its efforts to get stars to endorse televised versions of the Indian cinema. It has extended this spectatorial space into some kind of peripheral, perennially unstable and yet functioning economy with a rough-and-ready system of funding for its productions. It has also weathered a divide within its production processes, between those who control infrastructure—licensed stockists of film stock, lab owners and owners of dubbing theaters, editing suites, sound studios and other post-production facilities, all of whom routinely get banking and corporate-institutional support—and those who invest in *production*, bear the entrepreneurial risks of a film doing well or badly, and *never* receive institutionalized funding support. They do not receive support because they cannot, for to do so certainly would be to threaten the very *raison d'être* of why the cinema is so popular, the space the industry occupies.

This is the situation—an evidently backdated, relentlessly modernist, even Statist, situation, wedded to governmental support while at the same time aware of its peculiar illegitimacy—to which K. D. Shorey refers when he enumerates the problems that film producers continue to face. This is self-evidently not the situation that Bollywood faces. The old movie spectator, the member of Chatterjee's political society, would—and does—feel distinctly uncomfortable in plush new foyers with Pepsi soda fountains. And Bollywood, in its turn, quite explicitly qualifies for a range of corporate funding support systems.

Bollywood does however manage something else in its turn, it seems, something that none of its cinematic predecessors could quite achieve. It succeeds, on the whole, in mediating the transition into the new category of citizen-as-family-member while maintaining intact the cultural insiderism of film spectatorship. Few films being locally made in Bombay, Chennai, or Calcutta can aspire to such a transition. Few films, ergo, can claim international venture capital support.

Exporting the Spectator: New Sites for Modernism

"There is a near unanimity that the right kind of recognition would eventually lower the cost of an industry, where expenses and price of funds are mindboggling. Thanks to the well accepted practice of tapping undisclosed money, particularly the mega-budget ones, the string of financiers (mostly operating through fronts) extract a rate of return which is three to four times the interest a commercial bank would possibly charge. . . . This unpredictability has become inseparable with films. Immediately, I can't think of an evaluation procedure by which I can call a production viable," said a senior PSU bank official. Bringing the activity within the banking parlance of "productive purpose" appears to be the crux of the matter. "Is it an income generating asset? This is neither manufacturing nor trading nor agriculture nor self-employment," said a private bank official. . . . "We may consider the track record of a producer, personal investments and net worth and ability to repay if the production flops and then take a short-term loan backed by sound collaterals. But will this attract the filmwallas? They might get a better deal from sources they have been tapping so far, said an official of one of the older private banks. (Ghosh 1998)

Sushma Swaraj, then, was clearly making an intervention more complex than what the Film Federation of India necessarily saw as the issues, when

she offered "industry status" to the cinema. The problem was old, even te-
diously familiar; the circumstances, however, were brand new.

There is one crucially important sense, perhaps, in which the new international market opening up for Indian film could be continuing its
old symbolic-political adherences. It is possible that the Indian cinema's
modes of address have opened up a new category for spectatorial address
that appears not to be accounted for by, say, the American cinema after it
discovered the storytelling mode for itself and after numerous critics and
theorists went on to assume that this mode was globally relevant and that
"we all internalize at an early age a *reading competence* thanks to an exposure of films . . . which is universal among the young in industrial societies" (Burch 1990). If this is so, then in several places, like Nigeria, whose
distinctive reception of Indian cinema has been analyzed so remarkably
by Brian Larkin (2001) or among the Fijian Indians in Australia who
even make their own Hindi films on video, as examined by Manas Ray
(2000), or for that matter among audiences who still flock to Indian films
in Trinidad and South Africa, there could be people still going to these
films precisely for what Hollywood cannot be seen to offer. It is possible
that the cinema's addresses are entering complex realms of identification
in these places, which would definitely further the argument around the
nature of the cultural-political mediation that the Indian, or possibly the
Hong Kong, cinemas continue to allow.

Evidently, *this* was not the market that was pressuring Swaraj to define a law offering industrial status to film. Nor was this the market that
has film distributors and producers in Bombay in a tizzy, wondering how
they can rake in their megabucks or go corporate. In fact, a recent news
item about Burma and how popular Hindi films are there, speaks of print
rights of *Taal* being sold for $10,000, a "relatively high amount by Bur-
mese standards" (Jha 2000).

In the Bollywood sense of the export of the Indian spectator to distant
lands, I want to suggest another kind of export: the export of Indian nationalism itself, now commodified and globalized into a "feel good" version of "our culture." If so, then what we are also seeing is a globalization
of the conflict, the divide, central to nationalism itself: the divide of *democracy* versus *modernity*, now playing itself out on a wider, more surreal
canvas than ever before.[6] We do not know too much about this right now,
but in conclusion, I would like to state the following issues that could be
of relevance.

First, consider the question of *modernism*. If the civil- and political-society divide means anything at all, it shows how prevalent, foundational, and indeed how virtually unbridgeable the divides in India have been across the chasm of modernity. It is true that *something* has happened recently, which seemingly wipes them away as though they have never existed, and different people have tried to explain this erasure differently. Arjun Appadurai's famous formulation of "modernity at large," modernity cleansed of the mechanics of geographical belonging by the diaspora and the cyber-neighborhood, certainly offers the *terrain* on which this insiderism is acted out (Appadurai 1997). There do nevertheless seem to be larger and still unanswered questions, which might be asked both of the theorist but even more directly of the practitioner of Bollywood culture. For example, why now? The transition of cultural insiderism away from its heartland, away then from its historic political function of creating a certain category of citizen, and into something that informs the feelings of the visitor to the Brisbane night club, quoted earlier, who wants to go there to "assert her Eastern identity"—this transition would clearly have something basic to offer in its rewriting the *very trajectories of modernism* that have historically linked places such as India to the "West." Why does it seem so simple to pull off today when the Indian cinema has sought this transition to national legitimacy since at least the 1960s, without success?

A second question deals with the area of cultures resisting economic and political resolution. Bollywood clearly is reconfiguring the field of cinema in important ways. What does it pick as translatable into the new corporate economy, what is it that this economy leaves behind? This would be as important a cultural question as an economic one.

For example, I believe it is demonstrable that practically all the new money flowing into the cinema right now is concentrating on the ancillary sector of film production. On one side, software giants such as Pentafour and Silicon Graphics use film to demonstrate their products, so that it is unclear whether, say, Shankar's *Jeans* (1998), noted for all its digitized camerawork and produced by Hollywood's Ashok Amritraj, was more an independent feature film surviving on a pay-per-view basis or more a three-hour demo for Pentafour's special effects. On the other hand, the range of consumables increasingly visible on film screens—Stroh's beer in *DDLJ*, Coca-Cola in *Taal*, Swatch watches in *Phir Bhi Dil Hai Hindustani* —are symptomatic of the nature of funding that the cinema increasingly depends upon.

If so, it would be the final irony of the Bollywoodization of the Indian cinema that the very demand that the industry has sought from the government for so many decades could be the reason for its demise. The arrival of corporate-industrial-finance capital could reasonably lead to the final triumph of Bollywood, even as the cinema itself gets reduced only to a memory, a part of the nostalgia industry.

NOTES

Reprinted by permission of the publisher.

1. See http://www.bbc.co.uk/asianlife/film/indiansummer/index.shtml. Also, *The New Indian Express* (October 29, 1999) reports that "The opening titles of Sooraj Barjatya's forthcoming film *Hum Saath Saath Hain*, billed as the most cracking release this Diwali, will feature an important new player in Bollywood: Coca-Cola. The cola giant, in its bid to scramble to the very top of the Rs3500 crore soft drinks market, has spent a comparatively smaller amount, Rs1.5 crore, on branding Barjatya's family film and ensuring its release as *Coca-Cola Hum Saath Saath Hain*."

2. *Statistics on Film and Cinema 1975–77*, Paris: Office of Statistics, UNESCO, 1981.

3. Tejaswini Niranjana defines this newly forged relationship, in *Roja*, of a "techno-aesthetic" with a new category of the "national" subject: see Niranjana (1994).

4. Report of the Film Enquiry Committee (S. K. Patil, Chairman), New Delhi, Government of India Press, 1951.

5. See especially Prasad (1998) and Chakravarty (1993).

6. Chatterjee elaborates his "civil" versus "political" society argument by suggesting that although modernity was the main agenda for the former, democracy could be seen as the main issue addressing the latter. So, in effect, the entire debate around modernism, around high and low art, around a religious secularism versus theories of caste and religion, could be mapped around this often unbridgeable divide between modernity and democracy (Chatterjee 1997).

BIBLIOGRAPHY

Appadurai, Arjun. 1997. *Modernity At Large: Cultural Dimensions of Globalization*. New Delhi: Oxford University Press.

Banker, Ashok. 2001. *Bollywood*. New Delhi: Penguin Books.

Burch, Noel. 1990. *Life to those Shadows*, trans. Ben Brewster. Berkeley: University of California Press.

Chakravarty, Sumita. 1993. *National Identity in Indian Popular Cinema 1947–87*. Austin: University of Texas Press.

Chatterjee, Partha. 1997. "Beyond the Nation? Or Within?" *Economic & Political Weekly* 32, no. 1–2.

Cormack, Mike. 1994. *Ideology and Cinematography in Hollywood, 1930–39*. New York: St. Martin's Press.

Das Gupta, Chidananda. 1968. "The Cultural Basis of Indian Cinema." In *Talking About Films*. New Delhi: Orient Longman.

Diawara, Manthia. 1992. *African Cinema: Politics & Culture*. Bloomington: Indiana University Press.

Ghosh, Sugata. 1998. "Industry Status: Cinema May Find Itself Going Round Trees." *Economic Times*, May 12.

Jha, Lalit K. 2000. "Mania for Hindi Movies Sweeps Myanmar." *The Hindu*, February 29.

Kabir, Nasreen Munni. 2001. *Bollywood: The Indian Cinema Story*. London: Channel 4 Books.

Larkin, Brian. 2001. "Indian Films, Nigerian Lovers: Media and the Creation of Parallel Modernities." *Africa* 67 (3): 406–40.

Metz, Christian. 1982. *The Imaginary Signifier: Psychoanalysis and the Cinema*. Bloomington: Indiana University Press.

Moshavi, Sharon. 1995. "Bollywood Breaks into the Big Time." *Economic Times*, October 3.

Niranjana, Tejaswini. 1994. "Integrating Whose Nation? Tourists and Terrorists in *Roja*." *Economic & Political Weekly* 29 (3): 79–81.

Prasad, Madhava. 1998. *Ideology of the Hindi Film: a Historical Construction*. New Delhi: Oxford University Press.

Rajadhyaksha, Ashish. 1993. "The Epic Melodrama: Themes of Nationality in Indian Cinema." *Journal of Arts & Ideas* 25–26: 55–70.

Ray, Manas. 2000. "Bollywood Down Under: Fiji Indian Cultural History and Popular Assertion. In *Floating Lives: The Media and Asian Diaspora*, ed. Stuart Cunningham and John Sinclair, 136–84. Queensland: University of Queensland Press.

Sengupta, Ratnottama. 1999. "Taalis for the Showman." *The Times of India*, July 8.

Shukla, Sandhya. 1997. "Building Diaspora and Nation: the 1991 'Cultural Festival of India.'" *Cultural Studies* 11, 2 (July): 296–315.

Sivathamby, K. 1981. *The Tamil Film as a Medium of Political Communication*. Madras: New Century Book House.

Srinivas, S. V. 1996. "Devotion and Defiance in Fan Activity." *Journal of Arts & Ideas* 29 (January): 67–83.

Chapter 2

ılıllıllıllıllıllıllıllıllıllıllıllıllıllıllıllıllıllıllılı

Surviving Bollywood

M. Madhava Prasad

Origins

It is precisely the act of naming that is the most interesting aspect of Bollywood. It is a strange name, a hybrid, that seems to at once mock the thing it names and celebrate its difference. And in spite of a few murmurs of protest from the industry, the name has now come to stay. Today, the term "Bollywood" has become naturalized not only in the English-language media, which is probably the term's original habitat, but also the Indian-language press, not only among journalists but also film scholars. One kind of response to this development has been a sense of outrage, a feeling that someone has successfully conducted an operation of symbolic abduction, leaving us (meaning something like "real Indians") with the vague feeling that we have been cheated out of something precious, the right to name our own fantasies. One cannot blame people for feeling so, and indeed this sentiment itself is an integral part of the phenomenon. But neither should we limit ourselves to this nationalist framework if we want to make sense of this event of the rise of Bollywood. Beyond the disputes over the name, there is also a dispute over control over the thing it designates, and these will be the dual focus of this short consideration of the matter.

The origin of the term being obscure, there have been many claimants to the credit for coining it, and many theories as to its first usage. What is not often recognized is that the coining of the term was at least a two-step process which might not have occurred were it not for the chance juxtaposition of two pairs of rhyming syllables. In 1932, Wilford E. Deming, an American engineer who claims that "under my supervision was produced India's first sound and talking picture," writing in *American*

Cinematographer (12.11, March 1932), mentions a telegram he received as he was leaving India after his assignment: TOLLYWOOD SENDS BEST WISHES HAPPY NEW YEAR TO LUBILL FILM DOING WONDERFULLY RECORDS BRO-KEN.[1] In explanation, he adds, "In passing it might be explained that our Calcutta studio was located in the suburb of Tollygunge . . . Tolly being a proper name and Gunge meaning locality. After studying the advantages of Hollygunge we decided on Tollywood. There being two studios at present in that locality, and several more projected, the name seems appropriate." Whether or not Deming and his colleagues actually coined it, it is clear that this is an old term. Thus it was Hollywood itself, in a manner of speaking, that, with the confidence that comes from global supremacy, renamed a concentration of production facilities to make it look like its own baby. In those days already the supremacy of Hollywood was unchallenged throughout the world. The archive is full of admiring references by Indian filmmakers to the big Hollywood studios and industry giants like Cecil B. DeMille. We should note that the Indian film industry has always been dominated by admirers of Hollywood and that many standard features of Indian popular cinema derive from Hollywood films. In such an atmosphere, the collaborative act of renaming Tollygunge as Tollywood signals not so much an insinuation of cultural subalternity as the sense of international solidarity of film technicians. At any rate, it carries no trace of an intention to characterize the cinema of Tollygunge itself as in any way a derivative product. It is quite likely that Indian filmmakers in Calcutta and Bombay implicitly accepted their own second-rank status vis-à-vis Hollywood in terms of technical sophistication and storytelling skills, but this should not be confused with the more nationalist preoccupation with originality and embarrassment about derivativeness.

Deming and his hosts in Calcutta were renaming the locality, but there is no suggestion here that the name would also serve as an adjective to describe Indian cinema in general (although Calcutta in those days was a major production center). This fits very well with what I seem to remember from occasionally glancing at a Kolkata-based youth magazine called *JS* (or Junior Statesman, a publication of the Statesman group which, long before satellite television and MTV, was addressed to what must have been a very small elite Indian youth segment) which referred to the Bengali film industry as Tollywood. Bollywood is most likely to have come into existence by this route with a further act of phonetic transposition. There is no obvious way to get from Bombay to Bollywood directly.

Once Tollywood was made possible by the fortuitous availability of a half-rhyme, it was easy to clone new Hollywood babies by simply replacing the first letter. Thus, the Tamil film industry is referred to as Kollywood, because the studios are concentrated in an area of Chennai called Kodambakkam. I suspect (thus adding my own origin story to the many that are in existence) that it was the trendy young *JS* journalists who first adopted this way of slotting Hindi cinema into their otherwise largely Eurocentric cultural world. It is thus a mark of the indulgent lampooning that the Anglophone middle class subjected the Hindi cinema to in reviews, articles, and private conversations. For a long time the term was occasionally used in such discourse. In the 1990s, it began to be used with greater frequency, with Indian popular cinema attracting international attention as diasporic audiences pushed Hindi films into the box office charts of the American and British film markets.

Unlike this forgotten originary moment in Kolkata, it seems that the late renomination of Bollywood is of a different order of significance. Is it meant to suggest that Indian popular cinema is imitative and therefore deserves to be rechristened to highlight this derivativeness? Or is it in fact the opposite: an attempt to indicate a difference internal to the dominant idiom, a variation that is related to but distinct from the globally hegemonic Hollywood? Is it Indian cinema's way of signifying its difference or is it (inter)national film journalism and scholarship's way of re-inscribing the difference that Indian cinema represents within an articulated model of global hegemony and resistance?

The term seems to serve different purposes for different people. Thus, academic conferences on Bollywood tend to use the term loosely to refer to Indian cinema in general, whereas European television shows which feature Indian films might restrict the meaning to the popular genre, and then only to the blockbusters. Bollywood also, like Hollywood, refers to everything to do with the Bombay film industry, and there is growing interest both among international filmmakers and scholars in many of its auxiliary sectors, such as choreography, music, costumes, hairstyling. The meaning of the term may also vary from user to user: some mean by it Hindi cinema of the globalized present alone, whereas others just substitute it for Indian popular cinema, Bombay/Hindi cinema and other previously employed terms.

In this changeable form, the term Bollywood has since found a place in the vocabulary of the Anglophone national culture. Like certain processes of which we become aware only when they are almost over, we are right now witnessing the naturalization of Bollywood as the designation for what was previously known as Hindi cinema, Bombay cinema, popular cinema, and so on. It is tempting to think that this process of near-universal legitimation of Bollywood is a symptom of some other social and cultural processes with a wider significance. Can linguistic change be an index of social transformations and if so, how do we make sense of them?

In the last decade or so, since the term began to catch on, Indian popular cinema has undergone some major changes, and indeed could be said to have developed a new genre of sorts. We might be tempted to give the term some academic respectability by assigning it a definite signifier: those films that, since the early 1990s have evolved a new aesthetic that is marked by consciousness of the global presence of Indians and Indian cinema, a genre that is prevalent not only in Hindi but also in high-profile regional cinemas like Tamil. While such efforts might help to clarify the uses of the term, in the end it must be admitted that there is no hope of giving it a definite meaning. For its significance lies not in its strictly denotative function, but in the power that it has manifested in the last decade or so, of recentering Indian film culture around a new cluster of identifications. The rise to prominence of this term is undoubtedly a cultural symptom whose meaning remains to be deciphered. For naming is not only about the reality that is designated, but about the will of the one who names, the will to reconstitute an existing reality in its own image.

The new popular cinema referred to above has figured prominently in the emerging culture of India, where consumer capitalism has finally succeeded in weaning the citizens away from a strongly entrenched culture of thrift toward a system of gratification more firmly in its (capitalism's) own long-term control. They have produced yet another variation of the nationalist ideology of tradition and modernity, and, most interestingly, they have sought to relocate what we might call the seismic center of Indian national identity somewhere in Anglo-America. In other words, this new trend in the industry has brought the NRI decisively into the center of the picture, as a more stable figure of Indian identity than anything that can be found indigenously. While economists continue to be skeptical about NRI patriotism making a difference to FDI, culturally it is indisputable that the NRI is increasingly beginning to look like the sole guarantor of Indian identity. In this regard, the NRI productions themselves have lately become more important than the indigenous ones which, with a few exceptions like *Dilwale Dulhania Le Jayenge* (1995, Aditya Chopra), continue to pose the "return to roots" as the redeeming factor in tales of dislocation. The success of films like *Bend It Like Beckham* (2003, Gurinder Chadha) is an obvious indicator of how the NRI is once again functioning as a facilitator in the transition to a new mode of self-relation. "Once again," because the last time it was as television personalities that young NRIs held our hands when we were trying to find our bearings in an MTV world. One can discern here issues related to language, to the sociology of the Indian film industry including its audiences, and at the economic level, the local variations in the logic of commodification. Let us look at these one by one.

The Languages of Identity

Language, or the verbal discourse of Hindi film narrative, is one element that bears traces of movements and shifts in our sociocultural identity of which Bollywood is a symptom. The arrival of Bollywood coincides with a tectonic shift in the linguistic balance of forces within the Indian subcontinent. In order to grasp this point, we need to take a detour into what I will call the structural bilingualism of the Indian nation-state.[2] Structural bilingualism is a state of affairs where the multitude of Indian languages (here counted as one) function under the direction of a metalanguage in which alone the national ideology can be properly articulated. Although Hindi occupies a middle position between English and other Indian languages, by virtue of its status as a national language and the enormous influence of Hindi cinema across the subcontinent, it is in Hindi cinema that we can track a change that is decisive in terms of defining the linguistic order of new India. In this respect, Hindi cinema has witnessed a very significant transformation in recent periods: The role of Hindustani/Urdu as the metalanguage of Hindi cinema's ideological work has now been challenged by English. Of course, it is difficult to conceive of Urdu being replaced by English in a film without it becoming an "English film," but it is nevertheless the case that English provides the ideological coordinates of the new world of the Hindi film.

The general point here is that the social genre, which is the dominant genre beside which all others must seek to find a place, and which constitutes popular cinema's most significant contribution to the ongoing elaboration of India's cultural identity, must locate its narratives in a modern context. This is, interestingly enough, a compulsion born not out of any realist desire to reflect actually existing social conditions, but one deriving from the popular cinematic narrative form itself as it was inherited along with film technology from Western sources. The history of narrative cinema in India bears witness to the fact that from the beginning it included a romance plot which gradually came to be the main plotline.[3] This is a compulsion entirely attributable to the cinematic apparatus and its pedagogic role as the disseminator of modernity. There is a difference between Hindi and the rest of the Indian-language cinemas in this regard, because the Hindi cinema alone had, at its disposal, a ready-made language of universality that could be straightaway narratively deployed. This language was of course the Urdu component of the composite language called Hindustani. In the Indian context it alone had elaborated a discourse of love and a discourse of law—the two fundamental registers of universality. In Hindi cinema too one can easily picture the difficulty that might have confronted a language devoid of the Urdu component. Consider the songs Hindi film lead pairs sing: they are replete with erotic imagery and fairly elaborate conceits which require thought. But in the next moment, when they are relocated in a Hindu familial context, they re-emerge as virgin adolescents being fed and cajoled by their mothers and showing no signs of the intelligence that they displayed in the songs. Hindustani had a convincing depth to its languages of love and law, both of which had a long history of elaboration in India before the advent of modern cultural forms like the cinema.

Against this background, we can examine the Hindi cinema of the present. Of course, this cinema cannot really function without its Hindustani. Nevertheless, there are signs of change. Love, rather than *pyar, mohabbat,* or *ishq,* is today the reigning signifier for the privileged affect. English phrases and proverbs are liberally used to construct a web of discourse which the characters inhabit. The charms of Urdu, of course, continue to command a good price, but the language has now been reduced to its accumulated stocks of nostalgic sentiment, as was more than evident in the recent *Fanaa* (2006, Kunal Kohli). The old three-language formula of filmic Indian nationalism, for instance, has imperceptibly undergone a change: today, posters and credits no longer carry the title in Urdu script as a matter of routine.

While discussing these changes we should not lose sight of the significant countertrends that are also part of today's Indian cinema. If we take a film like the recent *Omkara* (2006), Vishal Bharadwaj's adaptation of Shakespeare's *Othello,* as an example, what we have is a sign of another kind of linguistic experimentation in the Hindi cinema, which would have been unthinkable in the commercial sector of the industry even a decade ago. We can see signs, beneath the nationalist and now diasporic preoccupations of the Bombay cinema, many trends that point to a cultural-linguistic recuperation of the Hindi-speaking regions, which are joining the general trend of cultural assertion. Reports about the growing popularity of films made in Bhojpuri and *khadi boli* seem to conform to this logic.

Sociology

But structural bilingualism has significance at a different level: today, it is the will of the English-speaking classes that prevails in giving a name and an identity to the Hindi cinema. Ajay Devgan recently told an interviewer that he disapproved of the use of "Bollywood" to refer to Hindi films. There is a lot of resentment against it, but it cannot be said that the industry has had no role to play in the popularization of its usage. Bollywood is also a product of developments within the popular Hindi cinema, notably the generational changes within the industry, which have brought to the limelight a group of sons of industry magnates and others similarly placed, as well as new generations of stars, most of whom are educated in elite schools, if not abroad. There is no reliable study of the sociology of the Indian film industry yet, but it is more than evident from the information available in the media and the films themselves that today the most powerful segment of the industry is controlled by a few big daddies (to put it literally). The sons and daughters of producers, directors, script writers, stars, and studio owners of an earlier generation are today some of the most prominent directors and stars. Their wealth, education, and age make them naturally a part of the global Indian culture. They are the leaders of the new Bollywood turn in the industry, and although a few people might disapprove, this generation is very much a part of the whole process of renomination that we are talking about. And their language of choice is English: the stories they tell rely increasingly on a Hollywood-style, English-dependent discourse of love, however derivative the end product might seem. This shift in the register of love toward English is also accompanied by a sharp fall in the importance of the register of law. This is a post-national aesthetic where the old dramatic courtroom confrontations seem to have lost their place (now only Govinda's films, which maintain continuity with the older film form, continue to rely on court-room scenes). Even the romantic register of Urdu tends to be more and more attenuated and fetishized in a compensatory move. These shifts in language are a pointer to a reconstitution of the ideological field in the moment of Bollywood.

Here too certain countertrends might be noted. While the daddy-led sector of the industry invests in an aesthetic that combines Western con-sumerist ideals and sentiments with the distinctive Indian features like dances and weddings, there are others who would abandon the Indian style altogether: there is today a more diverse range of experimentation going on in Indian cinema than at any time previously, and all of it is in the commercial sector. Whereas the daddy sector works to maintain con-tinuity while incorporating superficial changes, others seem to be making a sustained effort to break once and for all with this "Indian" style and its artifices. Their efforts are increasingly inspired by Hollywood and Asian cinema (*Zinda*), and the net effect of it all is still too early to gauge. But this does not look like Bollywood.

The Commodification of Fetishes

This brings us to the other means by which the word has been legit-imized: the discovery of Hindi cinema by the rest of the world includ-ing NRI filmmakers, which leads to a reification of its most obvious dis-tinguishing properties as constituting its permanent identity. Recently, much was made of the presence of a Hindi film song on the soundtrack of *Moulin Rouge*, and similar examples can be cited from various parts of the world. The pan-Asian production *Perhaps Love* (2005) used Farah Khan's choreography, and Jackie Chan's *The Myth* included a segment shot in India in a familiar Hollywood idiom. *Moulin Rouge*, for all its novelty, deviated little from the familiar Hollywood musical style, and in spite of the Hindi song, the Indian excitement about it being inspired by Hindi cinema was a bit desperate to say the least. But these news events should be located in a larger trend of commodification of film styles in a post-modern world where a new logic of commodification is in operation. More than the above instances, it is the example of the NRI directors that illustrates this trend.

While a lot of popular writing reflects such Bollywood sentiment, we should locate the work of NRI directors like Mira Nair, Deepa Mehta, Gurinder Chaddha, and Nagesh Kukunoor in this tendency as well.

Mehta, of course, has given ample indication of this line of thinking in her *Hollywood/Bollywood,* but the films of Mira Nair, and Chaddha's *Bend It Like Beckham* and *Bride and Prejudice* are also indicative of a similar proclivity. In this genre of NRI films, Bollywood is given a sort of dual status. On the one hand there is a link suggested between the moral-ideological framework of popular cinema and the moral-ideological world of older generations of Indians living in Western countries. In the narratives of struggle between generations, a staple of NRI cinema, Bollywood serves to pin the older generation to an ideological slot. At the same time, the affection that is nevertheless felt toward these older people—parents, aunts and uncles, grandparents—is transferred to Bollywood. Protagonists occupy a position of uneasy familiarity with this cinema: they are in daily contact with it, but their own temperaments are more local, Western, thus unable to identify with it.

The early films of Chaddha, Hanif Kureishi, Srinivas Krishna and others are all in this mode. But in time, as the market for these films grew, and the diasporic community quickly expanded, the sort of enclosed community of migrant Indians that the early films portrayed was replaced in some countries by a new and multitiered immigrant workforce. Unlike second- or third-generation British or American youth of Indian origin, these IT professionals and other workers were in love with their national cinema *and* young. The NRI filmmakers evolved a different aesthetic, less focused on the older community and more aware of the living connection with India that had been revived in the moment of globalization. Their films have thus played a significant role in commodifying Bollywood for the international market and for introducing to Indian audiences their own cinema in new packaging.

The successful commodification of Indian cinema as Bollywood in the international market is based on the idea of an unchanging essence that distinguishes it from Hollywood. It cannot have a history, or its history can only be a narrative of the spontaneous repetition of its innate predilection to sing and dance and cry. This agonistic relation to Hollywood is definitive. As a variant of international melodrama from the early capitalist era, Indian popular cinema did not undergo formal transformations comparable to those that signaled the advent of realism in Hollywood. Thus, it would be a mistake to regard the thematic elements of Indian popular cinema as reflecting the social realities of their time. Most of the thematic elements are variants of the ones popularized by stage melodrama in nineteenth-century Europe. Thus, Bollywood serves not only as the aesthetic of the spatially Other, but also as a revisitation of the Hollywood of the past.

In this moment of its commodification as a fetish object, the Hindi films that are named by Bollywood are also undergoing a change. As the symptom of a formal transformation, where form is understood not only as a dimension of textuality, but also in a larger sense as the set of relations between the elements internal to the text as well as those which constitute its habitat—its audiences, its economic structure, its ideological matrix, etc.—Bollywood is capable of affording us crucial insights into the changing modalities of Indian national identity in a globalizing world. Related to the above, "Bollywood" also signals the advent of a certain reflexivity, becoming a cinema for itself as it were, recognizing its own unique position in the world, the contrastive pleasures and values that it represents vis-à-vis Hollywood. This reflexivity is as much a form of self-awareness as it is a know-how that enables the Hindi film to reproduce itself for a market that demands its perpetuation as a source of cultural identity. At a time when Indian cinema is far more diverse than it has even been in the past, Bollywood is an attempt to hold on to the idea of an essence of Indian cinema. Indian cinema's marketability is becoming a matter of Indianness, which is its Bollywoodness. Bollywood keeps alive a sense of continuity amidst change.

In some recent films we get a distinct feeling that the intelligences involved in their production had bought into the Bollywood theory about songs in films, rather than spontaneously making films with songs which might have been the situation in earlier times. The desire for Bollywood is thus a desire for the reproduction of the difference that it represents on a world platform, which the industry itself, in its current reflexive moment, is responding to. It is this reflexivity and the demand it is responding to that can be said to constitute the very stuff of the new NRI film. But there are other dynamics at work, as we have briefly noted above, which are invested in transforming the Indian cinema scene, of getting rid of the old formats and establishing new logics of cultural production. Of course, people will continue to use the same term, Bollywood, even for this trend, since as we have noted above, it does not commit itself to any restrictive meaning. Nevertheless, the box office statistics seem to indicate that there is another way of classifying the products of Bombay which will give us another map of the territory, such as the one Ashish Rajadhyaksha[4] has tried to delineate, which will reveal objective limits to the scope of the term Bollywood and the fantasy that it embodies.

NOTES

1. I thank Madhuja Mukherjee for drawing my attention to this article.

2. Colonial bilingualism, as Veena Naregal has termed and studied it, is the historical factor of which the structural bilingualism of the independent Indian state is a sort of end-product.

3. This point has been demonstrated in detail in Subhajit Chatterjee's "Romance . . . ," unpublished dissertation, Manipal Academy of Higher Education/ Centre for the Study of Culture and Society, 2006.

4. See Ashish Rajadhyaksha, "The 'Bollywoodization' of the Indian Cinema: Cultural Nationalism in a Global Arena," in (*City Flicks: Cinema, Urban Worlds and Modernities in India and Beyond*, ed. Preben Karsholm. International Development Studies, Roskilde University Occasional Paper # 22, 2002.

Chapter 3

|||||||||||||||||||||||||||||||||||||||||||||||||||||||

Mumbai versus Bollywood
The Hindi Film Industry and the Politics of Cultural Heritage in Contemporary India

Tejaswini Ganti

On a July afternoon near Bombay's Nariman Point, people pushed and shoved, straining to get a glimpse of the film stars standing on the platform erected by the sea.[1] Two men simultaneously sounded their high-pitched horns shaped like elephant tusks, signaling to the drummers behind them to start beating their barrel-shaped drums. Policemen held back the crowds as men and women attired in hobbyhorses started swaying to the drumbeat. Women with their hair pulled back in buns encircled by garlands of jasmine and wearing maroon nine-yard saris in the Maharashtrian style (pulled between their legs and fastened in the back) followed, carrying brass platters of clay oil lamps. Following them were pairs of men and women dressed in colorful "folk" outfits—turbans, *kurtas*, and *ghagra-cholis*—dancing with each other. Residents of nearby apartment buildings gathered on their balconies to watch the events below. TV crews stood on the roofs of their vans taping the proceedings.[2]

The spectacle holding everyone's interest was not the shooting of a film, a frequent enough sight on the streets of Bombay, but a procession to commemorate the hundredth year of the arrival of cinema in India. On July 7, 1896, a representative of the Lumiere Brothers from Paris en route to Australia screened the first motion pictures in India in Bombay's Watsons Hotel. Exactly a hundred years later, on July 7, 1996, the Department of Cultural Affairs of the Government of Maharashtra in conjunction with the National Film Archives of India organized a series of public events in downtown Bombay to mark the day as an historic one. This program was the final event in a series of country-wide commemorations, organized by the Ministry of Information and Broadcasting's National Committee for the Celebration of the Cinema Centenary, which had started during the 26th International Film Festival of India (IFFI) held in Bombay in January 1995. At that time, the National Film Development Corporation (NFDC) commissioned an art director from the Hindi film industry to recreate the original venue of the Lumiere Brothers' first screenings at the Nehru Centre, organized a temporary film museum with items from landmark Hindi films, and produced a stage show "Cinema Cinema 100" in collaboration with the Hindi film industry as a tribute to a century of Indian cinema.

The commemorations organized by the state government of Maharashtra on July 7, 1996, were a combination of public and semi-public rituals inscribing the history of cinema in India onto the urban landscape of Bombay.[3] The key attraction was a procession of members of the Hindi and Marathi film industries to the site of the Watsons Hotel—now referred to as either the Esplanade Mansion or the Army-Navy Building—where the Chief Minister of Maharashtra unveiled a plaque affixed to the building proclaiming its historical importance. However, this event was declared a disappointment by the press because of a dearth of stars from the Hindi film industry. "Centenary fete lacks glitz," declared one headline, while another accused, "Bollywood has no sense of duty or history."

In this chapter, I examine the centenary commemorations staged by the government of Maharashtra to show how the history of cinema in India becomes an arena for the state to assert its distinct cultural identity. Mass media such as film and television have been the objects of study and critique mainly for the form and content of their texts. Here, I explore how the institution of cinema is incorporated by the regional state, in this case, the government of Maharashtra, into its vocabulary of cultural heritage. The commemorations reveal how the official history of Indian cinema as promulgated by national institutions like the Ministry of Information and Broadcasting and the National Film Archives is contested by a regional institution like the Department of Cultural Affairs of Maharashtra, a state which was at that time governed by the Shiv Sena—a political party rooted in regional, linguistic, and religious chauvinism. Although the Hindi film industry was articulated as a partner in the commemorations, the relative absence of its members from the events provides an insight into the relationship between the state and the industry. The commemorations also disclose how the history of cinema in Bombay becomes a site for the state to assert a particular cultural claim to the city itself. The centenary celebrations thus become the terrain of a cultural struggle for the city of Bombay.

I first provide a description of the commemorations, including the press reports prior to the events of July 7. Then I explain the apparent disjuncture between the stated purpose of the commemorations and their actual character. In the third section, I discuss how the press judged and evaluated the commemorations as a failure. Next, I detail the reasons for the film industry's lack of participation and describe its relationship with the government of Maharashtra. Finally, I situate the commemorations in the larger political and historical context of Bombay.

Marching through Time and Space in Bombay

Prior to July 7, articles appeared in the major English-language newspapers in Bombay announcing the procession of film personalities and the unveiling of the plaque on the former Watsons Hotel as the main features of the centenary celebrations. Some of the articles explained the impetus for the celebrations in terms of a corrective. "It's official—cinema started here," represented the events as fixing an oversight of the centenary celebrations initiated the previous year in Bombay by the Central government where, "in all the hoopla, the actual place where moving pictures first saw the light of day in India was totally forgotten" (Menon 1996a). The fact that the Watsons Hotel—the embodiment of the origins of cinema in India—had not been officially designated a landmark, was posited as a neglect of history that the current celebrations would rectify: "And at last a plaque will be put up at this building to remind posterity that cinema began here" (Menon 1996a). Another article, "Thespians and vintage cars will mark movie centenary," also explained the motivation for the celebrations in terms of an oversight, but one by the state government since special programs had been held in Calcutta and Bangalore in 1995 under the auspices of the centenary celebrations by their respective state governments; "the Maharashtra government thought it imperative to organize a gala function to salute the industry, which is one among the largest employers in the state" (Chaware 1996). The articles also remarked that the government was sparing no expense for the celebrations, describing them as a combined effort among the state government, the National Film Archives, and the Hindi film industry. The impending procession promised to be a "star studded" spectacle: "a galaxy of thespians decked up in period costumes . . . in a colourful procession decorated with vintage cars and buggies," (Chaware 1996) where "leading stars Dilip Kumar, Amitabh, Shahrukh, Manisha Koirala, Dimple, Jackie, Juhi Chawla, and others will participate" (Menon 1996a).

While the press represented the centenary celebrations as commemorating the hundredth year of the first screening of motion pictures in India, the government of Maharashtra presented the celebrations as commemorating a hundred years of Indian cinema. The Directorate of Cultural Affairs circulated invitations printed in English labeled, "Indian Film Centenary Celebration" which stated,

> The Cultural Affairs Department of the Government of Maharashtra with the active cooperation of the Indian Film Industry is celebrating the 100 years of Indian Cinema on Sunday, 7th of July 1996 in Mumbai. A grand procession of film artists, producers, directors, and technicians from the Hindi and Marathi film industry (sic) is being organized. The route of the procession is Tata Theatre (National Center for Performing Arts) to Subashchandra Bose Chowk (Kala Ghoda) to Y. B. Chavan Centre. Your presence on this historic day is earnestly requested.

The people signing off on the invitations were the President of the Film Federation of India (FFI), the Managing Director of the National Film Development Corporation (NFDC), the Director of Cultural Affairs of the Government of Maharashtra, the Secretary of Cultural Affairs of the Government of Maharashtra, and the Director of the National Film Archives. The card also listed the Chief Minister, two of his cabinet members, and renowned playback singer Lata Mangeshkar[4] as the key participants in the day's events.

Flagged off by the Minister for Cultural Affairs, Pramod Navalkar, the focal point of the procession was a large, navy blue, open-bed truck marked with a sign "Indian Cinema 100 Years" in Marathi, a model of a movie camera affixed to its roof, and a mural on the side depicting a scene from the 1936 Marathi film *Sant Tukaram* (Saint Tukaram). Most of the film personalities—actors, actresses, directors, producers, and technicians from both the Hindi and Marathi film industries—were either standing or sitting in this truck and waving to the cheering crowds of spectators lined along the streets. Following the truck were antique cars and horse-drawn carriages carrying the "veterans" of the Hindi film industry[5]— those members who are retired or not as professionally active—as well as officials of the government of Maharashtra. As the procession wended its way east and then north to the site of the Watsons Hotel, it was met with hundreds of people eagerly waiting behind police cordons, hoping to see some film stars.

Once the procession wound up at the historic site, the participants and spectators awaited the unveiling of the plaque by Chief Minister Manohar Joshi. The area underneath the portico of the building was covered with red carpeting and potted plants placed at intervals. Rows of chairs faced a small platform erected on one end. High above on the silvery gray wall of the building was a short white curtain with garlands of marigolds dangling underneath and a coconut placed on the ground below. Wizened old men were playing the shehnai.[6] Before the Chief Minister's appearance, Navalkar announced that theater owners in the state had agreed to exhibit Marathi films for 15 days in a year. His announcement was met with a burst of applause. By the time Joshi arrived, the small area was packed with spectators, photographers, and television cameras jostling each other for a clear view. After posing for photographs with film personalities flanking him on all sides, Joshi made his way to the wall and waited with the cord in his hand. Once the coconut was smashed against a rock on the ground[7] with the music reaching a crescendo, he pulled away the curtain to reveal the "plaque," a white canvas board with black lettering, that simply stated,

> Lumiere Brothers' "Cinematographe" was first screened here on 7th July 1896, at the erstwhile Watsons Hotel, thus sowing the seed of one of the most popular of the art forms of this century, cinema in India.

After a break for tea and refreshments in the Jehangir Art Gallery across the street, the entourage of film personalities, bureaucrats, officials, and spectators fortunate to have invitations shifted to the nearby Y. B. Chavan auditorium for the final ceremonies of the day, which involved inaugurations of the weeklong film festival and an exhibition of photographs documenting the 100 years of Indian cinema. Sixteen people—a combination of officials and film personalities—sat on stage against a graphic of a motion picture camera and the words, "100 Years of Indian Cinema" in Marathi emblazoned on a backdrop of marigolds. The ceremonies began with a moment of silence for the remembrance of Hindi film actor, Raaj Kumar, who had died two days earlier, and for all those before him. The Minister for Cultural Affairs, Pramod Navalkar, then presented Lata

Mangeshkar with a big bouquet of flowers and led her to a tall, brass oil lamp. Navalkar and Mangeshkar lit the lamp together, officially initiating the program.[8] State Minister for Cultural Affairs,[9] Anil Deshmukh, "released" the official program of the film festival by unwrapping a package tied in red ribbon, taking out a brochure entitled in English, "Celebrating the 100th Year of the Arrival of Cinema in Mumbai," displaying it to the audience and then distributing them to all of the guests present on stage.

The various government officials made short speeches about the historic importance of the occasion and the significance of cinema in India. Pramod Navalkar declared, "This is an industry where there are no divisions based on caste, language, religion, or region." The Director of the National Film Archives, Suresh Chhabria, asserted, "It is really the public of India that has taken cinema to their hearts and minds. Nowhere in the world has a public taken to cinema as much as has the public of India. It is really them we have to thank." The music director Ravindra Jain sang a song celebrating cinema that he had composed in honor of the function. After the speeches, the same Lumiere films—*Arrival of a Train*; *Workers Leaving a Factory*; *By the Seaside*; and *Baby's Dinner*—that were screened a hundred years ago, were screened that evening in the auditorium. After the screening, most people trooped upstairs to the exhibition of film stills, posters, and photographs organized by the National Film Archives to represent a visual history of the hundred years of Indian cinema. The space was packed full of people as well as television cameras which were documenting the event.

Maharashtra as the "Birthplace of Indian Cinema"

The commemorations were an assertion of Maharashtrian regionalism. What was striking about the entire day was the high visibility of representatives from the government of Maharashtra, to the near exclusion of the other organizers such as the NFDC, National Film Archives, and the FFI. Representatives from the Department of Cultural Affairs were the only ones to address the crowds at the start of the procession and at the plaque unveiling. While the managing director of the NFDC and the director of the Archives briefly addressed the audience during the auditorium ceremonies, the president of the FFI did not address spectators even once during the whole day. Except for the directors of the NFDC and the Archives, the former speaking in Hindi and the latter in English, almost every speech and commentary was conducted solely in Marathi, the state language, rather than a combination of languages like Marathi and Hindi or Marathi and English, a standard practice in official ceremonies when national institutions are involved. For example, during the 26th International Film Festival of India held in Bombay in January 1995, the Chief Minister at the time addressed the audience in Marathi, Hindi, and English, while at the Mumbai International Film Festival for short films and documentaries held in February 1996, all of the proceedings took place in English.[10] Unlike these events which had an "international" in their names and hence an implied audience of non-Indians, the implied audience for the centenary celebrations was not so much Indians in general, but exclusively Marathi speakers.

Although the invitation was titled, "Indian Film Centenary Celebrations," speeches by state officials completely focused on Maharashtrians and Marathi cinema. Maharashtra was declared the birthplace of Indian cinema and Maharashtrians, such as Seve Dada (Harischandra Bhatvadekar), who is credited with making the first film in India, and Dadasaheb (Dhundiraj Govind) Phalke, who made the first feature-length film in India, its progenitors. Laudatory statements about early filmmakers and the importance of the film industry to the cultural life of Bombay emphasized the Marathi film industry, rather than the Hindi film industry. The Chief Minister, the Minister for Cultural Affairs, and a few representatives from the Department of Cultural Affairs in their public addresses extolled the "pioneers"—Baburao Painter, Bhalji Pendharkar, V. Shantaram, Prabhat Studios—for their contributions to Marathi cinema. Nearly all of the proceedings, the signs in the procession and in the auditorium were in Marathi; the one visual representation of a film scene—the mural on the side of the truck—was from a Marathi film; the speeches focused on Marathi cinema; and even the actors and actresses who attended the procession were mainly Marathi speakers who worked in the Hindi film industry, the Marathi industry, or both. Rather than the centenary of the arrival of cinema in India or the centenary of Indian cinema, it appeared as if the centenary of Marathi cinema was being commemorated.

The focus on Marathi cinema to the exclusion of Hindi cinema at the commemorations can be understood as an effort by the state government to counter the dominance of Hindi cinema in the exhibits, festivals, and histories produced by institutions such as the Ministry of Information and Broadcasting, the NFDC, and the National Film Archives (NFAI). The photography exhibit organized by the NFAI as a part of the commemorations divided the history of Indian cinema into 12 sections, each with brief introductions and titles in English.[11] The first three sections were devoted to the beginnings of cinema in India, while the next three detailed the development of sound, the studio system, and filmmaking right after Indian independence. An entire section was devoted to the work of Satyajit Ray, while another section grouped together the "parallel cinema"—cinema working outside the commercial framework—as well as the "middle cinema"—films described as trying to bridge the gap between parallel and commercial styles of filmmaking. The one section about documentaries focused mainly on those produced by the Films Division, a government agency, reputed to be the largest documentary producer in the world. The emphasis of the exhibit, however, was on Hindi cinema, which was the normative category in the exhibit. The section about film music—"Film Music: World Within a World"—was completely oriented around Hindi film music, while the sections entitled "Popularity at its Peak" and "Modern Decades of Colorful Cinema" focused solely on Hindi films. Films in other languages—if not by Satyajit Ray or labeled as "art"—were arranged under the heading, "Different Regions, Different Worlds," where stills were shown from films made in 12 different languages.

Like the photography exhibit, the weeklong film festival of the "finest" in world and Indian cinema curated by the NFAI also had a heavy emphasis on Hindi films. Thirty-three films were shown in total from July 8–14, divided into the categories of World Cinema (11 films), Indian cinema (11 films), Marathi Cinema (5 films), and Documentary (6 films). Of the films screened in the category of Indian cinema, eight were in Hindi, while the other three were in Tamil, Bengali, and Manipuri. The Hindi films were mostly from the 1950s: Mehboob Khan's *Mother India* (1957), Raj Kapoor's *Awara* (Vagabond, 1951), and Guru Dutt's *Pyaasa* (The Thirsty One, 1957), are all regarded as "classics" and canonical texts in the study of Indian cinema. The separate category for Marathi films was explained in the introduction to the film festival brochure "as a special tribute to our host state" (Chhabria 1996).

The emphasis by state officials on the contributions of Maharashtrians to the development of cinema in India challenges the nationalist history of Indian cinema produced by institutions like the Ministry of Information and Broadcasting and the National Film Archives. These histories eschew mentioning the regional or linguistic identity of "pioneers" working in Bombay like Phalke and subsume everyone under the category "Indian" instead. For example, a pamphlet entitled, *"Bharat mein Cinema ke 100 Varsh: Ek Pariprekshya"* (100 Years of Cinema in India: A Perspective)[12] published by the Ministry of Information and Broadcasting and circulated in both Hindi and Marathi at the photography exhibit, states with regard to the first films made in India which happened to be in Bombay, "The century had not yet ended when one of India's professional photographers, Harischandra Sakharam Bhatvadekar imported a movie camera . . . and made 2 short films himself" (Rangoonwalla 1995: 1). The pamphlet is replete with statements where the regional/linguistic affiliation of filmmakers is mentioned only with regard to cities other than Bombay. Whereas Hiralal Sen in Calcutta in his efforts to film Bengali plays is described as "taking advantage of Bengal's rich theatrical tradition" (Rangoonwalla 1995: 3), R. G. Torne's film of his theater group in Bombay performing the Marathi play, *Pundalik*, is described in the pamphlet as simply "the first example of Indian creativity," with no mention that the play was in Marathi (Rangoonwalla 1995: 5). The pamphlet refers to Phalke's *Raja Harischandra* as "India's first totally indigenous feature film" (Rangoonwalla 1995: 5) while features made by others are referred to as "Bengal's first feature film" and "South India's first feature film" (Rangoonwalla 1995: 6).

The erasure of "Maharashtra" from the origins of Indian cinema and as the specific site of "Indian creativity" results in an attempt to reinsert the region into the narrative about the history of Indian cinema. The fact that the "birthplace" of Indian cinema is in Maharashtra and that many early "pioneers" of Indian cinema, including D. G. Phalke, labeled the "Father of Indian cinema," were native Marathi speakers is a source of regional pride, not just unique to the 1996 celebrations, but can be noted in earlier documents such as the *Report of the Committee of Secretaries on Demands of the Film Industry* compiled in 1986 in response to a series of grievances put forth by the Hindi film industry. The *Report's* introduction states:

> Maharashtra occupies a special place in the history of Indian Cinema. . . . Most of the pioneers of Indian cinema are from Maharashtra. . . . All of them, little remembered today, have played very important roles as trail blazers in the Indian film industry. . . . Even a cursory look at the landmarks of Indian Cinema during 1896–1931 shows the major part played by persons from this State in the development of this medium. (Committee 1986: 1)

Both the *Report* and the commemorations demonstrate how cinema is a mode of self-representation for the state government, a part of its "symbol pool" of Maharashtrian regionalism (Cohn 1987: 120). Since "Maharashtra" is a distinct regional entity created only in 1960 as a part of the linguistic reorganization of India, the commemorations, by reclaiming "Indian pioneers" as "Maharashtrian pioneers," replace one nationalist narrative with another.

No Glitz, No Glamour: The "Failure" of the Celebrations

The next day, stories appeared in the newspapers about how disappointing the event was for the crowds of spectators because Hindi film stars had not turned out in full force for the procession. "The much-hyped celebration of the 'Hundred Years of Cinema in India' was a lacklustre affair with no notable stars turning up for the show" (*Indian Express, 1996b*). In fact, this particular news article—"Centenary fete lacks glitz"—listed all of the stars who had not attended (in addition to those who had). Members of the Hindi film industry did participate in the procession, including its most visible members—actors and actresses, but not all of them are categorized as "stars." Hindi film stars are men and women in leading roles who not only have tremendous drawing power at the box office, but are national icons epitomizing a variety of attributes such as power, strength, sophistication, desirability, beauty, masculinity, and femininity. In that respect, none of the stars, with the exception of Nana Patekar—an actor especially popular in Maharashtra with close connections to the ruling party, Shiv Sena, and who made his way into Hindi films via Marathi cinema and theater—were present. Most of the other participants in the procession were actors and actresses from earlier eras—referred to as "seniors" or "veterans"—who played supporting roles which labeled them as "character artists" rather than stars, or producers and directors who did not have the same face recognition as even the former character artists. The newspapers' focus on the presence of stars as the definitive measure of the procession's success is an example of how the Hindi film industry is primarily defined by and identified with its stars.

In addition to citing the disappointment of hundreds of fans who were unable to see their favorite stars, the news reports also portrayed the government of Maharashtra as being unfairly burdened with such a momentous task without much help from the Central government or the film industry. "It was left to the Maharashtra Government to handle the celebrations since the birth of cinema took place in Mumbai" (*Indian Express*, 1996b) concluded a report that also pointed out how the Ministry of Information and Broadcasting had not sent a representative to either the procession or the inaugurations, even though it was the Ministry's idea originally to commemorate the centenary of cinema in the various film production centers.

Prior to the procession, articles in newspapers had described how the entire Hindi film industry was going to take part as "Bollywood has always respected seniority and experience" (*Indian Express*, 1996a), but afterward the same newspapers heavily criticized the Hindi film industry for its poor attendance and contrasted its apathy with the state government's enthusiasm, evident from it having "shouldered the funding of the celebrations" (Desai 1996). Pointing out that the function should have been more of a film industry's celebration than the government's, an article entitled "Bollywood lacks sense of duty and history" interpreted the stars' nonparticipation as a sign of their self-seeking nature:

> This indifference and ungrateful attitude is not uncommon in the film industry, it's all pervading in Bollywood. They easily forget they owe something to the industry which has given them name, fame, and fortune. They kick the ladder on which they climb. How can such persons whether they be veterans or young hero and heroine care to pay tribute to the pioneers of cinema, which does not fetch them any pay! (Desai 1996)

The editorial page of the *Times of India* characterized the lack of participation in the procession as an active gesture of ingratitude and disrespect to the industry's own heritage: "Most of the top film stars refused to join a procession organized by the Maharashtra government on July 7 to celebrate the centenary of Indian cinema. They saw no need to show their gratitude to the pioneers whose toil helps them to wallow in luxury today" (July 15, 1996).

The press accounts of the commemorations established a series of explicit and implicit oppositions between the Hindi film industry and the Government of Maharashtra. The blame for the "failure" of the commemorations was squarely placed on the film industry, while the state was represented as the guardian of cinematic heritage. The state was seen to have taken on the responsibility of properly memorializing an event, the significance of which the film industry, single-mindedly interested in profit, did not seem to understand or care. The press portrayed the state as a selfless actor for organizing and funding the commemorations, and the members of the film industry as bad citizens for not participating in them.

What is striking about the press-generated discourse is the rhetorical shift regarding the significance of the event. Originally described by the press as a commemoration of the first screening of motion pictures in India, the centenary celebrations, after their occurrence, were transformed by the press into a memorial to the history of Indian cinema. Hence, the celebration of the hundredth year of the arrival of cinema in India became a celebration of the hundred years of Indian cinema. The initial screening at the Watsons Hotel became an event invested with primeval importance—the "birth of cinema" in India, conflated with the birth of Indian cinema. From the point of view of the press, the magnitude of the event demanded that members of the Hindi film industry attend and pay obeisance to their predecessors.

The State as "Step-Mother": The Hindi Film Industry and the Government of Maharashtra

Why didn't more people from the Hindi film industry attend the procession? About the industry members who did participate in the procession, the Secretary of Cultural Affairs asserted, "Those who had the feeling for the cinema came" (Desai 1996). What about the others? The answer provided by the press, that the industry does not have a sense of history and is only concerned about the present, is a superficial assessment, overlooking the number of ways that the Hindi film industry commemorates itself and its history. In the same week as the procession, prominent members of the film industry[13] turned out for the release function of a book, *The Hundred Luminaries of Hindi Cinema*, which aimed to document and commemorate the lives and careers of members of the Hindi film industry. Eighteen months earlier, many members of the industry had participated in the NFDC-produced "Cinema Cinema 100," an elaborate, live stage show devised as a salute to the centenary of cinema. Conceived, designed, and directed by Subhash Ghai, a highly successful producer-director known for his lavish, big-budget sagas, the show took place in Bombay on January 15, 1995, and was broadcast live on the national television network. Unlike the July 7, 1996, procession in Bombay, which did not involve many members of the Hindi film industry, "Cinema Cinema 100" had the participation of top stars to lend it glamour as well as the participation of well-known music directors, directors, and other figures.[14]

Commemorations organized by the Hindi film industry in the past, such as the 25th anniversary (referred to as the Silver Jubilee) of the Indian film industry in 1938, the 25th anniversary of Indian talkies in 1956, and the 50th anniversary of talkies in 1981, designate 1913, the year of the first Indian feature film, or 1931, the year of the first Indian sound film, as milestones worthy of celebration. July 7, 1896, is a meaningless date for the film industry since the screenings at the Watsons Hotel which were by a European for other Europeans, as the hotel barred entry to Indians, did not involve anyone who could be identified as a progenitor or pioneer for the film industry. Veteran producer and former president of the Indian Motion Picture Producers Association (IMPPA)[15] G. P. Sippy, who actually attended the procession, commented that it was a sorry affair and questioned the logic of celebrating an event organized by a representative of the Lumiere Brothers, not the Lumieres themselves, in a place that did not even exist anymore.[16] He states, "You see Indian cinema is Bombay cinema, *Raja Harischandra* in 1913 by Dadasaheb Phalke" (Interview, October 14, 1996). The birth anniversary of Phalke continues to be celebrated annually by various trade associations.

Whereas the mainstream press had characterized the centenary commemorations as a failed event on the part of the industry, the film press characterized it as a failure on the part of the state to organize the event properly. An editorial in *Screen*, the weekly newspaper of the entertainment industry, asserted, "The general feeling in the industry was that it was not the industry's own event inasmuch as it was organised mainly by the state government of Maharashtra" (July 12, 1996). The editorial argued that despite the fact that "the way the proceedings were put together looked as though the arrangements were made hurriedly at the eleventh hour," and that the national committee which was formed to celebrate the centenary had ignored the Film Federation of India (the apex body of the film industry) till the last moment, the industry should have risen above such matters and participated in the procession in full force (*Screen*, July 12, 1996).

In my interviews with members of the industry, some of the reasons for not attending the procession included people being out of town,[17] as well as people feeling that they had done their duty by participating in the "Cinema Cinema 100" stage show, but the most consistent reason revolved around the issue of protocol, specifically how to properly invite people. "Too casual" was the frequent description of the state's invitation. Proper invitation protocol from the point of view of the film industry is a personal invitation. Instead, the Ministry of Cultural Affairs sent invitations to all of the various film organizations[18] and asked the heads of the organizations to invite their members to participate. Director Ramesh Sippy explained the inefficacy of such a method of inviting people:

> The invitation side hasn't been handled in a manner to get the best people there. In other words, they are artists and people of repute, they need not just a letter going out or something like that. They need somebody to call them, meet them, go and see them once and say, "This is the occasion, you must come and participate." It should not just be kind of something in the air, an announcement at some meeting somewhere—that everyone must participate. That's not enough. There should be a PR cell and a few people should be kept in charge to go to individuals and see that they participate. (Interview with author, July 8, 1996)

Sippy's comments do not apply solely to this event, but generally to industry practice. For any special occasion—premieres, *mahurats*,[19] audio releases, awards ceremonies—people are invited personally. Prior to the Filmfare Awards,[20] I observed the magazine's staff traversing the ends of Bombay delivering the invitations for the awards night personally to each and every invitee. Personal invitations are seen as a gesture of respect toward the invitee. Thus, when the Secretary of Cultural Affairs stated in a news report that there was just not enough time to invite everyone personally for the procession, it signaled the insincerity of the invitation. Not having enough time to invite people properly as a consequence of poor planning reveals the low priority assigned to the event. Actor/Producer Shashi Kapoor contrasted how he was notified barely 30 hours in advance about a meeting to organize the centenary celebrations with the one-year notice he had received from the Cinematheque Francais in Paris asking him to attend their Indomania film festival. He conceded, "The problem with our, especially anything to do with our government, vis-à-vis films, or the arts, is that they don't like to plan. They think they can do it at the last minute" (Interview with author, August 8, 1996).

Such a last-minute approach exemplifies to many in the Hindi film industry the mercenary attitude of the state toward the industry. The relationship between the Hindi film industry and the state, both at the regional and national levels, has been marked by ambivalence throughout the years.[21] While the industry represents itself in a perpetual state of financial crisis, the state views it as an infinite source of revenue. Veteran producer B. R. Chopra describes the contentious relationship between the state and the film industry:

> You find that the government is interfering with us quite a bit, putting restrictions on us quite a bit, and taking away the biggest slice of our earnings. The whole picture industry, whatever they've done, they've done all by themselves without the aid of the government. According to me the film industry has not been able to get the favor of the government, except when it serves the government's purpose. We have been fighting for the removal of entertainment tax for the last 20–30 years. Every time the promises go down, they look into it, but look into it only, they don't do it. The government keeps milking the cow; they've done precious little for its development. The only thing they've done is to develop the parallel cinema[22] and to help it. That's all, but they've not done anything for the common man's cinema. (Interview, August 14, 1996)[23]

Chopra focuses on the issue most abominable to the film industry, that of the entertainment tax levied by individual state governments on box office revenues, which transfers a significant portion of the industry's earnings into state exchequers. For example, entertainment tax collected in Maharashtra was 800 million rupees in the tax year 1994–95; 880 million in 1995–96; and in the six months from April 1996 to September 1996, 540 million rupees (*Film Information*, 1997). Most state governments practice protectionism on behalf of their state language film industries and subject films in languages other than their official language to higher rates of entertainment tax.[24] I use the term protectionism because higher tax rates translate into higher ticket prices. Since Hindi films are the only Indian films distributed nationally, they are the ones that bear the brunt of such taxation.[25]

The Hindi film industry and the government of Maharashtra have clashed on the issue of entertainment tax periodically. For example, in January 1997, when the government suspended the entertainment tax "relief" granted in September 1994, and increased the tax rate back to 50 percent from 33.33 percent of the box office gross,[26] movie theaters all across the state closed down in protest and reopened after a month to promises of the tax rate staying the same—only to have the government renege on its promise and reinstate the higher tax rate. After a series of negotiations with the industry, the Maharashtra government settled on a rate of 37.5 percent in May 1997. During the entire episode, the film trade press was filled with statements about the duplicity of the Maharashtra government in its dealings with the industry. When state officials tried to justify the reversal of the tax rate by stating that the concession had been a "gift" to the film industry for a year in honor of the centenary year of cinema, industry members pointed out the speciousness of their argument—when the previous administration (led by the Congress Party) instituted the lower tax rate in September 1994, it was not described as a "gift" and that the centenary commemorations of cinema took place afterward in 1995 and 1996.[27] The trade magazine *Film Information* retorted:

> Is the Sena-BJP (Shiv Sena and Bharatiya Janata Party coalition) government just looking for an excuse to not renew the concession? Your guess is as good as ours. But the least the government could have done was to have come up with a more plausible and believable excuse, not a lame one like this which on the face of it looks false. (January 11, 1997)

Other points of contention between the Hindi film industry and the state in Maharashtra include the imposition of a variety of other taxes like sales tax on equipment rental, difficulty in obtaining permission as well as the high charges to shoot in public spaces (roads, beaches, parks, municipal property) in Bombay, and inaction on the part of the state to crack down on video and cable piracy. During my discussions with filmmakers, the state's dealings with the film industry were frequently characterized as "step-motherly." Shashi Kapoor asserts:

> Hindi films have always had a step-motherly treatment by the government, which is very sad. Why go anywhere else, in Maharashtra, there are lots of financial facilities and helps when you make a Marathi film, but not when you make a Hindi film. (Interview with author, August 6, 1996)

Kapoor is referring to the government of Maharashtra's attempts to promote Marathi cinema. Marathi films have long been in the shadow of Hindi films, which are associated with more glamour, money, and fame, both nationally and internationally. Production of Marathi films dwindled from a peak of 35 films in 1993 to only 9 in 1997, while Marathi actors and actresses are increasingly drawn to Hindi films and television. Bombay has only two theaters and Pune, the cultural heart of Maharashtra, only one, which screen Marathi films as they are considered commercially unviable because of their limited audience (Ashraf 1997). Production suffers when exhibition outlets are few, so when Navalkar announced during the commemorations that exhibitors agreed to screen Marathi films for 15 days a year, it was characterized as a "boon" for Marathi filmmakers.

The state promotes Marathi cinema not just through its power to pressure exhibitors, but also through direct financial assistance. In 1994, the Congress administration offered a grant of 1.6 million rupees per film to Marathi filmmakers as a measure to revive the ailing Marathi film industry,[28] but filmmakers criticized the conditions accompanying the grants as unreasonable. In May 1997, under the Shiv Sena-BJP coalition government, the state announced that it would grant 1.5 million rupees each to 15 filmmakers every year without conditions. At the same time, the state also abolished the entertainment tax on Marathi films. Minister of Cultural Affairs, Pramod Navalkar, appealed to Maharashtrian actors, actresses, producers, and directors to "return" to Marathi cinema and expressed, "I hope our government's initiative will bring back the glory of Marathi cinema" (Ashraf 1997).

What differentiates the Hindi film industry from film industries in other languages is that it does not have recourse to a regional state apparatus that promotes its interests. Kapoor laments this lack of support for Hindi films, which he characterizes as "provincialism":

> You take a Hindi film to Karnataka and the cinema man has a preference for the Kannada film, even though you might have the hottest Hindi film which is a big, big success, but he will still prefer to have, because of this provincialism. I don't know why. They don't realize you see that in Hindi film, the Indian, so-called Indian who lives in the East, South, West, everywhere, he, that person, that audience is getting a touch of the neutral language[29] of the country, or the national language of the country. Whereas the provincial languages are not doing that. So Hindi films have always been fatherless, motherless *koi baap nai, koi nai hai, kuch nahin dethe* [there's no father, there's no one, they don't give anything]. Even the states, which are basically Hindi like UP, Madhya Pradesh, even they don't treat us well. *Samajh bhi nahi aata, yeh kya karenge* [Can't even understand, what they will do]. You look at the South, the way their

different state governments have helped them, the regional films, the regional film industry. It's nothing like that with Hindi films. (Interview, August 6, 1996)

The Hindi film industry is located in a state where the official language is Marathi rather than Hindi, unlike the rest of the film industries in India (Tamil, Telugu, Kannada, Bengali, Malayalam, etc.) which are located in states where the official language of the state and the language of filmmaking are the same. Other states promote filmmaking of their respective languages by offering incentives and subsidies, whereas Hindi films are not identified with any one particular state—exemplifying in Kapoor's words how Hindi films are "motherless and fatherless" with respect to any regional state apparatus. This "orphan" status can be understood as one of the factors that contribute to the national character of Hindi films and the film industry.

The concern for Marathi cinema while taxing Hindi films heavily positioned the government of Maharashtra as an opponent of the Hindi film industry's interests. The mainstream press's representation of the centenary celebrations belied the contentious relationship between the state and the Hindi film industry, as well as the irony of the state celebrating or "saluting" an industry which it did not support institutionally.

Mumbai versus Bollywood

Amidst the articles in newspapers praising the state government for planning the centenary celebrations, a lone article stood out for its criticism. "The monument to cinema in state of despair" asserted, "The Esplanade building—the birthplace of cinema in India—continues to deteriorate while the state government is busy spending crores on the centenary celebrations" (Menon 1996b). The article argued that a more fitting tribute to the centenary of cinema in India would have been to use the money spent on the procession to restore the building and convert a portion of it into a mini theater to screen documentaries and "good films." What becomes apparent if the commemorations are examined in the context of Maharashtra's political landscape of the late 1990s is that, rather than preserving cinematic heritage, they were an attempt to lay claim to the city of Bombay, consonant with the character of the Shiv Sena—the leading party at that time in the coalition controlling the government of Maharashtra and institutions such as the Ministry of Cultural Affairs.

Involved in city politics for over a decade, the Shiv Sena came to power at the state level for the first time in May 1995, in a partnership with the Bharatiya Janata Party. The Shiv Sena has been characterized as nativist (Katzenstein 1979), populist (Lele 1995), cultural populist (Heuze 1995), ethnic chauvinist, and all of the above (Patel and Thorner 1995). The Sena originated in 1966, in Shivaji Park—a heavily Maharashtrian neighborhood in Bombay's central suburb of Dadar—as a sons-of-soil movement raising a cry of "Bombay for Maharashtrians." Their goal was to rid Bombay of "outsiders," specifically South Indians, who were represented as disproportionately occupying white-collar, clerical jobs rightfully belonging to Maharashtrians (Katzenstein 1979). From its inception, the Shiv Sena has practiced a politics of exclusion articulated through violence, with the boundaries of who constitutes an outsider changing through the years (Lele 1995). The most inassimilable "outsiders" in its rhetoric are Muslims, and the Sena was heavily involved in carrying out organized attacks against Muslims during the riots that wracked Bombay in the aftermath of the Babri Masjid demolition in Ayodhya in 1992–93.

Symbolism plays an important role in the Shiv Sena's activities, including its attempts to appropriate the city (Heuze 1995: 230). One of the first things that the Sena did as soon as it came into power at the state level in 1995 was to officially change the name of Bombay to its Marathi equivalent, Mumbai. Within the first year of its administration, the Sena government renamed nearly a hundred places and institutions in Bombay after the preeminent icon of Maharashtrian nationalism, Shivaji, the seventeenth-century warrior king whose military exploits extended the Maratha empire over much of Central India, and from whom the Shiv Sena derive their name and identity as the "Army of Shivaji." The attempt to impose a Maharashtrian character onto Bombay, signified by the name change, reveals how Bombay's identity has been autonomous from Maharashtra. Bombay is described as the most cosmopolitan city in India in terms of the ethnicity, native language, and religion of its population. While Marathi speakers are the single largest linguistic group, they do not comprise a majority but about 45 percent of the population. Scholars have remarked how Bombay is not a "Maharashtrian" city and have argued that its heterogeneity has been one of the root causes of the Shiv Sena's emergence (Heuze 1995; Katzenstein 1979).

Historically, Bombay was separate from the center of Maratha power located in Pune, and Maharashtrians viewed the city with ambivalence, regarding it as a culturally alien, coastal enclave of foreign traders who had usurped Maratha political power (Kosambi 1995). After independence, when the national leadership agreed to the linguistic reorganization of India in 1955, the States Reorganization Commission recommended that Bombay State not be divided into separate Gujarati and Marathi states largely because of Bombay city where Marathi speakers were the largest language group, but Gujarati speakers dominated the city economically. Gujarat and Maharashtra were finally created as separate linguistic states in 1960 after a great deal of political turmoil as well as rioting in both the Marathi- and Gujarati-speaking districts of Bombay state. During this period, arguments were advanced for and against the inclusion of Bombay in a prospective Maharashtra. The arguments against the city's incorporation included: Marathi speakers were not in a majority in the city and their proportion was decreasing; Bombay was the trade center of all of India, not just of Maharashtra; Bombay was never a part of Maharashtra; and mainly non-Maharashtrians had developed the city by their capital and managerial skills (Katzenstein 1979: 46).

Although Bombay has not been readily recognized as a Maharashtrian city, it has been synonymous with filmmaking, identified as the "birthplace" of cinema in India—"It is in Bombay that Indian cinema was born" (Gangar 1995: 210). In addition to being the site of the first screenings of motion pictures in India, Bombay was also the site of the first film made in India—a wrestling match shot in the city's Hanging Gardens. Phalke's *Raja Harischandra*, the first Indian feature film, made its debut in Bombay's Coronation Cinematograph Theatre. Bombay's development into the center of film production in India was based on its position as the main center of commerce and manufacturing in British India. Film technology could take root and flourish in Bombay as capital from industrial and commercial activity flowed into filmmaking. For example, Phalke's first financier was a Gujarati textile tycoon, Mayashankar Bhatt. The increased profitability of the cinema enabled filmmakers to reinvest their gains in new productions and additional infrastructure such as studios, laboratories, theaters, and by 1925 Bombay had already become India's cinema capital (Gangar 1995: 218). By the early 1930s, the film industry was competing with the textile industry as the most important local industry in Bombay—bypassing it soon after with over 60 percent of India's

film production units in the 1930s located in the city (Dwivedi and Mehrotra 1995). By 1987, the film industry as a whole employed about 520,000
people (Gangar 1995: 219).

Through the lens of the Shiv Sena, the commemorations were an effort to contest the dominant identification of Bombay with the Hindi film
industry, encapsulated by the nickname "Bollywood." The seemingly unexpected emphasis on Maharashtrians and Marathi cinema in the commemorations was an attempt to assert the presence of Marathi cinema,
and hence Marathi identity in an urban landscape completely dominated
by Hindi cinema. Billboards, posters (in both English and Hindi), and
movie theaters in Bombay are overwhelmingly oriented around Hindi
films. Hindi filmmaking and film-viewing are woven into the urban geography and landscape of Bombay: many streets and intersections are named
for prominent film personalities; certain neighborhoods are marked as inhabited by film stars; film studios occupy large amounts of space in parts
of the city; public spaces serve as sets for film shoots; and stars' homes,
studios, and cinemas, all serve as landmarks in the city.

Scholars have argued that the Shiv Sena works at the level of popular
culture and mass appeal (Heuze 1995: 215), and that it "thrives by creating
spectacles" (Patel and Thorner 1995: xxix), referring to its sponsorship of
mass public prayer sessions and religious festivals. By drawing hundreds
of spectators and visibly transforming a portion of the cityscape for a day,
the centenary commemorations, specifically the procession and plaque
unveiling, were public spectacles characteristic of the Shiv Sena. Renovat-
ing the former Watsons Hotel and constructing a theater on the premises
to show "good" films, argued as a more fitting tribute to the occasion than
a procession, are not actions valued by the Sena as they would only be
noticeable and accessible to a limited, elite audience rather than a mass
public. In fact, some of the other publicized events of the commemorations such as seminars and workshops on cinema never took place, revealing how the commemorations were not about cinema as such, but
about cultural ownership of the city of Bombay.

The commemorations were an act of appropriating the city symbolically into Maharashtra. As the history of cinema in India is so entwined
with the history of Bombay, and cinema has become a prime signifier of
the city, by trying to reclaim the history of cinema as the sole province of
Maharashtrians, the Shiv Sena was reclaiming Bombay as Maharashtrian.
In the process, they erased from the history of cinema the contributions
to its development by other linguistic and ethnic groups in the city and

the great amount of cultural collaboration and fusion that has characterized the medium. The centenary celebrations communicated that since
Indian cinema was first created by Maharashtrians in Bombay, the cinema
and by association the city are Maharashtrian. Hence, Bombay is Mumbai
and not Bollywood.

Conclusions

The centenary celebrations of cinema in Maharashtra demonstrate how
something as fixed and precise as a date can generate multiple meanings.
July 7, 1896, the arrival of cinema in India, was transformed into the birth
of Indian cinema, which was then defined as "Marathi" cinema, since the
early pioneers were Maharashtrian. The commemorations reveal how a
regional identity seeks to redefine the "national" (Appadurai and Breckenridge 1995) by inserting itself into the historical narrative about Indian
cinema. Hence, a national event organized by the central government,
which in itself was a celebration of a world historical moment like the
100th anniversary of cinema, was appropriated by the state government to
assert specific claims about the history of cinema and the city of Bombay.
The commemorations demonstrate the symbolic significance accorded to
the institution of cinema by the state in India at both the national and
regional levels.

While the idea of Hindi films as being more national or equivalent to
"Indian" cinema is institutionalized in the discourse and history about
cinema in India with films in other languages referred to as "regional"
films and Hindi films referred to as "Indian" films, the example of the
commemorations in Bombay illustrates that Indian cinema is not a ho-
mogenous and absolute category, but created and re-created, and that the
dominance of Hindi cinema can be contested in extra-cinematic ways.
Such contestations around the history and institution of cinema in India
reveal that the study of cinema must encompass more than the filmic text
and the viewing experience, and see the cinematic institution as encompassing many forms of social practice.

ACKNOWLEDGMENTS

I would like to thank Lila Abu-Lughod, Nitin Govil, Brian Larkin, Ranjani Mazumdar, Radhika Subramaniam, and Adam Zeff for their comments and sugges-

tions. A special thanks to Vipul Agrawal for all of his help and invaluable feed-back at every stage of this chapter.

NOTES

1. An earlier version of this article appeared as "Centenary Commemorations or Centenary Contestations?—Celebrating a Hundred Years of Cinema in Bombay" in *Visual Anthropology* 11(1998): 399–419.

2. Fieldwork for this article was carried out in 1996, in Bombay, funded by an American Institute of Indian Studies junior fellowship for dissertation research.

3. This is not the first time that the history of Indian cinema is used to mark Bombay. In 1970, during the celebrations of the birth centennial of Dadasaheb Phalke, also known as the "Father of Indian cinema," the main road in the central suburb of Dadar was renamed Dadasaheb Phalke Road.

4. Lata Mangeshkar has been the leading female singer for Hindi films for 50 years and has been listed in the Guinness Book of World Records for having the most number of recordings credited to any one individual.

5. The majority of the film personalities who participated in the procession were from this category. However, the ones who sat in the cars were especially senior in terms of their age—octogenarians such as the actor K. N. Singh, and producers such as G. P. Sippy and B. R. Chopra.

6. An oboe-like instrument played in North India during ceremonial occasions such as weddings, funerals, and religious festivals.

7. Breaking a coconut is a common feature of Hindu ritual which has been imported into all types of nonreligious ritual practice where it functions as a moment of inauguration, signifying auspicious beginnings.

8. Lighting an oil lamp is also a feature of Hindu ritual which has been incorporated into secular ceremonies of inauguration.

9. Subordinate to the Minister for Cultural Affairs; second level in the three-level ministerial hierarchy.

10. The IFFI 95 was sponsored by the Directorate of Film Festivals, Ministry of Information and Broadcasting, Government of India in collaboration with the Government of Maharashtra. The Mumbai International Film Festival for Documentary, Short, and Animation Films was sponsored by the Government of India's Films Division, NFDC, and Ministry of Information and Broadcasting along with the Government of Maharashtra's Ministry of Culture.

11. The exhibit was badly organized. Many of the stills were unlabeled or incorrectly labeled. Even when labeled, stills were not consistently marked with basic information such as title and year, much less producer and director. The stills were not presented chronologically within the sections but were arranged in a rather haphazard way.

12. The quotations are from the Hindi version of the pamphlet; all translations are mine.

13. These included the actors Amitabh Bachchan, Shashi Kapoor, Anupam Kher, Manoj Kumar, the actresses Nadira and Dimple Kapadia, as well as the director Ramesh Sippy.

14. The show included performances by Madhuri Dixit, Juhi Chawla, Manisha Koirala, Shahrukh Khan, Anil Kapoor, Saif Ali Khan, Sonali Bendre, Vinod Khanna, Ajay Devgan, and Amrish Puri, as well as appearances by Ashok Kumar, Raaj Kumar, Asha Parekh, Rajesh Khanna, Dev Anand, Shatrughan Sinha, Shabana Azmi, Anupam Kher, and the Kapoor family, to name a few.

15. Established in 1937, IMPPA was for several years the most influential trade organization in the film industry.

16. Sippy is mistaken about the building—it does exist, but under a different name.

17. The summer months of May to August are a popular time for members of the film industry to either take vacations abroad to escape the heat and then rain, or to shoot in Europe and North America.

18. There are a variety of organizations representing the various sectors (producers, distributors, exhibitors, laborers, technicians, musicians, actors, dancers, etc.) of the film industry. Some examples include the Cine Artists Association which represents actors, the Film Makers Combine which represents directors, the Federation of Western India Cine Employees which represents 18 unions, and the Indian Motion Pictures Producers Association which represents producers.

19. Mahurat is a Sanskrit word that refers to an auspicious (calculated astrologically) date and time on which to start any new venture. The most common use of the concept is during Hindu wedding ceremonies. Within the film industry, a mahurat is a ritualized announcement of a new production.

20. The oldest system of awards dating back to 1953 for Hindi films, instituted by the English-language film magazine, *Filmfare*, published by the *Times of India* Group.

21. Cinema has been an object of state regulation in India since colonial times through censorship, taxation, allocation of raw materials, and control over exhibition through the licensing of theaters. Cinema has also been a "problem" warranting the attention of government commissions, inquiries, and seminars in postcolonial India. See Eric Barnouw and S. Krishnaswamy, *Indian Film* (New York: Oxford University Press, 1980) and Sumita Chakravarty, *National Identity in Indian Popular Cinema 1947–1987* (Austin: University of Texas Press, 1993) for a discussion of the relationship between the Indian State and the Hindi film industry in the 1950s.

22. Chopra is referring to the establishment of the NFDC and its mandate to develop and promote "good cinema" which in India has always been defined against the Hindi film industry and its goals of box office success. Filmmakers

working outside the dominant paradigm receive loans from NFDC to make films, but many of these films are never released theatrically because of a lack of an alternative distribution and exhibition network. NFDC funded films have been the ones that tended to receive the National Awards granted by the Indian government.

23. Chopra is referring to the most common rhetorical division of the film-going audience in India posed by members of the film industry, journalists, bureaucrats, and intellectuals: that the "masses" watch commercial films while the "classes" or elite audiences watch the art or parallel films.

24. For example, in 1997, West Bengal's tax rate (of the box office gross) was 41 percent for non-Bengali films and 16 percent for Bengali films. In Karnataka, the entertainment tax rate on non-Kannada films was 52 percent, while Kannada films were exempt from entertainment tax.

25. English-language films released in these states would also be taxed at a higher rate.

26. Generally, members of the film industry represent the entertainment tax rate as a percentage of the box office's net receipts. For example, when they assert that the entertainment tax is 100 percent it actually is 50 percent of the box office gross; when the rate is 50 percent according to the industry, it is 33.33 percent of the gross. Thus, in January 1997, when the Maharashtra government increased the tax rate, it was represented in the trade press and by industry members as an increase from 50 to 100 percent. The rate that was eventually settled on is represented as 60 percent.

27. The reduction in the entertainment tax rate in Maharashtra was instituted by a Congress-led government in September 1994 for one year, which was then renewed for another year by the Shiv Sena and BJP coalition government in September 1995. In September 1996, the government extended the rate until December 31, assuring the industry that the reduced rate would continue, but on December 24, the government decided to discontinue the reduced rate from the New Year. The previous time that cinemas had closed down in Maharashtra was in October 1986, in a similar dispute regarding the entertainment tax.

28. In contrast, the average budget of a Hindi film in 1997 was about 60 million rupees.

29. Of course the language riots that occurred in South India in 1965, especially in the state of Tamil Nadu, over the adoption of Hindi as a "link" language, belies the "neutrality" of Hindi. However, to Kapoor, a Punjabi born and brought up in a multilingual city like Bombay where the conflicts over language had centered around Marathi and Gujarati, Hindi may appear "neutral."

BIBLIOGRAPHY

Appadurai, Arjun, and Carol A. Breckenridge. 1995. "Public Modernity in India." In *Consuming Modernity: Public Culture in a South Asian World*, ed. Carol A. Breckenridge, 1–22. Minneapolis: University of Minnesota Press.

Ashraf, Syed Firdaus. 1997. "State Gives Marathi Films a Leg Up." *Rediff on the Net*, Bombay, www.rediff.com, May 14.

Chhabria, Suresh. 1996. *Celebrating the Hundredth Year of the Arrival of Cinema in Mumbai July 7–14*. Mumbai: Prabhat Chitra Mandal.

Chaware, Dilip. 1996. "Thespians and Vintage Cars Will Mark Movie Centenary." *Times of India*, Mumbai, June 30.

Cohn, Bernard S. 1987. "Regions Subjective and Objective: Their Relation to the Study of Modern Indian History and Society." In *An Anthropologist among the Historians and Other Essays*, 100–135. New York: Oxford University Press.

Committee of Secretaries, Government of Maharashtra. 1986. *Report on Demands of Film Industry*. Bombay: Director, Government Print and Stationery, Maharashtra State.

Desai, M.S.M. 1996. "Bollywood Lacks Sense of Duty and History." *Indian Express*, Mumbai, July 9.

Dwivedi, Sharada, and Rahul Mehrotra. 1995. *Bombay: The Cities Within*. Bombay: India Book House.

Film Information. 1997. Government's Bluff. Bombay, January 11.

Gangar, Amrit. 1995. "Films from the City of Dreams." In *Bombay: Mosaic of Modern Culture*, ed. Sujata Patel and Alice Thorner, 210–24. Bombay: Oxford University Press.

Ganti, Tejaswini. 2000. "Casting Culture: The Social Life of Hindi Film Production in Contemporary India." Ph.D. diss., New York University.

———. 2004. *Bollywood: A Guidebook to Popular Hindi Cinema*. London: Routledge.

Heuze, Gerard. 1995. "Cultural Populism: The Appeal of the Shiv Sena." In *Bombay: Metaphor for Modern India*, ed. Sujata Patel and Alice Thorner, 213–47. Bombay: Oxford University Press.

Indian Express. 1996a. "Top Billing for Veterans in Bollywood Procession," July 1.

———. 1996b. "Centenary Fete Lacks Glitz," July 8.

Katzenstein, Mary Fainsod. 1979. *Ethnicity and Equality: The Shiv Sena Party and Preferential Policies in Bombay*. Ithaca, N.Y.: Cornell University Press.

Kosambi, Meera. 1995. "British Bombay and Marathi Mumbai: Some Nineteenth Century Perceptions." In *Bombay: Mosaic of Modern Culture*, ed. Sujata Patel and Alice Thorner, 3–24. Bombay: Oxford University Press.

Lele, Jayant. 1995. "Saffronization of the Shiv Sena: The Political Economy of City, State and Nation." In *Bombay: Metaphor for Modern India*, ed. Sujata Patel and Alice Thorner, 185–212. Bombay: Oxford University Press.

Menon, Sri Prakash. 1996a. "It's Official—Cinema Started Here." *The Metropolis on Saturday*, Mumbai, July 6–7.

———. 1996b. "The Monument to Cinema in State of Despair." *The Metropolis on Saturday*, Mumbai, July 6–7.

Patel, Sujata, and Alice Thorner, eds. 1995. *Bombay: Metaphor for Modern India.* Bombay: Oxford University Press.

Rangoonwalla, Firoze. 1995. *Bharat mein Cinema ke 100 Varsh: Ek Pariprekshya.* New Delhi: Ministry of Information and Broadcasting, Directorate of Advertising and Visual Publicity.

Screen. 1995. "Who Cares!" Mumbai, July 12, vol. 45 (43), page 8.

Times of India. 1996. "Barmaids and Stars," July 15.

Chapter 4

||||||||||||||||||||||||||||||||||||||||||||||||||||||

Hollywood, Bollywood, Tollywood
Redefining the Global in Indian Cinema

Shanti Kumar

Given the dominance of Hollywood productions in the global media industry, academic and journalistic debates over the rapid increase in transnational flows of television and film have emphasized the potential for either homogenization or fragmentation of national cinemas and television cultures around the world (Gupta and Dayal 1996; Herman and McChesney 1997; Thussu 1998).[1] However, little attention has been focused on the ways in which the globalization of production practices outside Hollywood has significantly transformed the circulation of films and television programs around the world.

In terms of Hollywood's role in film and television production, John Hannigan, Michael Sorkin, and Eric Smoodin, among others, have argued that fantasy cities (such as Universal Studios) and theme park cities (such as the Disney kingdom) in the United States contribute to the globalization of a postmodern culture that is primarily based in a capitalist system of profit and pleasure (Hannigan 1998; Smoodin 1994; Sorkin 1992). However, such Hollywood-centered approaches do not adequately attend to the significant role that cultural location plays in our understanding of capitalist profit and pleasure in the transnational media industries.

In this chapter, I seek to redress this gap in the dialogue by exploring the transnational characteristics of global television and film production in one specific cultural context outside Hollywood—Ramoji Film City in Hyderabad, India. I posit that the emergence of RFC represents a new kind of entertainment-based culture in India that is partly invested in claiming a share in the transnational enterprise of film and television production, and partly interested in creating a postcolonial alternative to the Hollywood-centered world of capitalist profit and pleasure. I examine how RFC's one-stop shop of outdoor locations and indoor studios is enabling foreign and domestic filmmakers to imagine and create hybrid mediascapes that resemble prominent cultural landscapes from all over the world.

Mediascapes is a term coined by Arjun Appadurai to describe the diversity of media images that is constantly produced and reproduced by new media technologies in the global cultural economy (Appadurai 1996). Appadurai's formulation of mediascapes provides a useful framework to examine how the production practices at RFC have emerged at the intersection of global, national, regional, and local flows of media and popular culture in India.

I posit that the creation of new, hybrid mediascapes at RFC represents the rise of a new transnational vernacular in Indian cinema that is inflected with regional variations and local traditions even as it seeks newer markets around the world. In doing so, I argue, it has engendered new ways of imagining the interconnections of the global, the national, the regional, and the local in Indian cinema. By focusing attention on the global, national, and local mediascapes at RFC, I seek to highlight the transformative role of Indian cinema in what Appadurai has called the work of imagination in the global cultural economy.

An Armchair Tour of RFC

A city within a city, Ramoji Film City (RFC) is the largest, most comprehensive, and most professionally planned film production center in the world. According to the *Guinness Book of World Records*, it has surpassed Hollywood's Universal Studio in both size and the range of media facilities offered. With over 7,500 employees working in 29 departments, RFC can accommodate the production of 20 international films at any one time, and cater to at least 40 Indian films simultaneously. Over 1,200 acres of the Film City have already been developed, and plans are afoot to use the remaining 800 acres to create dubbing studios and mythological sites that will recreate gardens, temples, forts, and palaces depicted in Hindu epics such as the Ramayana and the Mahabharata.

Located at an hour's driving distance (approximately 40 kilometers) from the twin cities of Hyderabad and Secunderabad, RFC is a one-stop facility that claims to offer "the best of pre-production, production and post-production facilities for any kind of film or television show."[2] Promoting RFC as "the Land of Movies," publicity brochures promise "an out of the world experience" for visitors and filmmakers alike:

> Ramoji Film City, the land of films & fantasy, where dreams turn to reality. A strong favorite of the film fraternity, the world's largest Film City is enchanting, enthralling and spellbinding at the same time. Amidst the rocky Deccan Landscape, in the heart of Andhra Pradesh, the magic of make believe is a heady and engulfing surprise, as you are confronted with the Film City's splash of colour and charm. Glamorous, surreal, and breathtakingly beautiful, it's [sic] mind-boggling mammoth proportions, scores of unbelievable sets and fantastic landscapes offer more than just a glimpse into the thrilling and exciting world of film and television. Grandeur, glamour and professionalism combine to present a truly out-of-this-world experience.

Indian films have always been celebrated for their "splash of colour and charm" and are almost always made to look "glamorous, surreal, and breathtakingly beautiful." The art of commercial filmmaking in India—which is popularly if somewhat inaccurately called Bollywood—is well known for its "mind-boggling mammoth proportions, scores of unbelievable sets and fantastic landscapes." From the earliest times in the Indian film industry, filmmakers expended great amounts of time, energy, and money to travel around the world in search of the perfect setting for the most extravagant song-and-dance sequences in their films. Therefore, the "out of the world experience" promised by the publicity brochures at RFC is not something new to on-screen representations of extravagant sets and fantastic locales in Indian cinema.

What makes RFC a rather new phenomenon in Indian cinema is that for the first time foreign and domestic filmmakers can make an entire film from pre-production and production to post-production in a single studio that provides multiple outdoor locales and diverse indoor settings. Since its opening in 1997, six foreign films and over 500 Indian films in languages such as English, Hindi, Kannada, Telugu, and Tamil have been produced at RFC. *Maa Nannaki Pelli* (My Father's Wedding) was the first Telugu film shot entirely at RFC in 1997. The first Hindi film shot in RFC was *Bade Miyan Chote Miyan* (Big Guy, Little Guy) in 1998.

RFC is the dream project of Cherukuri Ramoji Rao, the owner of the Eenadu media group in the South Indian state of Andhra Pradesh. The

Eenadu group is one of the largest media conglomerates in South India, and Ramoji Rao's business empire consists of several English- and Telugu-language periodicals, including the widely read newspaper, *Eenadu*; a multilingual satellite television network, ETV; a film distribution banner, Ushakiron Movies; and a financial services group, Margadarshi.

When Ramoji Rao launched *Eenadu* in 1974, it had a modest beginning—a single edition, hand-composed newspaper which was printed on a flatbed press in the coastal town of Visakhapatnam in Andhra Pradesh. From the beginning, Ramoji Rao intensely researched the Telugu newspaper industry and used creative editorial and marketing strategies to sell *Eenadu* to advertisers and readers alike.

To set itself apart from its competition, *Eenadu* drew upon local dialects and colloquial idioms to present headlines and stories, provided colorful photographs and captions to draw attention, and used sarcasm and wit to analyze news events. By 1989, *Eenadu* devised a strategy to further localize its coverage by inserting a tabloid devoted to local events in the broadsheet edition of each relevant district every day. To gather local news for the tabloid inserts, *Eenadu* created a network of stringers across the state who were paid a small fee if their news item was published in a daily.

The stringers based in cities and small towns across the state corresponded with editors by telephone and made arrangements with bus companies to carry their reports to the district headquarters, where *Eenadu* employees collected them. To obtain local classifieds and display advertisements for each of its district tabloid inserts, *Eenadu* hired thousands of sales people to convince local businesses of the virtues of advertising. By the late 1990s, *Eenadu* had transformed into a major regional-language newspaper, with daily editions from ten towns, which had cornered 70 percent of Telugu daily circulations (Jeffrey 2000).

When Eenadu Television—or ETV, as it is popularly known—was launched in August 1995, there was great anticipation among Telugu-speaking audiences who were already familiar with the parent company's powerful influence in Telugu media, thanks largely to the success of the daily newspaper by the same name. Leasing a high-quality transponder on the INTELSAT satellite system, and uplinked from Padduka near Colombo, Sri Lanka, Eenadu began television transmission with an ambitious 17½-hour service of entertainment and film-based programming. Elated by the audience's response to its Telugu-language fare in Andhra Pradesh, Eenadu earnestly expanded its network into other Indian states, and offered viewers across the country programming in the regional language of their choice.

A veteran producer and director in the Hyderabad-based Telugu film industry—or Tollywood as some fans call it—Ramoji Rao recognized that filmmaking in India is a rather tedious and expensive venture because the production calendar can often be interrupted by unpredictable weather, unreliable electricity, inappropriate set designs, and inflexible star schedules.[3] Realizing that a more reliable environment and a well-organized production schedule could dramatically reduce the time, the cost, and the resources required to make a film in India, Rao set about the ambitious task of developing a one-stop studio in Hyderabad.

Planning for the Film City began in 1991, and Rao acquired a barren stretch of 2,000 acres in Anjapur village located at the outskirts of Hyderabad. Soon a team of architects, designers, and developers started work on the plans to create the largest film studio in the world, with over 500 locations for outdoor and indoor shooting.

In addition to being billed as the world's largest one-stop shop for foreign and domestic filmmakers, RFC is a popular tourist site, with over 2,500 visitors coming to the city every day. In order to reach the Film City, visitors have to either take a city bus or arrange a private mode of transport. The day tour begins at 9:00 a.m. and ends at 6:00 p.m. Once at the imposing black gates of the RFC, visitors are greeted by security, and reminders to purchase tickets for the package tour. The visiting charges are Rs200 per head on Sunday and Rs150 per head on weekdays. For children over the age of three, the ticket costs Rs150 on Sunday and Rs100 on weekdays. For visitors who want to take their own cars, the ticket cost is Rs700 per person. After a brisk security check, visitors are allowed to get into one of the many waiting buses of RFC. A short bus ride on a winding road around rolling hills, the sprawling RFC comes into full view.

To begin the tour, visitors are dropped off at Eureka Point—"The Fun Place" which is the starting and ending point of the package tour. Architecturally designed to resemble a historic fort from the ancient period of the Mauryan Empire, Eureka can be accessed via a drawbridge. From here the package tour begins, as visitors are escorted by well-trained guides into jumbo-sized red buses. The buses take the visitors to the Sun Fountain, which is adorned by a huge statue of the mythological character, Surya, holding the reins of three horses.

Since visitors are not allowed to take food or beverages into the Film City, no fewer than four restaurants are located at the Film City. Alampana restaurant claims to bring its guests authentic Mughalai cuisine all the way from the Royal House of Awadh. For those who like vegetarian cuisine, served in Indian "thali" style, Chanakya is the place to go. While Ganga Jamuna serves South Indian cuisine, Gunsmoke provides a taste of fast food from the Wild Wild West.

The meticulously cultivated gardens in RFC, known as Shangri La, have been carefully designed to create a breathtaking view of perennial trees and flowers which are always in full bloom. The gardens are laid out in distinct patterns to give a film director the creative flexibility to shoot one sequence in the Swiss Alps or the Arizona desert, and turn the cameras and the crew in a different direction to shoot another sequence in Kashmir or in Mysore. For instance, the appropriately named Two-in-One garden appears like the famous Mughal Gardens from the outside, and resembles the Brindavan Garden in Mysore from the inside. The Arizona garden, on the other side, has 25 varieties of cactus plants, and when filmed against the backdrop of a setting sun it can be made to look like a picturesque desert in the southwestern region of the United States.

Throughout the Film City, tourists can visit merchandise stores located in the theme parks of Maurya, Maghadha, Black Cat Warehouse, Frontier Land, and Meena Bazaar. Meandering through the gardens, parks, stores, and restaurants, visitors can slowly find their way back. Those tired of walking can take the returning bus to Eureka. From Eureka Point, all visitors are asked to board the RFC bus which drops them off at the security gate of the main entrance.

For visitors who desire more than a day trip, RFC also offers packages for holidays, honeymoon couples, and state-of-the art conferencing facilities for corporations. For the newlyweds, RFC has a honeymoon package which, as travel-india.com describes it, is for those who don't want the run-of-the-mill tourist destination. The travel-india.com website goes on:

> Besides a comfortable stay in Sitara, a five-star hotel within the RFC complex with the normal complimentary freebies thrown in, a minifilm unit complete with make-up artist, director, cameraman and the equipment to help you capture unforgettable moments of your honeymoon. Sitara has one of Asia's best health clubs, where guides identify the workstation that Shah Rukh Khan used during the shooting of one of his films. And you could take your pick of some of the more exotically named suites: Cleopatra, Zorba the Greek, and Mughal-e-Azam with décor to match.[4]

But what travel-india.com neglects to mention is that all this comes with a steep price tag. A one-day stay at Five-Star Hotel Sitara for a couple costs Rs4800 (with food allowance up to Rs1000). For the more economically minded, there is the Three-Star Hotel Tara, where a one-day stay costs Rs1890 (with food allowance up to Rs600). For its corporate clients, RFC has special package deals which include accommodation at the five-star hotel Sitara, use of conference facilities, a well-equipped business center, and a health club. For conferencing or teleconferencing needs, clients can use Startrack, the conference hall, which comes with an attached banquet hall called Taj Mahal. The health club in Sitara, called Samson and Delilah, which according to a reviewer is "one of the best health clubs in Asia with top-of-the-line equipment such as Vecra multigym and Sybex" (Suresh 1998: 46).

Samara, the office complex at RFC, provides office spaces and air-conditioned suites for film producers and their production crews. The RFC has its own travel agency, transport and telecommunication network to look after ticketing, airport pickups, car rentals, and other requirements. If a film director or a television producer requires something that is not readily available in the studios or the outdoor locations, it can be created from scratch by Maya, the set construction division at RFC.

Spread over an area of 300,000 square feet, Maya (also the Sanskrit word for divine magic) employs over 1,000 skilled carpenters, sculptors, and craftsmen who can quickly transform an art director's creative ideas into cinematic reality. The furniture division, Harmony, also has a pool of carpenters and artisans who are trained to build furniture and decors for "Indian," "Chinese," "European," or "American" set designs. If the need of the day is a ready-made prop, a filmmaker can visit the prop supply division, named Parade, which houses a wide variety of objects from the most mundane to the more exotic in a six-story building. Whether it is a bicycle or bullock cart, a French chandelier or a Chinese lantern, a filmmaker can probably find it in Parade.

By offering the entire gamut of services necessary for producing a film, RFC has introduced the concept of "turnkey packages" in India at a time when many of the major film studios in Mumbai are content to offer only shooting floors. According to Rao, the concept of creating a Film City as a one-stop shop for turnkey packages emerged from his desire to provide filmmakers efficient ways to "save time, energy and resources and focus on creative excellence, executional quality, economical schedules

and meticulous planning" (Suresh 1998: 50). After Rao successfully introduced the concept of turnkey packages for film productions at RFC, other
studios in south India, such as the MGR Film City in Chennai, have followed suit in offering similar one-stop services for film productions.

Remapping Hollywood, Bollywood, and Tollywood

The unique selling point of Ramoji Film City is that it is a self-contained
world of flexible authenticity. Although located in one place at the outskirts of Hyderabad, RFC provides film and television producers a vast
variety of flexible locales, some clearly identifiable by name (such as the
Hawa Mahal) and others more spontaneous (such as the 20 or so gardens
on the premises). Having total control over all aspects of production gives
RFC an enviable ability to rebuild any location for a shoot on short notice.
This ensures that no location will become jaded from repeated exposure.

Some of the outdoor locales and building facades in RFC are clearly
recognizable, since they are rather stereotypically marked as "North Indian," "South Indian," "Western," or "Japanese." In the "North India" section of the Film City, for instance, there is an exact replica of the ancient
Fort City of Fatehpur Sikri near Agra. There is a replica of the Taj Mahal
too, but it can be easily converted to resemble a mosque with a backdrop
of a crescent moon at night. Similarly, a building with a front elevation
that resembles the Golden Temple in Amristar, Punjab, has a rear elevation that looks like a shopping center. Film directors who need to create middle-class marketplaces or shopping centers in their films often use
these facades at RFC. These facades can be changed or removed at a moment's notice because the buildings in the shopping centers at RFC are
built using plaster of Paris. So, if a director wishes to blow up the shopping center for a film sequence, an explosion can be created in such a
way that the facades explode but the underlying structure of the building
remains intact.

A North Indian Shopping Center is located right next to a South Indian shopping center at RFC. While the North Indian shopping center
was used to create the "chor bazaar" in *Bade Miyan, Chote Miyan*, the
South Indian shopping center has been featured in the Telugu films such
as *Mechanic Mamayya* (Mechanic Uncle). In RFC, the "chor bazaar" (the
crooks' market) and the local police station are conveniently located right

next to each other. For shooting the more serious criminal acts, there is a Central Jail complex with five different types of built-in prisons, but if necessary the prison interiors can be quickly converted into hospital wards.

In RFC one can travel from Mumbai or Calcutta to London or New York in a few minutes. A street consisting of the front elevations of several high-rise buildings is long enough for three films to be shot at the same time. With a few modifications, the high-rise buildings can be made to resemble a busy street in London, or an upscale neighborhood in Mumbai, or a scenic ski resort in the Swiss Alps. All the buildings are made of plywood, and there are no interiors to shoot in. A hero or heroine can only be shown entering these buildings, but the rest of the film has to be shot in one of the indoor shooting floors. These high-rise buildings in RFC can be seen in several Hindi films such as *Bade Miyan, Chote Miyan, Joru Ka Gulam* (Wife's Slave) *Salakhein, Anari No. 1, Jodi No. 1, Dulhe Raja, Tujhe Meri Kasam* (My Promise to You), *Khushi* Happiness), *Ek Aur Ek Gyarah* (One and One is Eleven), and *Supari* (Beetle Nut). Telugu films such as *Nuvve Kavali* (I Want You), *Narasimha Naidu, Samarasimha Reddy, Badri, Yuva Raju* (Crown Prince), *Vamsee, Murari, Palanati Bhramanaidu,* and *Vasantam* (Spring Festival) have also used the streets in RFC.[5]

RFC provides filmmakers with several multipurpose buildings which can be converted into a school, college, or a courthouse. Most of the buildings can be modified quickly to resemble homes in a city or a town or a village. Each of the buildings is elaborately decorated with doors and windows to create an "authentic" sense of urban or rural lifestyles. A building with a glass facade serves as the offices of the State Bank of India, but the other side of the building is not part of the bank but is the front elevation of a college. Another building consists of a front elevation that looks like a hospital, while the two side elevations are that of a church and a library. The fourth elevation of the building is designed as an airport with a curbside on the exterior, a ticketing area in the interior, and a model airplane cabin.

If air travel is not part of a director's plans for a film shooting, RFC provides a railway station that consists of two elevations—one for an urban station and another for a rural station. The front elevation of the railway station can be made to read "New Delhi" or "Mumbai" for a Hindi film, and changed to "Vijaywada" or "Vishakapatnam" for a Telugu film. The railway station comes complete with a special train. The wheels of the train do not run on a railway track because they are made with tires which are usually used for trucks. The train does not have an engine, but a tractor can be hooked up to the railway compartments to move them along the "tracks." The railway station at RFC can be seen in many Hindi films such as *Bade Miyan Chote Miyan, Joru Ka Gulam, Tujhe Meri Kasam,* and *Khushi.* The railway station also appears in many Telugu films such as *Santosham* (Happiness), *Indra,* and *Khadgam* (Armor).

RFC also has a bus station which has been prominently featured in the *Coolie No. 1,* and Govinda, the hero in the film, worked as a coolie in this bus station. A roadside *dhaba* (restaurant) is also available for the heroes, the heroines, and villains to eat out in a film. A long street lined with lampposts can be transformed into a two-lane highway by replacing the lampposts with milestones showing "Calcutta 400 kms" or "Mumbai 300 kms" for a Hindi film, or "Vijayawada 400 kms" or "Vizag 300 kms" for a Telugu film. Car chase scenes and the kidnapping of heroes and heroines can also be shot on the same street. There are 27 different varieties of lampposts in RFC, and no two streets have the same type. All the lamp posts were imported from Singapore and Malaysia. Fantasy Street is the highest point in RFC. Over 75 percent of the Film City is visible from this point. By removing the lamp posts and creating some fog with a fog-making machine, Fantasy Street can be changed to resemble a misty road in the South Indian hill station of Ooty, or a foggy lane in the mountainous terrain of the Swiss Alps.

By using the outdoor locales and indoor facilities at RFC, an international filmmaker can save up to 40 percent of the production costs if the film is shot entirely in the Film City.[6] If the same filmmaker also chooses to embrace the turnkey concept and use the facilities at RFC for postproduction, the savings could be as high as 50 percent of the total costs in a comparable studio in Europe or North America. In the past, foreign films were made in India only if the story was centrally about Indians, as in the case of Richard Attenborough's *Gandhi* (1982) or David Lean's *A Passage to India* (1984). However, in recent years, several foreign films, such as *Centipede* (2004), *Crocodile 2: Death Swamp* (2002), *Nightfall* (2000), *Panic, Quicksand* (2002), and *In the Shadow of the Cobra* (2004) have been made at RFC.

Directed by Ted Nicolau and executive produced by Ramoji Rao and David A. Jackson, *In the Shadow of the Cobra* is about the search for an ancient tablet believed to be a road map to the legendary Lost Temple of Faramundi and its hidden treasures. In *Crocodile 2: Death Swamp,* a criminal carrying stolen money and gold hijacks a plane that crashes in a Mexican swamp, where the survivors are terrorized by a giant crocodile.

Centipede is a horror film directed by Gregory Gieras and executive produced by Eduardo Castro and Ramoji Rao. The story of *Centipede* revolves around a group of extreme sports enthusiasts from the United States who travel to India to explore the Shankali caves, where they encounter a 14-foot-long mutant centipede that attacks and kills them one at a time. Explaining the reasons for shooting an American film at RFC instead of using a Hollywood studio, Terry Hoffman, Associate Producer of *Centipede*, explains, "Cost is definitely a factor but the overall production values are great too" (Choudhury n.d: n.p).

The director-actor duo of Sam Firstenberg and Michael Dudikoff also produced an American film entitled *QuickSand* entirely at RFC. The film was shot on a budget of $3.7 million in a four-week schedule. *Quicksand* is set in a military base in Arizona where the commanding officer (Michael Dudikoff) of a military base in Arizona is murdered, and his daughter (Brooke Theiss) is the prime suspect. Production designer Robert Jenkins used the outdoor locations and sets at RFC to recreate the military base in a synthetic landscape which resembles a typical—or a stereotypical— desert in Arizona. Firstenberg acknowledged that lower production costs combined with a highly skilled technical workforce at RFC induced him to make his film entirely in India (Theodore 2001).

Although most of the foreign films shot at RFC so far have been low-budget, B-grade movies, Ramoji Rao plans to co-produce big-budget films with well-known directors and producers in Hollywood. In February 2003, RFC announced that it was finalizing a contract with Goldie Hawn to co-produce her film *Ashes*. As part of the deal, the details of which are closely guarded, it appears that Rao will provide RFC's facilities to Hawn free of charge in return for a 30 percent stake in the co-production of the film with Hawn's Cosmic Entertainment/Clear Light banner. According to Arun Kumar, manager of international marketing for Ramoji Rao's Ushakiron Movies, Hawn's *Ashes* is the first among 24 joint projects with Hollywood that will be produced at RFC in the coming years (Chaudhuri 2003).

In this sense, Ramoji Rao's ambitious vision of developing the Film City as a transnational studio to attract foreign producers is in line with Hyderabad's growing reputation as a popular center for the "outsourcing" of high-tech skills in the increasingly globalized South India. The software industry is already a booming business in South India, and the Hi-Tech

City in Hyderabad has run into serious competition from other equally capable contenders like Bangalore—often called the silicon valley of India. Although there is a healthy rivalry between these two South Indian cities in the information technology sector, there has been hardly any discussion of their role in the global entertainment industry.

The entertainment industry is a multi-billion-dollar enterprise worldwide, but the Indian share in the business is minimal, to say the least. In this context, the film studios of Hyderabad, led by RFC, have done well to gain a "toehold" in that market. Although officials at RFC are reluctant to divulge the figures, industry sources estimate that the production and post-production costs in RFC are about ten times lower than a similarly equipped studio in Hollywood (Financial Express 2000). On an average, its costs anywhere between Rs15,000 to Rs25,000 a second to produce special effects in India for cinema. However, in Hyderabad it averages Rs7,500 to Rs12,000 per second for films, while it costs up to Rs250 per second of crude SFX for TV. For instance, the 18.5 minutes of SFX in Kamal Hasan's *HeyRam*, done at the Ramoji Film City over a seven-month period, would have cost upwards of Rs10 crore in a studio in the United States. Though RFC is reluctant to divulge the figures, industry sources estimate the same would cost just under Rs1 crore (Financial Express 2000).

However, the complex articulation of global, national, regional, and local mediascapes at RFC cannot be understood merely in terms of "outsourcing" from Hollywood. To go beyond the "outsourcing debate," it is important to remember that a fierce competition is also raging *within* the Indian film industry as the Hyderabad-based Telugu film industry, Tollywood, is seeking to compete with the national hegemony of the Hindi film industry, Bollywood, which has traditionally been based in Mumbai or Bombay. Moreover, filmmaking is cheaper in Hyderabad than Mumbai by about 30–40 percent, so many Hindi filmmakers are looking toward RFC as a more economical, efficient, and convenient location for shooting films with regional, national and global appeal (Financial Express 2000).

Redefining the Global

Highlighting the growing transnational appeal of the Indian cinema industry, Carla Power and Sudip Mazumdar tell readers of *Newsweek* that "America Isn't the Only Country That Knows How to Spin and Export Fantasies." Arguing that Bollywood is going global, they write:

The West may have the biggest stalls in the world's media bazaar, but it's not the only player. Globalization isn't merely another word for Americanization and the recent expansion of the Indian entertainment industry proves it. For hundreds of millions of fans around the world, it is Bollywood, India's film industry, not Hollywood that spins their screen fantasies. Bollywood, based in Mumbai, has become a global industry. India's entertainment moguls don't merely target the billion South Asians, or desis, at home; they make slick movies, songs and TV shows for export. Attracted by a growing Indian middle class and a more welcoming investor environment, foreign companies are flocking to Bollywood, funding films and musicians. The foreign money is already helping India's pop culture to reach even greater audiences. And it may have a benign side effect cleaning up an Indian movie business long haunted by links to the underworld. (Power and Mazumdar 2000: 52)

Even the government of India seems to have taken note of this trend, and the Press Information Bureau (PIB) led the charge with an announcement that Indian cinema has become global (Raina 2000). The inducement for the government of India to make what the PIB called an unambiguous proclamation that Indian cinema has arrived on the international stage was the first International Film Festival Awards held in London 2000. According to the PIB news release, the global reach of the function was symbolized by the presence of Hollywood and European filmmakers and stars, along with the Indian veterans like Dilip Kumar and Amitabh Bachan [sic] at the function (Raina 2000). Countless e-zines on the Web, dedicated to Bollywood cinema, have also joined the chorus. Shyam Barooah of Apunkachoice.com who finds Indian spice sprinkling the world of cinema, writes:

Indian films are well and truly going global, that's for sure. Until recently, the products of the desi film industry were confined to the sub-continental market, except for a few off-beat art films, which made it to the international film festival circuit. The situation has undergone a sea change of late. In the last two-three years, film exports have been growing at over 80 percent and the Indian Motion Picture Association predicts exports will more than double in the near future. (Barooah 2000: n.p.)

India Today, the leading English news magazine in India and in the Indian diaspora, seems to agree with this growing sentiment among Bollywood aficionados, as evidenced by the following headline: "Bollywood has gone global, powered by the diaspora dollar [and] with a little effort it could challenge Hollywood." Arguing that the Global Indian is engendering a transnational chutney culture, *India Today*'s Shankar Aiyar and Sandeep Unnithan write:

> Globalisation has always been confused with Americanisation. If India has its way, it won't. The technological advances of the past decades have seen Indian movies make money in places like Japan witness Muthu's conquest in 2001 and desi music emanating from the unlikeliest of sources think Nicole Kidman singing in *Moulin Rouge*. Despite much clamour, India hasn't quite become a power to reckon with on the world stage. No Bollywood film crossed over into mainstream western theatres, though *Monsoon Wedding* reached the all-time Top 10 foreign box-office hit list in the US and *Bend it Like Beckham* was a hit in the UK. Bhangra pop and Bollywood remixes got clubbers dancing but didn't break out of the world music ghetto. But as India-inspired fiction discovered ever-new stars, some homegrown, some diasporic, Salman Rushdie's voice found many echoes across the globe and proved that cultural imperialism didn't necessarily speak with an American accent. (Aiyar and Unnithan 2003: n.p.)

As is evident from this sprinkling of news reports from a variety of sources, there is a buzz about Indian cinema going global in recent years, even as there is a clear recognition that Bollywood is still a very minor presence in the transnational entertainment industry. The entertainment business is a multi-billion-dollar enterprise worldwide, but in terms of sheer dollar values, the Indian share in the business has been minimal. India's movie exports grew from a paltry $10 million at the end of the 1980s to $100 million by the end of the 1990s, and were estimated to be over $250 million in 2000. However, when compared with Hollywood's $6.7 billion profits from foreign markets in the year 2000, some interesting contrasts begin to emerge between the world's largest film industry in Bollywood and the world's richest film industry in Hollywood.

For instance, while the total revenues in Indian cinema were an impressive $500 million in 2000, these numbers pale in comparison to Hollywood's $9.2 billion in ticket sales. Global merchandising and DVD sales rake in another $4 billion, which puts Hollywood's total revenue at over $13 billion in 2002 (Aiyar and Unnithan 2003: n.p.). However, one of the reasons that is often given to account for Bollywood going global is that the Indian entertainment industry is now recognizing the economic incentives of catering to its relatively affluent and culturally passionate diaspora, which is estimated to be 25 million around the world. The Indian diaspora in the United States and Britain have accounted for about 55 percent of international ticket sales for the Bollywood blockbusters *Taal* and *Kuch Kuch Hota Hai,* which grossed U.S.$8 million in foreign markets. But as Power and Mazumdar remind us, Bollywood films have always had millions of Indian and non-Indian fans in the Middle East, Africa, Southeast Asia, and Eastern Europe:

> Romany Gypsies in Eastern Europe tune in to India's Sony Entertainment Television, as do Hindi film fans in Fiji and the Philippines. In Israel . . . *Dil to Pagal Hai* is playing to packed houses in Tel Aviv as Halev Mistagya (Crazy Heart). In Arab countries, fans opt for Hindi movies over Hollywood ones. . . . In Tanzania's capital, open-air theaters screen the latest Indian romances, with interpreters standing in front of screens translating story lines. In Zanzibar, Swahili-speaking schoolgirls skip down the streets singing Hindi love songs despite not speaking a word of Hindi. (Power and Mazumdar 2000: n.p.)

Power and Mazumdar quote the noted Hindi film director-producer Subhash Ghai, who expresses confidence that Indian entertainment products have been globally accepted. Ghai further argues that in terms of international appeal no other cultural product except Hollywood has such a sweep. Shekhar Kapur, the Indian-born, London-based director of *Elizabeth,* goes one step further and predicts that the Western dominance of the cinema will be over in 10 years. Kapur writes:

> Here is a prediction: in its first week Spider-Man made $150 million and everybody was zonked out. Ten years from now, Spider-Man will make $1 billion in its first week. But when Spider-Man takes off his mask, he'll probably be Chinese. And the city in which he operates will not be New York, it will be Shanghai. And yet it will be an international film, it will still be Spider-Man. (Kapur 2002: 9)

The reason for this radical shift within a decade, Kapur argues, is that the American entertainment industry is becoming heavily dependent on foreign markets as fewer and fewer films are being funded within the United

States. In 2001, one-third of all Hollywood productions were funded by German banks, and by the end of the decade Kapur believes, most of the funding will be Asian [and] the next big studio will be Asian. His argument goes somewhat like this: the main Asian markets led by Japan, China, and India constitute 80 percent of the world population. In India alone, almost 60 percent of the country's one billion strong population is under the age of 30 years. Since the global entertainment industries mostly desire consumers in the 15–30 demographics, Kapur feels that the Asian markets will be the preferred targets for films and television programs produced in the next decade. Gazing through the crystal ball even further into the future, Kapur predicts:

> In 15 years from now, we won't be discussing the domination of the Western media but the domination of the Chinese media or the Asian media. Soon we will find that to make a hugely successful film, you have to match Tom Cruise with an Indian or a Chinese actor. What you are seeing with films such as the *The Guru* is just the tip of the iceberg. (Kapur 2002: 9)

The Guru (2001), produced by Hugh Grant's London-based company Working Title, is one of the very few Hollywood films featuring an Indian actor (Jimi Mistry) in the lead role opposite Hollywood stars like Heather Graham and Marisa Tomei. However, it would be far-fetched to suggest that transnational films like *The Guru, Monsoon Wedding, Bend It Like Beckham,* or even Bollywood blockbusters like *Lagaan* and *Devdas* would even make a dent into Tom Cruise's profit margins around the world with films like his *Mission Impossible* movies, including MI 4 that will surely be produced within the decade.

Therefore, some of Kapur's predictions about the coming Asian dominance in the entertainment industry in the next 10 to 15 years may be wishful thinking, and it will take more than a Chinese Spider-Man weaving his magical web over the streets of Shanghai to disrupt Hollywood's hegemony over production, distribution, and exhibition in the transnational entertainment industry in the next ten years.

While one-half-billion-strong audiences in the 15–30 demographics in India may have the numerical strength to attract the attention of many transnational media corporations, it is rather unlikely that Hollywood will revamp its scheduling and promotional strategies aimed at the big Oscars ceremony in March every year to accommodate the Hindu festivals of Dusserah and Divali in October and November. However, one of Kapur's predictions has already come true: the world's biggest film studio, Ramoji Film City, is indeed now in India and that may induce us to pause and consider some of the other things about the Asian future of the transnational entertainment industry in the next ten to fifteen years.

NOTES

1. An earlier version of this chapter, "Mapping Tollywood: The Cultural Geography of 'Ramoji Film City' in Hyderbad," appeared in *Quarterly Review of Film and Video* 23 (2006): 129–38.

2. Quoted on the Ramoji Film City website.

3. "Tollywood" refers to the Telugu-language film industry based in the state of Andhra Pradesh in South India. The name "Tollywood" is derived from the concept of naming commercial film industries in India in relation to the commercial film industry of "Hollywood" in the United States. Although it was first used in the context of the Bombay-based Hindi film industry (Bollywood = Bombay + Hollywood), the concept was soon extended to define other Indian-language cinemas such as Tollywood (Telugu Cinema) and Mollywood (Malayalam cinema). The naming of the Telugu film industry as "Tollywood" serves a dual function for fans and media critics alike: it enables them to compare and contrast the commercial success and popularity of their native film industry in relation to the global might of Hollywood, and it also helps them to draw distinctions and parallels between the regional clout of Telugu cinema and the nationalist appeal of Hindi cinema.

4. See http://www.travel-india.com.

5. Film titles which refer to proper names of characters have not been translated into English here.

6. Breza, "Ramoji Film City Woos World": http://www.rediff.com/entertai/2002/may/29ram.htm.

BIBLIOGRAPHY

Aiyar, S., and S. Unnithan. 2003. "Bollywood's Flight: The World A Stage." *India Today.*

Appadurai, A. 1996. *Modernity at Large: Cultural Dimensions of Globalization.* Minneapolis: University of Minnesota Press.

Barooah, S. 2000. "Indian Spice Sprinkling in the World of Cinema." Retrieved April 6, 2004 from: http://www.apunkachoice.com/scoop/bollywood/20001126-1.html.

Chaudhuri, H. 2003. "Goldie Hawn to Shoot in Ramoji Film City?" *Times of India*, February 27.

Chitti, P. C. 2000. "IT Effects—Cyberabad Emerging Specialist in 3-D Animation." *The Indian Express*, May 13.

Choudhury, S. n.d. "The Plot Thins: Red Tape Fetters the Ramoji Rao Film City's Hollywood Dream." *Outlook*.

Financial Express. 2000. "IT Effects: Cyberabad Emerging Specialist in 3D Animation." May 13.

Gupta, V. S., and R. Dayal. 1996. *Media and Market Forces: Challenges and Opportunities*. Delhi: Concept Publishing.

Hannigan, J. 1998. *Fantasy City: Pleasure and Profit in the Postmodern Metropolis*. New York: Routledge.

Herman, Edward S., and R. W. McChesney. 1997. *The Global Media: Missionaries of Corporate Capitalism*. London: Cassel.

Jeffrey, R. 2000. *India's Newspaper Revolution: Capitalism, Politics and the Indian-Language Press, 1977–99*. New York: Oxford University Press.

Kapur, S. 2002. "The Asians Are Coming." *The Guardian*, August 23.

Kuriakose, R. 1997. "Down in the Clouds." *The Week*, October 19.

Power, C., and S. Mazumdar. 2000. "America Isn't the Only Country That Knows How to Spin and Export Fantasies." *Newsweek International*, February 28.

Raina, R. 2000. "Indian Cinema Goes Global." Press Information Bureau, Government of India, Available at: http://pib.nic.in/feature/feyr2000/faug2000/f2908 2001.

Smoodin, E., ed. 1994. *Disney Discourse: Producing the Magic Kingdom*. New York: Routledge.

Sorkin, M., ed. 1992. *Variations on a Theme Park: The New American City and the End of Public Space*. New York: Hill and Wang.

Suresh, K. 1998. "Reel Estate Tycoon." *Advertising and Marketing*, November 15, pp. 46–50.

Theodore, S. 2001. "International Quality at Cheaper Cost: Hollywood Magic to Be Woven in Hyderabad." *The Statesman*, March 25.

Thussu, D. K., ed. 1998. *Electronic Empires: Global Media and Local Resistance*. New York: Arnold.

Chapter 5

The Globalization of "Bollywood"

The Hype and the Hope

Daya Kishan Thussu

From Kenya to Kazakhstan and from Morocco to Malaysia, Indian films have found an eager audience. As India integrates further into a globalized free-market economy, Indian films are likely to have a global reach attracting new viewers, beyond their traditional South Asian diasporic constituency. In this chapter, I aim to map this phenomenon, examining the hype associated with globalization of Indian cinema and the hope that it may generate more pluralist global cultural interactions. I will examine how a combination of national and transnational factors, including deregulation of media and communication sectors, the availability of new delivery and distribution mechanisms as well as growing corporatization of the film industry, has contributed to global visibility of popular Indian cinema.

Demonstrating robust annual economic growth of 8 percent in the past few years, India is increasingly viewed internationally as an emerging economic and political power. One manifestation of this status is how India's popular culture is being perceived outside India, particularly within the metropolitan centers of the globe (Goswami 2004). "The Rise of India" was the main theme of *Foreign Affairs*, one of the world's most influential foreign policy journals, in July-August 2006, while *Time* magazine ran a cover story in July the same year on "India Inc.: Why the world's biggest democracy is the next great economic superpower—and what it means for the rest of us" (*Time*, July 3, 2006). The globalization of the mainstream Indian film industry, popularly known as Bollywood, also reflects this phenomenon.

The number of academic books and articles that have been published in the past few years is another indication that researchers in media and communication fields are now taking the world's most prolific film industry more seriously. Film schools in the United States and Europe traditionally have only been interested in a few avant-garde filmmakers from India, notably Satyajit Ray, as part of the study of World Cinema, or "Third Cinema." In terms of audiences too, the only international viewers interested in such "high-brow" cinema were on the festival circuit. What is new and potentially an exciting development, witnessed at the turn of the century, is that popular Indian cinema (predominantly, though not exclusively, Hindi cinema) has acquired an international profile, second only to Hollywood. Hindi films are shown in more than 70 countries and are popular everywhere where South Asians live, but also in the Arab world, in central and southeast Asia, and among African countries.

India's $3.5 billion Hindi film industry based in Mumbai (formerly Bombay), the country's commercial hub and a center of cosmopolitan culture, has witnessed extraordinary growth—Indian film exports jumped twenty-fold in the period 1989–1999 and have continued to grow since —and represents an excellent example of media flows emanating from the global South rather than from the North (Thussu 2006b). One key reason for its size is the huge domestic market among India's vast population —numbering one billion, reflecting the place that cinema has as the most popular form of entertainment, cutting across regional, linguistic, class, creed, gender, and generational divisions. Films have also contributed to the burgeoning popular music industry, as a mainstream Indian film is unlikely to succeed without a prominent musical score (Mishra 2002; Pendakur 2003; Kaur and Sinha 2005).

In terms of production and viewership, "Bollywood" is the world's largest film industry, which employs more than 2.5 million people and sells over 4 billion cinema tickets annually: every year a billion more people buy tickets for Indian movies than for Hollywood films. In addition to productions from Bollywood, strong regional centers provide films in India's other main languages, notably Tamil, Bangla, Telugu, and Malayalam, generating a multivocal audiovisual feast that circulates among the distinct geo-linguistic diasporic and national groups. For at least three decades, India has been producing more films annually than any other country in the world, including the United States (see Table 1) and, despite the globalization of the mainly U.S.-based media transnational conglomerates, this trend has not changed. If anything, globalization seems to have provided a much-needed fillip to Indian filmmakers to expand

TABLE 1
The World's Top Ten Film-Producing Nations

Country	Number of Films			
	1974	1984	1994	2004
India	432	829	754	946
United States	242	366	635	611
Japan	333	333	251	310
China and Hong Kong	146	253	340	276
France	234	161	115	203
Italy	231	103	95	134
Spain	112	75	44	133
United Kingdom	88	44	70	132
Germany	80	75	57	121
Russia	—	—	90	120

Source: Based on data from *Screen Digest*, June 2005.

beyond the national and diasporic geocultural territories and aim for a global audience through "cross-over" films (Desai 2004; Kaur and Sinha 2005). Although still very small in comparison with export earnings of Hollywood, this represents a remarkable development, given the overwhelming dominance of the U.S. film industry in global film production and distribution (Miller et al. 2001; Waterman 2005).

Even in countries with highly developed local film-production networks and markets, U.S. films dominate foreign imports, and, given the proliferation of dedicated film channels across the world, it is unlikely that the dependence on U.S. imports is diminishing. And yet India is one of the few countries where Hollywood barely gets a look in—at only 5 percent of the film market (as against 70–90 percent in European markets). This may be due to Indian cinema's relationship with its rich and complex cultural background (Vasudevan 2000). Traditionally, the cinema in India has been rooted in the "idea of India" as a pluralist, secular, and socialist country of continental dimensions with its multilayered and multifaceted society.

Globalization of Indian Cinema—The Historical Context

Cinema has a long history in India, with the first feature-length film, *Raja Harishchandra*, based on the life of a mythological king of ancient India, being released as far back as 1913. In the silent era (1913–1931), more than 1,200 films were made in India, and as India entered the sound era in

1931 with the first talkie—*Alam Ara*—the pace of filmmaking consistently increased: from 84 in 1932, to 173 in 1942, to 233 in 1952, to 315 in 1962 (Rajadhyaksha and Willemen 2000). Even before India won its independence from British colonialism, films from India were being exported to southeast Asian and African nations (Barnouw and Krishnaswamy 1980).

As for other Indian media, anti-colonialism profoundly influenced and defined Indian cinema in its formative years. Progressive organizations such as the Indian People's Theatre Association were directly involved in filmmaking, fostering a message of nation-building and social harmony. Their 1946 film *Dharti Ke Lal* (Children of the Earth), directed by well-known writer Khwaja Ahmad Abbas, was the first Indian film to receive widespread distribution in the Soviet Union, while the 1957 feature *Perdesi* (Foreigner) was the first Indo-Soviet co-production. Satyajit Ray's debut film *Pather Panchali* (Song of the Little Road), released in 1955, won international critical acclaim and continued to run for more than seven months in New York, setting a new record for foreign films released in the United States and putting Indian cinema on the world map. Raj Kapoor's 1955 film *Shri 420* (Mr 420) became immensely popular in the Soviet Union, while Shambhu Mitra's film *Jagte Raho* (Stay Awake) won the Grand Prix at the Karlovy Vary Film Festival in 1957. Indian films, especially those championing socialist themes, such as Bimal Roy's *Do Bigha Zameen* (Two Bigha of Land) and Raj Kapoor's *Awara* (Vagabond), were also widely shown in Maoist China, the latter being the most popular Indian film in that country (Aiyar 2006).

For audiences in other Asian countries, as well as in Africa and the Arab world, Indian films had a huge appeal, with their melodramatic narrative style and a storyline which emphasized dichotomies between the just and the unjust, enlivened with song-and-dance sequences. They tended to find it easier to relate to these themes, as Brian Larkin has shown in his study of the reception of popular Indian cinema among Nigerian audiences (Larkin 1997).

Exporting Indian Cinema to the West

The deregulation of India's media and communication sector in the 1990s enabled Indian filmmakers to promote their films to the Indian diaspora based in the West. In 1995, *Dilwale Dulhaniya Le Jayenge* (The Brave Heart Will Take the Bride), starring Shah Rukh Khan, was the first major film to focus on an Indian family based in Britain and was a huge commercial success—the film had a ten-year uninterrupted run in a Mumbai cinema until 2005. The hitherto unexplored export potential of Indian films came to light when the 1998 love story *Kuch Kuch Hota Hai* (Something Is Happening), directed by Karan Johar, featured in British weekly top 10 film lists. Subhash Ghai's love story *Taal* (The Beat), and Suraj Barjatya's 1999 musical extolling the virtues of extended family, *Hum Saath Saath Hain* (We Stand United), were the first Indian films to make it into the top 20 in the trade magazine *Variety*'s box office chart. Johar's 2001 family drama *Kabhi Khushi Kabhi Gham* (Sometimes Happiness, Sometimes Sorrow) exploited diasporic dilemmas effectively to rake in box office takings, making it one of the most successful Hindi films in both the United Kingdom and the United States, home to a sizable and economically prosperous Indian diaspora (see Tables 2 and 4) (Punathambekar 2005).

Advancements in digital technology and the availability of satellite and cable television have enabled the tremendous increase in the number of Indian films being shown outside India. In Europe, for example, the opening up of the audiovisual market both to pan-European and international operators changed the television landscape, with a twenty-fold increase in the number of channels available to audiences in the past decade and a half—from 93 in 1990 to more than 1,700 in 2005—with entertainment channels showing the most robust growth. Movie channels increased from just 5 in 1990 to 136 in 2005, while ethnic channels, which did not exist in 1990, climbed to as many as 51 (Thussu 2006a).

"Bollywoodization" of Television

As in Hollywood, there is a close connection between India's film factories and the small screens across the country and among South Asian diasporic communities. The changing global broadcasting environment and the availability of digital television and online delivery systems has led to the proliferation of Bollywood or Bollywoodized material on television almost to a saturation point—from soap operas to movie-based countdown and game shows, to sport and even news networks. The globalization of Indian television has ensured that Indian films are being watched by a varied international television audience, making it imperative for producers to invest in subtitling to widen their reach.

In 1999, B4U (Bollywood for You), Britain's round-the-clock digital

Hindi movie channel, was launched, which by 2006 was available on eight satellites in more than 100 countries in North America, Europe, the Middle East, Africa, and South Asia. In the coveted U.S. market, it was available on the Dish Network, while in Europe it was part of the Sky network and in the Middle East could be accessed through the Pehla or Al Awael bouquet. Other major players, Zee Network (India's largest media company), Star Plus (part of Rupert Murdoch's News Corporation), and Sony Entertainment Television, are increasingly using Hindi film-based programming to reach an international market (Thussu 2006a).

This unprecedented expansion of television in the early 2000s, and particularly the emergence of dedicated film-based pay channels, has given the movie industry a huge boost. Prominent among them are Zee Cinema (part of Zee Network), Max (part of Sony), Star Gold (part of News Corporation), and Filmy (part of Sahara Group). Publicizing Bollywood through television—now reaching the global Indian—has become a key marketing strategy. One indication of the Bollywoodization of television is the amount of airtime that television networks tend to give to telecasting annual film awards—which have evolved into a mini industry. Zee was the first network to recognize the advertising potential of such programs—peppered with live song-and-dance routines by top stars from Bollywood. Since their inception in 1998, the annual Zee Cine Awards have become a major showcase for Indian cinema. They went global in 2004 by hosting the award ceremony in Dubai, followed a year later in London and in Mauritius in 2006, all three places chosen with an eye on the diasporic demography. The so-called Bollywood Oscars, Awards of the International Indian Film Academy, launched in 2000, were broadcast live from London's Millennium Dome to more than 122 countries, reaching 600 million viewers. The subsequent awards have covered various parts of the globe: Sun City, South Africa (2001), Kuala Lumpur (2002), Johannesburg (2003), Singapore (2004), Amsterdam (2005), and Dubai (2006).

The Old Imperial Capital and the New Bollywood

London, the old imperial capital, has played a crucial role in the globalization of Indian cinema. It is a vital link in the global distribution of Hindi films and a center of Indian media operations in the West, besides being home to a huge Indian population, part of Britain's more than 2 million strong South Asian diaspora. It is not surprising then that among Western nations, Indian cinema has its highest profile in Britain.

In 2001, Indian director Mira Nair's *Monsoon Wedding*, a light-hearted account of a wedding in a wealthy family in India, was awarded the Golden Lion for best picture at the Venice film festival, while the British-born Asif Kapadia's *The Warrior* won the London Film Festival's prestigious Sutherland Trophy. A year later, the first Indian-Hollywood co-production entitled *Kaante* (Thorns) was released, starring India's best-known actor, Amitabh Bachchan, who was voted by a BBC online poll as the greatest star of stage and screen and immortalized in wax at London's Madame Tussaud's. He was the first Indian film personality to merit this accolade.

Subhash Ghai's 2001 film *Yaadein* (Memories) was premiered at the British Academy of Film and Television in London, an event organized by Star TV. The film entered the UK Top Ten in just one weekend. In 2002, the British Film Institute organized *ImagineAsia,* "a hugely successful, all-singing all-dancing masala festival" which "broke new ground on several fronts: introducing a broader appreciation and mainstreaming of South Asian film cultures to a cross over audience in the UK; launching a raft of new publications and educational materials; successful NFT (National Film Theatre) seasons and talks; new theatrical and DVD releases, young peoples events; touring exhibitions, screenings and talks around Britain" (Rughani and White 2003: 9). In 2004, a reality show on Britain's Channel 4 followed a group of British hopefuls as they underwent auditions and tests to compete for a star role in a Hindi film. *Bollywood Star*, broadcast at prime time on a major terrestrial channel, gave the Indian film industry huge exposure among the general British television audience. Indian films are regularly reviewed in major British newspapers.

TABLE 2

Top Hindi Films in the United Kingdom: 2000–2004

Film/Year	Gross Box Office (£ million)	Cinemas Released	Production
Kabhi Khushi Kabhi Gham (2001)	2.50	41	Yash Raj Films
Veer Zaara (2004)	2.01	60	Yash Raj Films
Devdas (2002)	1.74	54	Eros International
Kal Ho Naa Ho (2003)	1.67	38	Yash Raj Films
Mohabbatein (2000)	1.10	29	Yash Raj Films
Main Hoon Na (2004)	0.96	46	Eros International
Mujhse Dosti Karoge (2002)	0.80	32	Yash Raj Films

Source: UK Film Council, 2006.

This apparent mainstreaming of Bollywood is also to be witnessed in the manner in which Hindi films are released in the United Kingdom. For more than a decade now, commercial Indian films have been released not just among small "ethnic" cinemas but in multiplexes across the country, as new patterns of migration have meant that in most major British cities there is a sizable South Asian population. Given the currency exchange rate between the United Kingdom and India (at the time of writing 1£ = 80 rupees), the British market is seen as extremely lucrative. However, distribution remains a controversial issue; as Tables 2 and 3 demonstrate, the best performing Hindi films in the United Kingdom came from only two major production houses and distribution networks. Low-key distributors for small-budget films, often aesthetically more sophisticated than the average Bollywood fare, face serious hurdles to reach a wider audience as the diasporic market seems to be dominated by star-studded, big-budget films.

TABLE 3
Distribution of Hindi Films in the United Kingdom: 2000–2004

Distributor	Number of Releases	Box Office Gross (£ million)	Top Performing Title
Eros International Ltd.	80	13.94	*Devdas*
Bollywood Films	36	1.79	*Ek Hee Rishtaa*
Spark Entertainment	28	2.24	*Fiza*
Venus Entertainment	23	1.52	*The Hero*
Gurpreet Video Intl.	21	0.91	*Aankhen*
Yash Raj Films	18	12.23	*Kabhi Khushi Kabhi Gham*
Tip Top Entertainment	7	0.94	*Andaaz*
Shree Krishna Film	6	0.84	*Haan Maine Bhi Pyar Kiya*
Venus Films	6	0.65	*Dil Ka Rishtaa*

Source: UK Film Council, 2006.

TABLE 4
Million-Plus Grossing Hindi Films in the United States: 1999–2005

Film/Year	Gross Box Office ($ million)	Theaters Released	Distributor
Veer-Zaara (2004)	2.92	88	Yash Raj Films
Kabhi Khushi Kabhi Gham (2002)	2.90	73	Yash Raj Films
Hum Saath-Saath Hain (1999)	1.99	60	Eros
Taal (1999)	1.98	44	Eros
Kal Ho Naa Ho (2004)	1.78	52	Yash Raj Films
Salaam Namaste (2005)	1.43	63	Yash Raj Film
Main Prem Ki Diwani Hoon (2003)	1.23	60	Rajshri
Mohabbatein (2000)	1.07	53	Yash Raj Films
Kaante (2002)	1.04	29	Media Partners
Yaadein (2001)	1.00	56	Tips

Source: http://www.boxofficeguru.com/f2.htm.

Creating a Culture of Corporatization

The globalization of the Indian film industry is manifested by its gradual corporatization, spurred on by a change in perception by the Government of India, which is becoming increasingly aware of the export potential of India's entertainment industry. In 1999, it passed a law exempting film export earnings from tax. The decision of the state-run Industrial Development Bank of India to finance films has also made a difference, as producers can now receive loans from banks and do not have to depend on questionable financial sources. Financing of commercial cinema in India has traditionally been a complex operation, with funding sometimes being provided by syndicates with "underworld" contacts. Keen to launder their profits, cash transfer rather than checks was the industry norm, with little financial transparency. Despite a more liberal investment environment, only one in ten films are financed through organized institutions such as banks (Das 2006).

With the globalization of media industries and availability of new modes of delivery—through satellite and cable as well as online mechanisms—film producers can now recover costs through subsidiary rights: overseas, TV, video, DVD, and Internet download sales. The growth of the music industry and the existence of several international music corporations in India have contributed to a major new stream of revenue— by 2005, music rights for films were sold for 100 million rupees, instead of 1 million rupees in the early 1990s. Increasingly, more and more entertainment companies are listed on the Bombay Stock Exchange. When in 2000 filmmaker Subhash Ghai went public with his production company, Mukta Arts, it was hailed a groundbreaking development for the industry.

In the past five years, according to industry reports, financial institutions such as the Industrial Development Bank of India sanctioned Rs1.8 billion for movie projects, of which Rs900 million have already been distributed. Bank of India has financed Rs250 million for five movies, while since 2004, the Export-Import Bank of India has financed Rs580 million for nine movies. Though the interest rates are very low on such loans, they are offered only to well-established film companies. Many banks appear to be keen to fund such films which have a potential to earn foreign currency revenues in the overseas market (Das 2006).

Another significant contribution to the culture of corporatism has been the growing interest of nonmedia corporations in the film business.

A key example of this trend is Adlabs, part of the Reliance Infocomm, one of India's top industrial houses, which is now involved in film production, processing, exhibition, and distribution. The Sahara Group—a major presence in the television industry in India—is also making forays into film production through its Sahara Motion Pictures Division. Its deal with production house K Sera Sera to hire ace directors Ram Gopal Varma (maker of the Indian version of *The Godfather* called *Sarkar*), and Madhur Bhandarkar (whose *Page 3* received both critical and commercial success) has led to the production of several hit films.

International players such as Sony and Star are also entering the film business in India: prominent examples include the 2003 film *Ek Hasina Thi* (Once There Was a Beautiful Woman), co-produced by Murdoch's Twentieth Century Fox, and noted director Sanjay Leela Bhansali's movie *Saawariya* (Beloved), partly financed by Sony (Das 2006). With the growing corporatization of the film industry and progressive Americanization of popular culture, corporations both national and transnational, including Coke, Pepsi, and Intel, are increasingly warming up to the idea of in-film advertising and sponsorship and merchandising deals.

"Crossover Cinema"? Hype and Hope

The corporatization may help make the Indian film industry more professional and financially efficient, but how might it impact on the themes of films? Will filmmakers be tailoring their scripts to suit a global audience? How does the content cross cultural and linguistic boundaries? Though such diasporic filmmakers as New York–based Mira Nair (director of *Monsoon Wedding*) and the British-born Gurvinder Chaddha (director of such crossover films as *Bend It Like Beckham* and *Bride and Prejudice*) have acted as a bridge between Western and Indian popular cinema, their films are specifically aimed at Western audiences. For a Hindi-language Indian film—with its primary audience in India—to cross over to a wider international audience is a much more daunting task.

One of the more successful of the latter was the 2001 film *Lagaan* (Land Tax), produced by Aamir Khan, which was nominated for the Best Foreign Film at the Oscars and more recently listed at number 14 among the "50 films to see before you die" in a special program on Britain's Channel 4 television in July 2006. Hollywood-style marketing, with a premiere in London's West End, made *Lagaan* (which had a British actress,

Rachel Shelley, in a leading role) a candidate to cross the cultural divide that keeps the majority of Britons from watching Indian films. The film combines the two key aspects of Indian cultural life—cinema and cricket—against a colonial backdrop and the setting of the traditional Indian village. Sony Entertainment Television Pictures released *Lagaan* globally on June 15, 2001, in 40 theaters in the United States alone, as well as in Britain, Japan, China, Malaysia, Hong Kong, South Africa, Middle East, Australia, and New Zealand, and the film was subtitled in English, French, German, Arabic, and Mandarin. In Britain, *Lagaan* hit the box office top 10 and became a talking point even among non-Asian filmgoers.

Lagaan was followed by another Indian attempt at crossover cinema. *Asoka*, an ambitious film produced by superstar Shah Rukh Khan, told the story of India's greatest emperor, the ruler of the Mauryan dynasty (322–185 B.C.), famous for waging bloody campaigns, who gave up war to become a Buddhist monk, spreading the message of Buddha across Asia. Khan criss-crossed continents as part of a publicity blitzkrieg to promote the 120-million-rupee film, the first historical Hindi-language film in nearly two decades. *Asoka* received good coverage in Western media—it was the first Indian film to employ a British publicity firm to promote it, with posters on the London Underground. The film was released in more than 80 cinemas across the United Kingdom. The book, *The Making of Asoka*, by journalist Mushtaq Shiekh, published at the time of the film's release, marked the beginning of a trend in film marketing (Shiekh 2001). Since then, the marketing of films has taken on new dimensions—with online advertising and mobile publicity. Despite such efforts, Hindi films have not been able to make a significant dent into Hollywood's territory. It is still rare to find many Westerners, or for that matter, Chinese, queuing up to watch a Bollywood film.

It can be argued that corporatization and chasing crossover audiences has led to the advent of a new kind of cinema, a hybrid cultural product that fuses the language of Hollywood with the accent, slang, and emotions of India. Indian filmmakers appear to be aiming to reach the coveted Western markets, privileging scripts which interest the diasporic audience—by 2004, exports accounted for nearly 30 percent of the industry earnings (FICCI 2004; UNESCO 2005).

It is not unusual to see Indian filmmakers adapting Hollywood plots to Indian tastes, in the process refiguring the Hollywood hegemony in a hybridized product. The desire to maximise the global audience is seen in the increasing popularity of the Manhattan-in-Mumbai genre of movies, where either the hero or the heroine is an NRI (Non-resident Indian), based in the West mostly speaking Hinglish dialogues (a mixture of Hindi and English).

The film producers appear to be primarily interested only in the "secondary" markets—the demographically desirable NRIs, reflected in the themes of some recent big budget films. The 2003 mega hit, the Nikhil Advani-directed love triangle *Kal Ho Na Ho* (If Tomorrow Comes), was the first mainstream Indian film set entirely in the United States. Yash Chopra production's 2005 film *Salaam Namaste*, which dealt with the issue of a live-in relationship, was the first Hindi film to be based in Australia. A year later, Karan Johar's *Kabhi Alvida Na Kehna* (Never Say Goodbye), a film starring, among others, Shah Rukh Khan, which centered on a cross-couple romance and adultery, had virtually no reference to India at all. Most of the dialogue in the film was in English or Hinglish as the film was about young Indian-origin professionals living in New York. The film generated controversy in India as it seemed to legitimize extramarital affairs and divorce, still not socially acceptable for most Indians. Both director Johar and star Khan were defending the new value system of globalized Indians in an hour-long special program on NDTV (*We the People*, August 20, 2006, NDTV) as well as a half-hour special on CNN/IBN, another 24/7 news operation in India. Despite such controversies at home, the film did extremely well in the targeted market, generating £749,243 in its opening week in the United Kingdom, while in the United States it grossed $1.5 million in its first week, according to media reports.

To attempt to reach beyond the diasporic audience may be seen in the increasing presence of Western actors in Indian films. Filmmakers want to use the hegemonic superiority associated with Western media and cultural artefacts to gain Western as well as other non-South Asian audiences. British actress Antonia Bernath had a prominent role in Subhash Ghai's 2005 film *Kisna—the Warrior Poet*, which was shot simultaneously in Hindi and English, with the English print shortened by an hour to accommodate the Western audience. Another British actress, Annabelle Wallace, played the lead role in a bilingual romantic comedy *Dil Jo Bhi Kahey* (Whatever the Heart Says), which also starred Amitabh Bachchan. British actor Toby Stephens, previously cast in *Lagaan,* had a major appearance in the 2005 historical film *Mangal Pandey: The Rising,* set in nineteenth-century India, while British actress Alice Patten starred in the 2006 hit *Rang De Basanti.*

Hollywood/Bollywood

These trends toward corporatization and globalization indicate growing convergence between Bollywood and the West. The British government sees Bollywood as a source for foreign exchange: there was a buzz in the entertainment business when it was announced that the 2007 "Bollywood Oscars" ceremony will be held in Yorkshire. In December 2005, Indian and British governments signed a joint agreement to promote film co-productions. A much more significant synchronization is taking place between the world's biggest and its richest film factories. Plans for joint ventures between Indian film producers and Hollywood giants received a boost with the decision of the Indian government to allow foreign companies to invest in the Indian film industry. In 2000, the Indian government allowed the Foreign Investment Promotion Board to approve 100 percent Foreign Direct Investment ventures in filmmaking, financing, production, distribution, and exhibition. Now major Hollywood companies such as Columbia Tristar, Paramount, and Universal Pictures are contemplating co-productions in India.

This policy shift conforms to general pro-business orientation of post–Cold War Indian governments. Both the Indian film industry and the government are keen to explore global markets, as was evident at the 2001 Cannes Film Market when private producers joined hands with the state-run National Film Development Corporation in setting up an India Pavilion to market Indian films. A delegation from the Indian film, television, and music industries, headed by India's then Information and Broadcasting Minister Sushma Swaraj, visited the United States in 2001, meeting, among others, Jack Valenti, president of the Motion Pictures Association of America, to persuade Hollywood to invest in Indian entertainment industry and also to bring Indian films into the mainstream distribution circuit in the United States and globally. Pricewater Cooper valued the entertainment and media sector in India at $7 billion in 2004, and it was expected to grow at about 14 percent in the next five years to reach over $10 billion by 2009 (FICCI 2004).

As a UNESCO report noted:

Indian film production is progressively catering to foreign audiences. Although small by comparison with American productions, the revenues generated by Indian movies abroad have registered a ten-fold expansion in the last 10 years. For the estimated $990 million earned by the Indian film sector in 2004, revenues from overseas have already reached $220 million. Today the value of Indian cultural and creative industries is estimated at $4.3 billion. This sector is growing at an annual rate close to 30 percent, and analysts forecast that exports may continue to grow by 50 percent in the coming years. An important factor in this impressive performance is that Indian companies are succeeding in bringing international audiences to the cinemas, in addition to the traditional diaspora communities of the USA, the United Kingdom, and the Middle East. This strategy includes expansion to nontraditional countries, both industrialised and emerging, such as Japan and China. (UNESCO 2005: 44)

Already, some indication of Bollywood's look-east attitudes are discernable: leading Indian composer A. R. Rahman, who wrote the music for Andrew Lloyd Webber's West End musical hit, *Bombay Dreams*, created the score for a Chinese film *Warriors of Heaven and Earth*. The success of the 2005 Chinese film *Perhaps Love*—the first musical since the 1950s and made with expertise from Bollywood—is indicative of the potential of media collaborations among major non-Western cultures, involving the world's two largest populations and its two biggest diasporas: 35 million Chinese, 20 million Indian (*People's Daily* 2005).

The Indian government and the corporate world see Indian popular culture as part of India's "soft" power. Bollywood stars and singers were a key part of the closing ceremony of the 19th Commonwealth Games in Melbourne in 2006, promoting the 2010 Games in New Delhi, while during the 2006 World Economic Forum in Davos, Switzerland, a $3 million public-private promotional campaign called "India Everywhere" included shows organized by Bollywood choreographer Shiamak Davar.

This "soft" power is anchored in India's software industry, which earned as much as $17.2 billion in export revenue in 2005 (NASSCOM 2006). The world's largest distributor of Hindi films—Eros International —which began trading on the London Stock Exchange in 2006—has collaborated with Intel to deliver its content over broadband to consumers around the globe, and started a digital service with RTL, Europe's largest TV company, to make Indian movies available for on-demand delivery on the continent. It also announced plans to launch its content on Movielink, a leading broadband movie download service in the United States, owned by a joint venture of Metro-Goldwyn-Mayer, Paramount, Sony, Universal, and Warner Brothers. Commenting on these developments, Kishore

Lulla, Chairman and CEO of Eros International, said: "It marks the coming together of Hollywood and Bollywood. Our visions are aligned and we are confident of being able to offer a compelling consumer proposition" (quoted in press release available at www.erosentertainment.com).

Many Indian film companies, including Yash Raj Films, have set up hi-tech studios for outsourcing work from Hollywood, while Mukta Arts has opened a film academy called Whistling Woods, to train professionals in all departments of film production and distribution. Sahara's Hindi movie channel Filmy has launched a Hollywood dubbed movie segment. As the plans for joint ventures between Indian film producers and Hollywood giants mature and materialize, Indian films are likely to become more visible in the global market. However, there is a lurking danger that with Hollywood production houses dominating film financing, Indian films might lose their cultural distinctiveness.

Indian cinema can scarcely match the economic prowess of Hollywood. Even within India, Indian media companies are relatively poorly resourced: only three media companies find a place in a survey of top 500 Indian companies conducted in August 2006 by *The Economic Times*, India's leading financial newspaper, with a market capitalization of Rs9.3 billion; the top media company was Zee Telefilms, ranked 142nd. In contrast, Hollywood giants have huge revenues: in 2004, Hollywood accounted for 80 percent of the world's film business, half of its revenue generating outside the United States (Waterman 2005). In terms of earning revenue from film exports, India is no match for the United States—India's share in the global film industry, valued in 2004 at $200 billion, was less than 0.2 percent. India barely merits a page in the 552-page *Movie Business Book* (Squire 2006). In Britain, where Indian cinema has its best performance outside India, the Hindi film market accounted for just 1.1 percent of gross box office in 2004 (UK Film Council 2006). Economically, Indian cinema may take a long time to gain the kind of export revenue that Hollywood earns, but culturally its influence could be more tangible.

There is hope beyond the hype about globalization of Bollywood. In an era of the Pentagon-declared "long war" against "terrorism," Indian cinema and its culture may emerge as an important corrective to the excesses of Hollywood's representation of the Islamic "other." It is important to remind ourselves that had British colonial powers not partitioned India, it would have been the world's largest Muslim country. India has a long tradition of a composite culture and, with a few exceptions, mainstream Hindi cinema has projected a positive picture of Islam. It is hard to find another culture where the recent head of state is a Muslim, the current Prime Minister a Sikh, and the leader of the ruling party an Italian-born Catholic, in a country where more than 80 percent of the population is Hindu. Most important: the biggest contemporary Bollywood star, Shah Rukh Khan, is a Muslim. Being rooted in such a syncretic culture, Indian cinema is well placed to deal with diversity in a globalized world.

BIBLIOGRAPHY

Aiyar, P. 2006. "Bollywood's China Link." *The Hindu*, March 19.
Barnouw, E., and S. Krishnaswamy. 1980. *Indian Film*, 2nd edition. New York: Oxford University Press.
Das, S. 2006. "Bollywood Banks on Corporate Route to the Big League," March 21: http://www.indiantelevision.com/special/y2k6/film-finance.htm.
Desai, J. 2004. *Beyond Bollywood: The Cultural Politics of South Asian Diasporic Film*. London: Routledge.
FICCI. 2004. *The Indian Entertainment Industry: An Unfolding Opportunity*. Mumbai: Federation of Indian Chambers of Commerce and Industry.
Foreign Affairs. 2006. "The Rise of India." July-August.
Goswami, K. 2004. "Bollywood . . . the New Hollywood?" *Variety*, October 3.
Kaur, R., and A. J. Sinha. 2005. *Bollyworld: Popular Indian Cinema through a Transnational Lens*. New Delhi: Sage.
Larkin, B. 1997. "Indian Films and Nigerian Lovers: Media and the Creation of Parallel Modernities." *Africa* 67 (3).
Miller, T., N. Govil, J. McMurria, and R. Maxwell. 2001. *Global Hollywood*. London: British Film Institute.
Mishra, V. 2002. *Bollywood Cinema: Temples of Desire*. London: Routledge.
NASSCOM. 2006. *NASSCOM Strategic Review 2006*. Mumbai: National Association of Software Service Companies.
Pendakur, M. 2003. *Indian Popular Cinema: Industry, Ideology and Consciousness*: Cresskill, N.J.: Hampton Press.
People's Daily. 2005. "Musical Movie 'Perhaps Love' Hits Box Office Record." December 7, *The People's Daily* (English web edition). Available at: http://english.people.com.cn/200512/07/eng20051207_226188.html.
Punathambekar, A. 2005. "Bollywood in the Indian-American Diaspora: Mediating a Transitive Logic of Cultural Citizenship." *International Journal of Cultural Studies* 8 (2): 151–73.
Rajadhyaksha, A., and P. Willemen. 2000. *Encyclopaedia of Indian Cinema*, 2nd edition. New Delhi: Oxford University Press; London: British Film Institute.
Rughani, P., and A. White. 2003. *ImagineAsia Evaluation Report*. London: British Film Institute.

Shiekh, M. 2001. *The Making of Asoka*. New Delhi: HarperCollins.

Squire, J., ed. 2006. *The Movie Business Book*, 3rd edition. New York: Simon & Schuster.

Thussu, D. K. 2006a. *International Communication—Continuity and Change*, 2nd edition. London: Hodder Arnold and New York: Oxford University Press.

———. 2006b. "Mapping Global Media Flow and Contra-Flow." In *Media on the Move: Global Flow and Contra-Flow*, ed. D. K. Thussu. London and New York: Routledge.

UK Film Council. 2006. *Statistical Report (2005–06)*. London: UK Film Council.

UNESCO. 2005. *International Flows of Selected Cultural Goods and Services 1994–2003*. UNESCO Institute for Statistics, Paris: United Nations Educational, Scientific and Cultural Organization.

Vasudevan, R., ed. 2000. *Making Meaning in Indian Cinema*. New Delhi: Oxford University Press.

Waterman, D. 2005. *Hollywood's Road to Riches*. Cambridge, Mass.: Harvard University Press.

Part II

||||||||||||||||||||||||||||||||||||||||||||||||||||||||||||||

Texts and Audiences

Chapter 6

‖‖‖

Our Violence, Their Violence
Exploring the Emotional and Relational Matrix of Terrorist Cinema

Vamsee Juluri

It may be a nice thing that the issue of violence has not dominated debates about Indian cinema as it has those about Hollywood. Although violence is increasingly apparent in the gangster movies of the last decade, and also in the much discussed example of Hindu-Muslim conflict movies, the thought that this is a cinema that has emerged from the genre of the mythological, from movies like the beloved *Maya Bazaar* (1957 Telugu), with its battle scenes of politely dueling arrows and verses, is reassuring rather than threatening. However, neither Indian cinema, nor the real world it is situated in, are free of violence, either in the form of direct aggression, or in more indirect, structural forms. It is therefore the aim of this chapter to explore the question of violence in contemporary Indian cinema, not so much in terms of other questions such as communalism, but squarely in the terms of violence itself; or, to put it another way, from the social-philosophical perspective of Gandhian nonviolence.

The main question this chapter examines is whether violence is presented in the narratives of Indian cinema as an aberration from human nature, or whether violence is "naturalized" as something inevitable, eternal, and irrevocably entwined with human nature in particular, and nature in general. Furthermore, if Indian cinema represents violence in far more complex ways than Hollywood cinema, as I believe, how do these representations engage with questions of cultural difference as a possible cause of national and international violence? To further situate this chapter in the context of its title's ambitions ("our violence and their violence"), I would also like to propose it as a discussion of what Indian movies would think of the "clash of civilizations" argument (Huntington 1993).

These questions have come out of a concern primarily with "their violence." It is my belief that the way in which violence is represented in Western media, popular culture, and even in Western scholarship about media and violence, particularly in the post-9/11 context, makes enormous presumptions about cultural difference and human nature. As I have written elsewhere (Juluri 2005), there is a tendency to naturalize violence in the West, particularly along lines of cultural difference that is best critiqued by turning to some of Gandhi's writings on violence, cultural difference, and human nature. While this chapter does not attempt to systematically compare differences in Western and Indian media representations of violence, it does propose a broader theoretical framework in which such differences may be better understood.

My thesis is that the ways in which Indian cinema represents violence are far closer to some of the main philosophical precepts of nonviolence than their sometimes crude and jingoistic manner would suggest. In other words, even if Indian cinema has its own array of others, domestic and otherwise, and even if the enemies of Indian cinema narratives (who are, of course, often just plain old bad enemies of India, whether it is the legendary Mogambo or someone more neighborly) are depicted in ways that are far from sensitive or politically correct (especially by Hollywood standards), it may be possible to discern a set of concerns and constraints in their moral universe that resonate with the philosophy of nonviolence.

I would like to propose in this chapter an alternative framework from either those that have been used to study media violence in the Western academy such as the effects school, and even the critical and cultivation approaches (Morgan 2002), and those that have been used to address, in passing, questions of violence while discussing religious nationalism in Indian cinema studies (Vasudevan 2001).

The particular examples I would like to focus on here are the Hindi film *Mission: Kashmir* (2000, Vidhu Vinod Chopra) and the Telugu movie *Khadgam* (2002, Krishna Vamsi), which have no dearth of violence, religious conflict, and what has become the de rigueur endeavor in recent Indian cinema to differentiate the good and the bad other. However, the stories of these films, apart from the familiar terrorist theme, also address issues that I believe are best read through the perspective of Gandhian nonviolence.

In other words, I would like to propose that even though these films may be clearly committed to the ideological cause of India's integrity, which has of course been defined in recent years in increasingly un-Gandhian and militaristic ways in movies like *Roja* and *Bharateeyudu* (Niranjana and Srinivas 1996), their readings may be equally valid at other levels, particularly what I would call their "emotional and relational matrix." The embedding of the narratives—and of course depictions of violence—in Indian cinema in an emotional and relational matrix forms the foundation for what I would like to suggest is their nonviolent or Gandhian sensibility (even if Gandhi himself is rejected as a symbolic figure here; a point implicit for instance in *Bharateeyudu*, where there is a much greater admiration expressed to the militant Subhash Chandra Bose in the freedom struggle rather than Gandhi).

Emotions and relations may be more than the formula that producers sometimes reduce them to (Ganti 2004: 182–83). They are better seen as the moment of negotiation between postcolonial audiences and melodramatic texts of the very conditions of their existence (Martin-Barbero 1993). Although it may be premature to overstate what happens to this matrix in the reception process, it may be safe to assume from our own experience and also from the various audience studies carried out in India (Dickey 1993; Mankekar 1999; Juluri 2003) that issues of emotional experience and relationship-based narratives are quite important to the way audiences see not only media, but also their own selves, and the world. As a first step, this chapter outlines how we may engage with the emotions and relations that play out in the narratives of Indian cinema, and connect these with broader questions about film violence, and the philosophy of nonviolence.

Gandhian Nonviolence and the Emotional/Relational Matrix

While I will not digress at great length here into the question of why Gandhi belongs in critical media studies, or more accurately, why post-9/11 media studies needs Gandhi, it would be useful to outline some of my main arguments. My contention is that the post-9/11 media in the United States have naturalized the view that violence is caused by cultural differences, and even that human nature and nature in general are essentially violent—and these views are only partially critiqued by the chief media studies approaches of cultural studies and cultivation research because of their own epistemological limitations (Juluri 2005). These epistemological limits derive from the "technicism" of Western philosophy in contrast to Gandhian epistemology's emphasis on emotions and ethics as necessary conditions for the production of good and accurate knowledge (Nandy 1987).

From a Gandhian view, as I hope to show, the problem with even critical approaches to media in the West is that their critique focuses on an instrumental notion of violence (for instance, violence as a tool of capitalism, or of patriarchy) but does not quite engage with violence as a relatively autonomous notion. From a Gandhian view, the central question for media studies perhaps would be not so much whether the media depictions of violence represent ideologies about capitalism or patriarchy or religious fundamentalism, but really whether they represent the ideology of violence. Indian cinema, in my view, challenges the ideology of violence, while "their violence" perhaps does not.

At the outset, it may help to clarify that these claims are based on Gandhi's writings, and his belief in nonviolence as a universal philosophy, and not on a simplistic cliché of nonviolence as not hitting back if someone hits you, which the Jesuit nonviolence scholar Simon Harak compares to defining marriage as not sleeping with someone other than your wife (Harak 2000), or even of a not so simple cliché of nonviolence as nothing more than a technique for political expression or worse, a tool for corporate aggression management. Gandhi's belief, very simply, is quite the opposite of the claims made by the ideologies of violence in Western media. Gandhi first of all rejected the notion that violence was caused by cultural differences, or "clash of civilizations," and also questioned the myth that nature or human nature is innately violent. Gandhi's faith was in the duty of human beings to recognize the existence of violence—as an aberration or burden—in their "thoughts, words, and deeds" and to actively minimize this, as well as their dependence on systems of violence.

Gandhi's argument was based on the idea of human subjectivity as enmeshed in a balance of duties and obligations (Iyer 1973; Parekh 2001). In other words, for Gandhi, human beings (whether the police officers or terrorists in Indian cinema) are relational beings, whose agency unfolds in their ability to recognize their debts to society, family, and nature, to repay them. The condition of this agency is that human beings perform their lives in a relational matrix, and this performance of duty or obligation is fundamentally an emotional one. In other words, the Gandhian subject of Indian cinema does not stoically do his job in a cool *Terminator* sort of way, but exists as a feeling, experiencing subject. What this implies is that emotional experience is the basis of how one situates oneself in the relational matrix, and actively does the right thing and seeks out the right place by surrendering to the appropriate emotions. For example, the feeling of gratitude may position the subject in an appropriate way in relation to his parents, while hatefulness clearly would not.

Specifically, there are three themes in Gandhian thought that are relevant to the present critique of the question of the ideology of violence, and which may be usefully examined in the light of the examples of Indian terrorist cinema: Gandhi's rejection of the notion that violence is caused by cultural differences (Gandhi 1993: 18), Gandhi's overall emphasis on the notion of duty or obligation (Parekh 2001: 51), and Gandhi's distinction between acknowledging the bare minimum violence that living entails and for which one must repay one's debts and blindly accepting that nature is inherently violent (Gandhi 1927: 257).

Nonviolence in Mission: Kashmir and Khadgam

While a traditional media analysis of these movies would reveal no dearth of depictions of acts of violence, what I propose in this section is an alternative reading of the narratives of these films in the context of the Gandhian critiques of the ideology of violence mentioned above. In other words, if we are to probe the question of what is the message about violence and human nature that underlies these stories, my hypothesis is that we will see a story about violence that is very different from the instrumentalist, emotionless, professionalized sort framed within a shallowly culturally relativistic way as we do in Hollywood movies. The underlying message about violence and human nature in these movies is closer to a Gandhian conception about universalism, duty, and human nature, albeit within the terms of an action-filled and visually violent narrative.

Mission: Kashmir, briefly, tells the story of a young Kashmiri militant, Altaf (Hrithik Roshan), and his relationship with his foster father, the police officer Inayat Khan (Sanjay Dutt), foster mother Neelima (Sonali Kulkarni), a father-figure type Afghan terrorist mentor, Hilal (Jackie Shroff), a romantic partner, Sufi (Preity Zinta), and finally, the future of world peace, if only in the Indian subcontinent. The tense premise is that as a child, Altaf was adopted by Khan after the latter killed his parents while leading an assault on militants. The young Altaf finds out, runs away, and comes back all grown up years to later to avenge his parents.

Khadgam takes place in post-globalization Hyderabad, where an aspiring Hindu actor and his Muslim auto-driver friend save the city and the nation from the Muslim character's long-lost brother, who has resurfaced in the city after a training session in a "Pakistan terrorist training camp" in order to unleash terroristic violence and negotiate the release of a militant mastermind from Indian custody.

Both *Mission:Kashmir* and *Khadgam* appeared in the context of not only the spate of Hindu-Muslim and India-Pakistan related movies of the 1990s beginning with *Roja* (Dirks 2001), but, in the case of the latter, it also has the distinction of being one of India's first post–September 11 movies. *Khadgam* not only makes explicit references to 9/11 in the form of digs at Osama Bin Laden, and for good local measure, Pakistani General Musharaf, but also heightens this with allusions to what was widely perceived in India as the local, albeit foiled, 9/11, the December 2001 attack on the Indian Parliament.

There are three broad themes that run through these stories that are of relevance to a nonviolent reading: universalism (whether violence is coded as caused by religious differences or as an aberration from a universal, nonviolent trans-religious human nature), duty and obligation (the ways in which violence is located as the outcome or lack thereof of ethical choices made by the main characters within an emotional-relational matrix), and finally, the question of human nature itself. I take up each of these issues in the following sections.

Universalism versus "Clash of Civilizations"

Both movies place the emphasis on religious universalism. In *Mission: Kashmir*, this claim is set up early in the story, when the young Altaf, who has been adopted by Khan and his wife Neelima, expresses his surprise at discovering that his loving foster mother is a Hindu. He wonders how Khan, a fellow Muslim, could have married a Hindu. "Just like anyone else," he replies, in a nonchalant assertion of universalist sensibility. The discovery of this openness against the implied past prejudice against Hindus in the young Altaf is also signified in the following scene when he accompanies Neelima to a temple, where he secretly rings the temple bell.

These moments are once again furiously evoked at a climactic moment toward the end of the film, when Khan tries to convince Altaf that he must make a choice between getting his revenge and saving Kashmir, and by extension, humanity (the diabolic plot named Mission: Kashmir involves blowing up the Hazrat Bal Mosque and Shankaracharya Temple so that Hindus and Muslims blame each other and go to war). Altaf then has to make the ethical choice whether to carry out the mission, for which he has been both nurtured, and misled, by his mercenary Afghan mentor, or whether he finds his will, located in the memory of his love for his adopted Hindu mother, to save Kashmir from holocaust, whether he will, as I have written elsewhere, "save the world for mom" (Juluri 2001).

The narrative in *Mission: Kashmir* sets up and ultimately centers on the choice between a religious universalism expressed in not so much the language of Hindu-Muslim unity under the guise of the nation (as in *Khadgam's* all embracing animated Indian flag flying through the arches and alleyways of Charminar) but in the plain terms of everyday, relational, universalism ("we got married just like anyone else"). This value is, however, also emphasized in a more dramatic form in the context of a key song in the film, Rindu Posh Maal, which contrasts a televised song-and-dance performance by Shankar Mahadevan and party with its fervently universalist lyrics. The words express universalism in multiple ways, as the rising above differences (Music knows no creed or caste, Music knows no borders), as the unity of different religions (Music has the Gita and the Koran), and as an acknowledgment of the human condition (Music heals broken hearts). However, the rising intensity of this verse is set off against shots of Altaf's men infiltrating the TV station, hurting its workers, and ultimately, blowing up the TV tower.

The explosion signifies a potent moment in the film (it also heralds the interval) not only by showing a close-up of Altaf declaring this a "birthday gift" to his nemesis, Khan, but also by suggesting that the explosion is an enormous act of betrayal. Altaf gains access to the TV station through his childhood sweetheart, Sufi, who does not know anything about his violent past or intentions. At the interval, the sides are drawn, between the right thing (music, universalism, human condition, love), and the not-so-right one—which is not necessarily violence, or anti-state violence, but simply, betrayal of trust.

A third and final act of expressing univeralism as an opposite of inhumanity occurs in an iconic moment toward the end of the film, which is set in a dramatically dark and misty backdrop of ruined houseboats and sullied waters. A piece of paper lies crumpled in the oily waters, and on it are inscribed three religious symbols: the Om, the cross, and the crescent, suggesting a different sort of equality for different religions here, that of an equal doom in the face of inhumanity and violence. This also refers back to a moment in the title song of the movie, when a single lotus bud sinks into a swamp to the singing of the haunting song Dhua Dhua ("Smoke Smoke").

Khadgam's universalism is less subtle, and perhaps a tad more didactic (and this may have something to do with its simpler emotional-relational matrix, as I show below), but expresses itself strongly as well. Interestingly, the title of the film, and its title song, are an evocation of force as a legitimate and necessary condition for the existence and protection not so much of the state, but of certain cherished ideas such as universalism and perhaps even ahimsa. The title song introduces the "Khadgam" (sword) as the "foundation stone of world-peace" even as images of national heroes like Mahatma Gandhi and the Queen of Jhansi are displayed (for a celebration of a weapon, it is useful to note that all the other nationalistic heroes, especially Subhas Chandra Bose and Alluri Seetarama Raju, get only one picture each, but Gandhi gets three).

The seemingly strange celebration of force as the foundation of Gandhian ideals (peace, universalism, Gandhi himself), reappears elsewhere in the movie as well. A song extolling the colors of the Indian flag not only implies the usual association in Indian popular sensibility of saffron with Hindus, white with Christians, and green with Muslims, but also explores other symbolisms. For example, green is associated in the song with a tiny sapling, and its struggle, its force, in breaking through the earth. To celebrate the birth of a plant with the invocation of a weapon is perhaps one of the most innovative and unusual ideas I have ever seen in a movie.

The first use of force in the protection of the universal dharma occurs in the third scene of the movie (the very first scene takes place in a "Pakistan Terrorist Training Camp" where orders are being issued for a truly wicked-looking man to go back to India and create havoc). A busload of Hindu pilgrims (with shaved heads, evoking a return from a pilgrimage to the holiest of shrines in Andhra Pradesh, Tirupati) has wandered by mistake into a Muslim neighborhood, where they are being chased by an angry mob demanding revenge for the Gujarat riots. They are stopped by one man, the auto-driver Amjad (Prakash Raj), who keeps the mob at bay not only with his passionate arguments, but also by waving a club at them. A key point in his argument is his response when one of the mob members accuses him of not being a good Muslim. He asks, "What sort of a Muslim are you? You just returned from jail for killing your wife."

The confrontation ends, symbolically, with the call to prayer, and Amjad, looking for water to wash and begin his namaz, grabs a bucket from the Hindu pilgrims' bus. The bucket even has holy markings on it, and the legendarily sweet waters of Hyderabad have once again kept Hindu-Muslim brotherhood. The expression of universalism in *Khadgam* then drifts into the expected moments of iconic unity (the flag, Hindu and Muslim boys in religious outfits) and reasoned debate (a police officer arguing with the dreaded terrorist mastermind during interrogation about the idea of universalism and India).

It is also expressed in a less exalted manner in the context of what has been a big point of contention in the communal politics of popular culture in India; the India-Pakistan cricket match. The protagonists have just learned about their army officer friend's savage death at the hands of Pakistani-supported militants, when they see a crowd of Muslim youth celebrating India's defeat in a cricket match by burning the Indian flag. The flag-burners are duly beaten.

Despite this touchy reference, both movies value universalism, although it is expressed in different ways ranging from the modern-state discourse to other, folk-religious sensibilities, such as *Khadgam*'s street lingo lyrics, "Iswar Allah Yesu, okate kathara baasu" (Aren't they all the same, dude). However, what is important to reading these films from the perspective of Gandhian nonviolence is not only their seeming refutation of the clash of civilizations thesis by positing conflict as caused not by religious "differences" between Hindus and Muslims but as stoked by an inhuman greed for power and money. Hilal, despite his talk of Jihad, is just a mercenary. The critique of Musharaf and Osama in *Khadgam* is paired with a parody of the state of Andhra Pradesh's indebtedness to the World Bank and the make-it-big desperation of its youth in a song that mimics the Hindi hit "Lift kara de." The key basis of this universalism, as I show in the following section, is that it rests on not just a sloganistic celebration of "Hindus" and "Muslims" as "Indians" but instead on a deep-rooted sense of duty and obligation in what I call the "emotional-relational matrix" of the narrative.

Duty and Obligation in the Emotional-Relational Matrix

The universalist notion of religion in these movies rests on the assertion through the dialogues as well as narratives that religion is not an empty label that justifies violence, but simply a form for ethical conduct. However, what is interesting is the way in which the characters express such an understanding of true religion as an eschewing not so much of violence, but of what has been set up in the story as the unjustifiable grounds for violence—namely, a failure of the individual to live up to the obligation that his or her position in the relational/emotional matrix places in terms of what is expected to be appropriate conduct (which may or may not be violent).

For example, although the goal of the evil conspirators of *Mission Kashmir* is the destruction of India, the ethical choice for the hero is presented not as that, but instead as choosing between "love and hatred" and interestingly, between "Kashmir and holocaust." Altaf is asked, repeatedly, by his adoptive parents (including the father figure against whom he has a vendetta) and his childhood sweetheart, to make this choice, but what is important here is that the ethical choices here are not set up as mere exercises in free will enacted by a rational, agential, individual actor, but instead as moments of contingent agency predicated upon the precise balance of gains and pains that each character has at that moment in the story. It is a more complex, causally entwined idea of choices rather than a freewheeling individual one.

The way in which these causes and effects are entwined is, of course, in the terms of what each character has given to the other, what their relationship is, and what they stand for. In other words, each character is implicated in relationships, not only in categories like son or mother, but also in qualitative and emotional terms, such as love, forgiveness, vengeance, and so on. The table below maps out the main characters in *Mission: Kashmir* in an emotional-relational matrix.

Emotional-Relational Matrix of Mission: Kashmir

	Altaf	Khan	Nilu	Hilal
Altaf	*	Son *Revenge > Forgiveness*	Son *Love*	Protégé *Trust > Punishment*
Khan	Father *Guilt > Love*	*	Spouse *Love*	Enemy
Nilu	Mother *Love*	Spouse *Love*	*	none
Hilal	Mentor	Enemy	none	*

(The table may be read as follows: the first line of each row represents what the character in this row is to each of the characters in the columns, and the second line summarizes their emotional bond. For example, Altaf's relationship with Khan is that of a son's, motivated by revenge, which later turns to forgiveness, and so on).

What we find is that it is in the emotional-relational matrix that there is an unfolding of the ethical position of Indian cinema about violence. The stories reinforce the idea of duty and obligation in order to imply that violence is neither natural, nor the inevitable outcome of cultural or religious differences. In fact, even when there has been violence in a character's life, it is something that has to be stopped right there in this moral universe. Altaf is justified in his anger at Khan for having killed his parents, but ultimately, has to forgive him; for his anger ends up taking more lives and causing more hurt than what he had even intended.

A similar situation is also set up in *Khadgam*, albeit in a less complex level. The main villain of the story is Azhar, the long-lost younger brother of Amjad, whose starting grouse does seem to be one of victimization in communal violence, but whose background is a militant mission masterminded in Pakistan. *Khadgam* does not create much complexity in terms of who owes what to whom, especially since there are other parallel stories that are also developed. The main character, Koteswar Rao (Ravi Teja), is in fact an aspiring actor, and his story plays out as a very contemporary critique of the politics of hereditary privilege and the desperate centrality of the casting couch in the Telugu film industry. There is yet another story, narrated in flashback, centered on an increasingly common feature in South Indian films, the tragedy of the first lady love. The police officer, Radhakrishna (Srikanth), is especially aggrieved because his fiancée has been killed in a shoot-out by Azhar, before the latter's escape and subsequent reappearance. The emotional-relational matrix of the relevant characters may be mapped out as below:

Emotional-Relational Matrix of Khadgam

	Amjad	Azhar	Koteswa Rao	Radhakrishna
Amjad	*	Brother *Love > just anger*	Friends *Affection*	Becoming friends *(Mis)understanding*
Azhar	Brother *Deceit*	*	Minimal *Quiet anger*	Enemy *Vendetta*
K. Rao	Friend *Affection*	Minimal	*	Minimal
R'krishna	Becoming friends *(Mis)understanding*	Enemies *Vendetta*	Minimal	*

It is interesting that the emotional and relational matrix of *Khadgam* does not appear as strongly developed as that of *Mission Kashmir*. The main ethical choice in this movie is left to Amjad, who has to disown his own brother, whom he loves very much, when he realizes that his brother was deceitful and is actually a terrorist. Azhar asks his brother to join him, as the film reaches an explosive-strapped, hostage-trembling climax. But at this point, Amjad, who has previously also expressed outrage at how Muslims are asked to always prove their loyalties, makes a clear choice that he values his ethical choice more than his misguided brother.

The rest of the characters are defined by their low to moderate involvements with each other, and the only intensities arise in the context of flashbacks of past tragedies, and unfinished business with killers and such. It is also interesting that the narrative of *Khadgam* does not revolve around female characters (except for the personal revenge angle) on the same level as *Mission Kashmir*. Perhaps that too contributes to its attenuated narrative sophistication.

Conclusion: Human Nature and Violence

Although *Mission Kashmir* (and *Khadgam*) do not advocate nonviolence in a simple sense of refraining from violence, what they do, to lesser and greater degrees, is to situate the violence in the movie as an ethical choice made by characters within the context of their location in the matrix. Violence, in other words, is not condemned for its mere existence, but is refuted as unethical, evil, and cruel when it violates the expectations of duties and obligation (which are also emotional expectations, such as the expectation of love or forgiveness as opposed to vengefulness) that are demanded of the character in such a position.

To this extent, the choices that characters make in this movie are reminiscent of the Gandhian injunction to "minimize violence" for the sake of reducing one's obligation to the world, and to also recognize the cyclicality of violence (Parekh 1997). Whether this sensibility translates into an outright expression of faith in the nonviolence of human nature remains to be explored, but perhaps the violence of Indian terrorist cinema is still careful, occasional lack of subtleties notwithstanding, not to insinuate itself as a representation of an innately violent human nature. After all, the theme of recognition has been so important to Indian movies (Chakravarty 1993) in stories of long-lost brothers reuniting in profound nationalist allegories (such as *Amar Akbar Anthony* or MTV India's famous promo spoofing it). In these movies, though, the recognition is not only of one's self, but also of the conditions of our existence, and the role of violence in it, and the compunction to reject it. Perhaps this would also extend, in audience reception, to an interpretation of human nature as not necessarily violent, and cultural differences as no rigid causes of civilizational clashes, and future studies could explore this.

As far as these stories go, there is perhaps some hope that there is far more of the philosophy of nonviolence embedded in "our violence" than our present academic perspectives can give credit for, and it is my belief that recognizing this potential would be a useful step in bringing academics and the world that they study a little closer together.

BIBLIOGRAPHY

Chakravarty, S. 1993. *National Identity in Indian Popular Cinema, 1947–1987.* Austin: University of Texas Press.

Dickey, S. 1993. *Cinema and the Urban Poor in South India*: New Delhi: Cambridge University Press.

Dirks, N. 2001. "The Home and the Nation: Consuming Culture and Politics in *Roja.*" In *Pleasure and the Nation: The History, Politics, and Consumption of Public Culture in India*, ed. R. Dwyer and C. Pinney, 161–85. New Delhi: Oxford University Press.

Gandhi, M. 1927. *An Autobiography, or the Story of My Experiments with Truth.* Trans. M. Desai. Ahmedabad: Navjivan.

Gandhi, M. 1993. *The Penguin Gandhi Reader*, ed. R. Mukherjee. New Delhi: Penguin.

Ganti, T. 2004. *Bollywood: A Guidebook to Popular Hindi Cinema.* New York: Routledge.

Harak, S. 2000. "Afterword." In *Nonviolence for Third Millennium*, ed. S. Harak, 229–34. Macon, Ga.: Mercer University Press.

Huntington, S. P. 1993. "The Clash of Civilizations?" *Foreign Affairs*, Summer.

Iyer, R. 1973. *The Moral and Political Thought of Mahatma Gandhi.* New Delhi: Oxford University Press.

Juluri, V. 2001. *Lessons from Indian Cinema*, http://www.poppolitics.com.

Juluri, V. 2003. *Becoming a Global Audience: Longing and Belonging in Indian Music Television.* New York: Peter Lang.

Juluri, V. 2005. "Nonviolence and Media Studies." *Communication Theory* 15 (2): 196–215.

Mankekar, P. 1999. *Screening Culture, Viewing Politics: An Ethnography of Tele-*

vision, Womanhood, and Nation in Postcolonial India. Durham, N.C.: Duke University Press.

Martin-Barbero, J. 1993. *Communication, Culture and Hegemony: From the Media to Mediations.* Trans. E. Fox and R. White. London: Sage.

Morgan, M. ed. 2002. *Against the Mainstream: The Selected Works of George Gerbner.* New York: Peter Lang.

Nandy, A. 1987. "From Outside the Imperium: Gandhi's Cultural Critique of the West." In *Traditions, Tyrannies and Utopias: Essays in the Politics of Awareness,* ed. A. Nandy, 127–62. New Delhi: Oxford University Press.

Niranjana, T., and S. V. Srinivas. 1996. "Managing the Crisis: Bharateeyudu and the Ambivalence of Being Indian." *Economic and Political Weekly,* 30 November, pp. 3129–34.

Parekh, Bhiku. 1997. *Gandhi.* Oxford and New York: Oxford University Press.

———. 2001. *Gandhi: A Very Short Introduction.* Oxford and New York: Oxford University Press.

Vasudevan, R. 2001. "Bombay and Its Public." In *Pleasure and the Nation: The History, Politics, and Consumption of Public Culture in India,* ed. R. Dwyer and C. Pinney, 186–211. New Delhi: Oxford University Press.

Chapter 7

‖‖‖

Exoticized, Marginalized, Demonized
The Muslim "Other" in Indian Cinema

Kalyani Chadha and
Anandam P. Kavoori

As a nation, India has traditionally sought to define its post-colonial identity in secular, multiethnic terms, characterizing itself as a country where diverse faiths, languages, and cultures co-exist peacefully within the boundaries of a single state. Thus, even though the country was formed out of a partition marked by bloody communal violence in 1947, India's self-definition has typically been one of a tolerant, even syncretic, society that has assimilated and absorbed significant cultural and religious differences. In this particular characterization of the country, India is a melting pot whose distinctive strength lies in "its ability to transform invasion into accommodation, rupture into continuity, division into diversity" (Khilnani 1997: xvi).

Yet, despite the frequently articulated belief in the notion that India exemplifies a unique example of "unity in diversity," in reality, the nature of India's selfhood has been far more contested than the ritually celebratory accounts of Indian nation-building would suggest. As Khilnani writes:

The truncated colonial territories inherited by the Indian state after 1947 still left it in control of a population of incomparable differences: a multitude of Hindu castes and outcasts, Muslims, Sikhs, Christians, Buddhists, Jains and tribes; speakers of more than a dozen major languages (and thousands of dialects); myriad ethnic and cultural communities. This discordant material was not the stuff of which nation states are made; it suggested no common identity or basis of unity that could be reconciled within a modern state. (1997: 151–52)

And, although in the initial decades after independence, the state appeared to have managed to hold together these disparate groups based on an amorphous sense of "Indianness," over time, this conception has been increasingly corroded by a variety of conflicts that have developed across the Indian landscape. While these conflicts have taken multiple forms ranging from the ethnic and the linguistic to the caste-based, particularly significant among these have been the frequent eruptions of communal violence between Hindus and Muslims.

According to a report issued by the National Integration Council in 2005, the number of instances where tension was generated between the majority and minority communities has increased over the years, indicating declining levels of tolerance between them. In fact, between 2000 and 2005, India witnessed an annual average of 800 communal incidents of varying intensity, that ran the gamut from relatively small-scale, local clashes to full-blown riots of the type that occurred in Gujarat in 2002, resulting in the deaths of over a thousand people and the widespread displacement of Muslim communities through a process of ethnic cleansing (National Integration Council 2005).

Not surprisingly, such developments that reflect the struggle over India's identity have significantly undermined the carefully constructed conceptions of pluralism and secularism that informed the postcolonial state under Nehru. But despite fears about the deeply divisive impact of the Hindutva movement on Indian society, there is a sense within the country that certain sectors of Indian life have remained immune to the type of sectarian divisions that have become increasingly manifest in a number of political and social institutions.

One such sector in popular perception is the Hindi film industry, which is routinely held up as an exemplar of secularism. As Iqbal Masud, a noted film critic, has argued:

> It is in the domain of popular cinema that the diverse cultures of India met and negotiated their differences. They did not merge but worked in harmony. In fact, harmony is the key word in Indian cinema. It is the one Indian cultural-industrial structure that has resisted separatism. It is because of this element that Indian cinema has become over the past fifty years—despite its many distortions and contradictions—a major instrument of national consolidation, a true unity in diversity. (1997: n.p.)

In a more popular vein, Shashi Tharoor has commented:

In India, popular cinema has consistently reflected the diversity of a pluralistic community. The stories they tell are often silly, the plots formulaic, the characterizations superficial, the action predictable. But they are watched and made by members of every community in India . . . the film world of Bollywood embodies the very idea of India's diversity in the way in which it is organized, staffed and financed and in the stories that it tells. (2001: n.p.)

And finally, in yet another affirmation of the secular nature of Hindi cinema, Laleen Jayamanne, commenting on *Mother India,* has written:

That an iconic film embodying the struggle of a humble peasant woman who is allegorized as Mother India should be made and played by two Muslims is perhaps not so remarkable in that the Indian film industry has been immune to the kind of racism that has come to pervade wider social and political life in the wake of Hindu fundamentalism. (2002: n.p.)

Thus, the popular Bombay-based Hindi film industry is often cited as a social microcosm of India, a world where the members of the majority and minority community work together to produce a staggering output of anywhere between 150 and 200 films on an annual basis. Further, in making the case for the secular environment of the film industry, it is frequently pointed out that not only are Muslims comparatively well-represented within its ranks in the form of writers, lyricists, composers, producers, and directors, but that "some of the most popular film stars of Hindi cinema, both male and female, have been Muslim" (Ganti 2004: 23).

In addition to acknowledging the on- and off-screen prominence of Muslims in the film industry, scholars have also pointed to the pervasive influence of a "Muslim ethos" (Masud 1997) or the "Islamicate roots" of Hindi cinema (Kesavan 1994). In this context, the reference is not to Islam in a religious sense, but rather, to "the social and cultural complex historically associated with Islam and Muslims, both among Muslims themselves and even among non-Muslims" (Kesavan 1994: 246). Included among the elements of the Islamicate/Muslim culture that are believed to have influenced Hindi cinema are Urdu, a language traditionally associated with Muslims in India and one that has provided the vocabulary and idiom for countless Hindi films, and a range of images and archetypes derived from the eighteenth- and nineteenth-century culture of the Muslim elite in the northern Indian state of Awadh that have been liberally employed in Hindi films over the years (Kesavan 1994). As Kesavan points out:

> While the house of Hindi cinema has many mansions, its architecture is inspired by Islamicate forms. The most obvious example of these Islamicate forms is Urdu . . . any number of examples can be cited to show how the stock emotions of Hindi cinema are named and evoked by Urdu. . . . But Islamicate empire bequeathed to Hindi cinema much more than a medium and vocabulary: it provided it with images of the good life, a model of the man about town, a stereotype of cultivated leisure and the ingredients for rentier decadence. All of the above were derived from a part-fantasised vision of nawabi Lucknow, which was nostalgically remembered as the last bastion of Islamicate culture. (1994: 246–51)

But while the impression of what has been called the Muslim ethos as well as the prominence of Muslim artistes in Hindi cinema is undeniable, often obscured in this discussion has been the larger and more significant issue of the representation of Muslims within the narratives of Hindi cinema. Taking this issue as the point of departure, this chapter will argue that while Muslim characters have never been absent from the master narrative of Hindi cinema in the manner experienced typically by minorities in Hollywood, and that the Hindi film industry may indeed be "one of the few sites in India where Muslims are not marginal and even enjoy some success" (Ganti 2004: 24), the portrayal of the community itself has nevertheless remained deeply problematic, with Muslims being *othered* in a sustained fashion in commercial Hindi cinema. Indeed, it would appear that the rare instances of the cinematic representation of Muslims that deviate from this norm, films such as *Garam Hawa, Gaman, Bazaar, Salim Langde Pe Mat Ro, Anjuman* and *Mammo*, have more often than not been produced by non–commercially oriented filmmakers, operating outside the aesthetic and conceptual framework of the Bombay-based film industry.

Within mainstream Hindi films, the cinematic *Othering* of Muslims has occurred through a variety of strategies of representation ranging from exoticization and marginalization to demonization, that are widely recognized by anthropologists as critical to the production and maintenance of social and cultural difference. While anthropological discourse has focused on the use of these strategies primarily in the context of colonized societies, where rulers used them to construct and fix "native" identities, they have also been used to represent minority groups within diverse national contexts. This is certainly true in the case of the Muslim community whose portrayals in Hindi films over the last 50 years have followed the exoticization-marginalization-demonization pattern, more or less sequentially during that time. In other words, while representations of Muslims in terms of their exoticism dominated the early post-independence period of the 1950s and 1960s, these were followed in the 1970s and 1980s by films in which Muslim characters were increasingly marginalized, only to be succeeded by a series of ultranationalistic films dating from the early 2000s, in which they are demonized, typically through a conflating of Islam with terrorism and Muslims with Pakistan. In other words, this chapter argues that even though it is these most recent representations that have raised concerns that the Hindi film industry is moving away from its traditional secular moorings and succumbing to the regressive forces of communalism, the representation of the Muslim as Other has in fact been a long-term trend within the discourse of popular Hindi cinema.

The Exotic Other

The early incarnations of this trend, whereby Muslims were portrayed in terms of exotic otherness, can be traced back to the category of popular historical films such as *Pukar*, (1939), *Tansen* (1943), *Humayun* (1945), *Shahjehan* (1946), *Baiju Bawra* (1952), *Anarkali* (1953), *Mirza Ghalib* (1954), *Jahan Ara* (1964), *Noorjehan* (1967), and *Mughal-e-Azam* (1960), that were typically based on characters connected with the Mughal court, as in the case of films such as *Tansen, Baiju Bawra,* and *Mirza Ghalib*, or on storylines based on the reigns of various Mughal emperors, who were the last Muslim dynasty to rule India, prior to its conquest by the British. For instance, while *Pukar* and *Noorjehan* focused on the reign of Emperor Jehangir, the films *Shahjehan* and *Humayun* drew on the lives of rulers of the same names. *Mughal-e-Azam* or The Great Mughal, a megabudget spectacular that retold the popular story of the ill-fated romance between Prince Salim and a beautiful slave girl Anarkali, causing him to rebel against his father Emperor Akbar who opposed the relationship.

While *Mughal-e-Azam* best epitomized the historical genre (with its lavish sets, elaborate song-and-dance numbers, and ornate Urdu speech), the common thread connecting films of this type was the fact that they portrayed Muslims exclusively as kings or elites who inhabited a world that was spatially, linguistically, and culturally not just removed but distinct from the one occupied by its viewers. Indeed, whether one looks at *Pukar, Humayun, Taj Mahal, Jahan Ara,* or *Mughal-e-Azam,* they are universally characterized by the use of complex Persianized Urdu dialogue and stylized mannerisms that were believed to reflect the etiquette of the Muslim Mughal court. Thus, even though historical films emphasized the ideal of Hindu-Muslim unity and presented the rule of Mughal emperors such as Akbar as based on notions of justice and partnership with non-Muslims such as the Rajputs (Masud 1997), by representing Muslims only as members of the ruling class who generally spoke, dressed, and behaved differently from the norm, they rendered them a group distinct and separate from the mainstream.

If the so-called *shahenshah* or "emperor" films laid the foundation for the representation of Muslims as exotic others, this perception was immeasurably enhanced by films that were termed the "Muslim social." Influenced by the quasi-historical traditions of the Parsi theater, this category of film emerged as a significant popular genre in the years following India's independence and enjoyed considerable crossover appeal, attracting both Hindu and Muslim audiences throughout India (Farooqui 2001).

But what were the Muslim socials? As their nomenclature would seem to suggest, these were films that centered their narrative on the Muslim community and issues related to it. And indeed this was true of films such as *Elaan* (1947), which in the words of Iqbal Masud offered a critique "of the ghetto-like quality of certain segments of the Muslim middle class and emphasized the need for Western education of Muslim youth" (Masud 1997: n.p). However, it is important to recognize that *Elaan* was an anomaly and that, despite the conceptual implications of the term "Muslim social," in effect, these films explored a rather limited terrain in that they were almost exclusively focused on the lives of the "*ashraf,*" or former aristocratic elites of the Northern Indian state of Awadh, a very minor part of the Muslim community in India.

Moreover, Muslim socials did not focus on socioeconomic or political issues pertinent to the *ashraf* community itself, which had experienced a significant socioeconomic decline as a result of the thinning of its ranks caused by the migration of many of its members to Pakistan as well as a loss of hereditary landholdings due to land reform in the post-independence period. Instead, romantic relationships and family dramas constituted the bulk of their subject matter and through the characters and the contexts in which these characters operated, these films effectively constructed Muslims as exotic others. As Mohammed Farooqui puts it, "films like *Mere Mehboob, Bahu Begum, Chaudhvin ka Chand* and *Pakeezah*, all depicted an idealized Muslim world where Nawabs lived with all their grandeur and idiosyncrasies intact. Shairi (Urdu poetry), qawwali (form of singing) and the tawaif (courtesan) were their leitmotifs. This was the cinematic equivalent of a golden past" (Farooqui 2001: 1).

Thus, geographically, Muslim socials were almost always located in the city of Lucknow, the capital of the erstwhile state of Awadh, and were filmed so that the city's Islamic architecture represented by domes, minarets, and scalloped arches interspersed with frequent glimpses of the crescent moon—all of which reflexively constituted signifiers of the Muslim or Islamic, in the context of the South Asian subcontinent (Kesavan 1994) —were in the forefront. Similarly, the Muslim characters who populated the city of Lucknow were more often than not a stock ensemble: nawabs or scions of the former nobility who lived in elaborate *havelis* (mansions); burqa-clad women, fleeting glimpses of whose unveiled faces were enough to inspire passionate devotion; and tawaifs or courtesans whose "kothas" or houses of ill-repute were venues to which men frequently repaired, whether in the pursuit of love or to drown sorrows caused by romantic disappointment.

In fact, films synonymous with this genre, such as *Chaudhvin ka Chand, Mere Mehboob, Bahu Begum,* or *Pakeezah* typically were melodramatic romances involving precisely such stereotypical characters. For instance, the storylines of both *Chaudhvin ka Chand* and *Mere Mehboob* were based on men briefly glimpsing an unveiled woman's face, followed by a romance bedeviled by misunderstandings or family opposition. Other blockbusters like *Pakeezah* involved a romance between a courtesan and an aristocratic hero, with all the expected complications. These films were also marked by the use of a stylized and flowery form of Urdu, which, according to Rachel Dwyer, "reminded the listener that Urdu was the language of poetry and indeed of a great high culture (*tehzeeb*) and of formal manners (*adab*), whose rules and performance give delight in their elaboration" (2004: 89). Indeed, the protagonists of the Muslim socials were usually languid aristocrats, elaborately garbed in "Muslim" attire (men in sherwanis and women in ghararas), who seemed to have little to occupy them and appeared to be completely consumed by an adherence to notions of *tehzeeb* (culture) and *adab* (formal manners). As Parsa Venkateshwar Rao (1997: n.p.) notes:

The Muslim characters in these films spoke a strange and stilted Urdu
—which a majority of non-Urdu speakers took for a sophisticated and
delicate language—and recited verse at every turn, spent an enormous
amount of time saying their hellos and goodbyes—elaborate *adaabs* and
khuda hafizs. They were mostly from *nawabi* families, and they almost
always came from Lucknow. All they ever seemed to do was to move in
and out of their *havelis*, occasionally visiting the *tawaif's kotha* as one
would perhaps a movie-hall, and falling in and out of love.

Further, such representations of Muslims constructed by Muslim socials
did not reflect the fact that not only was the community quite heterogeneous in terms of language, culture, region, and socioeconomic status,
but that even the bulk of Muslims from Awadh were not Urdu-spouting,
mansion-dwelling aristocrats, but ordinary peasants, workers, and craftsmen. However, for large segments of the Hindi film audience, these films
do seem to have created an enduring image of Muslims imbued with a
certain mystique that rendered them a profoundly exotic "other," distinct
from the majority community, so distinct that in fact the very world they
inhabited on screen rarely had a non-Muslim character!

The Marginal Other

Although the construction of Muslims as "exotic others" constituted the
dominant mode of representation of the community during the 1950s
and 1960s, this pattern underwent a significant shift, primarily due to the
gradual disappearance of the Muslim social from the screen. Thus, even
though the early 1980s saw the release of some films that could be considered typical of this genre, including blockbusters such as *Nikaah*, both
in terms of themes and representational strategies, these films seemed to
take their cues from the 1950s. In fact, by the 1970s, mainstream films featuring significant Muslim characters became something of a rarity within
popular Hindi cinema.

Instead, there emerged a new mode of representation that was deployed in relation to the Muslim community: marginalization. The hallmark of this mode was the casting of Muslim characters in limited roles,
always subordinate to the leading players who were almost exclusively
portrayed as Hindu within the cinematic narrative. In other words, while
Muslim protagonists were present in the narrative and not entirely erased,

they only appeared in the margins, with their appearance conforming to an implicit representational code. They were typically cast to represent certain "Muslim" occupational stereotypes such as the skull-cap-wearing, prayer-bead-holding *maulvi* (preacher), *darzi* (tailor), pan-chewing *qawwali* singer, *hakim* (practitioner of traditional medicine), or as the good-hearted *mujrawali* (courtesan), and almost served as props to add color to the mise-en-scène, usually through idiosyncrasies of language, dress, or behavior. On the occasions when Muslim characters played larger roles, it was inevitably in a "supporting" capacity either as the hero's sidekick who accepted *prasad* (offerings from Hindu religious services) from the hero's mother and allowed his sisters to tie a rakhi on his wrist, as the loyal retainer who died in service to his employer, as the family friend/neighbor who arrived on cue to dispense wise counsel and participate in family weddings and celebrations (for e.g., Khan in *Maine Pyar Kiya*), and of course, the weak-kneed, god-fearing Rahim *chacha* (village/community elder) who made a plea for peace and harmony, a role played to particular perfection by character actor A. K. Hangal in popular films such as *Sholay* (1975).

Compared to the 1950s and 1960s, the representation of Muslims in Hindi films thus clearly underwent a significant shift in the 1970s and 1980s, notably in the sense that Muslims no longer appeared as distant aristocrats who seemingly inhabited a world of their own, but were instead depicted as "common or garden variety Muslims who did not speak the flowery Urdu of the *shahenshahs* (emperors) or the *nawabs* (aristocrats) but the patois of the street" (Masud 1997: n.p.) and were located within the larger context of Indian society. However, this emergence of the everyday Muslim, it is important to understand, did not imply a radical redefinition of the "Muslim" in mainstream Hindi cinema. As the discussion above indicates, Muslim characters were rarely more than adjuncts to "Hindu" protagonists.

Indeed, not only were substantial roles for Muslim characters few and far between during this period (Pran playing the Pathan Badhshah Khan in *Zanjeer* and Rishi Kapoor as Akbar Allahabadi in *Amar Akbar Anthony* or Amitabh Bachan in *Coolie* are among the few that come to mind), even these characters were defined in deeply stereotypical terms, marked by certain outward signifiers or what Umberto Eco has called "explicit codes," such as names, appearance, mannerisms, as well as religious practices such as the performance of *namaz* (daily prayer) or visits to *dargahs* (Muslim shrines) that constituted the only basis for the construction of their "Muslim identity" within the context of Hindi films. For instance, in *Zanjeer*, Pran was identified as a Muslim by virtue of his name, henna-colored hair, and shalwar kameez (a dress identified with Pathans). Similarly, in *Amar Akbar Anthony*, Rishi Kapoor's Muslimness was indicated (in addition to his name and dress) by his occupation as a singer of qawalis, while in *Coolie*, Amitabh Bachchan wore a badge with the number 786 which is sacred to Muslims.

Thus, while Hindi films from the 1970s onward included Muslim characters in their general storylines, a development frequently cited as evidence of the industry's embrace of secular ideals, like the Muslim socials that preceded them, they revealed little about the ethos of the Muslim community in India, its internal issues and divisions, or its relationship to the majority. As Fareed Kazmi states, "the characterization of Muslims is delineated in terms of abstractions. They emerge as stereotypes represented by well-defined signs of speech, appearance, dress, social and religious practice . . . ignored are the real-life men and women with distinct class positions, social backgrounds and individual disposition" (Kazmi 1994: 239–40). Consequently, despite their presence within mainstream films and a shift from their portrayal as exotic others, the systematic "othering" of Muslims continued apace, this time through a process of marginalization whereby they had a token presence but were never integral to the narrative.

The Demonized Other

This mode of representation which dominated the 1970s and 1980s underwent a considerable shift when the casting of Muslim protagonists in marginal roles was replaced by their appearance in more significant roles within numerous Hindi films, by the late 1990s and early 2000s. However, in this altered pattern of representation, while Muslim protagonists certainly had a more substantive presence within the master narrative of Hindi cinema, they were frequently cast in negative roles. Thus, whereas in the previous two decades their presence had been marginal but benign, Muslim protagonists now began to increasingly appear in a variety of negative roles whether as criminals (*Farz* and *Angaar*), small-time crooks (*Love Ke Liye Kuch Bhi Karega*), power-hungry politicians (*Bas Itna Sa Khwab Hai*), corrupt police officials (*Shool*), and as Pakistani aggressors fighting valiant Indian military forces in films such as *Border*, *Sarfarosh*,

Indian, and *LoC Kargil,* that focused on the conflict between India and Pakistan. Similarly, in the blockbuster of 2001, *Gadar: Ek Prem Katha* (Revolution: A love story), ostensibly a love story between a Sikh boy and Muslim girl set against the background and aftermath of the partition of 1947 that divided India and Pakistan, Muslim characters including the heroine's family, who hold her hostage until she is rescued by her Sikh husband, are "shown to be despicable, with their minds twisted with hatred of India" (Agarwal 2001: n.p.).

In keeping with this trend toward the demonization of Muslim characters within Hindi cinema is their frequent representation as terrorists engaged in acts of violence against the Indian nation. As Manisha Sethi puts it:

> A perceptible shift occurred in films through the turbulent 1990s and beyond, that of deploying aggression as one of the defining characteristics of the minority community. So while earlier Muslims usually appeared in "character" roles such as the hero's friend or a childless man who adopted the orphaned hero when he was young (*Vidhaata,* Amar Akbar Anthony), by the 1990s they were wearing the villain's boots. It is perhaps ironic that the silver screen which seems at the moment to be obsessed by the theme of terrorism, invariably of the Islamic type, is swamped by Muslim characters like never before. (Sethi 2002)

Indeed, such portrayals have emerged as *the* leitmotif of a series of recent films. Emblematic of this emergent genre of cine-patriotic films are simplistic good versus evil plots, in which Muslim protagonists are typically defined as violent, evil, driven by a visceral hatred of India and a single-minded desire to destroy it. For instance, in films such as *Qayamat: City under threat, Jaal, Hero, Ma Tujhe Salaam,* and *Yeh Dil Hai Aashiqana,* to name but a few, Muslim characters are involved in plots aimed at unleashing terror in India. Even a film like *Mission Kashmir,* which seemingly attempts to provide a more complex view of militancy in Kashmir, ultimately resorts to stereotypical characters such as Hilal Kohistani, a militant fundamentalist from Afghanistan, who, financed by Pakistani and Saudi backers, spouts the rhetoric of jihad and seeks to recruit young men in his war to "liberate" Kashmir from India.

In other words, there is no substantive attempt in this or other films that focus on terrorism, to portray the complexities of the political situation in Kashmir and its manipulation by politicians on both sides or of the factors that underpin militancy in the region. Instead, their narratives tend to identify terrorism almost exclusively as the result of the evil machinations of India's neighbor and archrival Pakistan, carried out either by infiltrators or misguided local recruits. As Syed Ali Mujtaba puts it:

> Kashmiri militants are shown as gun-toting bearded guys wearing skull-caps and fighting the Indian security forces. The Kashmiri militant linkage moves further in a linear direction to identify with Pakistan and Taliban. Characters dressed up in Afghan outfits with scarves over the shoulder are shown mouthing some Arabic words while scheming to launch jehad against India. The villain in these recent films caricatures "bin Laden" and looks like a typical Muslim priest holding a rosary in hand, counting beads, and spitting fire against India. The painting of the Taliban, Pakistanis and Kashmiris are all done with the same brush. (2004: n.p.)

But even though Pakistan is identified as the evil nation responsible for terrorism, the implications of these films for the Muslim community within India are very clear. By their tacit conflation of Islam with acts of violence against the Indian nation, these films indicate that Muslims living in India are either agents or supporters of Pakistan and that Muslims have to *prove* their loyalty to the nation-state. And indeed, when the token "good" Muslims do appear on the screen, they do not typically undertake the process of what Amit Rai (2004) has called "claiming and performing" their allegiance to the Indian nation. They do this either by expressing their devotion to India in patriotic speeches such as the one delivered by Fiza, the leading character of the film of the same name, or through "protesting religious discrimination which translates into an assertion of inclusion in the national family," as in both *Sarfarosh* and *Mission Kashmir*, where Muslim characters resist attempts to question their loyalty to the nation based on their religious identity (Rai 2004). And most dramatically, they prove their patriotism by making the supreme sacrifice for their country. For instance, in the film *Indian*, the Muslim character Rahim dies while aiding the hero in his mission, while in *Ma Tujhe Salaam*, the good Muslim al-Baksh dresses as a Rajput warrior going into battle and gives up his life in the fight against his disloyal master who wants to break away from India and establish an independent territory with Pakistan's help. However, despite the occasional addition of patriotic Muslim characters, the dominant representation of Muslims in recent years has tended to be negative, with Muslims appearing as the enemy, both without and within.

Further, while such representations largely originated in the late 1990s, a time when the Hindi film industry increasingly offered up "push button patriotism, easily orchestrated by stirring songs and air-brushed images of heroes saving the endangered nation" (Rao 1999: n.p.), it is undeniable that "normalcy," in popular Hindi cinema, has been reserved for Hindu characters, particularly those of Northern Indian provenance. Indeed, the industry has traditionally Othered minorities by representing them almost exclusively through stereotypes, reducing members of minority groups to a set of cultural, linguistic, or behavioral archetypes. Hindi films are replete with examples of Christian protagonists appearing typically as drunken Goans, kindly parish priests, or villainous sidekicks named Robert or Michael in the case of men, and as bar girls, cabaret dancers, or gangsters' molls (usually called Mona or Lily) in the case of women. Similarly, members of the Sikh community have been represented as possessing more brawn than brains, Parsis as absent-minded buffoons, while Muslims have been variously exoticized, marginalized, and demonized within the master narrative of commercial Hindi films.

Secular in Name

This then brings one back to the issue of just how inclusive and secular is the Hindi film industry. The industry itself, as well as many observers, has long claimed that it is characterized by a secular ethos, pointing both to the pluralistic composition of its workforce as well as the fact that "the dominant trend within Hindi cinema has been the omission of conflicts driven by communal identity and a deliberate representation of communal fraternizing," or Hindu-Muslim bhai bhai best exemplified in films such as *Amar Akbar Anthony* and *Coolie* (Virdi 2003: 75). However, despite the Hindi film industry's attempts to project a world unmarred by communal divisions, in effect its purported secularism always had significant limits, as the representation of minorities in general and Muslims in particular demonstrates—limits that were defined in large measure by well-established, if unfounded, ideas of what audiences find acceptable and appealing.

Moreover, in recent years, as the Hindi film industry has become "more comfortable in the shadow of saffron" (Salam 2005: n.p.), even this claim has become increasingly questionable. As actor Farooq Sheikh puts it, "whatever prevails in the society is bound to reflect in films. Bollywood is the safest place to reflect perceived social reality . . . the truth does not have to come into the picture" (quoted in Salam 2005: n.p.). As for the industry's fabled pluralism, while it is true that the combine of Aamir, Saif, Salman, and Shahrukh are among the industry's biggest stars, it is nevertheless important to recognize that not only has their entry into the industry been facilitated (in most cases) by their families' ties to the industry, but that (barring their names) they seem to have avoided any type of identification with a Muslim identity or even with the Muslim community. Indeed, none of these stars, with the recent exception of Aamir Khan, have ever played a Muslim character, even though they have appeared in films that have featured Muslim protagonists. And in what is perhaps the most telling commentary on the line that Muslim stars walk, superstar Shahrukh Khan, also known as King Khan for his larger than life image, has felt it necessary to publicly state in an interview that while he is a Muslim, he is also a "true blue Indian" and that "no one can take this right away from him,—in a truly secular industry, such a performance of identity would be unnecessary" (Gupta 2003).

BIBLIOGRAPHY

Agarwal, Y. 2001. "Competing Visions of Nationalism." Retrieved September 20, 2006, from: http://www.india-syndicate.com/polit/ya/6june001.htm.

Dwyer, R. 2004. "Representing the Muslim: The 'Courtesan Film' in Indian Popular Cinema." In *Mediating the Other: Representations of Jews, Muslims and Christians in the Media*, ed. T. Parfitt and Y. Egorova, 78–92. London: Routledge.

Farooqui, M. 2001. "Death of the Muslim Social." Retrieved September 15, 2006, from: http://www.mid-day.com/columns/Mahmood_Farooqui/2001/November/17541.htm.

Ganti, T. 2004. *Bollywood. A Guidebook to Popular Hindi Cinema*. London: Routledge.

Gupta, S. 2003. "Talking with Shahrukh Khan." *The Indian Express*, p. 32.

Jayamanne, L. 2002. "Review of Mother India by Gayatri Chatterjee." Retrieved September 10, 2006, from: http://www.sensesofcinema.com/contents/books/02/23/mother_india.html.

Kazmi, F. 1994. "Muslim Socials and the Female Protagonist: Seeing a Dominant Discourse at Work." In *Forging Identities: Gender, Communities and the State*, ed. Z. Hazan, 226–43. New Delhi: Kali For Women.

Kesavan, M. 1994. "Urdu, Awadh and the Tawaif: The Islamicate Roots of Muslim Culture in Hindi Cinema." In *Forging Identities: Gender, Communities and the State*, ed. Z. Hazan, 244–57. New Delhi: Kali For Women.

Khilnani, S. 1997. *The Idea of India*. London: Penguin Books.

Masud, I. 1997. "Muslim Ethos in India Cinema." Retrieved September 5, 2006, from: http://www.screenindia.com/fullstory.php?content id=9980.

Mujtaba, S. A. 2004. "Bollywood's Caricatures." Retrieved September 2, 2006, from: http://www.himalmag.com/2004/february/cpmmentary_3.htm.

National Integration Council Meeting Report. 2005. Retrieved September 20, 2006, from: http://www.hvk.org/specialarts/mnic/mnic.html.

Rai, A. 2004. "The Muslim "Other" in Bollywood." Retrieved September 10, 2006, from: http://www.shobak.org/islam_comments.php?id=147_0_31_0_C.

Rao, M. 1999. "Patriot Games." Retrieved September 2, 2006, from: http://www.humanscapeindia.net/humanscape/hs0999/hs9995t.htm.

Rao, P. V. 1997. "Sardari Begum, A Shyam Benegal Film Premiered on Television." *Biblio: A Review of Books*, vol. 2, no. 5.

Salam, Z. U. 2002. "Regressive Trend." Retrieved September 10, 2006, from: http://www.hinduonnet.com/the hindu/fr/2002/10/11/stories/2002101100050100.htm.

Salam, Z. 2005. "Between We and They." *The Hindu*, July 2.

Sethi, M. 2002. "Cine-Patriotism." Retrieved September 2, 2006, from: http://www.samarmagazine.org/archive/article.php?id=115.

Tharoor, S. 2001. "Classic and Contemporary." Retrieved September 2, 2006, from: http://www.hinduonnet.com/2001/09/02/stories/13021366.htm.

Virdi, J. 2003. *The Cinematic ImagiNation: Indian Popular Films as Social History*. New Brunswick, N.J.: Rutgers University Press.

Chapter 8

||||||||||||||||||||||||||||||||||||||||||||||||||||||

The Mirror Has Many Faces
The Politics of Male Same-Sex Desire in BOMgAY *and* Gulabi Aaina

Parmesh Shahani

Section 377 of the Indian Penal Code formulated in
1833 states that any person who voluntarily has carnal
intercourse against the order of nature with any man,
woman, or animal, shall be punished by imprisonment
for life. Carnal intercourse against the order of nature
includes the acts of sodomy, fellatio and cunnilingus.

With this simple declaration of the harsh reality surrounding homosexuality in India, the doors of India's cinematic closet were thrown open in
December 1996 as *BOMgAY*—the country's first "gay" film—was screened
at Bombay's National Center for the Performing Arts. The provocative
12-minute film captured a complex and nuanced slice of upper-middle-
class homosexual life in Bombay city. In the months and years that followed, as Riyad Vinci Wadia, the film's director, blazed a trail of media
frenzy across India's tabloids with his bold clothes and diva-esque antics
at the high-society soirées, *BOMgAY's* bold theme and gritty visuals made
it the toast of the international film festival circuit.

BOMgAY's declaration of urban Indian homosexuality as "gay," its
upper-class origins and packaging, and the fact that it was in English,
might have led to it being feted in San Francisco and Berlin, but it was
not something that sections of Indian homosexuals connected with. They
had to wait until *Gulabi Aaina* (*The Pink Mirror*, 2003) was released—a
campy, soap-opera-like romp with fabulously attired *kothis*.[1] This was the

first film to deal with the country's unique drag queen culture, and more important, the first significant film dealing with male same-sex desire to be made in Hindi.

Wait a minute! Is this chapter really about Bollywood? Aren't the two films that I've mentioned above the never commercially released, film festival kind? Why talk about these films in an anthology on "Bollywood"? Isn't there any queer material from Bollywood?

[SLOW DISSOLVE]

Flashback 1: Queer Bollywood

Commercial Bollywood cinema has a long tradition of films with comic sequences or songs featuring cross-dressing male stars, or any number of songs featuring *hijras*.[2] Indeed, as a number of recent articles demonstrate, it is possible to read queer desires in Hindi films.[3] And there are, of course, a handful of explicitly gay-themed Bollywood films, such as the landmark *Mast Kalander* (1991) featuring Bollywood's first out and out "gay" character, Pinku. If Hollywood's gay characters were either comic or villainous, Pinku is both (Sinha 1991). In a few rare cases, we can even find complex gay characters in films like *Bombay Boys* (1998) and *Split Wide Open* (1999), or "sensitive" portrayals of *hijras* in films like *Bombay* (1995), *Tamanna* (1997), and *Darmiyaan* (1997). There have also been villainous *hijras* in films like *Sadak* ("Street," 1991), and the reality-inspired *Shabnam Mausi* ("Aunt Shabnam," 2005, a biopic of a high-profile Indian *hijra* who was elected as a member of the legislative assembly in the Indian state of Madhya Pradesh), and lesbian-themed films like *Fire* (1998) and *Girlfriend* (2004). In 2005, *My Brother Nikhil*, dealing with the trials and tribulations of an Indian gay champion swimmer who is found to be HIV positive (based on the real-life story of swimming champion Dominic D'Souza) was well received in urban India.

[FADE TO BLACK]

Director's Note

First, I consider Bollywood to signify not just the cinema that emerges out of the Bombay film industry but a state of mind. It seeps into everything else around, especially with other creative content in India. Second,

I wish to focus on moments of transition—when ideas, thoughts, and ideologies that were previously unarticulated finally found voice, and the two films that I discuss in this chapter are both pioneering efforts in this direction. Riyad Wadia's *BOMgAY* is acknowledged as India's first gay film, while *Gulabi Aaina* has the distinction of being India's first *kothi* film (Thomas 2003). Third, these two films stand out as being the most Bollywood-like for me personally and arguably, the most significant non-commercial "queer" films to have emerged from India in the past decade. They have been followed by a succession of films like Tirthankar Guha Thakurta's *Piku Bhalo Achhey* ("Piku Is Fine," 2004), Ligy J. Pullappally's *Sancharam* ("The Journey," 2004), T. Jayshree's *Many People, Many Desires* (2004), Rangayan's *Yours Emotionally!* (2005), and Ashish Sawhney's *Happy Hookers* (2006). But it would not be incorrect to think that none of these would have been possible without the pioneering efforts of *BOMgAY* and *Gulabi Aaina*. Fourth, I find that these two films reflect quite brilliantly some of the contentious issues that I observed during my fieldwork for my forthcoming book on the contemporary Indian gay scene which I will discuss in this chapter. I will address key themes of both these films and examine their commonalities and their differences. I will attempt to relate these themes with ongoing debates about the problems that arise while trying to bracket ethnic sexualities into predefined categories, and suggest that rather than polemic positions, what both these films offer us are just two different shades in the entire spectrum of cinema dealing with alternative sexuality in India. I will intersperse my discussions about the films with my own fieldwork experiences encountered while conducting research for my book *Disco Jalebi: An Ethnographic Exploration of Gay Bombay*. I will also intersperse my narrative in this chapter with Bollywood-inspired interludes from my own life. I hope that, like the song-and-dance sequences in the best of Bollywood films, these interludes will enrich rather than distract, and nuance my argument further instead of irritate. A caveat: in case it isn't already clear by now, I'd like to set the record straight and clarify that I am primarily writing about homosexual men in this chapter—and more specifically, two identity-based categories of homosexual men: gay men and *kothis*.

[FADE IN]

EXT. CROWDED STREET IN SANTACRUZ, BOMBAY. DAY

Dancing Queens

The sky is pouring as my rickshaw makes its way to the Humsafar Center. I have known Ashok Row Kavi and company socially—we have had many common friends—but I have always hesitated when invited and backed off, citing some excuse or the other. This time, two months before I leave for the US in 2003, there's a big group of people I know going for a special Sunday High meeting, so I decide to finally take the plunge. From the outside the building looks old and unimpressive— but inside, the atmosphere is pure magic.

As I enter, two fabulous drag queens in saris sprinkle rose water, fold their hands in a dramatic namaste and hand me a gajra (bracelet) made of small jasmine flowers strung together that I wear on my wrist in total filmi style. There are beautiful diyas (oil lamps) placed all round and soft pink curtains that cascade down the walls. There are white mattresses placed alongside the walls with rose petals scattered all over them. It is Indian style seating, arranged specially for the mujra (courtesan dance) performance that is to be the highlight of the evening. I sprawl on some cushions and exhale. Why was I so scared to come here all these years?

Needless to say, the dances are spectacular—they're all my favourite mujra songs—Chalte Chalte from Pakeezah, Maar Daala from Devdas and Hoton Pe Aisi Baat from Guide. The crowd is going crazy, hooting and whistling with every swirl of hips, every lowered glance, every twitch of the lip. I recognize the movements and mannerisms. Last year, I took some business clients from out of town to the famous Topaz dance bar in central Bombay and witnessed a dreaded gangster nonchalantly shower a basketful of 500 rupee notes over the heads of the gorgeous fully clothed girls on the floor, who were winking and coyly making and breaking eye contact the same way as the drag queens at Humsafar are doing; except today, there's no money bring showered, but only warmth and appreciation. It is mesmerizing—the vocabulary of the erotic dance. I feel that I have always known it—and I have, in a way, having grown up on Bollywood. I suddenly realize that this is my first real contact with Indian drag queens—I have seen quite a few in the US while on vacation, but here, the connection is much more immediate. These are my songs, my music, my people, and I watch the entire show with a foolish grin on my face. Maybe some day, I might be able to perform like them. . . .

[FADE OUT]

BOMgAY Times

BOMgAY consists of six short poems written by Raj Rao, set to striking visuals and sequentially linked with inter-titles to construct a "quasi-socio-political frame" (Wadia 2000: 320).[4] This "frame," written in academic language, muses on the position of the gay "self" in Indian society, privileges coming out and embracing one's "gay" identity, and denounces the closet as a place for hypocrisy and self-denial. The full text reads:

> In 1991, the National Family Health Survey estimated that over 50 million Indian men have sex with other men. Of these, more than 12.5 million men are exclusively homosexual. At the heart of Indian society is a belief that a compromise brought about by a "collective" living is far more desirable than the stridency of "individual" expression. A notion of "self" is coterminous with the socialized self. The individual that seeks to speak finds solace in the ambivalent anonymity of the underground. Unfortunately, fear and debasement become the close companions of pleasure and self esteem. The purity of love subverted, the twisted soul escapes into a world of fantasy. The individual spirit purges itself by reveling in its victimization. Emboldened by the inadvertent structures of urbanism, a band of victims strive to create a society that respects the individual. An alternative "collective" is born, and with it the commoditization of its myriad ideologies. The love that dare not speak its name now sits across the table and debates its cause. The protagonists are self-respect and accountability. The antagonists are hypocrisy and self-denial.

Wadia clearly states that the film is not intended to be a realistic portrayal of the overall Indian gay scene. For him there is no such thing as an "Indian" gay community and all that BOMgAY is attempting to do is "portray the emergence of a small gay community that dwells in Bombay and who choose to interpret the word 'gay' as practiced and loosely defined by the cultural social and ideological expressions as seen in the western hemisphere" (Wadia 2000: 322). This westernized slant is evident in all aspects of the film, whether in its very name, the fact that it is entirely in English, the pink triangle symbolism of the opening titles' stylish imagery, the jazz that serves as the film's music score, or the MTV-style camera work, lighting, and editing.

The title of the film is especially significant. Bombay was renamed as Mumbai in November 1995 by the right-wing BJP–Shiv Sena coalition government in power, in an attempt to revert the name of the city from something that the British gave it to its supposedly rightful and more authentic past. Insisting on Bombay, but queering it with a bold pink "g" and the pink triangle gay icon below it was Wadia's way of reclaiming a recently lost heritage as well as mapping an emerging new space. In the communally charged atmosphere of 1996, *BOMgAY* also sounded emphatically cosmopolitan. Further, Wadia's team on *BOMgAY* consisted entirely of acquaintances (gay and straight) from Bombay advertising agencies, men who belonged in an upper-middle-class milieu, and the film is undoubtedly a reflection of their collective sensibilities.

The characters of all but the first vignette ("Opinions") are upper class, and even in the first vignette, the middle-class bachelor is shown in a dominant class position—leisurely reading the morning newspaper as he supervises the maidservant washing his clothes. In the other vignettes, the protagonists are either tie-wearing office yuppies ("Underground"), pumped-up college students indulging in orgiastic fantasies in beautiful Victorian libraries ("Lefty"), a gay couple in a slick apartment, decorated with risqué art and cool blue lighting ("Enema"), wealthy foreign tourists visiting the city's landmark "gay" locations ("BOMgAY"), or fabulous jewelry-wearing aesthetes dining in a penthouse overlooking the city's skyline ("Friends").

The nudity in the film is graphic. *BOMgAY*'s library sequence, where naked muscular long-haired men eat fried eggs off the protagonist's chest and fuck him violently in the ass, never ceases to draw a collective gasp from audiences, no matter where it is screened. Anal references in the writing also evoke similar responses. The film is clearly a provocation—a political and social manifesto, a declaration of gay lifestyle and an open call to elicit a reaction from those that agree to disagree as well as its opponents.

[SLOW DISSOLVE . . .]

Flashback 2: Behind BOMgAY

The Bombay of *BOMgAY* didn't suddenly appear out of nowhere. The city had a distinct underground "gay" scene even in the '70s and '80s. Popular cruising spots included the Chowpatty beach, the Gateway of India promenade, Maheshwari Gardens, Cooperage Park, the Bandra, Churchgate, and Dadar train stations, and the ever-popular local train compartments.

Bombay's first full-fledged gay hangout was a tiny bar called Gokul located in a bylane behind the five-star Taj Mahal Hotel in south Bombay. Saturday evenings at Gokul's become a regular event on the gay social calendar of Bombay during the 1980s. From the beginning of the 1990s, private dance parties began to catch on. These were either hosted at the homes of rich volunteers, in rented bungalows on the beaches of faraway Madh Island, or at city-based venues like rented public halls or school premises. The private party phase coincided with the decline in the popularity of Gokul and the rise of Bombay's second gay hangout—Voodoo, a dance club, also located in South Bombay's touristy Colaba area. Unlike Gokul's casual and conversation-oriented atmosphere, Saturday nights at Voodoo were loud, brash, noisy, and for all practical purposes, standing room only.

In the decade since *BOMgAY*'s first screening, the city's gay scene has changed rapidly. While the underground geography portrayed in the film still exists, the city's homosexuals have started organizing collectively and jostling for visible social space (Ahmed 2003). There are now regular gay nights in bars and clubs being organized as a way for homosexual men to network, as well as a wide variety of other social events and meetings (Gezarri 2003). There are Internet newsgroups, websites, and blogs dedicated to queer issues, popular gay chat rooms on leading national portals, marches, film festivals, legal petitions in the country's supreme court challenging section 377, and so on.[5] There is also a steady flow of empathic gay-related stories in the country's mainstream newspapers and magazines, where the reportage has shifted from the oh-wow-we-have-gay-people-in-India-too type of coverage of earlier years, to more in-depth coverage of the wide range of issues that affect the city's queer scene. For instance, India's first gay magazine *Bombay Dost* grew by leaps and bounds through the 1990s and also spawned The Humsafar Trust, the country's first Non-Governmental Organization (NGO) to deal with issues relating to homosexuality.

These changes in urban environments have been paralleled by a spurt in academic and activist discourse that traces the ancient origins of Indian homosexuality, in the process questioning the imposition of Western norms of "gayness" on the Indian homosexual population. Authors like Ruth Vanita and Saleem Kidwai have challenged the Western-centric narrative of homosexuality and also refuted the argument that same-sex desire as a category was the invention of nineteenth-century European sexologists. They have tried to demonstrate "the existence in pre-colonial India of complex discourses around same-sex love and also the use, in more than one language, of names, terms, and codes to distinguish homo-erotic love and those inclined to it" (Vanita 2002: n.p.). This categorization is very significant—these ancient discourses are the sources from which a large number of non-gay-identified sexual minorities in contemporary India, including *hijras* and *kothis*, derive their sense of identity, and this identity is very different from that of the urban gay identity that attracts attention. As a report released by the Naz Foundation says:

> In South Asia the socio-cultural frameworks are supremely gendered, and often sexual relationships are framed by gender roles, power rela-tionships, poverty, class, caste, tradition and custom, hierarchies of one sort of another. Here for many men/males we have gender identities, not sexual identities. The phrase males who have sex with males, or men who have sex with men is not about identities and desires, it is about recog-nizing that there are many frameworks within which men/males have sex with men/males, many different self-identities, many different contexts of behavior. (Khan 2000)

A complex and nuanced understanding of ancient and contemporary In-dian homosexuality that academics and activists have arrived at over the years is a much-needed step forward. However, unlike the public brou-haha surrounding the country's gay and lesbian communities, India's *kothis* have remained largely unnoticed by the mainstream media. Thus, *Gulabi Aaina*'s release in 2003 was a momentous occasion for *kothis*. *Gu-labi Aaina*'s director Sridhar Rangayan (a founder-trustee of the Humsafar Trust as well as Executive Editor of *Bombay Dost*) has been at the epicen-ter of Indian gay activism for the past decade. His inspiration for the film came from Bollywood-inspired drag numbers that he had seen performed at parties in Bombay city over the years. Rangayan was disturbed that the opportunities for Indian drag queens to perform were diminishing, ironically, as the number of gay parties occurring in the city continued to increase. So he decided to make a film that "portray[ed] drag queens with empathy and celebrate[ed] their life," with characters that were "com-pletely Indian and rooted in its culture, paying homage to Indian Bolly-wood divas and songs and speaking in Hindi" (Pandohar 2004: n.p.).

FADE OUT.

[INT: DARK SMOKY CLUB. NIGHT]

"Pricked by a Thorn"

My friend, the poet and writer R. Raj Rao, is visiting Bombay from Pune where he lives and teaches, and he asks me to meet up with him at the infamous Voodoo club. For six days a week, the place is a seedy pickup place for the Arab tourists that congregate in the area to pick up cheap hookers. But every Saturday night, it undergoes a fabulous transformation as hordes of gay men descend upon it and make it their own. Though it is located just off the street where I live, I have only been there once, with Riyad, maybe five years ago.

I arrive late, a little before midnight, pay Rs. 250 to the old Parsi owner sitting at the counter and swing open the door. It is a lot smaller than I remember. I walk straight on to a packed dance floor. There is a tiny DJ booth to the right, a basic bar to the left. The walls are scribbled with neon graffiti, there are strange colored shapes spray painted on to the ceiling. Very 80s. There are a few tables arranged towards the back of the club, and a metal staircase that leads to a mezzanine observation lounge, as well as passages that lead to a more private lounge in the back of the club, and to the toilets adjacent to this lounge. This is the "make out" lounge with soft sinkable sofas, slightly tattered, and even lower lighting than the rest of the club.

I climb up the metal staircase and position myself midway, leaning on the railing, arms folded, just like I'd seen Riyad do the last time. From my perch, I can scan the crowd, predator-like. I lean over and chat with Raj, who is dancing on the floor with someone he has just met. I make polite conversation with an older guy and discover to my surprise that he is the uncle of A, former fuck buddy, brief crush, and now soul brother. Uncle is a jet-setting global academic, and this is his first time out to a gay place in Bombay. I wish him all the best and continue sight-seeing.

Tonight, I am horny and angry. B has just told me online that he has slept with a girl back in Boston, I don't know whether he is lying or not —but I despise myself for being head over heels in love with a stupid 18-year-old Venezuelan boy who has only just begun exploring his sexuality. I seek revenge. Someone random, someone I will never meet again. I see a possible candidate. A cute white guy, standing by himself in a corner of the club. He's skinny and geeky, exactly my type. American? Maybe not. Perhaps European or Israeli. I wonder whether I should descend and make a move, but before I do, Xerxes bags him and within five minutes, they're the centre of attraction on the dance floor, groping each other all over.

I look away disappointed. Back to the desis. On the floor, there is an assortment of men of all ages, sizes, and shapes, merrily dancing away. This is not Gay Bombay crowd—it's more mixed—though I do see some familiar faces from the Gay Bombay parties. One of these is Kirit. He is about 5 and a half feet tall. Not more than 20. Perhaps younger. Very thin with a smooth body exposed due to the fact that his T-shirt is raised to his nipples as his hips gyrate feverishly. He is surrounded by a pack of hungry wolves, but his eyes are closed as he dances. He moves confidently, assuredly, slickly. I was such a dork at his age—pondering over my sexuality, wasting all those years being scared.

With his eyes closed, Kirit looks a little bit like B, and that does it for me. I alight, cut through the crowd with practiced ease, and whisper into his ear while nuzzling his neck that he's the sexiest person I've seen all week. It's a really lame line, but Kirit giggles and pulls me close to him. On the floor, we fondle each other's dicks and try to tongue each other's mouths out. Ten minutes later, we're on the sofa in the make out lounge, kissing fervently. I unzip his jeans and pull him to me, but he wants to go back and dance to Kaanta Lagaa ("Pricked by a Thorn")—the hot new Bollywood remix that the DJ has just begun playing—understandably, a gay dance floor favorite. We can do it after this song, he winks, as he zips up and prances back on to the floor.

I sit for five minutes on the sofa by myself. What the fuck do I think I am doing? And stupid, stupid boy. What kind of an idiot is he, wanting to "do it" with someone he's just met in a club. Does he do this often? I want to go back to the dance floor, slap him and educate him about safe sex and being careful. But I slink away home quietly, and jerk myself off in the bathroom.

FADE OUT

Thinking Pink

The story of *Gulabi Aaina* revolves around four characters—two drag queens Bibbo and Shabbo, Mandy, and Sameer. Bibbo is a fashion designer and she considers Shabbo, a performing artist, her daughter. Mandy, the new queen on the block, is a westernized gay teenager being groomed by

Shabbo to become more "Indian." The straight-appearing Sameer is an aspiring actor, hoping to get a break in the film industry using Bibbo's contacts (Bibbo is a costume designer for many stars). Most of the action of
the film deals with the machinations of the two queens and young Mandy
to get the attention of the hunky Sameer.

Rangayan's emphasis on the vernacular pervades all aspects of the film.
Unlike the corporate executives of *BOMgAY*, the two queens here are
lower-rung workers within the Hindi film industry. They use public transport and prefer "rum and cola" to the more exotic cocktails that Mandy
wants to conjure up for them. They desire branded products and place a
premium on powder "imported from Paris," but also use homemade face
packs and local cosmetics for their daily regimen. Not only do they embrace middle-class conventions, they subversively sneer at any attempts at
being too elite, or westernized. The English-speaking Mandy is the butt of
their jibes; his ignorance of *kothi* culture provides the queens an opportunity to explain its intricacies to him.

The film is shot in a TV soap-operatic style, using all the mainstream
clichés currently in vogue within the Indian television industry—the constant use of slow motion at dramatic moments, extreme close-ups, absence of long shots, jarring background music, and over-emphasized fa-
cial expressions and gestures are all conventions that any television viewer
in India would be familiar with. The partial nudity in the film is very conventional. There is one shower scene of the muscular Sameer in which the
camera pans over different parts of his body, but never on his buttocks
or genitalia, instead lingering for the longest time on his firm chest, in
a manner not unlike the conventional representations of heroines (and,
of late, the heroes as well!) in Bollywood films. In terms of structure, the
plot follows the norms of introducing the characters, quickly alternating
between humor, pathos, song and dance sequences and romance, introducing conflict, and resolving it with a happy ending.

One should note that Rangayan and his entire film crew have their
roots in the commercial Indian television and film industry, which by
and large is separated from the advertising industry that *BOMgAY* had
its roots in, along class lines. Rangayan has added to the televisual conventions a generous spattering of Bollywood-inspired song-and-dance sequences, camp mannerisms and colorful bitchy dialogues, full of terms
and nuances familiar to *kothis*. He also raises the issue of AIDS/HIV,
which is something that *kothis* and other MSM in India are supposed to

be at a much higher risk for than gay-identified men. *Gulabi Aaina* thus becomes as equally a significant manifesto for *kothis* as *BOMgAY* is for India's gay-identified males.

Conflict

The film's exhibition over the past several years at venues throughout India made the *kothi*-gay divide quite visible. I was present at its premiere screening in Bombay in 2003 and found the audience to be polarized. The South Bombay gay crowd stuck together, making snide remarks about the film and its vernacular drag lingo, while the *kothis* and their friends raved to each other and the director about how good it was. My ex-boyfriend, who had accompanied me for the screening, was extremely uncomfortable with its in-your-face-take-it-or-leave-it attitude. He was not alone in his discomfort. As I discovered, several gay-identified individuals I interviewed had based their identity and sometimes, their entire life, battling the notion that a gay person is "a pansy effeminate guy." They prided themselves on the fact that they were just like everyone else and were deeply vested with creating a culture where it is okay to be "straight-acting" gays. There was a discomfort with drag, and a resigned tolerance to it in public places was limited to *Western*-style drag. Thus, a Malaysian drag group that came down for the World Social Forum was invited to perform at a Gay Bombay dance party, but Indian drag groups have been constantly ignored at such events.

Class differences and language barriers were another flashpoint. It was clear that for most of the people I spoke to, their interactions with those beyond their class boundaries were limited. The hypocritical nature of some of these prejudices was quite evident—while there was resentment among upper-class, gay-identified people to interact socially with people from the non-English-speaking classes, many of them had no qualms about exoticizing them in their sexual fantasies or even picking them up for random sexual escapades when they desired so. There was also another important issue that I became concerned about during my research—the lack of attention paid to HIV by the upper-class, gay-identified men, either because they felt themselves to be perhaps not as much at risk as other queer populations, like the *kothis*, or because of plain ignorance.

[JUMP CUT]

Same Same, Poppy Same!

Now, despite seeming to be radically different, I want to suggest that these alternative points of view (presented within *BOMgAY* and *Gulabi Aaina* and reiterated via their reception by their gay and *kothi* constituencies), in fact, speak to each other. We can see this conversation take place through the many similarities between the two films.

Both films make strong political statements for the case of their protagonists, though *BOMgAY* does it more explicitly than *Gulabi Aaina*. Both films are unapologetic and in fact quite celebratory about their sexuality. Rangayan says, "The characters [in *Gulabi Aaina*], whether they are drag queens, gay or bisexual, offer no apologies for being what they are. They do not curse their fate and grovel at anyone's feet because they are homosexuals" (Pandohar 2004: n.p.). Likewise, Wadia said that he "was clear about one thing when we started the ideating process [for *BOMgAY*]: we were not going to fall shy or act coy just to please some societal norms. We were going to make a short film as we saw it . . . an important work of socio-politics that needed to be made" (2000: 317).

There is a near absence of women characters in both these films. In *BOMgAY*, the only female characters are the maidservant and neighbors that appear in the first vignette ("Opinions"), while *Gulabi Aaina* has absolutely no female cast members. Thus, both films are situated in completely self-contained universes, whether gay or *kothi*. It is significant that these self-contained universes also completely exclude any presence of the protagonists' family members. Familial relations in both *BOMgAY* and *Gulabi Aaina* consist of affinity groups constructed over the years. I find this affirming, even though it contrasts with the ground realities that I observed, experienced, and recorded in Bombay. My research findings indicate that for most homosexuals in India, whether gay identified or *kothi*, the blood family plays a huge role and coming out is, more often than not, not a viable or desirable option. They live with the constant tensions that arise due to the negotiation of a dual existence. In this sense, both these films are quite Bollywood-like in their fantasies!

I am not sure whether the class-positioning of both these films is as crystal clear as it initially seems. Despite *Gulabi Aaina*'s avowed vernacular slant, it is ultimately set in the upper middle class. The queens constantly use English slang while addressing each other, even as they deride

Mandy's English accent. When they are planning a date for Sameer and Mandy at the end of the film, their plan consists of "a table for two," "a candle-light dinner," and "a disco." And if there is an Indian drag *mujra* (courtesan dance) at the beginning of the film, there is a Western drag cabaret number toward its end. Bibbo's home is decked with feathered boas, red lace curtains, swathes of gold lamé, posters of almost nude macho hunks, and images of Ardhnareshwar (an incarnation of the Hindu God Shiva as half man-half woman) on the walls. The villa is palatial by Bombay's space-crunched standards, and certainly does not look like a place that a film-industry worker could afford. It is a flamboyant middle-class drag queen's camp fantasy, ultimately as unreal in its possibility as the images of oversized penises in the bathroom of the protagonists in *BOMgAY*'s "Enema" vignette.

Likewise, despite *BOMgAY*'s overt snobbery, its underlying basis is the poetry of Raj Rao, which arises from a very strong lower-middle-class ethos. While most of the poems are translated into upper-class settings on screen in *BOMgAY*, this does not mean that middle- and lower-middle-class characters and settings are erased completely. Thus, in "Underground," we see the characters of Raju (19, office boy in Bora Bazaar), Gulab (22, waiter at Satkar), and Pandu (50, coolie at VT Station), and the harsh world of hustlers and stinky railway station toilets, while "Opinions" gives us a glimpse of life in a middle-class city chawl (Kundu and Basu 1999).[6]

Ultimately, both films are a blend of fantasy and reality—the very real existence, as well as the imaginative possibilities, of two significant subsets of Bombay's queer population. What I find satisfying is that neither of them offers an ultimatum to the audience to force its particular version of Indian homosexual identity down their throats. Instead, they both offer viewers choices: of characters, situations, and viewing positions. If *Gulabi Aaina* has its ethnic queens as its stars, it also has a very comfortable westernized Mandy assert, "I am gay," and an equally comfortable bisexual Sameer.

Both films also tackle, at various levels, serious issues faced by the homosexual community-at-large in India. Homophobia and gay bashing are graphically depicted in *BOMgAY*, while the specter of HIV, though completely ignored in *BOMgAY*, raises its head in *Gulabi Aaina*. I am disappointed though, by the superficial way that it is handled and its repression at the film's ending as something to be tackled another day. Both films offer sharp critiques of the sexual hypocrisies of straight society. Consider this dialogue exchange from *Gulabi Aaina*:

> *Bibbo*: There were so many after us [at the party].
> *Shabbo*: Because we were in drag—they were all straight otherwise.
> *Bibbo*: Straight my foot. Pussy or bum, no one leaves a bubble gum!

They are also self-critical—*BOMgAY*'s narrator derides himself for being a post-colonial pimp for the sex tourists from abroad to whom he shows Bombay's exotic gay locales. Likewise, Shabbo and Bibbo's bitchy commentary to each other is laced with venomous truths about their promiscuity, their manipulations of men, and their past mistakes.

An inability to get a censor certificate for public viewings in India is another aspect that binds these two films together. While *BOMgAY* did not bother applying to the censors, *Gulabi Aaina* was refused "even an adult certificate, because the censor board termed it full of vulgarity and obscenity" in 2003.[7] Interestingly, on appeal in 2006, the censor board refused to issue a certificate, arguing that the film wasn't sensitive enough to the issues of the transvestites![8] Thus, the question of the films' widespread distribution is moot in any case and the only audiences that will possibly see both these films are those attending the homosexual community screenings, and film-festival cognoscenti. The chance of either of these films reaching the heterosexual mainstream seems remote.

[WIPE IN]

Hum Saath Saath Hain

In light of the above discussion, I posit that instead of positioning the two films against each other, we read them with each other, as initial pieces in the mosaic of Indian homosexual representation. Rather than polemical positions, what both these films offer us are just two different shades in the entire spectrum of queer cinema that is possible in a multilayered society like India. We could similarly think of the *kothi*/gay divide as not really a divide but as diverse family members dealing, in their own ways, with separate, but connected issues. At least, this is how I choose to see it, after spending some time conducting research in the field. As I mentioned earlier, while I did find several points of conflict between gay identified men and others, I also found a tremendous amount of cooperation, across class, language, and other barriers. For example, the Gay Bombay social group (which caters largely to gay-identified upper-middle-class men in the city) and the Humsafar Trust (an institution that runs a community center for homosexual men, and also focuses a lot on HIV prevention issues, and is patronized by men who identify as gay as well as *kothis*, and also *hijras*) had mutually decided to hold their weekend events every alternate Sunday, so that cross attendance would be possible. I attended one such Sunday High meeting at the Humsafar Trust premises that dealt with the rising problem of male hustlers in Bombay city, and I noticed the presence of several Gay Bombay regulars there. I also realized that the Gay Bombay group had begun to structure some of its dance parties as fundraisers for projects organized by Humsafar and other LBGT groups in the city and country at large, such as the Larzish LBGT film festival in Bombay in 2003, or the Calcutta Pride walk of 2005.

Within the larger queer movement, it is easy to get caught up in infighting and identity politics and lose sight of the larger common objective that all sexual minorities are fighting against—for example, the repeal of section 377 in India. A strategic interventionist approach would recognize that gay, *kothi, hijra,* and other identities are important on the ground, and in people's lives, however reductionist they may appear to be theoretically. It would also recognize these identities as constructs—ways of seeing and being. It would further self-consciously define certain essential qualities of these identities if needed, and reshape others, to achieve larger goals. Adopting a strategic essentialism would mean maintaining separate LBGT sub-identities, but tweaking them when needed, and compromising on them, if the situation demanded it. I agree with Nayan Shah's viewpoint when he writes that "we need not fear that differences or a lack of predetermined unity will produce irreconcilable divisions. It will help us develop communities which are stronger and more self-affirming" (Shah 1993: 127). On this path to self-affirmation, I believe that *BOMgAY* and *Gulabi Aaina*, just like the similar and different viewpoints they represent, walk together, hand in hand.

NOTES

1. A Hindi language term used to denote homosexual men in India who identify/dress/perform as women. "*Kothi* is a feminized male identity which is adopted by some people in the Indian subcontinent and is marked by gender

nonconformity. A *kothi*, though biologically male, adopts feminine modes of dressing, speech, and behavior and would look for a male partner who has masculine modes of behavior" (Narrain 2004: 2–3).

2. The term *hijra* refers to "a socially constructed role for a group of men with religious and cultural significance, whose primary belief is around the religious sacrifice of their genitalia and who act as women in exaggerated styles" (Khan 1995: n.p.).

3. See *Journal of Homosexuality* 39, no. 3/4 (2000).

4. These poems are part of a larger, yet-unreleased book of poems with the same title. Raj Rao is one of India's leading gay writers. His works include *The Boyfriend* (2003) and *One Day I Locked My Flat in Soul City* (1995).

5. The two most widely known websites are http://gaybombay.org and http://www.humsafar.org.

6. A chawl is "a set of small multi-storied residential units, constructed mostly in the nineteenth century, to accommodate industrial workers particularly in Bombay. These are sometimes described as 'inner city, run-down, walk ups.'"

7. "The Pink Mirror," *B. News* 85, March 11, 2004, p. 17. Retrieved from: http://www.solarispictures.com/reviews9.htm

8. Personal conversation with Sridhar Rangayan, Cambridge Mass., June 30, 2006.

BIBLIOGRAPHY

Ahmed, Z. 2003. "Gay Bombay Comes Out." *BBC News Online,* June 19. Retrieved from: http://news.bbc.co.uk/1/hi/world/south_asia/3001126.stm.

Gezarri, V. 2003. "India's Gays See Small Improvement in Cultural Outlets." *Chicago Tribune,* September 10.

Gopinath, G. 2000. "Queering Bollywood: Alternative Sexualities in Popular Indian Cinema." *Journal of Homosexuality* 39 (3/4): 283–97.

Kavi, Row Ashok. 2000. "The Changing Image of the Hero in Hindi Films." *Journal of Homosexuality* 39 (3/4): 307–12.

Khan, Shivananda. 1995. "Cultural Constructions of Male Sexualities in India." Naz Foundation International.

Khan, Shivananda. 2000. "*Kothis,* Gays and (Other) MSM." NazFoundation International.

Kidwai, R. 2005. "Real Cheer Dims MLA Jeers." *The Telegraph,* May 18. Retrieved from: http://www.telegraphindia.com/1050519/asp/nation/story_4758092.asp.

Kundu, Amitabh, and Somnath Basu. 1999. "Words and Concepts in Urban Development and Planning in India: An Analysis in the Context of Regional Variation and Changing Policy Perspectives." *Northern India,* Working Paper No. 4, UNESCO. Retrieved from: http://www.unesco.org/most/p2basu.htm.

Narrain, Arvind. 2004. *Queer: Despised Sexuality, Law and Legal Change.* Bangalore: Books For Change.

Pandohar, Jaspreet. 2004. "Loud and Proud: India's Hidden Gay Community Comes Out of the Closet." *Desi Magazine.* Retrieved from: http://www.solaris pictures.com/reviews7.htm.

Rao, Raj R. 2000. "Memories Pierce the Heart: Homoeroticism, Bollywood-Style." *Journal of Homosexuality* 39 (3/4): 299–306.

Shah, N. 1993. "Sexuality, Identity, and the Uses of History." In *A Lotus of Another Color: An Unfolding of the South Asian Gay and Lesbian Experience*, ed. R. Ratti, 113–32. Boston: Alyson.

Sinha, Gayatri. 1991. "Bollywood Goes Gay with Abandon." *Indian Express,* April 21.

Thomas, S. 2003. "India Finally Enters Gay World." *Asian Age,* January 31.

Vanita, Ruth. 2002. "Homosexuality in India: Past and Present." *International Institute for Asian Studies Newsletter* 29, Amsterdam.

Wadia, Riyad. 2000. "Long Life of a Short Film." In *Queer Asian Cinema: Shadows in the Shade*, ed. A. Grossman, 313–23. New York: Harrington Park Press.

Chapter 9

||||||||||||||||||||||||||||||||||||||||||||||||||||||||

"Bring Back the Old Films, Our Culture Is in Disrepute"
Hindi Film and the Construction of Femininity in Guyana

Atticus Narain

One of the major sources of cultural renewal for Indo-Guyanese is Hindi films. They watch as if their very existence depends upon it, and in terms of identity it does. While Hindi films cater to diverse international audiences, there are few studies that examine how such films frame the expectations of audiences—as in the Guyanese case—for whom these films are the primary sources of cultural confirmation. Even as Hindi films construct a moralistic caricature of Indian mores, they authenticate a notion of "Indianness" for Guyanese whose ties to the subcontinent have long been severed. In the context of persistent ethnic hostility between Afro-Guyanese and Indo-Guyanese, Indian films denote a cultural "intactness" amongst complicated conceptions of an imagined community. Between 1838 and 1917, 200,000 Indians were transported as indentured laborers to Guyana, where they became a significant population. Guyana—still overwhelmingly agrarian—presents an interesting case in which the (ex-)colonial antagonists (Afro- and Indo-Guyanese) operate within a space largely vacated by British agents of colonialism.

Attempts by Indo-Caribbean scholars to wrestle with the dominance of Euro/African and black/white paradigms highlight the historical and cultural eclipsing by their black counterparts. Their invisibility is also compounded by the diasporic hegemony of South Asian writers from North America and Britain, and from Indian writers (Mehta 2004). Re-addressing the misrepresentation of Indians in the Caribbean is often weighted in narratives that formulate an alternative and incommensurable system of meaning that closes off the possibilities of a dialectic between "blackness" and "brownness." A shared sense of historical struggle in the works of Kumar (2000) and Prashad (2000) offers a refreshing narrative of interconnections absent in many other accounts.

Historical and cultural contextualization of the specificities of the Indo-Guyanese experience problematizes their inclusion in the conceptualization of wider South Asian diasporic and film politics. The intellectual recognition and growth in interest on Indian diasporas' global reach has produced a homogenization that speaks of and to an already articulated audience. Excited conversations with film viewers in London, Guyana, Delhi, and Calcutta reproduce with stark similarity a discourse that serves to highlight the Bollywood-inspired culture "effect" (Mishra 2002; Rajadhyaksha 2003). Ethnographies that have focused on Indian cinema practices and its flows also offer useful comparisons: Dickey (1993), Abu-Lughod (1995), Fuglesang (1994), Mankekar (1999), Ray (2004), and Uberoi (2001). There may be room to speak of a diasporic imaginary born out of a loose, shared, and inspired set of overlapping global relations, whose currency maintains a conception of the Indian nation (Mishra 2002: 237). However, heterogeneous linguistic and national differences inspire caution over the quick adoption or utilizing of this transnational cultural sphere to work as diaspora politics. Such analyses and infotainment exchanges are inadequate to explain fully the racial, class, and gender specificities that infringe upon the experience of Indians in Guyana. As Kumar writes,

> Indians in India have monuments we in Trinidad [and Guyana] are making them, there is so much taken for granted, we are in the process of rooting ourselves. . . . Assembling fragments to make a different whole . . . You aren't going to understand us with Indian categories. (2000: 97)

Immigrants "arrive" under very different circumstances, positioned by various discourses contingent upon their "host" environments. Race, class, and history heavily inform how diasporas are received and represented through public narratives of arrival and settlement. The historical, social, and political construction of Indianness in Guyana is predominantly in opposition to Afro-Guyanese identity. Indo-Guyanese are no longer replenished by "fresh" Indians from India and today are comprised of fourth and fifth generations whose loyalties are not limited to the "mother country." Often, South Asian Diaspora studies are characterized by particular post-colonial movements from periphery to the center that engage in specific histories of race, immigration, and citizenship (Sharma, Hutnyk, and Sharma 1996). These are extremely important but cannot be straightforwardly applied to understanding the Indian diaspora of Guyana whose history of arrival, length of "settlement," historical, and antagonistic relations with other ethnic groups generates a different politics of nation and identity.

The old diaspora is situated through a specificity lodged in classical capitalist development of nineteenth-century labor. These classes were bonded to plantation regimes whose contact with India was ruptured, and have subsequently existed as a pure imaginary space of epic plenitude (Mishra 2002; Jayawardena 1980). The "new diaspora" "of late modern capital" is dominated by economic migration (and others), and is characterized by an "unbroken" contact with the homeland. Race and ethnicity for the new diaspora are linked to questions of justice, self-empowerment, representation, equal opportunity, and definitions of citizenship. Mishra's diasporic distinction (2002: 235) acknowledges the historical specificities of coerced migration that operate and are articulated differently under colonialism and post-colonialism. Similarities may exist between diasporas and their processes of political life, but emphasizing these, I argue, undermines the specificity of the Indian experience in Guyana. Although Indo-Guyanese are currently producing their own subjects based in North America who participate in the politics of the "new," they highlight the ambiguous relationship between those who return and reside that generates a host of unifying and contested claims around Indo-Guyanese identity, one of which is centered around femininity.

This chapter unravels a system of differentiation that enables an articulation of Indian identity that is contradicted by the acts of viewing. Old films are championed for their traditional values but never watched. New films are scorned for their lurid content but eagerly consumed. This dialectic presents areas of contestation and offers an understanding of how Hindi films ignite competing but complimentary realms of identification around different conceptions of femininity. Initially, this is presented through a distinction made by viewers between old and new movies. The ambiguity surrounding boundaries of exclusion is significant, for it serves as a strategy to demarcate attitudes and characteristics of femininity. A moral panic is circulated that frames the discourse on femininity and is linked to cinema as a space for women not to attend. Using Prasad's

(1998) analysis of the kiss in Hindi cinema, I demonstrate how filmic representations simultaneously undermine and compliment local notions of femininity.

A Vignette to Work With

On a night with the Ganesh's, like many spent before, the respectful bonds between mother and daughter were temporarily disrupted. Mother and daughter sat on the sofa facing me as I swung in the hammock, relaxing after a sumptuous meal. Early on their maternal drive took pity on this lone male and they insisted that I pass by both before and after my visits to the cinema to be fed. A single man going home and fending for himself was unthinkable; I obliged and ate well. The thirty-year-old daughter, Bipti, is unmarried and lives at home with her mother, father, grandmother, and brother. In a place where marriage is a distinctive rite of passage and defining principle of womanhood, she was nearing the danger zone of expiry. This scenario for an older Indian girl/woman with such potential is an unusual one—a fact that is never wasted by the family, who taunt and tease her on her untouched, intelligent, and marriageable qualities, perfect for Indo-Guyanese abroad who come in search of a "traditional" Indian girl. Their teasing no doubt hid serious anxieties and unexpectedly these exploded.

A friend passed by to invite Bipti to a wedding in Trinidad, a 90-minute flight away. Her mother laughed out loud, signaling the absurdity of the proposition. The conversation strategically changed to a local wedding. After her friend left, Bipti, with casual and controlled anger, told me, for the benefit of her mother, "She never lets me go out." In fact, neither mother nor daughter left the house much and attempts to take them to the cinema were never successful.

Both sat side-by-side facing me as I witnessed the unfolding of subject matter that neither wanted aired but was now out in the open. Bipti continued, "She would not even let me go to the club in town with my own brother, my own brother." Kavita (mother), for her part, proffered a reason for being overly protective. "You remember the time your cousin from outside (America) hit you in the face?" Bipti cried out, "Oh God," her eyes wide and amazed that her mother would bring this up. Her mother continued, "Yes, her cousin from outside wanted to go to the Roxy cinema (2 minutes walk) to meet some boys who like to drink." "How old was she?" I asked. "The cousin was 14 and Bipti was 25. The cousin then hit she in she face and she fell into the wardrobe, it made such a loud noise that she father and uncle come up from downstairs to see the commotion. Then it was arranged for the cousin and she to go to the cinema with the uncle, but Bipti did not want to go. The uncle took the cousin and she met up with the boys anyhow. When I was her age I was never allowed to go alone, always with others or with Uncle and certainly never allowed to go see an English movie. That is when I watched plenty Indian films. I use to go to Monarch, Roxy and Devan. I liked those old films like Waqt, Suman Kalin Pool, Milan, Dosti, Ek Phool do Maali. The women of old were naturally beautiful not like now they wear so much makeup."

Bipti got up, went to the fridge to get some chocolate for herself, a little respite from the barrage, and was scolded for eating too much at her age. She put the chocolate back, sat down and changed the topic so obviously that we all exhaled a little chuckle and mum clasped her hands as though to signify the end of that. The hierarchy was challenged, a brief altercation ensued, and the matriarch resumed her rightful position. Bipti's feeling of suffocation and frustration emanates from her lack of control over her movement in contrast to her brothers. The memory of visiting the cinema for Bipti produced a set of antagonistic positions: her cousin challenged the boundaries of female behavior, but she was constrained by social and cultural expectations. The restrictions that Bipti faced reflect more widely held beliefs, and are shaped by a range of religious, social, and political norms that define femininity.

The exchange between mother and daughter also foregrounds cinema's role in shaping patterns of socialization. The process of meaning-making around the space of the cinema hall is, at its core, a question of defining and circumscribing women's position in that space. I examine conflicts surrounding the cinema hall, and responses to specific films to interrogate how cinema becomes an integral part of the social and cultural history of Indo-Guyana. I argue that the importance of cinema is articulated in terms of a seemingly rigid dichotomy around past/old and new/present films that are, in turn, invoked to critique the inadequacies of "Indian" culture. Let me begin then by addressing cinema's fall from grace in Indo-Guyana.

Old Films: Highlighting the Best Aspects of "Our" Culture

The call for the return of films like *Boot Polish* (1954), *Dosti* (1964), and *Pakeezah* (1972) was strong. Viewers state that their stories are better, the emotional drive strong, and the messages for the family are clean. Furthermore, the promotion of mythological salvation, hard-working Hindu ethic, well-defined gender roles, codes for moral and religious self-conduct were all cited as positive attributes of such films. Old films are good, and they tackle proper idealistic concerns through their clear-cut narratives that privilege the rural peasant. Underlying these narratives is a masculinity that puts the struggle of providing for the family within a larger allegory of national independence onto the male (Kaali 2000: 170). Post *Mother India* (1957), the struggle is transformed into one that feminizes the nation and woman becomes the key symbol for an array of social and political issues (Chakravarty 1993; Virdi 2004). Filmic representations of the limits and possibilities of female positionality are legitimated and re-enacted through discussions between old and new films that inform Indo-Guyanese social relations.

One could argue that the older generation prefers older films and the younger newer films. This arises out of parental attempts to uphold tradition against the forward march of modernity being embraced by a younger generation. For example, in the absence of their parents teenagers often relayed their preference for the dancing and fashion prominent in new films for their modern ethos. When parents were present, these same teenagers dismissed new films, citing the same reasons their parents would. This was played out on several occasions where verbal fluctuations were matched by physical transformation. On leaving the house, bodies were covered, hair tied back, and shoes were covered or slippers worn. On the way to the cinema, jeans were rolled up, flesh revealed, hair styled, and makeup applied. Their transformation is not surprising and is consistent with the repeated themes of divisions between parents and children. Parents stick to the old ways where change is slow if not frozen and the young have to negotiate the traditional with the demands of the new. Viewers situate and critique new films for their ability to corrupt the young, and despite rigorous monitoring and guidance parents can never police completely their children's film-viewing activities. For viewers, old films mark cultural continuity and social stability. The conflict between old and new films is mirrored by a generational split that in itself is a site of struggle over maintaining authority.

The boundaries between old/new films are ambivalent, and revolve principally around representations of women. The proliferation of representations that go beyond the dutiful passive female archetype challenges local codes that govern gender relations. This presents a possible split for viewer loyalties, but also illustrates the friction between speaking and living through ideal conceptions of self. Viewers are quick to perpetuate generous identifications of their "culture" with the "correct" representation in old films. However, in most cases, Hindi films are simultaneously celebrated and rejected and what is disparaged by some is openly appreciated by others. This sets up a struggle between modernity and tradition that is not simply generational, but intrinsically linked to attempts at maintaining cultural and social cohesion.

Films screened at cinemas and television schedules provide a useful place to interrogate the contradictions in viewing new films. Black and white films are never shown at the cinema, rarely on television, serve as fillers for late-night schedules, and are derided for their slow pace. Old films are designated one slot on channel 69 on Sunday afternoons, and as the proprietor informed me, it was his way of reaching out to a section of the community that he felt was unaccounted for. When I suggested to the staff at the Astro to screen an old film, I was met with laughter. Films made prior to the 1980s are not screened in the cinema, and perhaps it is here that the seamless boundary between old and new films could be disrupted. Films post-1980 are viewed because of the popularity of the stars in relation to their present success in contemporary films. Double-bill screenings of favorite actors and their films contribute to a collective actor and film historiography. For instance, watching two films starring Shahrukh Khan, one can hear laughter that goes beyond the recognition of the slapstick humor, and as I turned to ask the woman several rows away if this was Khan's first picture, nodding enthusiastically, she says yes. Her admiration is attributed to her favorite star, but also speaks to a certain nostalgia about the ways films used to look, the narrative and representational devices, special effects, and fashions of the time. In these nostalgic moments, Žižek states, "the real object of fascination is not the displayed scene, but the gaze of the naïve 'other' absorbed, enchanted by it" (2000: 529). Viewing old films produces a collective remembering that in turn validates the importance of the moral and traditional values that viewers invest in them.

While viewers express admiration of old films, they only watch new ones. Often, during or after an interview, the fiercest opponents of the new films would declare that they have watched many a new film, showing no sign of recognizing the contradiction in their position. Or as in the case of Pundit G, who mischievously replied, "I have to keep up to date with what the youth are watching," some viewers recognize the inconsistencies of the position against new films. Between these dialogues is a tension that uncovers the space occupied by realism and myth, the "pull of the everyday, the normal, the contemporary against that of the imaginative, the unexpected, and the timeless" (Chakravarty 1993: 119). They coexist to form an "imaginative truth" and participation "is not a case of split existence, since such a split is postulated on a divide between the real and the imagined, something that Bollywood disavows" constantly (Ray 2004: 162). Both myth and realism are "impersonating phenomena" for "realism as a particular set of conventions points always to the larger traditions and belief systems within which those conventions are embedded, with a mythic structure or image often embodies the most real though indirect expression of the ways of seeing and believing of a society and its culture" (Chakravarty 1993: 119).

This friction between fluid and static meaning produces an instability embodied in the dialectic of old and new films. This separation demonstrates how Indo-Guyanese viewing regimes punctuate their ideological polarizations. As one viewer retorted, "you know sometimes I really wonder if they take the stories from our lives, because it is like watching ourselves on screen."

The conceptualized category of old films offers homogeneity, comfort, and security through an investment of an ideal film type that best projects Indian mores. Old films are assigned a special fixed historical position and their absence from present screen representation lends them a sense of authenticity. In the following section, I explore the process that enables the watching of new films whose narratives seem to tear at the heart of viewer sensibilities.

Female Representation in New Films

Only recently have new films been locally termed Bollywood, and this coincides with Mishra's claim that it refers to a specific mode of address linked to the shift in seeking out the diaspora located in the West (Mishra

2002). Interviewing one of the organizers of a new multifaith television channel generated the following discussion on the role of Hindi film in society:

> I am happy that the cinemas are closed down, it was destroying the fabric of our society. Years ago families could watch a film together now they can't. Bollywood is not Indian—in fact it's against our culture. The sense of hostility, aggressiveness, revenge and half nakedness of love always existing between only two people and of families not approving of love-always need antagonistic stories that are not true to Hinduism. Bollywood is more a hindrance than help. Its to do with Americanism and commerce more than anything else-older films had morals-dress and language was good, in fact the English in the subtitles was so good that we could learn good grammar.

This non-identification with viewers repeatedly places the speaker outside of associating with the viewers being lambasted. The relaxing of Indian censorship is blamed for the deterioration in Indo-Guyanese society. The proliferation in sexually explicit content is, for him, utterly inappropriate. His response hinges on a moral and educational discourse whose disapproval targets the devaluation of the female body. Consider these responses from two female university students:

> Yes! Guyanese practice their culture more; they perform marriage ceremonies the same way like dress and ritual and Indian films strengthen our beliefs as Hindus. The bride and groom dress traditionally with sari etc. and the bride treats her husband as God himself.
>
> I dislike the crying the submissiveness of women and the unreal. I wonder if people do that in India, do Indian women cry like that? Is it cultural? On the one hand there is no realism yet I watch Indian films when I feel depressed and want to see the world as light and fluffy and you are always guaranteed of a happy ending. Indians wouldn't put up with the submissive role that the women play yet the values presented are commendable. Women always appear to be virgins respectable unlike Western women. There is so much patriarchal conceit. I hate how the women are always goody two shoes, good looking, and hair is never out of place. My mum use to say that women always walk with their own bag of breeze. Today films are de-collateralized from their tradition and is part of the westernization and the need to tap into the markets abroad.

Key to these testimonies are the possibilities and limitations of woman-hood defined through their relations to film. Both uphold notions of fe-male piety, and while the first respondent does so in straightforward fash-ion, the second respondent voices a disagreement that is overridden by visual pleasures. These statements reflect how female representations of the body are empowered with an agency detached from their producers. Hindi film narratives are "potent mediators of the lived experience of the body, our own and others, giving us ways of conceptualizing and describ-ing the body" (Callen 1998: 401). Films demarcate a site to outline the hierarchical social order that govern gender relations. This is not to sug-gest a one-way traffic of meaning because how the body is located, given meaning, and consumed is culturally and historically specific.

One need only count the many girls named Sita in Guyana to realize the importance of this personification of womanhood as a standard to be endorsed, if only in name. Sudhir Kakar, for instance, argues that Sita's ego ideal still governs the inner imagery of individual men and women as well as the social relations between them in both traditional and modern sectors of the Indian community (1978: 68). Given the importance of this mythology, it is not surprising that the sentiments of womanhood repro-duce notions of purity, chastity, self-sacrifice, and a singular faithfulness to men. Put another way, the Sita ego brings the historical into the frame to reveal the position of women as important to the stability of social for-mation that is threatened by contemporary representations of femininity.

Thus, the position of women falls into the common duality of uphold-ers and transgressors of cultural value (Chakravarty 1993; Virdi 2004), burdened with the responsibility of maintaining the boundaries of com-munity. Larger ideals around Indianness are maintained through discus-sions on film at the level of a vocalized withdrawal from looking. It is as though a collective mandate in response to the differentiation between old/new films is circulated and endorsed to disguise the fact that their consumption still persists. On the one hand, a relationship with film is being tested that provides a profoundly unstable economy of discourses, and one of a continued contracted voyeurism. The unstable economy is the meeting between public consumption of private space offered through representation.

Visual representations of intimate exchanges that were once confined to premarital signification, typified in the eve of the wedding night, are no longer adequate. These have given way to more potent and explicit rep-resentations that infringe upon cultural norms of acceptability. "Families can't go to the cinema anymore," said one concerned mother, "because the content is too crude and we have to monitor what our children view." Contemporary narratives violate their visual sanctuary amidst overlapping conflicts of interest. Why this preservation of old films if no one watches them? Why are people not boycotting new films?

Prohibiting Sexual Acts, Displaying the Body

As Prasad argues, kissing (or the lack thereof) in Indian cinema demonstrates processes of situating the female body through public representations that negates a language around sexuality. He argues that the function of prohibiting the kiss is attributed to an "Indian culture" that "blocks the centrifugal force unleashed by the kiss that would threaten the integrity of the culture" (Prasad 1998: 97). It is necessary to expand the metaphor of the kiss to include an array of signifiers that do the same work. This incorporates and acknowledges the claims of viewers that films of today deploy far more than the kiss to evoke the private in the public. The sexual scenario represented in the kiss or the rain-soaked sari has given way to include: dress styles, body contact, direct gazes of desire and intent, dream sequences, and dance scenes located in nightclubs and bars instead of the idyllic and pastoral settings of the Swiss Alps. It is precisely this expansion of the private that has brought the local sensibilities of Hindi film consumption into disrepute.

Prasad suggests that the private, symbolized by the kiss, exists in the public domain through its visual circulation but is not necessarily of the public (1998: 93). Hindi films thus create a coexistence of negation and celebration through particular representational strategies that ambiguously blurs the real and unreal. What takes place in the viewing of films is a meeting between private and public actions, and representational strategies deployed in film help keep what might appear as ideological conflict separate. Consider viewer responses to the film *Paap* (screened in 2004).

In *Paap*, the pious and noble female seduces the male protagonist. Both are rolling across kitchen tops, simulating the sexual act whose climax is erased by the revelation that this is in fact a dream. Thus, the shock factor is firmly put in its place, as unreal, and we can relax. The dream sequence is one technique deployed to circumvent the problem of actually depicting the sexual act. The sequence makes visible almost naked bodies for communal inspection. Within the larger narrative of the film is a double representation of femininity. Outside the dream, the woman is presented as coy, humble, and naïve and her clothing, hair, and physical presence all work to establish her aspirations to perform the "Sita" figure. In the dream, she transforms into a vixen and is able to actualize her physical desires. The duality between positive/negative and feared/desired coexist and function interchangeably, bringing to the surface the ambivalence of the female archetype. An ambivalence that embodies a "double ideological profit" (Žižek 1999: 94), for it simultaneously signifies the boundaries, limits, and fissures of female positionality. They are both the producers and pollutants of culture, whose bodies need to be controlled through a patriarchal representational framework. This is re-enacted by Kavita's over-protection of her daughters' attendance to the cinema. Or, as performed by the boys who talk of securing a "good wife" yet on the streets, parade their sexually explicit desires.

Hindi film narratives continually uphold "official" and "unofficial" conceptions of femininity that appear diametrically opposed. This apparent contradiction exists within an "idealized moral universe" (Thomas 1989: 15) that is made possible through a variety of representational devices. Therefore, the complexity of femininity is offered to the viewer but is strategically reduced to a perpetuation of a singular female ideal. This "displays the female body for communal inspection, consists of a retreat of the sexual act itself into a zone of privacy while exhibiting the evidence of its consummation" (Prasad 1998: 91). It is a representation disguised through a form of "narrative arrest" that positions the dream outside yet clearly within the film.

Withdrawing before the kiss, before engagement, or after the dream sequence, "cinema produces and maintains an illusion of a community" (Prasad 1998: 104) and this, only with the active complicity of the audience, is made possible through shared cultural references. This illusion is endorsed and maintained, at one level, in the participatory responses of the audience in the cinema. An example of this is the arrival of a film called *Girlfriend* (2004) that sparked huge protests in India, causing some cinemas to be burned down.

The film was promoted as groundbreaking in its treatment of lesbianism. And for viewers, such as those at the Mayal cinema in Guyana, *Girlfriend* was little more than a story about an obsessive woman fantasizing about her flat mate. The film's screening had attracted a lot of curiosity over the possibility of a girl-on-girl kiss and this was reflected in the higher than usual attendance. The suggestive moments of a kiss produced much anticipation, screams, laughter, and encouragement. Unlike the responses in India, the titillation far outstripped any revulsion or violation of Indian values. No, Indo-Guyanese laughed, wolf-whistled and, because it was daylight, people's faces were easily recognizable, marked by sheepish smiles of forbidden pleasure. The frequent possibility of the kiss produced a feeling of collective naughtiness as looks of disbelief were exchanged that suggested "I'm not looking at this filth" but heads soon turned toward the screen. These shared glances and retorts serve as collective policing over what is not acceptable, and the community effect is produced and maintained and viewing safely resumes. This is a prime example of a duality at work that governs the rules of sexual display while at the same moment presenting the female body for erotic inspection (Prasad 1998: 93).

The community effect is stabilized through Hindi films' idealized cultural and moral universe, and local "ways of seeing" attribute to a visual clarity that stays within the boundaries of viewer sensibilities. This is how visual ideology works, not a dreamlike illusion built to escape reality, but rather, it is in its basic dimensions a social construction of fantasy that serves to support real social relations. In order for fantasy to work, the fantasy scenario that regulates the subject's identification must not be too alienating. For example, what if the sequence was not a dream, or the couples did not withdraw, or the lesbians did in fact kiss? The fragile relationship between difference and similarity allows ideology to function as possible attainment through identification. This identification must not be so identical as to render it a "real" representation. It is within this refractive mimetic image/gaze relation that Hindi films serve to provide ideals to be attained and desired. The Hindi film matrix at once serves to reinforce an ideological premise yet problematizes their strategic claims over identity.

The absence denied through the prohibition of not representing the kiss within the collective activity of viewing functions as "the agency that decides instead of us, in our place" (Žižek, quoted in Prasad 1998: 97). This is central to a notion of cinematic democracy—power without leadership—a coercion through which the cinema is devoid of any authoritarian rule. It enables free-floating associations that reproduce the community effect in ways unlike the political dogma attempting to reclaim these cultural spheres. Prasad warns that "the real stakes of the ideology project of Indian popular cinema lies in prohibiting representations of the private, this cinema blocks the recognition of the break down of pre-capitalist community bonds and the learning of new modes of solidarity based on the shared interests of the working class" (1998: 104). Therefore, traditional values continue to be invested in truths that can never be attained. This is demonstrated in the discourses that surround the female body and its attachment to old and new films as articulated by viewers. The difference between verbal and visual practices presents a duality that works together to negotiate and maintain notions of femininity.

Conclusion

I have examined how femininity is constructed by presenting a selection of ethnographic encounters: an overprotective mother, loitering boys, female absence from cinema, and the act of lesbians kissing on the screen. The mother-daughter relation highlighted the need to guard female sexuality to uphold status and social standing. These ideals are undermined by Hindi films' shift in narrative focus that is echoed by viewer responses. The discourse on femininity circulates an ambiguous distinction between old and new films and is legitimated through cinema's association as an undesirable space for female attendance. Hindi films' representational strategies and the sites of their reception present an array of conflicting contradictions, an overarching one being the repeated verbalized position of "we don't watch" and the actual practice of looking. Verbal responses help uphold an ideal logic that is identified in a romanticism embodied by old films. This is undermined by the looking practices of Indo-Guyanese who solely consume new films.

New films offer dynamic Indian subjectivities that critique and transcend the local, restrictive "cane field coolie" paradigm. The apparent tension between verbal and viewing practices is resolved through a duality in film and by audience participation. On the one hand, Hindi films evoke traditional values punctuated with modernist sensibilities through various representational strategies. Through their collective responses, the audience either accepts or rejects values fitting for the "community." Thus, the call and response of the spectators serves to outline the boundaries of acceptance and structure the social function of the ideal. Film content and audience engagement combine to convey the contentious issues around femininity being policed in the cinema in a non-authoritarian way that draw from an insider culturally specific frame of reference.

Indian cinema simultaneously reinforces cultural and religious significance appropriated as "tradition" and provides an aspirational capital-

inspired milieu of abroad. This is ambiguous for viewers because the geopolitical boundaries have shifted in ways that undermine their temporal
security in particular representations and spectatorial investments in India. The transition from an imagined geopolitical India to a fluid global
Bollywoodized diaspora reconfigures the field of Indianness and problematizes how Indo-Guyanese position themselves. For an older generation, this raises questions of their nostalgic relationship to film whereby
cinema-going was linked to a historical political and cultural era of pros-
perity. Perhaps for the younger generation this is part of an ongoing continuum; from nineteenth-century religious temples, to cinemas in the
twentieth century, that is now superseded by the neon nightclub lights of
the twenty-first century. Here cinema and its cultural and moral attributes
come to occupy another social space, where both sexes can participate
in Bollywood's modernity free from the prying eyes of their parents and
raises further questions of locating femininity.

BIBLIOGRAPHY

Abu-Lughod, Lila. 1995. "The Objects of Soap Opera: Egyptian Television and the
Cultural Politics of Modernity." In *Worlds Apart,* ed. Daniel Miller. London:
Routledge.
Callen, A. 1998. "Ideal Masculinities: An Anatomy of Power." In *The Visual Cul-
ture Reader,* ed. N. Mirzoeff, 401–14. London: Routledge.
Chakravarty, S. S. 1993. *National Identity in Indian Popular Cinema 1947–1987.*
Delhi: Oxford University Press.
Dickey, Sarah. 1993. *Cinema and the Urban Poor in South India.* New York: Cam-
bridge University Press.
Fuglesang, Minou. 1994. *Veils and Videos: Female Youth Culture on the Kenyan
Coast.* Stockholm: Stockholm University/Almqvist and Wiksell International.
Hetherington, K. 1997. *The Badlands of Modernity: Heterotopia and Social Order-
ing.* London: Routledge.
Jayawardena, Chandra. 1980. "Culture and Ethnicity in Guyana and Fiji." *MAN*
19: 430–50.
Kaali, S. 2000. "Narrating Seduction: Vicissitudes of the Dexed Subject in Tamil
Nativity Film." In *Making Meaning in Indian Cinema,* ed. R. Vasudevan, 168–
90. New Delhi: Oxford University Press.
Kakar, S. 1978. *The Inner World.* New Delhi: Oxford India Paperbacks.
Kumar, Amitava. 2000. *Passport Photos.* Berkeley: University of California Press.
Mankekar, Purnima. 1999. *Screening Culture, Viewing Politics.* Durham, N.C.:
Duke University Press.

Mehta, Brinda. 2004. *Diasporic (Dis)locations.* Kingston, Jamaica: University of the West Indies Press.

Mishra, V. 2002. *Bollywood Cinema, Temples of Desire.* New York: Routledge.

Petro, P. 2000. "Mass Culture and the Feminine: The 'Place' of Television in Film Studies." In *Film and Theory: An Anthology,* ed. R. Stam and T. Miller, 577–93. Oxford, U.K.: Blackwell.

Prasad, M. M. 1998. *Ideology of the Hindi Film: A Historical Construction.* New Delhi: Oxford University Press.

Prashad, Vijay. 2000. *The Karma of Brown Folk.* Minneapolis: University of Minnesota Press.

Rajadhyaksha, A. 2003. "The Bollywoodization of the Indian Cinema: Cultural Nationalism in a Global Arena." *Inter-Asia Cultural Studies* 4 (1): 28–34.

Ray, M. 2004. "Chalo Jahaji: Bollywood in the Tracks of Indenture of Globalization." In *City Flicks, Calcutta,* ed. P. Kaarsholm, 140–82. Calcutta: Seagull Books.

Sharma, Sanjay, John Hutnyk, and Ashwani Sharma. 1996. *Dis-Orienting Rhythms: The Politics of the New Asian Dance Music.* London: Zed Books.

Thomas, R. 1985. "Indian Cinema: Pleasures and Popularity." *Screen* 26 (3–4): 116–31.

Thomas, R. 1989. "Sanctity and Scandal: The Mythologization of Mother India." *Quarterly Journal of Film and Video* 11 (3): 11–30.

Uberoi, Patricia. 2001. "Imagining the Family: An Ethnography of Viewing Hum Aapke Hain kaun." In *Pleasure and the Nation: the History, Politics and Consumption of Public Culture,* ed. Rachel Dwyer and Christopher Pinney. Delhi: Oxford University Press.

Virdi, J. 2004. *The Cinematic ImagiNation: Indian Popular Films as Social History.* New Brunswick, N.J.: Rutgers University Press.

Wright, E. W. 1999. *The Žižek Reader.* Oxford, U.K.: Blackwell.

Žižek, S. 1999. *The Ticklish Subject: The Absent Center of Political Ontology.* London: Verso.

Žižek, S. 2000. "Looking Awry." In *Film and Theory: An Anthology,* ed. R. Stam and T. Miller, 524–38. Oxford, U.K.: Blackwell.

Chapter 10

||||||||||||||||||||||||||||||||||||||||||||||||||||||||

"From Villain to Traditional Housewife!"
The Politics of Globalization and Women's Sexuality in the "New" Indian Media

Padma P. Govindan and Bisakha Dutta

Aitraaz was challenging because I didn't just play a bad girl, I played a sexually aggressive character. . . . This character is the absolute antithesis of what I stand for. Sonia is not a character I empathize with. I will never play a sexually deprived woman again. I do not wish to be typecast as some kind of sex kitten. Right now, I'm happy playing the stereotyped Hindi film heroine, because that can be equally challenging.

—Priyanka Chopra, actress

The Bombay film industry in the twenty-first century, or "Bollywood," as it is commonly known,[1] exemplifies what Appadurai (1996) has termed "mediascape": it taps into a large complex repertoire of images and narratives from a global cultural warehouse.[2] Within this mediascape, Indian actresses represent a nexus, an intersectionn of different discourses around issues of sexuality, desire, agency, and representation. Global media flows are registered on several levels in the Indian film actress's presence—the clothes she wears, the choreography of the dances, the settings for the dances, the music—each is a hybrid product that innovatively incorporates the "global" within existing Bollywood idioms.[3] In this chapter we explore how representations of Indian female sexuality are shaped by these global media flows. We contend that these representations are governed by a paradox: actresses are expected to represent globalized images of a liberated female sexuality, but are still circumscribed by shifting yet narrow definitions of "Indian" femininity. This paradox is amplified by the burgeoning of Indian media outlets, a phenomenon that, rather than expand the subject positions for actresses, regulates and disciplines them within limited definitions of selfhood and sexuality. The global flows of media products and the existing media ecology set the stage where a "traditional" understanding of Indian womanhood, replete with references to archetypes such as Sita and Draupadi, is rehearsed for the contemporary era through global idioms. In this ecology, the distinction between "admirable" and "trashy" roles is coded by representations of female sexuality that reiterate an existing hierarchy among Bollywood actresses. As a result, success for the Bollywood film actress is contingent upon strategic negotiations and presentations of her sexual self. Notwithstanding global media flows within a bounded media ecology, as this chapter illustrates, the public presence of female sexuality continues to be guided by very narrow definitions of what is permissible.

The media ecology we refer to is a system of outlets that establish a self-contained feedback loop. They refer to each other in their content and mimic production practices. For instance, song-and-dance sequences from films are often extracted and migrate from screen to the stage to television. Or, film magazines often comment on stars and these commentaries then set the terms on which the film industry characterizes the actors and thus delimits their career choices. In each instance, two or more media outlets feed each other.[4] This feedback loop characteristic of a bounded media ecology has always existed in India, but today media outlets are no longer limited to the three film magazines of the seventies or film-based programming on the state-run television station Doordarshan. Rather, over the last decade, since the liberalization of the national economy, the media scene has witnessed a proliferation of outlets; however, this enlarged media space has not expanded the subject positions available to actresses as one would predict, especially with respect to their sexuality. Rather, even as contemporary actresses actively negotiate their public personas using global media archetypes for female sexual agency, media representational practices repeatedly fetishize these women as "feminized" bodies, subjecting them to a voyeuristic male gaze—their sexual and gendered selves continued to be circumscribed.[5] Caught between these competing subject positions, contemporary Indian actresses have very little room for maneuvering. This media environment is particularly pernicious for actresses the media label as "item girls" because, although their star status hinges on their sexualized persona, this public display of sexuality also binds their careers within the "item" roles. Strategies for resistance or subverting hegemonic norms of Indian womanhood through the media, consequently, are very limited.

The chapter is divided into three main sections. First, we provide some historical background on the new media environment and describe the cross-cutting global flows that characterize the contemporary national landscape. Next, we outline the ways in which "respectable" and "cheap" female sexualities have been depicted in Indian films, and finally, through two case studies we explore the boundaries of the space allocated to "item girls" in which to maintain and increase their agentive status in the contemporary mediascape.

Liberalization and Indian Media

Following four decades of Nehruvian socialism, the Indian government liberalized the economy in 1991, relaxing restrictions and controls around various sectors of the economy. This economic liberalization was propelled by the International Monetary Fund, which had granted two loans to the Indian government. Consequently, state-run projects and government subsidies were replaced in favor of a more Westernized, consumerist-oriented model: import restrictions and duties were relaxed; significantly for the Indian media, rules governing foreign investment were relaxed. This economic liberalization paved the way for the establishment of a number of Indian and multinational media companies, such as MTV India and Sony Television. These changes coincided with the spread of satellite technologies that led to the establishment of Zee TV and STAR TV (a division of Rupert Murdoch's News Corporation), providing Indian television audiences with a wide range of viewing choices.[6]

As in other countries, the presence of multinational media corporations has resulted in a vertical and horizontal consolidation of the Indian entertainment industry. Media corporations have developed interests in film production and distribution, television reporting, programming, music videos, album production and distribution, print media, advertising, and event management. This trend has led to "managerial techniques" of entertainment production (Naregal 2004: 531). Within the realm of Hindi films, the conglomeration of media interests with television programming has led to a shift in style. Despite the initial fears of the film industry that satellite television would be competition, the two have settled into a symbiotic relationship. Satellite channels offer the film industry an exponentially increased ability to promote and market their films through television previews, programming that features song-and-dance sequences, and the purchase of telecast rights to popular films. Television shows (as well as print media) in turn depend on the film world—its music, award ceremonies, and celebrity gossip—for programming and articles. At the same time, new trends within the film industry have emerged with exponentially increased possibilities for publicity and marketing that television programming offers, along with the phenomenon of well-known directors marketing their films for an affluent NRI community and the resultant increase in film budgets. Directors and producers have become more attentive to production qualities, the storylines have started to include well-choreographed song and dance sequences, the sets and costumes have become more lavish. Through these stylistic gestures devised to retain their audiences, Hindi films have come to mimic a style of production—polished and westernized—that already existed in television and print.

Although media outlets have expanded significantly over the past decade, the bounded nature of the feedback loop has also amplified. For example, cable channels such as MTV-India and [V] TV depend heavily on Hindi film songs for programming, even as Hindi films now have started to compete with the look of music and entertainment channels. Thus, song-and-dance sequences are now staged and directed to look like music videos precisely so that they can be aired on music video channels as advanced film publicity. This phenomenon is not new in India, as the popularity of *Chitrahaar,* the Doordarshan program from the 1970s comprising song-and-dance sequences, testifies. However, the expanded media outlets have made the symbiotic relationship between films and television programming more readily apparent.[7]

The presence of the multinational media corporations and the proliferation of satellite channels have made available for Indian audiences a vast array of images from around the globe.[8] The formerly sheltered Indian media now have to compete with their global counterparts, a trend heralded by a new glossy, cosmopolitan look. However, these shifts in style and presentation subtly mask the reproduction of hegemonic and (ultimately) patriarchal social structures.[9] The globalization "project," as it were, necessitates an uncomfortable cooperation: films, television shows, print media, and advertising all inform each other in terms of style of presentation and feed each other material for the sake of perpetuating a consumerism of aspiration among the public.[10] The proliferation of media outlets, instead of encouraging a variety of subject positions, has in fact shrunk the field of possibilities; products in the Indian mediascape are homogeneous in message and appearance. David Harvey captures how the competition central to market-driven economies sets the stages for this attenuated field of representation. "Heightened inter-place competition should lead to the production of more variegated spaces within the increasing homogeneity of international (or global) exchange. But . . . it ends up producing . . . a 'recursive' and 'serial' monotony" (1990: 295). In the rest of this chapter we explore how this "recursive," "serial monotony" is reproduced in the celebrity journalism culture with an emphasis on representations of female sexuality.

Our use of the term media ecology to describe this new environment in India is informed by the writing of Stuart Cunningham and Elizabeth Jacka. They use it to refer to "a sense of the delicate balance of interlocking factors—if one element is changed, it will have effects throughout the whole system . . . the popular cultural forms that exist in that society and their relationship to dominant forms" (1996: 16–17). As a result of this self-referential system, we contend that the expansion of "celebrity" media venues has resulted, paradoxically, in the continued limiting of subject positions that are available to Hindi actresses. Further, because the media tap into a limited visual grammar and repertoire of images in representing female sexuality, the spaces available for resistance or transgression are very limited.[11] Television shows, print media, music videos, and films all provide grist for each other's mills. By interviewing the same celebrities, broadcasting images of those celebrities, and using each other as news and programming sources, these media outlets each set themselves up as a site for sexual regulation and surveillance, and the women celebrities who provide subject matter must in turn act within that sphere as self-regulators of their sexual image.[12]

Representations of Female Sexuality

Our analysis is informed by Michel Foucault's understanding of power "as the multiplicity of force relations immanent in the sphere in which they operate and which constitute their own organization; the process which, through ceaseless struggles and confrontations, transforms, strengthens, or reverses them" (1977: 92). Sandra Bartky extends this analysis of power to offer a gendered view, one that contends that women in patriarchal societies internalize disciplinary procedures and self-regulate their bodies and sexuality.[13] In patriarchal societies there is no need for external surveillance mechanisms to control women. We extend these insights to the realm of the Indian media industry to underscore the mechanisms through which representations of virtuous and wanton female sexuality help discipline women but also the modalities through which women participate in limiting female subject positions.[14]

In the Indian public sphere, actresses have to locate themselves strategically within a limited rubric of sexual identities—the vamp, the virgin, or some blurring of the two. Although the meanings and content associated with these identity categories are constantly shifting, the necessity of having a label of sexual identification for actresses remains unquestioned in the Bollywood hierarchy.[15] As Karen Gabriel asserts, "It indicates the privileging of a specific desire and the consolidation of hierarchy through gender relations. . . . its availability already indicates the practices of desire as moderated in gendered terms" (2002: 54). Thus, even when actresses or celebrities try to resist these categories within the field of media representations, their "rebellions" are subverted and recuperated within patriarchal definitions of sexuality. This problematic of the representation of female sexuality is compounded by processes of globalization: because of the increasingly public and easily commodified nature of their personas, actresses must find a satisfactory convergence between the characters they play on screen and their "real" personalities through various media outlets. Their presentations on-screen are either altered to match their personalities off-screen, or vice-versa, but both of these strategies are ultimately reproductive of the same patriarchy that disciplines and regulates women's sexuality.[16]

More than in other countries because of the popularity of the Hindi film industry and the strong fan base that exists, actresses are not merely performers, but celebrities whose aura is defined, produced, maintained, and constantly negotiated by the media. It is de rigueur for performers to promote their films in daily talk shows, radio programs, and newspaper interviews. Television, radio programs, and newspapers will then promote the film, which will, presumably, attract viewers. Thus, in order to draw audience members, the performer has to not only advertise the film, but his or her own presence in the film as well. Thus, the viewers of the television program not only want to see the movie, but they want to see that person in the movie. Thus, successfully constructing a celebrity persona hinges on a careful calibration of "revealing" the individual personality and highlighting the continuities or contrasts between that "real" person and the character.[17] Indian actresses, in their quest to create a seamless persona between their reel and real sexualities, must negotiate these identities in the bounded media ecology we described earlier in the chapter.

Much has been written about the scopic pleasures of consuming the celebrity, but this chapter also seeks to interrogate how actresses in Bombay maintain celebrity.[18] The actor must constantly use those outlets in order to both re-establish and redefine the contours of his or her celebrity persona. In other words, the celebrity acts as a mediated and contested ground between the individual performer and larger media structures; or, as James Lull states in *Media, Communication, and Culture,* "People routinely select and weave mediated, publicly available symbolic representations into the particular cultural condition's discourses" (2000: 174). Given the particularities of representing feminine sexuality in the Bombay film industry, actresses' selections of "publicly available symbolic representations" take on a specific meaning in constructing themselves as sexual beings and celebrities.

The main female lead in Hindi films has often been represented as an idealized woman, and historically her body language, appearance, and behavior as a character coded her status as a heroine within the film. Throughout most of Hindi film history, the heroine could be identified by her dress,[19] her chastity, and her character's inevitable marriage. Traditionally, the virgin's love songs were often filmed as fantasy or dream sequences, where the heroine was "imagined" to be dancing in erotic poses with the hero. As Jyotika Virdi writes, "the song and dance sequences stand in for sex scenes. The focus is particularly on the heroine, the fetishized female sexualized through close attention to her costumes, graceful body movements, and carefully angled shots that heighten scopic pleasure. . . . [she feigns] an unawareness of [her] sexualized body and the camera's voyeuristic gaze" (Virdi 2003: 146). Thus, the virgin could be (and often was) cast in an eroticized light, but it was rare that the actress directly communicated the sexuality of the character to the audience.

Unlike the virgin, the vamp is a trope in Hindi films that occupies a more complex and difficult discursive location, both within the diegetic space of the narrative and the culture at large. As with the virgin, key markers in dress, status, and behavior code for her position, however, she was often the only female character with the sole and exclusive right to exhibit physical pleasure and desire directly to the audience.[20] She was rarely a heroine, or even a secondary character, and usually appeared in the film for one or two of what were (and are still) euphemistically referred to as "item," or cabaret songs. Helen, the best-known vamp of the 1960s, typified these sexual markers: "not so much the 'wicked' woman as the 'naughty,' sexually alluring, immodest one, coded by her erotic and nimbly performed dance numbers. . . . Located in the public sphere, in the world of men, she [was] somehow bereft of a man of her own. Desired by all, yet loved by none . . . within the pleasures and dangers of a liminal but exciting nightlife, the role enacted . . . is that of the 'bad,' undomesticated woman" (Virdi 2003: 168). Because of the frequent casting of the vamp as a cabaret girl, as a character she could also afford the audience member a site of "double viewership": the audience member could reasonably claim to be observing the film audience that was watching her, thus removing the actress twice from the audience.[21]

However, Karen Gabriel observes the gradual disappearance of the vamp as a separate character from Hindi films. "The emergence of a new media environment in the late eighties in India impacted directly on sexual imagination and possible sexual practices, in bringing images of different lifestyles, kinds of relationships, and ways of representing and managing these" (2002: 59). The coding of the vamp/virgin binary has not disappeared entirely from Bollywood films; rather, aspects of the vamp have been incorporated in the presentation of the character of the heroine. Today, women who play vamps in Bollywood films must more actively negotiate the nexus between their film roles and the presentation of their personal lives.[22] In the section that follows, we outline different strategies of sexual presentation by two "vamps" in the Hindi film industry, one former and one current: Priyanka Chopra and Mallika Sherawat.

Negotiating Sexuality

To unpack the trajectory of the celebrity status of "item girls," we examined some print media outlets, such as *Bombay Times, Filmfare,* and *India Today.* While we pay attention to the biographies celebrity journalism has produced for Chopra and Sherawat, in the case of the former we examine how she re-authors her persona while with the latter we highlight her strategic embrace of a rebellious sexuality.

First Encounter

Asambhav, starring Priyanka Chopra as a nightclub singer who falls in love with an Indian soldier played by Arjun Rampal, opened in 2004.[23] The two protagonists work together to bring the terrorists to justice: this includes Chopra performing in several "cabaret" scenes at the club, assorted miscreants being shot, beaten, or tortured for their knowledge of the president's whereabouts. To provide an aura of the glossy, cosmopolitan style we alluded to earlier, the film includes a nightclub scene with a young white woman, whose purpose in the diegetic space is only to add Western "glamour," since she neither understands the conversations in Hindi that take place around her nor contributes in any other manner to the narrative movement.[24]

Chopra's dance numbers in the film are memorable and striking, particularly because of her attire. During one of the songs, "Koi Aayega," Chopra twirls in a glittery red gown, cut high to reveal her legs. She is next shown in a green chiffon bra and skirt that highlights the (presumably fake) tattoo on her back.

Chopra at this time was recognized as being a borderline A-list/B-list actress, but these days is steadily entrenching herself safely in the ranks of A-list. The films that Chopra starred in at the beginning of her career coded her as a vamp, and scenes such as the one we outlined above reinforce this characterization. In order to ascend to a position of influence within the Hindi film industry, Chopra has been engaging in a process of re-authoring her persona through other media outlets—primarily in her interviews with newspapers and magazines. By using the circularity of the Indian mediascape, Chopra demonstrates an implicit understanding of the vexed confluence of her public presentation and her screen persona, and the necessity of using already existing outlets of surveillance in order to construct an acceptable image of her sexuality—a new image that both utilizes and disavows her sexual desire. Richard Dyer contends that "the powerfully, inescapably present, always-already-signifying nature of star images more often than not creates problems in the construction of character. . . . What analysis is concerned to do is to discover . . . where the contradictions are articulated . . . and to attempt to see what possible sources of 'masking' or 'pseudo-unification' the film offers" (1979: 129–31). In the case of Chopra, the opposite can be argued: that the inescapably present nature of her former character image presented, to herself at least, a concrete problem in the construction of her star image, and that the key lies in observing how she uses new vehicles of celebrity construction to "pseudo-unify" the meeting point between the sexuality of her characters and the sexuality of her real being.

"I Can't See Myself Kissing On Screen Anymore"

Chopra, who catapulted her film career by starring in sexualized roles like her character in *Asambhav*, has publicly declared her determination to no longer "expose."[25] In a January 2005 interview with *Bombay Times,* Chopra asserted her new identity as a modest woman: "I hate the 'sexy seductress/sizzling' tags I have. 'Sizzle' for an actor is great but for people to think that you can only look sexy and not be an actress is very annoying" ("I Don't Know How to Act," January 10, 2005). She echoed these sentiments in a *Filmfare* interview: "I will not kiss or expose from now on. . . . Yes, I did wear shorts and swimming costume in *Andaaz*, my debut film. . . . [But] I realize that I'd never be comfortable wearing those costumes again. Nor can I see myself kissing on screen. Not any more" ("I Can't See Myself Kissing on Screen Anymore," January 2005).

Regarding the film *Aitraaz*, in which she played a seductress out to ruin her employee's life when he rejects her sexual advances, Chopra emphatically asserted that her choice to remain modest was not compromised. (*Aitraaz* was released in January 2005. It is based on the 1994 Hollywood film, *Disclosure.*) "I made the decision even before I accepted *Aitraaz*. If you've seen the film, you'll notice there is no uncalled-for exposure. . . . Nor is there more than the required intimacy" (*Filmfare,* January 2005). In April 2005, *Filmfare* held their annual screen awards and Chopra was awarded "Best Performance in a Villainous Role" for *Aitraaz*. In her acceptance speech she stated that "*Aitraaz* was challenging because I didn't just play a bad girl, I played a sexually aggressive character. . . . This character is the absolute antithesis of what I stand for. I'm a very emotional person; I'm not in the least bit aggressive. . . . The most difficult part was lending the character a certain dignity. My biggest fear was that I shouldn't come across as a cheap woman. . . . That said, Sonia is not a character I empathize with. I will never play a sexually deprived woman again. I do not wish to be typecast as some kind of sex kitten. Right now, I'm happy playing the stereotyped Hindi film heroine, because that can be equally challenging" (emphasis added, *Filmfare* 2005). Thus, despite having been through the "phase" of making sexy films, Chopra positions herself here as having emerged with her innocence, graciousness, and virtue intact.

The implication is that one can play the vamp for a while, without it becoming a permanent part of oneself—but only provided that the actress in question makes the transition in a timely manner.

It is noteworthy that Chopra, in a December 2004 interview with *Film-fare* prior to the release of *Aitraaz*, stated that women like her character in *Aitraaz* don't exist in India, explaining that "I don't think such things happen in our country, because women are brought up on different values in our culture." This instance offers an excellent vantage point to examine the re-authoring of persona: having been brought up in Australia, Chopra has adopted a strangely proprietary air toward Indian "culture" in describing both her role and the possibility of Indian women identifying with her in *Aitraaz*, inserting herself into a discourse that may or may not have been familiar to her prior to her entry into the Indian media world.[26] It is clear that she was elaborating on what *she perceived* to be a commonly held attitude toward women's sexuality—one is either a pure woman or a whore. At the same time, having made the decision to act in several films that would technically put her in the "whore" category, Chopra actively utilized the media outlets at hand to mark the boundary between herself as an individual and the roles she plays.

Her place in the existing mediascape requires Chopra to straddle a constantly shifting boundary. Even more striking is Chopra's insistence in her December 2004 *Filmfare* interview that "you can't blame, negate, or praise anybody for [exposing]. I think an actress like Mallika Sherawat has a lot of guts. I would never be able to talk the way she does." Chopra does not have the option, in the panoptic media ecology she inhabits, to openly condemn actresses whose "sizzling" demeanor she has often been linked with. By vacillating between implicit condemnation and overt endorsement, Chopra is able to publicly reconcile her public persona as "sexy" with her supposedly inherent gentleness and girlishness—but her ambivalence has the effect of silencing what could be a slowly opening discourse over women's sexuality—in effect, flattening the terrain of other actresses' possible choices.[27]

Chopra's choices of roles and career are strategies of self-surveillance as she continues to work her way from successful B-list actress to powerful A-list actress. In this context, other media outlets, such as magazines, television interviews, and newspapers, become the vehicles by which women like Chopra negotiate the vagaries and potential pitfalls of constructing their personal sexuality. Richard Dyer describes the construction of the celebrity character as such: "Stars . . . collapse this distinction between the actor's authenticity and the authentication of the character [he or she] is playing. . . . The star phenomenon orchestrates the whole set of problems inherent in the common-place metaphor of life-as-theater, role-playing, etc., and stars do this because they are known as performers, since what is interesting about them is not the character they have constructed . . . but rather the business of constructing/performing/being a 'character'" (emphasis added: 21). Having begun her career as a vamp actress, Chopra is in a process of re-authoring her biography and persona as a fundamentally "gentle" person, feminine, and somewhat childlike in her attachment to her parents. In much the same way that old Hindi films constructed "item" dance numbers as club performances in order to place the ownership of the voyeuristic gaze upon the diegetic audience in the film, so Chopra has constructed her film roles as more performative than innate —she has painted her "real" personality as markedly different from her previous screen roles, thus making it possible for her to distance herself from those roles and secure more "virtuous" film roles for the future.[28]

Sisterhood Is Powerful (?): Mallika Sherawat and Embracing Sexuality

The popular news magazine *India Today* devoted a January 2005 issue to India's youth, with the magazine cover proclaiming: "What They Think, Do, and Want to Be." The magazine covered a range of issues regarding youths' attitudes toward careers, family, sexuality, and entertainment. In an essay contributed by Mallika Sherawat entitled "Come On India, Let's Be Honest," the actress asserts: "[Things] are changing so fast. Our elders didn't have the world thrust in their face by satellite TV and the Internet, with Western icons telling us how we should dress, dance, and get off with each other. Every culture influences the other today and we are fast becoming citizens of the world. I am sorry, I like being someone who is found attractive not only by the young Indian, but by young people everywhere. I take that back. I am not apologizing. I am entitled to it" (115).

Sherawat, who actively identifies as a member of the Hindu Jat, or farmer caste, started her career as a model in Delhi. Her birth name is Reema Lamba, which she shed when she came to Bombay to start her film career. Her most well-known film to date, released in May 2004, is *Murder*, which was loosely based on the 2002 Hollywood film, *Unfaithful*. Sherawat plays a wife who is unfaithful to her husband, and then plots with her lover to have him murdered. The film garnered much public attention for its explicit sex scenes and suggestive song-and-dance numbers. In a May 2004 interview with *Filmfare*, when asked whether she was comfortable with her image as a highly sexual woman, Sherawat responded as such: "I would just like to ask you one question: If a chemical drug like Viagra is accepted by society and by the world to ignite desire, then what is the problem with my audio-visual drug called cinema which ignites desire? Both are doing the same thing!" When later asked whether other Indian actresses are too conservative, although Sherawat equivocated in much the same way as Chopra with regard to judging her peers, she did not appear to be implicitly condemning them: "I think that more than the actresses, the whole image of this so-called sati-savitri is unnatural . . . [but] I am no one to talk about other actresses. I am just talking about myself, the way I want to live, and I think I have made my choice" (emphasis added: "In 'Murder' It Goes Much Further Than Kissing!": May 2004).

It is particularly striking that Sherawat seems to have such a grasp on the nature of representations of femininity in Hindi films—her invocation of the traditional Hindu image of virtuous womanhood, a sati-savitri, or literally "woman of eternal sacrifice"[29] superficially echoes Chopra's own statement that "women are brought up on different values in our culture." However, the implications of each actress's statements are wildly different—while Chopra means to assume the mantle of virtuous Indian womanhood by denying the existence of an aggressive sexuality in Indian women, Sherawat positions herself as openly dismissive of such a willfully blind attitude: "Why was *Murder* such a controversial film? Do you think married women are not having affairs in India?" (*India Today* 2005: 115). In addition, she explicitly states her choice, her agency, in assuming the image of an aggressive sexual presence in the May interview with *Filmfare*, and makes it clear to the reader that she is aware of the implications of her decision: "I would rather be an outsider than be a conformist. Because to conform is to die."

On many counts Sherawat's determination to be honest is admirable, as is her grasp of the machinery behind the construction of the virgin/vamp dichotomy in Hindi films. However, in spite of her bravura in the face of such public judgment, Sherawat also displays a kind of vulnerability in her "sex-bomb" status: "I don't mind jokes or pranks per se, because I have a good sense of humor, but when any joke crosses its line of decency and ends up humiliating me, then that hurts" (*Filmfare*, May 2004). For her to recognize the secondary status that her films accord her and to still actively seek such roles and defend her decision to play them speaks of an admirable courage. In many ways, her career decisions are resistive, at least on a personal level.

Resistance versus Transformation

The question remains whether her personally constructed image of sexual bravura and daring is truly transformative in a larger sense—whether Sherawat's personal questioning of the authenticity of the "stereotyped Hindi film heroine" has translated into transgressive or intelligent film roles. Sherawat clearly has a keen understanding of the demands of the global media ecology—that the choices offered to the consumer in a competitive media industry compel the entertainer to put forth a product that can also compete with the other offerings on the market. Nevertheless, her acceptance of such market forces has led to a startling lack of self-awareness with regard to her own roles and public persona, despite her insightful understanding of the construction of other celebrity and film personas. As Srimati Basu so astutely observes, "Transgression may be negated through speaking—by bringing certain forms of sexual behavior into discourse, one may render them 'docile' by defining and regulating them, incorporating them into the ideologies of dominant discourse" (2001: 185). Sherawat proves herself capable of underscoring the absurdities of one discourse—the discourse that states that Indian women should be docile, modest, and self-sacrificing—but not the other discourse of voyeuristic, heteronormative pleasure that informs the first one. The roles she plays are that of the "immoral" seductress who is inevitably punished at the end of the film—an odd reworking of the very "vamp" stereotype that Sherawat publicly disavows.

Richard Dyer relates his analysis of the "star" persona to Herbert Marcuse's attack on popular culture in a way that is most illuminating of this particular situation. Marcuse maintains that in contemporary society creativity has been reduced to the role of maintaining the status quo: "the vamp, the national hero, the beatnik, the neurotic housewife, the gangster, the star, the charismatic tycoon . . . are no longer images of another way of life but rather freaks or types of the same life, serving as an affirmation rather than negation of the established order" (1964: 59). In contrast, Dyer asserts that "differences in appearance are not, in a visual medium, necessarily superficial, and stars need also to be seen in the context of their roles and their filmic presentation. Examination of stars' images reveals complexity, contradiction, and difference" (1979: 13–14). For Sherawat, recognition of one discourse's implications requires the ignoring of another. Despite her appropriation of the persona of an open-minded provocateur, her films are based not upon active exploration of sexual politics or even the power dynamics at play in sexual imagery, but on empty titillation. Ultimately her filmic presentation is rife with stereotypes about the "tragic vamp" character in Hindi films. These contradictions do not allow for a smooth transition from personal image to public persona.[30]

Despite the ringing call to honesty in Sherawat's essay for *India Today*, she ultimately reinforces and reproduces the same images of a heteronormative, fetishized female body—her strategy of "embracing sexuality" fails to take note of the element of coercion inherent in producing an eroticized body for physical commodification. Undeniably, there is a seductive and potentially transformative possibility in embracing these images as an individual—particularly in exploring the erotic components at play in creating such power-laden images.[31] Nonetheless, Sherawat's tactical negotiations do not represent an informed, complex understanding of the power relations at work in commodifying female sexuality, or a knowing, self-aware embrace of fetishization that could transform the fetishized image's content and symbolic meaning. Rather, hers is a strategy that, while somewhat agentive, is also reproductive of the very discourses of power and knowledge that Sherawat exhorts other Indians to liberate themselves from. In attempting to disentangle herself from the virgin/vamp dichotomy, she has instead only further lodged herself in the Indian mediascape's patriarchical codings of women's sexuality.

Using/Being Used by the Gaze

Actresses in the Bollywood mediascape internalize and make organic the panoptic gaze of the industry they inhabit, and as a result, must draw together the strands of various contradictory and hybrid sexual expectations.[32] In this new globalized media, women are expected to "move" the media product through selling a fetishized, eroticized packaging of female heterosexual desire, but must also demonstrate a coy disavowal of this desire and its implications in order to advance to the ranks of top-tier actresses. Thus, the rigorous disciplining of public responses necessary for reconciling these conflicting dictates results in a kind of sexual ambivalence among these celebrities, an ambivalence that translates into a narrative schizophrenia in their self-presentation.

Christopher Pinney's insightful observation underscores the point: "'Cultural agency implies a much wider field of symbiotic flows in which it is impossible to identify stable interests" (2001: 19). If, as Pinney argues earlier, "desires and aspirations are mediated through—and articulated by—cultural strategies and idioms which necessarily imply the apportionment of power" (16), then these actresses' struggle to maintain a level of success and name-recognition implies an abdication of agency, even as it affords momentary instances of transgression. Even that which appears to be transgressive—filmic demonstrations of sexual desire, public declarations of sexual self-acceptance—is subverted in order to advance or protect the actress's celebrity status.

Ultimately, the slippages we have described in our readings of Priyanka Chopra and Mallika Sherawat are evident throughout the media industry as symptoms of the globalization process. The rapidity of the changes in the Indian media industry place all women in the odd position of both highlighting and denying their own sexuality, but without the private sphere that allowed Indian women celebrities room for negotiations and transgressive behavior. If the media outlets have become more vigilant, so too have the actresses. When the gaze is directed inward, the field for boundary events and transformative agency is narrowed and the public discourse surrounding women's sexuality is circumscribed as well.

NOTES

1. The word "Bollywood" is considered problematic within the Hindi film industry (see Prasad, in this volume). There are many members of the Indian media world who find the term offensive and condescending in its implication that Hindi films are mere replicas of Hollywood movies. However, as Tejaswini Ganti notes, "'Bollywood'—a tongue-in-cheek term created by the English-language press in India in the late 1970s—has now become the dominant global term to refer to the prolific and box-office oriented Hindi language film industry located in Bombay. The Oxford English Dictionary has had an entry for the term since 2001" (2004: 2). Given the word's ubiquity and recognizability, we will be using it throughout this chapter.

2. Appadurai uses the term mediascape to "refer both to the distribution of the electronic capabilities to produce and disseminate information . . . and to the images of the world created by these media" (35).

3. The *New York Times*'s review of the 2004 film *Veer-Zaara* describes the confusion that many newcomers to Bollywood feel upon encountering the genre's idioms: "[American] moviegoers, [may] find the Indian film industry's tastes a little over the top, may not be able to get past cinematic device . . . shamefully obvious, but over-the-top is part of the fun. In Bollywood, a single musical number can move through a dozen different settings with as many glamorous wardrobe changes" ("Lovers Sing in the Rain (and Elsewhere)," *New York Times*: November 13, 2004).

4. See John E. McGrath's study (2004) of reality television shows for an effective analysis of media surveillance and agency in bounded mediascapes: "Such radical potentials for behavior under surveillance, while they may indicate paths towards agency, do not imply a voluntaristic relation to the effects of surveillance . . . active engagement in surveillance practices . . . by women is less a choice than an inevitable result of the shaky relations of these subject positions to the certainties of the symbolic" (89).

5. Laura Mulvey describes this fetishism as "the most semiotic of perversions, screening and shielding by means of an object that is, unavoidably, also a sign of loss and substitution . . . invested in an acknowledgement of its artifice" (1999: 319). Although the fetishization of the female body in Bollywood films may partially represent loss as Mulvey describes it, it also seems to me that on the part of the audience there is also a kind of pleasure in these films that cuts deeper than a mere substitution for "real sex"—the act of viewership itself is enjoyable. There are several authors who criticize Mulvey's construction of the "male gaze" for being overly simplistic and ignoring the ways in which women themselves consume and absorb sexualized media images. For an excellent criticism, see Shohini Ghosh's essay, "Looking in Horror and Fascination (2005: 34).

6. David Page and William Crawley's study of satellite television, *Satellites over South Asia*, offers an excellent description of this phenomenon: "The new popular satellite channels have been powerful agents of a new consumerism. . . . [They] appeal to the viewer as a consumer in a liberalized Indian economy where personal choice has become a new ideology" (2001: 141).

7. See Henry Jenkins: "Media convergence is more than simply a digital revolution; it involves the introduction of a much broader array of new media technologies that enable consumers to . . . recirculate media content. Media convergence is more than simply a technological shift; it alters the relationship among existing technologies, industries, markets, genres, and audiences" (2004: 116).

8. See Sreberny-Mohammadi's essay, "The Global and the Local": "One other basic shift that the global flow of mediated products and the establishment of culture industries in the Third World creates, is that documented by Horkheimer and Adorno toward consumption of mass-mediated culture. That is culture, from being local lived experience becomes media product, with the implicit danger that what is not reflected on television no longer has cultural worth" (2000: 352).

9. Patriarchy refers to the social, cultural, and material structures by which a male, heterosexual way of being is privileged.

10. See William Mazzarella's critique of this process of globalization: "In the new dispensation, Indian consumers were supposedly no longer members of a merely national market; rather, they were graduating to membership of a globally interlinked series of segments" (2003: 262).

11. It is possible to understand this as a disappearance of "safe spaces" for actresses in which to make autonomous or at least semi-autonomous decisions in experiencing sex and relationships; even activities conducted within the realm of the private sphere have come under the purview of media surveillance.

12. See Bhabha and what he terms the "the stylistics of connivance" (1994: 145).

13. See Bartky's seminal essay, "Foucault, Femininity, and the Modernization of Patriarchical Power" for an analysis of Foucault's panopticon in the context of modern women's practices of embodying femininity through regulating their bodies and sexual behavior, such as wearing makeup, dieting, and choice of clothing.

14. Foucault illuminates the problems with anti-repressive hypotheses of power quite wittily: "These conditions explain the fact that 'anti-repressive' discourse would be a genre that circulates so obstinately between university auditorium and analytic couch" (1978: 160). Sue Scott and Stevi Jackson elaborate: "Although Foucault himself pays little attention to gender and regards the regulation of women's sexuality as only one form among many, feminists have found much in his work useful. In particular, it allows us to see female sexuality as constructed and reconstructed in complex and often contradictory ways, rather than as simply being repressed" (1996: 9).

15. This refers to "exposure," the term given to the showing of flesh or wearing of skimpy costumes in Bollywood films; "a specific code of clothes, body, and body language" (Dwyer 2001: 267).

16. As Jyotika Virdi states in *The Cinematic ImagiNation*: "As actors they perform—directed by male fantasies and patriarchical values. . . . Star texts—the lives of film stars occupying public space and knowledge—are useful counterpoints to constructions in film narratives" (2003: 61).

17. P. David Marshall has an excellent analysis of this process in his chapter, "The Cinematic Apparatus and the Construction of the Film Celebrity," in *Celebrity and Power: Fame in Contemporary Culture*: "The activity of creating a celebrity from film involves coordinating the reading of the star by the audience outside the film. . . . it is the solving by the audience of the enigma of the star's personality that helps formulate the celebrity: the audience wants to know the authentic nature of the star behind the screen . . . [however,] the relationship that the audience builds with the film celebrity is configured through a tension between the possibility and impossibility of knowing the authentic individual" (1997: 89–90).

18. This kind of speculation is usually the fodder of tabloid magazines, but it is important to remember that those media outlets, along with television shows and music videos, represent precisely the ongoing nature of celebrity construction on the part of the actor. See Maureen Orth's assertion in *The Importance of Being Famous*: "In the celebrity-industrial complex, reinvention and transformation are games and, increasingly, no one is noticing just how radical these transformations are becoming" (2004: 68). I particularly like Orth's connection between capital and global forces and the shaping of celebrity.

19. Before marriage the heroine usually sported *salwaar-kameezes*, a combination of leggings and a long tunic; after marriage, *saris*, a 6-yard draped cloth with blouse and petticoat, as a mark of her status as both "womanly" and "adult" (Dwyer 2000: 185).

20. "In the glory days of Bindu and Helen, the vamps were the only screen women who were allowed to wear shocking costumes, gyrate erotically, drink whiskey" (Mehta 2004: 363). See also Moorti (2003: 355–76).

21. Asha Kasbekar describes this phenomenon as such: "[Any] erotic voyeurism on the part of the film spectator is disavowed by the deliberate mediation of the diegetic spectator, who is determined as the true owner of the voyeuristic gaze. . . . it allows erotic contemplation of the female body but simultaneously disavows any prurient intention" (2001: 306).

22. See Katherine Frank's ethnography of American strip clubs (2002): "Perhaps it is time to begin exploring the context and meanings of different kinds of visibilities, especially those that are commodified. . . . How are different voyeuristic practices situated within broader discourses and understandings of identities, relationships, and consumption?" (31).

23. Subtitled as "The Impossible," the film documents the soldier's attempts to shield the president of India from Pakistani terrorists—terrorists who finance the nightclub where Chopra's character performs.

24. Transnational flows of media are such that the appearance of non-Indians as extras in Bollywood films has become *de rigueur*: "No longer are India and the West presented as antithetical or constituting a binary. . . . Visually, east and west have melded into the liminal migratory space of the diaspora. The Other or alterity appears . . . only as a spectatorial backdrop against which a global Indian identity is performed" (Moorti 2005). Apparently the majority of *Asambhav* was filmed in Switzerland.

25. Chopra starred in her first film in 2003, the hit *Andaaz*. In it, as in her subsequent films, she made a name for herself through her revealing costumes and highly suggestive dances. It appears that she is currently attempting to publicly disavow her decisions to act in those films in favor of more "traditional" roles.

26. Winner of the Miss India and Miss World titles (in 1999 and 2000, respectively), Chopra was raised in Australia, and was entered into the Miss India

pageant on a whim by her mother and brother. As she described it in the 2005 interview with *Bombay Times*, "The Miss India contest was not planned. I was studying for my [engineering] board exams. My brother, along with my mother, sent in my pictures on the quiet. . . . From high school I went directly to Miss India." She describes herself in that interview as "childish in some ways. . . . I need my mom with me all the time."

27. After the initial writing of this piece, we discovered an article authored by Chopra in the December 2005 issue of *Filmfare* in which she discussed her attachment to the color pink in the "My Obsessions" section of the magazine. (The entire article is devoted to this topic.) It is difficult not to read this statement as a metaphor for Chopra's intended transformation from vamp to respectable (and sexually modest) star: "I remember I used to wear a lot of black and white when I first joined the industry . . . these days, I've stopped wearing black. I find it very dark and I think it doesn't go with my personality. It's pink all the way now." Chopra then goes on to describe her mother and younger brother's reactions to her pink obsession, ending with this thought: "When you say pink, the first word that comes to my mind is feminine. Hearts . . . baby pink dresses. I'm very fond of babies, especially girls, and I love to see them in frilly pink dresses. They look so cute!" The implication is clear: Chopra is painting herself as an innocent daughter and sister who is demure, sweet, and loving—and no longer the sophisticate who wore black.

28. See Beroze Gandhy and Rosie Thomas's essay on star personae, "Three Indian Film Stars": "They do not simply transgress: stars are represented as finely balancing their transgressions with personifications of ideal behavior especially . . . in the domains of sexuality" (1991: 125).

29. The mythological underpinnings of this ideal can be traced to the Indian epic, *Ramayana*, and the virtue of its main female character, Sita. Ironically, *Ramayana* itself was made into a spectacularly popular Indian television serial for the government-run channel Doordashan in the 1980s. In describing the construction of Sita's femininity and sexuality for the television, Purnima Mankekar states that "the television serial *Ramayan* depicted Sita as the epitome of Indian Womanhood by focusing on her chastity, passivity, fidelity to her husband and his clan, and, most importantly, her forbearance. The serial characterized Sita as a devoted wife (a *sati*) rather than a powerful woman (*shakti*)" (1999: 210). It seems that Sherawat is drawing upon popular images of sexuality in Indian media—and recognizes the deep embeddedness of that imagery in history and mythology.

30. A helpful way of conceptualizing the problematic nexus between character and persona can be culled from Appadurai's observation that modernity is "irregularly self-conscious and unevenly experienced" (1996: 3).

31. In his work *Saint Foucault: Towards a Gay Hagiography*, David Halperin articulates this use of power with regard to sadomasochism in a way that is quite illuminating for the purposes at hand: "As we have seen, sadomasochistic eroticism

uses 'discipline' strategically not only to produce effects of intense pleasure but also in order to disarticulate personal identity and to disrupt the order of the self on which the normalization of the modern subject depends. . . . [it] can be understood as 'the purposeful art of a freedom perceived as a power game'" (1995: 111). The same could be said of a *conscious* exploration of the erotic possibilities implicit in the fetishizing of the female body in Bollywood films; however, we are reluctant to read the actions of either Sherawat or Chopra in this way.

32. See "Public Modernity in India": "[Public culture] is that space between domestic life and projects of the nation-state—where different social groups . . . constitute their identities by their experience of mass-mediated forms in relation to the practices of everyday life" (Appadurai and Breckenridge 1995: 4–5).

BIBLIOGRAPHY

Appadurai, A. 1996. *Modernity at Large: Cultural Dimensions of Globalization.* Minneapolis: University of Minnesota Press.

Appadurai, A., and C. Breckenridge. 1995. "Public Modernity in India." In *Consuming Modernity*, ed. Breckenridge, 1–17. Delhi: Oxford University Press.

Bartky, S. 1988. "Foucault, Femininity, and the Modernization of Patriarchical Power." In *Feminism and Foucault: Reflections on Resistance*, ed. I. Diamond and L. Quinby, 61–86. Boston: Northeastern University Press.

Basu, S. 2001. "The Blunt Cutting-Edge: The Construction of Sexuality in the Bengali 'Feminist' Magazine Sanada." *Feminist Media Studies* 1 (2): 178–96.

Bhabha, H. K. 1994. *The Location of Culture.* London: Routledge.

Cunningham, S., and E. Jacka. 1996. *Australian Television and International Mediascapes.* Melbourne: Cambridge University Press.

Dwyer, R. 2001. "Shooting Stars: The Indian Film Magazine, *Stardust.*" In *Pleasure and the Nation: The History, Politics, and Consumption of Public Culture in India*, ed. C. Penney and R. Dwyer, 247–85. New Delhi: Oxford University Press.

Dwyer, R. 2000. "Bombay Ishtyle." In *Fashion Cultures: Theories, Explorations, and Analysis*, ed. S. Bruzzi and G. P. Church, 178–90. New York: Routledge.

Dyer, R. 1979. *Stars.* London: British Film Institute Publishing.

Foucault, M. 1978. "Schizo-Culture: Infantile Sexuality." In *Foucault Live: Interviews 1961–1984*, ed. S. Lotringer, 154–67. New York: Semiotext(e).

Foucault, M. 1977. *Discipline and Punish.* New York: Random House.

Frank, K. 2002. *G-strings and Sympathy: Strip Club Regulars and Male Desire.* Durham, N.C.: Duke University Press.

Gabriel, K. 2002. *Translating Desire: The Politics of Gender and Culture in India.* New Delhi: Katha.

Gandhy, B., and R. Thomas. 1991. "Three Indian Film Stars." In *Home Is Where the*

Heart Is: Studies in Melodrama and the Women's Films, ed. C. Gledhill, 21–147. London: British Film Institute Publishing.

Ganti, T. 2004. *Bollywood: A Guidebook to Popular Hindi Cinema*. New York: Routledge.

Ghosh, S. 2005. "Looking in Horror and Fascination: Sex, Violence, and Spectatorship in India." In *Sexuality, Gender and Rights: Exploring Theory and Practice in South and Southeast Asia*, ed. G. Misra and R. Chandiramani, 29–46. Thousand Oaks, Calif.: Sage.

Halperin, D. M. 1995. *Saint Foucault: Towards a Gay Hagiography*. New York: Oxford University Press.

Harvey, D. 1990. *The Condition of Postmodernity*. Malden, Mass.: Blackwell.

Jenkins, H. 2004. "Pop Cosmopolitanism: Mapping Cultural Flows in an Age of Media Convergence." In *Globalization: Culture and Education in the New Millennium*, ed. M. M. Suàrez-Orozco and D. B. Qin-Hilliard, 114–40. Berkeley: University of California Press.

Kasbekar, A. 2001. "Hidden Pleasures: Negotiating the Myth of the Female Ideal in Popular Hindi Cinema." In *Pleasure and the Nation: The History, Politics, and Consumption of Public Culture in India*, ed. C. Penney and R. Dwyer, 286–308. New Delhi: Oxford University Press.

Lull, James. 2000. *Media, Communication and Culture*. New York: Columbia University Press.

Mankekar, P. 1999. *Screening Culture, Viewing Politics: An Ethnography of Television, Womanhood, and Nation in Postcolonial India*. Durham, N.C.: Duke University Press.

Marcuse, H. 1964. *One-Dimensional Man*. Boston: Beacon.

Marshall, P. D. 1997. *Celebrity and Power: Fame in Contemporary Culture*. Minneapolis: University of Minnesota Press.

Mazzarella, W. 2003. *Shovelling Dmoke: Advertising and Globalization in Contemporary India*. Durham, N.C.: Duke University Press.

McGrath, J. E. 2004. *Loving Big Brother: Performance, Privacy, and Surveillance Space*. New York: Routledge.

Mehta, S. 2004. *Maximum City: Bombay Lost and Found*. New York: Alfred A. Knopf.

Moorti, S. 2003. "Desperately Seeking an Identity: Diasporic Cinema and the Articulation of Transnational Kinship." *International Journal of Cultural Studies* 6 (3): 355–76.

Moorti, S. 2005. "Uses of the Diaspora: Indian Popular Culture and the NRI Dilemma." *South Asian Popular Culture* 3 (1): 49–62.

Mulvey, L. 1999. "Cosmetics and Abjection: Cindy Sherman, 1977–1987." In M *Feminism and Cultural Studies*, ed. M. Schiach, 319–32. New York: Oxford University Press.

Naregal, V. 2004. "Bollywood and Indian Cinema: Changing Contexts and Articulations of National Cultural Desire." In *The SAGE Handbook of Media Studies*, ed. J. D. H. Downing et al., 517–540. Thousand Oaks, Calif.: Sage.

Orth, M. 2004. *The Importance of Being Famous: Behind the Scenes of the Celebrity-Industrial Complex.* New York: Henry Holt.

Page, D., and W. Crawley. 2001. *Satellites over South Asia.* Thousand Oaks, Calif.: Sage.

Pinney, C. 2001. "Public, Popular, and Other Cultures." In *Pleasure and the Nation: The History, Politics, and Consumption of Public Culture in India*, ed. C. Pinney and R. Dwyer, 1–34. New Delhi: Oxford University Press.

Scott, S., and S. Jackson. 1996. "Sexual Skirmishes and Feminist Factions: Twenty-five Years of Debate on Women and Sexuality." In *Feminism and Sexuality*, ed. S. Scott and S. Jackson, 1–34. New York: Columbia University Press.

Sherawat, M. 2005. "Come on India, Be Honest." *India Today* 115, January 31.

Sreberny-Mohammadi, A. 2000. "The Global and the Local in International Communications." In *The Anthropology of Media*, ed. K. Askew and R. R. Wilk, 337–56. Malden, Mass.: Blackwell.

Virdi, J. 2003. *The Cinematic Imagination: Indian Popular Films as Social History.* New Brunswick, N.J.: Rutgers University Press.

Chapter 11

||||||||||||||||||||||||||||||||||||||||||||||||||||

Songs from the Heart

Musical Coding, Emotional Sentiment, and Transnational Sonic Identity in India's Popular Film Music

Natalie Sarrazin

The Hindi expression *dil se* (from the heart) is a common refrain found in film dialogues, titles, and song lyrics that captures the essence of Hindi popular film melodrama and its music. Dramatically, Indian cinema is long known for its dependence on melodrama as a primary vehicle of expression. Abounding in romantic sentiment and agonizing situations, Hindi film's melodrama is a well-discussed phenomenon, where over-emotive acting and emotional subjectivity dominate plot lines, characterizations, staging, dialogue, scenes, and songs.[1] Musically, Indian cinema is differentiated from other world cinemas due to its enthusiastic inclusion of film songs, with five to seven in each film, and their extra-cinematic popularity as the top-selling, independent popular music genre in South Asia.

In this chapter, I identify some common traditional and contemporary musical film song codes and their relation to melodrama, exploring how emotion and sentiments such as love are created and intensified through sound. In what ways does film music construct and exhibit aural representations of "heart"? How have Western aesthetics altered Indian film music expectations? What is the impact of the transnational environment on musical and visual representations of sentiment? I also identify recent changes in film song sounds and codes for ways in which music engenders "heart" to negotiate a new sonic Indian identity in a global context.

"From the Heart"

According to Dissanayke, the term melodrama, derived from the Greek word song, means a romantic and sentimental play that contains songs and music deemed appropriate for enhancing the situations presented on stage (Dissanayake 1993: 1). Although the term *dil se* or "heart" must be understood within the context of Indian cinematic melodrama that makes "all interiority exterior" (Dwyer 2000: 150), there is a difference between decoding all emotion as melodrama and understanding it as cultural sentiment. Song lyrics are certainly one logical and rich source for cultural and emotional analysis, but few expressive mediums convey more information than that of sound, where centuries of historical and cultural resonance can be embedded in a single pitch, melody, rhythmic cycle, and most specifically vocal and instrumental timbres. Film songs, therefore, are in unique positions to aurally illustrate cultural concepts such as emotion and "heart" to their audiences, relying on pre-composed concepts of emotional sentiment and common codes of musical understanding.

From *Purab aur Paschim* (1970) to *Swades* (2004) and beyond, dozens of films have villified the West for its lack of "heart" by cinematically reinforcing a selfless, loving, giving India with songs and dialogues that construct notions of proper Indian identity and values. In the opening monologue of Subhash Ghai's *Pardes* (1997), for example, Non-resident Indian (NRI) Kishorilal (Amrish Puri), upon returning to India from the United States: "Today, my India may have something to offer [the world] or not, but she has one thing in abundance, and that is love. In the US, love means give and take, but in India, it means give, give, give!"

This message ties into one of the primary expectations of heartfelt expression—which is the sincerity with which the message is delivered. The value of Kishorilal's invocation is his conviction and passion that sets the tone for the remainder of the film. In this context, "heart," conflated with the idea of love and giving selflessly, is understood metaphorically to include a sense of generosity, sacrifice, and renunciation—qualities associated with a nationalistic, feminized notion of long-suffering, Mother India (Mishra 2002: 83). This metaphor is extended further in the song "I Love my India" in which India is framed as the singer's homeland and beloved, and where the world is a bride, and India is the *bindi* (jewel) on her forehead. The remainder of the soundtrack follows suit with songs that blur the lines between the passionate love of lovers and passionate love of country and that are laced with the appropriate nationalistic or romantic sincerity.

"Heart" also implies having the capacity to emote—a function well suited to the expressive medium of music in general and singing in particular. Musically, principally in Indian classical music, voice is privileged as its sound is associated with the most fundamental human expressive characteristics. Cinematically, the embodied voice is one of the most powerful forces to transmit and elicit emotion. In addition, the ability to emote on screen conveys substantial character information to the audience. The act of performing a song is a reflection of the moral value of the characters themselves as well as the emotional content being conveyed. It implies the proper ethics and behavior, upstanding values, goodness, and the embodiment of Indian ideals as a hero or heroine.[2] Celluloid villains, for example, are never given license to sing, prohibiting the characters from crucial access to a mode of expression that fully humanizes them. Heroes and heroines, on the other hand, are required to emote through song, and what they are required to emote is the accepted constructs of love.

"Heart" also denotes emotion or sentiment in general (*rasa*). Raghavan states that for the audience '. . .the essential thing in poetry or drama is not story and character as such, but the emotion that they embody. . . . The emotional interest of a work centers on certain primary sentiments felt by all human beings' (1988: 264–65). Emotionally, Hindi cinema's melodies are in a prime position to exploit this central idea of *rasa* as well as to embody the performative aspects of "heart." Many film songs are either *raga* based or are pseudo-*ragas*,[3] which explore sentiments contained in the cultural associations of that *raga*. A composition in *sringar rasa*, therefore, may reverberate among knowledgeable listeners, conferring essential extra-musical aesthetics based in Indian historical codes. Even if a *raga* per se is unrecognizable by name by the audience, the visual coding and familiarity with romantic tales and couples will clue them in to their proper response.[4] The actor's on-screen performance contributes as well to the emotion-enhancing aspect of the song, as his or her emotions are perceived to emerge spontaneously from the heart. Indeed, the seemingly impulsive outbreak into song self-reinforces the concept in that the character is moved by strong emotion.

An intriguing example of this musico-emotional display can be found in Mani Ratnam's *Dil Se* (1997), with music by A. R. Rahman. The film itself is a vehicle through which central aspects of *sringar rasa* are examined. Each of the film songs represent the subtleties of love, such as obsession, desire, etc., and each song in the film incrementally marks the protagonist's total surrender to the emotion, ending in his ultimate sacrifice at the film's culmination.

Given its contemporary usage in films, "heart," emotion, and love seemed to be perceived as uniquely Indian constructs. And given a strong cultural background that intertwines sound and emotion, music as a medium is used to convey this primary emotional expression, where the vehicle of the song and the singing of the song converge to amplify the emotional experience for the audience. It is a form of identity that carries cachet, can be negotiated, and can contain transformative powers for the listener, as I will discuss further below.

Codes

As with all film, Indian cinema relies heavily on cultural, dramatic, and emotional codes to resonate the traditional and familiar. In a Hindi film, the act of a man putting *sindur* on a woman's forehead, for example, requires no further explication to an Indian audience that the couple was now married. Musical and cultural signifiers make film songs and sound powerful indicators of Indian identity by including indigenous musical aesthetics such as vocal timbres, *talas* and *ragas*, instruments, forms such as *ghazal*, *bhangra*, etc., familiar to its audiences.

In film picturizations, music is intensified through its conjunction with visual imagery as musical codes cement the relationship between sound and filmic image.[5] While some codes are traditional, others are either newly created or reinforced through duplication in other films or they combine aspects of both. The cultural, dramatic, and emotional codes described below provide common examples found in films. Even without the aid of visuals, musical film codes convey cultural, emotional, and dramatic information. The sound of a single instrument such as the *shehnai*, for example, is enough to transmit the proper associations to the viewer. As a musical cultural code, the sound of the oboe-like double-reed instrument *shehnai* has rich cultural connotations. Its sound is associated with processions and royal court ensembles. Its auspicious nature and association with royalty extends itself to the groom on his wedding day, and is used in marriage celebrations. For example, in the song "Kabhi, Kabhie" (Sometimes, 1976, by the film of the same name) sung by Mukesh and Lata Mangeshkar, the sound of the instrument is subtly placed but indicates a powerful symbol of the couple's relationship. Two-thirds of the way through the song, the two phrases "as the *shehnai* plays along the way" and "it is my wedding night and I am lifting your veil" occurs with the *shehnai* literally playing in between the two lines. By inserting this *shehnai* in this location, the sound not only underscores the idea of "marriage" by its mere presence and timbre, but it actually connects or "marries" the two lines together in a rather literal or concrete way as it metaphorically marries the on-screen couple. These interstitial timbres and instrumentation are certainly not accidental, and occur frequently in film song accompaniments to illustrate exactly such symbolic points.

Cultural codes can also be resignified over time depending on the film and audience. As more films reach international audiences, sounds take on new meanings. For example, in the song "Aaye ho meri zindagi mein" from Dharmesh Darshan's *Raja Hindustani* (1996), the sound of the *shehnai* remains intact as a traditional code in that it signifies a wedding. However, a few measures later, a sitar is heard as the camera shows a line of village girls carrying water pots on their head. In this instance, the Indian classical instrument, which normally symbolizes Indian tradition writ large, is extended to symbolize traditional tropes in general, including Indian village life.

Musical dramatic codes are used to affect the audience's interpretation of the drama itself. These can enhance mood, suspense, and action. In the case of Kamal Amrohi's *Pakeezah* (1971), music is used to illustrate the quick passage of time through use of a musical *raga* montage. The *tawaif* singer is in musical training, and in addition to a series of visual cuts, the music itself progresses through at least half a dozen *ragas* in just a few minutes. The exact indication of time is not given, but the viewer understands that many years have passed. In addition, the use of *raga* itself implicates the classical nature of the learning, enhancing the historical dimensions and time period for the viewer.

Given the propensity for conveying "heart" in Hindi film, emotional codes reign supreme. Some of the oldest and most prominent emotional codes in Indian cinema are found in the romantic films, most notably in the song duets. Love songs are associated with the predominant *rasa sringar*, which embodies love-in-union and love-in-separation with shades of erotic or romantic sentiment. The popularity of the romantic film genre relies on emotional love codes, which can embody associations with traditional Indian couples such as Radha and Krishna but also with romantic couples such as Romeo and Juliet.[6] Boy meets girl, falls in love, is separated, and then reunites is the basic foundation of the romantic film genre for both Indian and western romantic films.[7]

Love songs, either solos or duets,[8] are cinematically almost entirely corporeal and embodied for maximum emotional impact—that is, the camera frames the singer. Film love songs also intensify the couple's on-screen intimacy and are coded as private (either sung by hero or heroine or both) rather than communal or public, despite the context or number of people that might be included in the frame. Traditionally, a film's first half is dedicated to the private world of the lovers, and the second half to removing obstacles regarding caste, love marriage, family, class and/or religious difference, as well as familial reconciliation (Dwyer 2000: 163).

Visually, the couple is always alone, highlighting both intimacy and commitment. Although complicated by consumerist and material culture and tourist spectacle (i.e., travel to exotic locations, product placement), the duet retains traditional imagery and emotional resonances in which hero and heroine behaviors are reminiscent of the playfulness of Holi and Krishna's episodes with the *gopi*s (milkmaids). Duet imagery made popular by directors such as Yash Chopra often includes pastoral settings, nature, lush fields, and flowers. Nature and fruit symbolically show a woman's fertility and/or the man's desire for children (Dwyer 2000: 114). Cinematographically, a long shot and panoramic view capture the lovers in fields of flowers or vegetation, by oceans, waterfalls, and in other sensual "natural" settings.

The shot from above is important, as height or a rising up plays a role in establishing almost a sacred or mythic transcendence for the couple. The visual metaphor of rising or height is associated with the rising sentiments of the couple. Visual accompaniments in nature set the couple upon hilltops, ridges of mountains, along gorges, or climbing rocks at the seashore. The actor's movements augment the freedom and intensity of the moment, often with a long shot of the heroine running through blooming fields with the end of her sari or *dupatta* (scarf) flowing in the breeze. In urban settings, they are on top of buildings or, as in the case of *Dil Chahta Hai*, in a helicopter captured by crane shot above Sydney.

The sudden, rising orchestral violin "flourish" is the single most pervasive iconic musical sound pattern used across films to accompany the idea of height and frame the intimate love song. Found in the introduction of the love song, this prominent upward flourish of the violins is encoded to indicate *sringar rasa*, and can introduce the idea of budding romance or intimate romantic union.

The musical flourish coupled with visual images of height is familiar fare in Hollywood romances. But the rising violin motif or museme (musically representational meaning) used in Indian popular film has long outlived and out-impacted codes of other types. The swirling, upward flourish was in regular use by Raj Kapoor's *Sangam* (1964), although its heyday was in the 1960s–1980s.

The flourish's placement in the film also acts as a dramatic code in that it is usually most evident as the opening strains of a love song or as a cue to indicate an upcoming song. However, as the preponderant string section fades with newer, lighter musical styles, the flourish can also be found buried in the orchestration of a verse or refrain or may be eclipsed almost immediately by other melodies.

The isolated nature of these musical, visual, and dramatic codes indicates that the couple is occupying a fantasy world unto themselves. Rarely do others appear in the shot, and the wide vistas, cinematographic long shots, and relative freedom of restraint from onlookers, and especially from the eyes of disapproving relatives, returns the association to the music itself. The violin flourish, therefore, connotes this particular type of romantic freedom, and sets up the ensuing song content to indicate romantic anticipation and its temporary abandonment of social strictures in lieu of private romantic expression. This is an important emotional moment in Hindi film songs, and particularly important for an audience in which such private moments with a lover are difficult to achieve even in contemporary society.[9] The songs also tie into the historical snapshots of the *ragamala* paintings, Radha and Krishna moments in which the frame excludes outsiders and the lovers are prominent and isolated and free to express their relationship. Thus, despite the "love marriage" implication in such songs, Radha and Krishna nuances provide traditional, historical precedent for the social acceptability for such display. Because this code can be read as both traditional and modern, its popularity is guaranteed continuity.

Although still prevalent, this code is sometimes used only as an acknowledgment of the longstanding musical tradition. However, many of the more recent love songs have dispensed with the string flourish and rely only on the visual rising to refer to this love code.

Emotional and Narrative Intensification

Film songs not only introduce the audience to the proper emotion by which to respond, but also intensify that emotional experience through use of familiar and new or established visual codes. Songs can, however, further intensify emotions by subverting the film's narrative by repositioning the viewer's understanding of the temporal flow and trajectories of the storyline and its possible outcomes. Although a full examination of Hindi film music and narrative is beyond the scope of this chapter, a few points are worth mentioning here in terms of this emotional intensification. Songs have always been sites for flashback, memory, and spatial and temporal disjunctions in films (Gopalan 2002: 129). In the context of a film narrative's flow, songs are capable of transforming the narrative by manipulating the audience's perception of the story's trajectory. For example, Aditya Chopra's (1995) *Dilwale Dulhania Le Jayenge*, with music by the team Jatin-Lalit, was a surprise hit among NRIs and resident Indians alike. The film contains seven songs, three of which provide moments for this type of narrative transformation.

In the first song, "Meri khwabon hai," the heroine divulges dreams of her future husband to her mother. Desirable and appropriate shots of the film's hero are then interjected into her emotional fantasy, making the audience privy to the specific images of her future partner, while she herself is not. This scene provides the possible but most likely narrative trajectory of inevitable union, intensified by her unawareness of her own future.

During another number later in the film in which the couple is separated ("Na Jaane Mere"), the hero abandons the heroine at the train station without any indication of his return. The song is filled with flashbacks to important moments of the relationship, revealing images now colored by the belief that she will never again see her lover. It is by experiencing emotional turmoil in separation that the heroine ultimately realizes that she is in love. However, narrative tension is retained in that the heroine returns home and agrees to an arranged marriage to someone else to appease her traditional father.

The final revisiting of the relationship takes place when the hero returns to her. His sound lures the heroine from her parents' home, and they meet surreptitiously in a field. This duet represents the capitulation, during which scenes from the relationship are again replayed but this time are coded with images of the heroine as a "proper" Indian female wearing a sari, hence indicating her upcoming role as a proper Indian wife. This song "Tujhe Dekha" provides the audience with the assurance of their eventual union. Recontextualization, or shifting the narrative frame through song, provides opportunities for the viewer to re-experience alternative aspects of the plot through different emotional lenses, creating temporary but crucial tensions in the process.

Signature Sounds: Old and New

As I have previously discussed, Hindi film's traditional, signature sound as used in the love code flourish relied almost exclusively on the large string orchestra, which became the normative sound in post-Independent India (Arnold 1991: 166). Orchestral strings, associated with melodrama, underscores dialogues and songs highlighting the music drama in order to evince specific traditional emotions from audiences. For decades, film soundtracks relied on codes or, as some might say, clichés that seemed resistant to change. Despite being known for its eclecticism, such as film composers' Shankar-Jaikishan's use of South American rhythms of rumba and cha-cha in 1950s Raj Kapoor films or R. D. Burman's use of electric guitar or bongos in the 1970s (Arnold 1988), Hindi film songs seemed reluctant to add new instruments or alter the song form or structure in any appreciable way. Until the 1990s, film song composers relied on one major type of orchestration—the full orchestra, replete with large string section that lent the type of melodramatic soundtrack reminiscent of Western romantic stage and screen. Other types of orchestration occasionally used might include Indian traditional instruments, either folk or classical. While swooping, full-orchestral sound in the background score helped to propel the melodrama in the dialogues, for the listener, their impact on song accompaniments was mixed. The heavy orchestral sound continues to function as a melo-dramatic code, prompting the listener to disregard or overlook its musical intricacies somewhat, thus casting more attention on lyrics and the melody.

Contemporary music directors such as A. R. Rahman, Anu Malik, Shankar-Ehsaan-Loy, and Himesh Reshammiya have radically changed the core nature of this traditionally orchestral sound. In addition, these composers have resignified the traditional codes or dispensed with them altogether, thereby altering the expectations of delineation of "Indianness" in both domestic and exported films.

Contemporary Sound and the New Exoticism

Currently, Hindi film music straddles two worlds—traditional and contemporary, or rather national-oriented versus diasporic-oriented—and there are parallel musical soundtracks composed to accompany each of them. Many composers, although fewer and fewer, still incorporate the large orchestral sound and older codes in their film compositions. However, in films made during the 1990s and early 2000s, dramatic changes in orchestration began to vary the musical texture. Changes include increased experimentation with timbral colors including vocal timbres, choral harmony, and vocal ostinatos. Explicit instrumental codes associated with particular cultures and meanings were always incorporated, such as rhythms from rock, trance dance, disco, *bhangra*, *ras garba*, hip-hop, cha-cha, rumba, and classical *talas*. But an extended cultural worldview and its aesthetics means that the shakuhachi and West African drum ensemble now replace the once exotic Western electric guitar, saxophone, or even bongos. Melodies may or may not be *raga* derived, but music directors such as A. R. Rahman, Anu Malik, and others add chords and bass lines and other musical devices that not only allude to functional harmony, as was the case several decades ago (Manuel 1988), but are based on functional harmony. Interestingly, the classical drone, which is left out of the film song almost entirely since its inception, is now back, albeit in a modified form. Drone is reinterpreted and then reintroduced usually in the form of an ostinato pattern. This is one of the only examples of a "reincarnated" traditional sound added back into the Hindi film soundtrack rather than subtracted from the contemporary soundscape.

Nonlyrical song vocalizations (such as "ah," "oo," or vocables) in film songs have also increased, adding meaning through timbre, pitch, and melody rather than text. During the first interlude section of "Jane Kyom" from Farhan Akhtar's *Dil Chahta Hai* (2001), for example, music directors Shankar-Ehsaan-Loy add a thickly layered orchestration incorporating a didgeridoo, harmony, rock beat, and three different types of vocalizations. The first is a male vocal drone that is interspliced with the sound of helicopter blades that take the couple up over Sidney (rising code) while female soloist and mixed chorus imitate an American gospel/light jazz sound respectively.

The assimilation of Western aesthetics and Indian codes is commonplace from the technological standpoint as well. Inclusion of electronic and digitized sounds reinforced rhythmic tracks and bass lines pump up film soundtracks, and are even further pumped up in dance re-mixes of film soundtracks that inevitably follow. Global genres of Goan trance and pop *bhangra*, Punjabi folk music transformed in London, New York, and Delhi discos and sampled in hip-hop, are now soundtrack staples.

The contemporary, instrumentally "lighter" sound contains not only highly westernized, digitized, and synthesized sounds but use of world music sounds instruments as well as an increased use of regional Indian sounds. Ironically, the heightened presence of global sounds and music video filming and editing techniques are balanced by an increased use of local musics and references. The "discovery" and inclusion of specific, lo-cal Indian styles and sounds such as Malayalam choral singing from South India along with world beat sounds render the local as an exotic or for-eign element. This "new exoticism" is a result of the changing aesthetics of Hindi film sound, taking on the Western ideas of dabbling in intriguing world music, even if those sounds come from within India itself.

Playback Authenticity and Timbre

Playback singing is still a mainstay in Indian films, despite increased au-thenticity in other areas of the industry. Indian audiences seem to take little issue with it, and are able to minimize the discrepancy between the split between image and sound. For over 50 years, playback singer Lata Mangeshkar embodied the ideal in Indian femininity with a voice that emerged from screen heroines regardless of age.

Throughout the 1990s, fuller female timbres became more common-place, but were related to specific character types. Initially, this fuller vo-cal female sound was equated with a villager or folk/tribal woman whose sound was distinctly different from the heroine's. This folk/tribal timber had a throatier, rougher, richer quality, sometimes with an accent that ap-proximates specific local dialects that evoke lower castes and class. Vis-ually, she is pictured as a slightly older woman drawing her authority from resemblance to a familiar elder such as an aunt or older sister-in-law (*bhabhi*), but her jaded, aggressive, and sexualized demeanor strongly suggest a powerful negative figure of mother-in-law or *dakan* (witch) in-voking low caste, magic, and prophesy. A second female or tribal singer may be present in the picturization as well. Her sound typically mediates that of the first singer's, as can be seen in *Raja Hindustani*'s "Pardesi." This second female singer is deliberately identified with the heroine as her voice approximates the heroine's timbre and she often sings lyrics that express the subconscious thoughts of the heroine—those that would be unacceptable for her to sing herself. Such timbral changes mediated the still innocent, very Indianized sound of the female playback singer for international consumption.

Newer singers, however, must negotiate between recent transnational aesthetic demands, while maintaining the girl-like vocal quality that transmits the traditional notion of *sharam* or shyness still essential to the heroine's cultured, upper-caste character. Lata's legacy is still recognizable in the high tessitura and transparency of the upper registers. However, recently there is a suggestion of timbral fullness in the lower tessitura, a little warmer sound with more vibrato that indicates a capacity to exude much more feeling, which is often timbrally related to the sound stylings of Western pop singers.

One of the most dramatic changes found in films aimed at the international market, however, is that the traditional embodied voice of the hero or heroine is often substituted with the embodied voice-over, where the actor no longer lip-syncs to the vocal soundtrack. This perhaps is an acknowledgment of the cultural unacceptability of the technique of lip-synching in particular and the song sequence in general outside of Indian cinema. Directors such as Mani Ratnam take another step toward closing the gap between Bollywood and Hollywood by using the song as a non-diegetic background similar to that of a pop song soundtrack.

Musical Heart on a Transnational Stage

Within India itself, codes must be mutable to audiences from vastly different regions, cultures, and languages. It is not surprising, therefore, that these same codes can be read by NRIs and their children who have tenuous ties with India, or even for foreign viewers who have little knowledge of Indian traditional culture. In addition to the familiarity of the film musical and romantic couple as discussed above, the depth of emotional transference is also essential.

Music codes and songs not only embody specific cultural meaning and are capable of channeling emotional outpouring, but music can also perform as an agent of character metamorphosis stemming from deep sources of sensitivity and feeling to display India's true "heart" and humanity. This revelatory effect is, as I have argued, implicit in the act of singing the song, but is most obviously evident in the following examples from films produced for an international, diasporic audience.

In Asutosh Gowariker's *Swades* (2004) with music by A. R. Rahman, for example, music acts as a caste, cultural, and transnational leveler. In the first song, Shahrukh Khan (SRK) picks up a *sadhu* (holy man) while on his way to find his old nanny in a remote village. The larger context is that SRK is an NRI who works for NASA and, while living in "sterile" America, longs for his Indian roots and past, hence the desire to immigrate his nanny to the United States. In this first song, "Yun hi chala chal" (Go on, O traveler) SRK is driving his oversized luxury camper along dirt roads as the song begins. The *sadhu* sits beside him. A quick visual cut to the radio and SRK's fingers tapping on the steering wheel indicate that the song is emanating from the radio itself. The instrumentation is a simple clapping pattern along with a stringed-instrument-pitched sound somewhere in between a guitar and sitar. This deliberately noncommittal timbre indicates a vaguely Indian classical music sound that is then further coded (but not clarified) by indistinguishable vocables reminiscent of Indian classical *sargam*. As SRK grooves to the music, the *sadhu*, while listening, becomes increasingly absorbed by the sound. He literally and figuratively lets his hair down, and begins singing along with SRK. The playback singer, however, does not change from the *sadhu* to SRK, so the two are literally singing the song using the same voice. This opening is followed by electric bass, drum set, and the guitar, coalescing into a light jazz slightly funk style into which the *sadhu* can also enter. In this one musical moment, both men from two worlds are subsumed in the subtly Indian yet highly Western musical soundtrack.

With larger numbers of Indians living abroad and the escalating exchange of monetary remittance, cultural ideas, and material products, Indians at home are increasingly exposed to Western aesthetics. Even though the earlier dichotomous paradigm of traditional/India/good and modern/West/bad remains intact, there is a subtle shift. The premise of *Swades*, for example, contrasts India's warm, comforting, nurturing, colorful culture against the cold, alienated, steel-and-glass world of the United States. However, there is a perceptible change in emphasis from the protagonist's typical socially oriented and communal role to a more internal, psychological realm. The conflict can be resolved only by the hero's personal decision after a lengthy heart and soul searching reflected in correlated musical examples throughout the film.

Another example of personal transformation depicted through sound comes from Deepa Mehta's film *Bollywood/Hollywood* (2002), in which a Westernized and very independent Indian hero meets a woman whom he assumes to be of non-Indian origin. He coaches her to pass as an Indian in order to deceive his parents and avoid marriage, teaching her about Indian food, behavior, and linguistic customs. It is not until she sings an Indian song at a party, however, that we have full and final confirmation of her "Indian-ness." The song also melts the cynical hero's attitude toward love and marriage, revealing his true Indian heart.

In Nagesh Kukunoor's *Bollywood Calling* (2001), a third-rate American actor who is dying of lymphoma is brought to India to star in a film. Needless to say, the film includes what the actor concludes to be superficial melodramatic acting and song-and-dance numbers at which he initially balks but learns to embrace fully and with total abandon as he submits to the deeply seeded emotional heart that he holds within him. In other words, through song, he gets in touch with his "Indian" self. Upon his return to the United States, he sings one of the film's songs on the lawn of his ex-wife's house in the middle of the night to woo her back.

Dil Chahta Hai contains a powerful example that represents a cross-cultural recognition of musical heart. The film's heroine takes the hero to see an opera. Initially, he ridicules its vocal timbre and performance aesthetics—the over-emotive acting style in particular. Slowly, however, he begins to recognize the strong themes of love and sacrifice presented in the performance and is overwhelmed by them. Making a cultural connection between emotions allows him to transcend and erase divisions between the heroine and himself that existed.

In all of these cases, singing not only occurs, but "song" becomes a critical symbol of humanity as a crucial agent for personal transformation. Singing elicits an awakening of the protagonist's emotions displayed through song, and the performance itself transmits and relates various types of NRIs, Indians, and westerners to core values of love, family, and Indian identity.

Conclusion

The Indian diaspora in the last part of the twentieth century and beginning of the twenty-first has resulted in significant cross-cultural exchange, including both musical and film sensibilities and aesthetics. One of the most revealing facts about Hindi cinema is that, despite global flows, still nearly every film, regardless of genre, contains song-and-dance sequences. The ubiquity of the *masala* phenomenon assures that film music was and continues to be the most popular form of popular music in India, and that music remains one of the core identifiers of Indian identity in transnational space.

With the advent and quickening pace of globalization, transnational movement of NRIs between Europe/United States and India, the contrast between what is inherently "Indian" about the popular film music sound and what is foreign becomes a place of contestation and negotiation. Recent Hindi film song structure has begun to absorb outside musical aesthetics, increasing musical blendings and fusions from composers in the past decade creating the sonic appearance of a westernized sound available for Indian domestic and diasporic consumption. Cinema and its music help to define, with intense emotional clarity, ways in which Indians identify themselves or choose to separate themselves from other cultures.

Film music, at its most basic level, is used to create culturally meaningful codes that ensure emotional intensity for the audience while stretching to sustain traditional values for one type of audience as it satisfied the exotic curiosity of another. It is through codes that India's self-perception emotionally and culturally can be shared through song, and song is valued for its transformative ability. Song in this context functions as a particular type of universal emotional language, on the basis of an understanding of shared human emotions in addition to particular musical structures and forms that allow for transnational audiences to share symbolically in varying images of India. Additionally, music is capable of co-opting and exploiting film codes and conventions by subsuming and transforming the narrative itself to sustain and even convey values and sentiments of heart to all audiences. Music acts to "humanize" the West. If India cannot conquer the world culturally, economically, or spiritually, at least it can demonstrate on the silver screen that it has the market cornered on emotionality, love, and selflessness—qualities that it is willing and capable of sharing through music.

NOTES

1. See Prasad (1998); Wimal Dissanayake, *Melodrama and Asian Cinema*, Cambridge: Cambridge University Press, 2005; and Thomas (1995) for further discussion on this topic.

2. In rare cases such as the film *Baazigar* (1993), this promise is breached in that the hero, SRK, sings but is of immoral and low character in the film.

3. By pseudo-raga, I mean a melody that might indicate a *raga*-based composition that does not follow all of the strict rules of *raga* delineation.

4. For further discussion of the use of *raga* in Hindi film, see Morcom (2001).

5. According to Creekmur, the Hindi film song is served by the image and not the other, way around. Pamela Robertson Wojcik, and Arthur Knight, eds. *Soundtrack Available: Essays on Film and Popular Music*, Durham, N.C.: Duke University Press, 2001.

6. See "Tales of Love" in Dwyer (2000), 8–57.

7. For a more detailed exploration of this topic, see my forthcoming article in *Popular Music*.

8. Although they are referred to as duets, ironically, the hero and heroine almost never sing together, but alternate verses or phrases, thus musically reinforcing the cultural separation of genders.

9. In the new Shipra Mall in Delhi, for example, lovers wishing to remain somewhat out of view of the public eye occupy the benches on the very top floor.

BIBLIOGRAPHY

Arnold, A. 1988. "Popular Film Song in India: A Case for Mass-Market Musical Eclecticism." *Popular Music* 7 (2): 177–88.

——. 1991. *Hindi Filmi Git: On the History of Indian Popular Music*. Ann Arbor, Mich.: University Microfilms International. Ph.D. dissertation, University of Illinois at Urbana-Champaign.

Dissanayake, Wimal. 1993. "The Concepts of Evil and Social Order in Indian Melodrama: An Evolving Dialectic." In *Melodrama and Asian Cinema*, ed. W. Dissanayake, 189–204. Cambridge: Cambridge University Press.

Dwyer, Rachel. 2000. *All You Want Is Money, All You Need Is Love: Sex and Romance in Modern India*. London: Cassell.

Gopalan, Lalitha. 2002. *Cinema of Interruptions: Action Genres in Contemporary Indian Cinema*. London: British Film Institute.

Hogan, Patrick. 2003. "Rasa Theory and Dharma Theory: From the Home and the World to Bandit Queen." *Quarterly Review of Film and Video* 20: 37–52.

Manuel, Peter. 1988. "South Asia." In *Popular Musics of the Non-Western World*. London: Oxford University Press.

Mishra, V. 2002. "The Texts of Mother India." In *Bollywood Cinema: Temples of Desire*, 61–87. New York: Routledge.

Morcom, Anna. 2001. "An Understanding between Bollywood and Hollywood? The Meaning of Hollywood-style Music in Hindi Films." *British Journal of Ethnomusicology* 10/I, pp. 63–84.

Prasad, M. Madhava. 1998. *Ideology of the Hindi Film: A Historical Construction.* Delhi: Oxford University PRess.

Raghavan, V. 1988. "Aesthetics: Theory and Practice." In *Sources of Indian Tradition,* 2nd ed., ed. A. Embree, 264–73. New York: Columbia University Press.

Thomas, Rosie. 1995. "Melodrama and the Negotiation of Morality in Mainstream Hindi Film." In *Consuming Modernity: Public Culture in a South Asian World,* ed. Carol Breckenridge, 157–82. Minneapolis: University of Minnesota Press.

Vasudevan, Ravi. 1989. "The Melodramatic Mode and Commercial Hindi Cinema." *Screen* 30 (3): 29–50.

Part III

Beyond Film
Stars, Fans, and Participatory Culture

Chapter 12

IIIIIIIIIIIIIIIIIIIIIIIIIIIIIIIIIIIIIIIIIIIIIIIIIIIIII

Deewar/Wall (1975)

Fact, Fiction, and the Making of a Superstar

Jyotika Virdi

Amitabh Bachchan's performance in *Deewar/Wall* (Yash Chopra, 1975), and *Zanjeer/Chain* (Prakash Mehra, 1973) a few years earlier, transformed his initial middle cinema actor status into the now clichéd "angry man" figure, that insignia of his unprecedented stardom in popular Indian cinema. Understanding stardom, particularly Amitabh Bachchan's phenomenal success in the 1970s and 1980s, provided a significant impulse to Indian cinema studies in the late 1980s. His superstar status prompted canonization in more than a handful of scholarly works, and everything from his films and the tumultuous political period to his personal background and unusual physical appearance are configured in calibrating this success.

Acknowledged as a versatile actor playing comic and romantic roles in his early career, it was his rebellious, anti-establishment, hero-of-the-oppressed portrayal, ubiquitously named Vijay (literally meaning victorious), which became enormously popular across the working and middle classes in India and its overseas diaspora, dwarfing other popular stars of the time playing romantic roles that merely challenged the institution of the family (Sharma 1993: 171). *Deewar*, a critical prototype of a 1970s film, has prompted analysis of the iconic hero Bachchan popularized and comparisons to film heroes before and after him, who, to an extent, index continuities and ruptures in cultural flux.

Deewar is a benchmark film providing comparison with and insights into shifts in generic development two decades later in the 1990s, and with its 1950s antecedents. The spate of sophisticated, well-crafted, and successful gangster films, alongside 1960s-style romance films revived in the 1990s, together call for reconsidering the putative absence of genres in Hindi cinema. Exploring in any detail audience and industry shifts in the 1950s, 1970s, and 1990s that account for developing sharper generic conventions differentiating the film product is beyond the scope of this chapter. However, looking for earlier traces of the contemporary gangster film in the 1970s, tracking its novelties, and distinguishing it from 1950s' films such as *Awara* (Raj Kapoor, 1951), *Shri 420* (Raj Kapoor, 1955), or *CID* (Raj Khosla, 1956), can be instructive for understanding genre development and genre cycles, affording insights into cultural shifts manifested in filmic renditions. In this chapter I consider *Deewar* a master text that allows tracing the development of (the gangster) genre in Hindi cinema and the construction of Amitabh Bachchan's superstar status.

Star Text

Richard Dyer's search for Paul Robeson's cross-over appeal among white audiences from 1920 to 1945 paradigmatically suggests a conundrum surrounding Amitabh Bachchan: how does an elite ruling-class member become incontrovertibly a working-class hero, appealing to the middle class as well? Many have noted Bachchan's early career in middle cinema as a romantic hero, but that changed after *Zanjeer*, *Deewar*, and then *Sholay* (Ramesh Sippy, 1975), and despite a roller coaster career in the 1990s, he went all the way to being voted the millennial star in BBC's 1999 poll.

Dyer argues the star phenomenon includes everything: the films and publicity about the star's private life—the performance and the person, according to John Ellis (Ellis 1982: 104). Dyer identifies stars as commodities, labor, and the thing labor produces. First, the star is a person, a body, psychology, with skills to manipulate with the help of industry personnel—the director, screen writer, cameraperson, makeup artists, costume designer, publicists, and gossip magazine columnists who produce the image—and second, the star has personhood and a social reality (Dyer 1995: 2–3).

Critics discuss Amitabh Bachchan's unusual physical attributes—a figure of mobilization whose confident body language betrayed his upper-class origins, layering his working-class performance with a swagger that charmed both middle- and working-class audiences. His eyes conveyed the brooding introverted character, a figure of "masochistic fantasy" (Prasad 1998: 150) which together with his laconic dialogue delivered in a baritone voice and controlled body movements encapsulate restrained anger (Chakravarty 1993: 228–29; Mazumdar 2000: 243; Mishra 2002: 128; Prasad 1998: 141). Bachchan himself acknowledges a debt to screen writers Salim Khan and Javed Akhtar, crediting them entirely for *Deewar's* success and admitting a sense of loss after the screenwriter duo split in the 1980s: "I couldn't ever get that kind of intensity again, that power was missing" (Mohamed 2002: 124). Likewise, he acknowledges director Manmohan Desai's role in casting him in films from the late 1970s to the mid-1980s, each one an extraordinary box office success.

In addition to on-screen performance, star phenomenon encompasses the off-screen lives available through publicity material, collapsing the public/private distinction (Dyer 1995: 5–6). Vijay Mishra refers to this parallel text, astutely differentiating fanzines in the Indian context, divided by the cultural power associated with publications in English, the vernacular languages, and the overseas diasporic market that proliferate along with newer venues such as cable television and the Internet. However, contrary to Mishra's claim about the inadequacy of Dyer's and Ellis' models in India where large audience segments are excluded from such media, exposed only to the stars' film repertoire, gossip about stars spills over and circulates well beyond the literate fanzine constituency. Furthermore, though Mishra identifies songs as special to the Indian context, they are arguably easily accommodated in the star's performance along with acting skills—voice, dialogue, and dancing in musical numbers (Mishra 2002: 129–56).

Deewar—Polysemic Text

Yash Chopra's *Deewar* is marked by significant ways in which it articulates the historical moment of its production. The film resonates powerfully with the political turbulence of the early 1970s. *Deewar* is a richly polysemic text, skillfully woven for a heterogeneous audience, offering a range of possible readings. Without claiming to speak for the audience, the varied meanings it makes, or how variegated audiences "shift" the text to fit their own social positioning, I identify different skeins available within the text. Stuart Hall's idea that meaning is neither imposed nor passively accepted, rather, the audience, in some correlation with its own situation, arrives at it by negotiating competing textual strands, is particularly productive (1980: 128–39). *Deewar* simultaneously straddles readings consonant with a family melodrama, an action-thriller, a religious-mythical, and a radical-subversive text. The film's success lies in mobilizing more than one reading, ensuring its broad appeal. At another level the fictional film can be meaningfully read against Amitabh Bachchan's career configured by a film industry, a star system, and their relation to politics, the state, and the nation. This analysis interweaves readings of the text and meta-text.

In *Deewar*, Vijay (Amitabh Bachchan) and Ravi (Shashi Kapoor) are sons of a trade unionist, Anand Verma, who, defeated by management, feels disgraced, abandons his family, and leaves Vijay to grow up acutely aware of, humiliated, and victimized by the calumny his father faced, while raised by his suffering single mother. A dockyard worker, Vijay's fighting spirit propels him to a top underworld position, even as Ravi, his brother, receives an education and becomes a dedicated police officer. Vijay resolves to abandon the underworld when his girlfriend declares she is pregnant, a step meant to end the cycle of sons suffering humiliation because of their fathers. The decision comes too late; Ravi decides to arrest Vijay, who dies when the brothers clash. Ravi wins a police gallantry award and their mother's support, notwithstanding her deep attachment to Vijay.

India's political climate in the 1970s offers a textured backdrop crucial to understanding *Deewar*. Meaning in texts parallels social power, its distribution, and the political struggle for it (Fiske 1987: 255). *Deewar* appeared in 1975, roughly 30 years after independence (1947) in a decade markedly different from the first two post-independence decades. If the 1950s was a period of reconstruction, optimism, and hope, in the 1960s the nation was set back by wars against China (1962) and Pakistan (1965). Although this effectively ratcheted up nationalist fervor, by the late 1960s that dreamy "springtime" after colonial liberation was over (Brennan 1990: 57).

The hegemonic Congress party split in 1967 and the Indira Gandhi-led faction came to power. India successfully intervened on behalf of the Bangladesh liberation movement in the 1971 war between India and Pakistan, further boosting Indira Gandhi's image. However, in 1972–73 events took a sudden downturn: a failed monsoon led to food shortages and price rises aggravated by the influx of Bangladeshi refugees, and the 1973–74 oil shock intensified inflation and unemployment. Extensive state intervention in the economy created opportunities for corruption, spawned a get-rich-quick culture, and widened social disparities. Simultaneously, labor movements in the country gained strength: flashpoints were industrial strikes (like the paralyzing 1974 railway strike) and the student movement responding to J. P. Narayan's Mahatma Gandhi-style anti-corruption call for *Sampooran Kranti* (Total Revolution).

Indira Gandhi resorted to authoritarian politics to strike at labor movements culminating in the 1975 crackdown—the National "Emergency" declaration, lasting 19 months, in which citizens' fundamental rights were suspended and political persecution became the weapon against the opposition. Her attempt to stay in power through a reign of terror was shortsighted: in the 1977 election, after the Emergency was lifted, the Congress Party, which had dominated Indian politics for just under a century, was routed for the first time. The Emergency had set in circulation several stories about political repression, arrests of top figures who had fallen from favor with the ruling Congress. One such story was about the legendary smuggler Haaji Mastaan.

Deewar's narrative interestingly parallels Haaji Mastaan's—a dock worker turned powerful underworld Bombay don, who allegedly singlehandedly tackled a rival gang leader, Bakhia, attacking him in his home. Mastaan, prominent during the Emergency, was arrested under COFEPOSA (Control of Foreign Exchange and Prevention of Smuggling Act) by the Indira Gandhi government. Vijay's rise from a dockyard worker to powerful underworld don in *Deewar* is inspired by Haaji Mastaan's life (Mohamed 2002: 51) and the moment in the film when Vijay enters a rival gangster Samant's house to attack him is compared to Mastaan's attack on Bakhia. The parallel ends here. In the film, Vijay (Mastaan) kills Samant (Bakhia), though the hot-headed Mastaan supposedly had only threatened Bakhia and later went on to become the leader of a small Muslim Majlis Party in Bombay. The veracity of the film's representation is less important than the circulation of such stories about the criminalized political/public sphere.

Deewar deploys melodrama, addressing contemporary discourses within a moral framework: social injustice, state power, criminality, gender, and religion are braided together against the backdrop of early 1970s turmoil. Hall's concept of "negotiating" meaning suggests competing ideological strands struggle for dominance. While the multiplicity of strands open a text to multiple meanings, there are limits—not "any and every interpretation" goes (Gledhill 1988: 74). The range of textual meanings ultimately is circumscribed by historical conditions, codes, genres, and available forms. The film's reception, making meaning of it, is negotiated from particular social locations. Negotiation here implies an active audience reconciling conflicting interests between varied meanings to claim one that is its own.

A prominent strand in the film is the sympathetic representation of the struggling working class with Vijay as its emblematic figure. At the film's outset, in a flashback, Anand *Babu*, Vijay's father, a trade union leader, in a stirring speech reminds striking workers of their fight for education, health care, and housing. In carefully chosen rhetoric he argues that he isn't questioning why the rich have so much, but rather, why the food barrels are empty for the poor, a reference to contemporary food shortages —an artificial scarcity traders created to make an extra buck. Throughout the Emergency, State propaganda claimed to punish public enemies (like grain hoarders) and maintain "law and order," when in fact it strategically ignored unprecedented lawlessness.

Punished for his militancy, Anand Babu is shamed into a life of a defeated vagrant, a humiliation that becomes a driving force in Vijay's life, stamped on him (both literally and metaphorically). The tattoo on his body "my father is a thief," symbolizes Vijay's constant denigration, motivating a deep-seated rage. Writing the trauma on his body, literally branding the hieroglyphics of his oppression, also manifests itself in unerasable memories constituting his subjectivity: "the lines on the palms of one's hand" (fate) and "events impressed upon the mind and heart" (experience) "cannot be wiped out," he says.

Vijay's thinly veiled rage turns into an assertive demand for respect, self-consciously acknowledging his lower-class status and the resentment against it. As a young shoe-shine boy he refuses to accept money "thrown" rather than handed to him; later he flings a brick at the building contractor who humiliates his mother on the job, and as an adult he fights back against Peter—the Mafiosi in the dockyard who extorts *hafta* (protection fee) from all dock workers. His refusal to visit the temple signals his rebellion against religion, with its connotations of a Hindu acceptance of life's circumstances, of fate—the consequence of past life's *karma* (actions).

Life in the dockyard is an exposition of Vijay's strong working-class identity. Rahim, an elderly fellow worker, ponders the working-class condition: "for the past twenty-five years nothing but the workers have changed," he says, referring to *badli* (casual) workers, the flux of expendable migrants exposed to job insecurity and extortion by gangsters. A typical migrant worker sending his village money is killed for refusing to pay his *hafta* contribution. Vijay's solidarity with this defiance antagonizes Peter's men, but Rahim pleads for caution, for watching their step—

as the underprivileged must. Vijay, speaking in the voice of the emerging working-class generation, thunders: "what hasn't happened in twenty-five years will now; another worker is going to refuse the *hafta*." In the ensuing "fight" sequence Vijay single-handedly beats up Peter and his gang. Responding to his mother's fulminations against his bravado, Vijay invokes his father's "cowardice": "Did you want me to hide my face too and run away?" Vijay "externalizes his alienation from the cruel materialist world through anger, action and revenge" (Sharma 1993: 172)—the hallmark of his masculinity in innumerable *Deewar*-like films through which he heroically rewrites his history, circumstance, and destiny.

Unlike Vijay, the working-class figure who "makes it" climbing the underworld ladder, his brother Ravi, a cop, is the quintessential educated lower- and middle-class youth. Disheartened by the long unemployment lines before landing this job he complains, "even the last job won't be available," without "connections." Ravi voices the recognition dawning among disenchanted 1970s' educated youth—their education, degrees, and certification are worthless in a milieu where there just are no jobs. As a boy Ravi runs away from their sidewalk dwelling (the abode of the homeless in India) to gaze longingly at a phalanx of neatly dressed school children as the extra-diegetic music plays a famous nationalist song, "*saare jahaan se achcha, Hindustan hamaara*" (my nation, greatest in this world). This ironic comment, invoking nationalism cross-cut by class division, is further reiterated in the economic gulf that later separates Ravi from his girlfriend, Veera. Romance, of course, transcends their class distance, a difficulty suggested but contained by heterosexual love, Yash Chopra-style (Dwyer 2000: 147–67).

In the film's climactic moment Ravi and Vijay, grown far apart in their ways, meet under the bridge that was once their pavement dwelling, a reminder of shared origins. The extra-diegetic soundtrack replaying "*saare jahaan se achcha . . .*" (my nation . . .) lends a sardonic tone to this momentous meeting. In a charged scene they exchange how their opposing tracks have distanced them, leaving their specific histories, the different *avenues* available to each, unspoken, unsaid. Ravi's shot at getting an education, enabling a police officer's career, is lost in his rhetoric about *adarsh* (ideals) and *asul* (principles).

Class politics, however, hound Ravi. In a "police-encounter" Ravi shoots at a child he later discovers has stolen bread. He visits the child's parents, offers them food, but is rebuffed by the mother, who castigates the police state for protecting "big" criminals, while persecuting petty food theft. Her husband intervenes; silencing her he says, "My wife is uneducated," then waxes, "All stealing, of a cent or a million, is a crime. . . . If the thousands dying of hunger start stealing it'd create an impossible situation." Ravi discovers the man is a teacher by profession and is chastened. Such "common sense" dovetails with the analogy Ravi's boss later draws between law enforcement tackling crime and doctors, cancer. In these contested dialogical voices, arguably, the suggested alliance between education and the state silences—or nearly silences—the dissenting woman.

Her voice, a nagging reminder of deeper contradictions, resonates with Ravi's discovery—his own brother Vijay is a major contraband dealer, the criminal the unnamed woman says the state protects. *Deewar* marshals melodrama's quintessential power to exacerbate conflict by overlaying the public sphere with the force of searing personal emotions. Ravi resolves, in the name of the state and the law, not to protect Vijay and instead demands his signature on a statement confessing his crimes. Vijay protests, reminds Ravi of their past, their humiliating hardships, while Ravi repeatedly admonishes: "Will you sign it or not?" The altercation builds until Vijay declares he will sign the statement, confess his crimes, only if Ravi gets the signature of all those who wrote his humiliation—the ones who made their father sign himself as an outcast, fired their mother, and tattooed his life's ignominy onto his body.

Arguably, *Deewar* is distinct from the other Amitabh Bachchan "angry man" films in that the protagonist's anger is directed against a generalized power network unleashing everyday humiliation against the disenfranchised millions. While it is an individual hero's story, it is not about that hero's revenge against another *individual* industrialist, upper-class, bourgeois member. In all Bachchan films the protagonist rebels, clashes with powerful figures, whether representing state machinery or the criminal underworld. A surprising turn in the 1970s' films is the extent to which criminality is a metaphor for rebellion (Prasad 1998: 155). Fareeduddin Kazmi challenges this popular perception, arguing instead that against a thoroughly corrupted institutional machinery the Bachchan figure stands for vigilante justice, one that Karen Gabriel labels a "mode of masculinity" (Kazmi 1998: 138; Gabriel 2004: 265). The hero, a stand-in for subaltern rebellion, inevitably aligned with the Muslim minority (Kazmi 1998: 139; Mazumdar 2000: 249; Prasad 1998: 142), turns a past trauma, his private pain, and anger into a struggle for social justice, whether working on or against the side of law.

In *Deewar,* the potentially "subversive" rebellion is a stable though carefully contained strand in the film. For instance, the film's ending comes full circle, returning to its beginning—celebrating the trappings of state power. Ravi is receiving the police force's gallantry award, and the narrative unfolding in a flashback (perhaps his mother's memory) builds strong empathy for the lawless Vijay, which only intensifies when he is punished, shot, by his lawful police officer brother. Abruptly cutting back to an audience applauding Ravi for placing loyalty and public duty above the personal, the scene is shot almost like a curtain call at the end of a play, suggesting a make-believe performance. This attempt to impose closure, restore faith in, and valorize state power, its law enforcement, appears feeble, more like strategically appeasing state censorship by offsetting the wealth of sympathy accumulated for Vijay's (anti-state) heroism.

Other strands in the film contest the above reading and struggle to dominate the text. *Deewar* is classifiable as a "social"—a unique Hindi cinema genre, which Indian film critics assign to films with explicit social commentary framed in the melodramatic mode. In *Deewar,* conflicts involving economic and political power intersect family relationships, creating an emotionally charged story about sibling rivalry, Vijay's transgressive love for his mother, his inability to "separate" from her, and above all his pain.

Behind the anger is a body in pain, scarred by memories of a childhood traumatized by violence and loss, typically figured in the absence of one or both parents (Kazmi 1998: 140; Mazumdar 2000: 241). In *Deewar* the scar, literally carved on the body, produces a pain, which in many films becomes the alibi for rebellion/revenge, and finally closure, not uncommonly achieved through death. In *Deewar* it occasions reunion, a "psychic fusion" with his mother, who abandons him despite her excessive love (Sharma 1993: 176). Surrendering in the end to the state, to law, Vijay is well compensated by dying in his mother's lap, a defeat "masking victory," according to Prasad (1998: 150). Here the film is a throwback to the earlier classic, *Mother India* (Mehboob Khan, 1957), to which it is frequently compared, reiterating the powerfully enduring trinity of mother, god, and nation in popular Hindi cinema (Kazmi 1998: 143). The mother, a metaphor for nation and a site of contest, is conferred power and stands for Father's law. Death redeems Vijay's past, reuniting him with the mother, family, and nation (Lal 1998: 239–40; Mazumdar 2000: 246 and 249; Prasad 1998: 149).

A religious-mythic reading is equally plausible, of championing the devout's faith in the victory of uncomplicated good against evil. A sequence establishing Vijay's lack of faith frames him as a boy refusing to enter the temple, always waiting at the bottom of the stairs for his mother and Ravi. Cutting to the temple bells, the next shot, a major ellipsis, reveals a grown Vijay still at those temple steps. Ravi, also grown up, returns with his mother from the temple and symbolically the brothers walk away in opposite directions. They have different trajectories: the "right" one is to the temple and the "wrong" one leading to hell is punished with violent death. But first Vijay is humbled before the Gods he emphatically refused to have faith in.

The prospect of his mother dying challenges his beliefs: returning to the same temple steps, this time he enters, praying to spare his mother from punishment for his sins. She recovers, but in an act of retributive justice, he dies for his *karma*, shot while fleeing the temple. Endorsing the faith of believers, the final act seals the victory of the devout over non-believers in a framework of grand justice beyond the mundane everyday. Resonating with the characters in the epic *Mahabharata*, the mother in *Deewar*, like Kunti, suffers witnessing her son warring with his brothers and then dying in battle. Besides such inter-textual references, the power of faith is paid off in watching Vijay's resistance break down "when all other avenues are closed"—surrendering at the temple, begging for his mother's life.

Like other successful films of its ilk, *Deewar* blends together different genres. Melodrama combines with cops-and-robbers action, and thriller dynamics build on the suspense of heists, chases, fights, and an exposition of the underworld. The episodes are held together in a tight plot that moves swiftly, exploring the intrigue and mystery of dangerous urban spaces. *Deewar* introduced a new 1970s-style masculinity cultivated in Amitabh Bachchan's Vijay: withdrawn, intense, yet revealing a vulnerability that he galvanizes in his lone struggle against oppression. His agency is expressed through spectacular feats, physical strength, an excessive machismo that is as important as his intelligence and wit (Sharma 1993: 177–78).

Since the late 1990s, gangster films like *Satya/Truth* (Ram Gopal Varma, 1998), *Company* (Ram Gopal Varma, 2002), *Maqbool/Possessed* (Vishal Bhardwaj, 2003), and *Ab Tak Chappan/Fifty Six Yet* (Shimit Amin, 2004) have perfected this genre's conventions in the most carefully crafted productions yet produced in the industry. It focuses on tracing the allure and perils of the transnationally connected Bombay underworld, its sadomasochistic contours, which the protagonist negotiates, albeit doomed to self-destruction. Ranjani Mazumdar discusses the psychotic heroes in *Darr/Fear* (Yash Chopra, 1993) and *Baazigar/Gambler* (Burmawalla and Burmawalla, 1993), early figurations of a shift toward this self-destructive excess (Mazumdar 2000: 242). There is an apparent regression in the symbolic embodiment of the hero through the decades: in the 1950s (*Awara*, *CID*, and *Shri 420*) after his temporary descent into criminality, he repents, turns his back on it, hopeful for the future; in the 1970s, after 25 years of independence that hope turned into despair and anger; this was replaced in the 1990s' gangster films with deep cynicism.

Along with a new masculine ideal, *Deewar* makes visible inchoate codes of representing women. The pure, suffering mother and eager-to-please Veera, Ravi's girlfriend, are in sharp contrast to Anita, the heroine, paired with the male lead. Both the female love interests in the film function to support their men, characters whose internal conflicts are privileged. Anita gratefully accepts the otherwise self-enclosed aloof Vijay's confessions, but is bereft of her own narrative telling viewers why she drinks, or is unhappy. Yet emphatically autonomous, she controls her own sexuality, sleeps with a man of her choice without marrying him (striking for a 1970s Hindi film), and when she finds out she is pregnant is confident of raising a child independently—she tells Vijay she will not "force him to marry her." This becomes Vijay's transformative moment, fortifying him to abandon the underworld. Unrepentant, he desires only to not repeat history, inflicting the misery of the same inscription on his "son" (sic)—"his father is a thief." Anita, undoubtedly an unconventional heroine, in a strange narrative twist, is murdered, punished for her sexual transgression, falling back on Hindi cinema's earlier conventions of treating women like Anita, coded "western"/"other" (drinking, smoking, and scantily dressed).

As I have argued, *Deewar's* polysemy is capable of generating multiple meanings, and it is precisely this open-ended quality encompassing strands of family drama, action, religious, social, and political hermeneutic that ensures its appeal to a diverse audience. Anecdotally, I suggest how social situations affect textual reading. While interviewing audiences in a working-class Delhi neighborhood, my informant Mukhtiar, a 17-year-old high school dropout, compared rich-poor screen representations. Mukhtiar himself had worked at odd jobs since he was 13 and at the time was a bus conductor working a punitive 17-hour shift.

For Mukhtiar the screen representation of the arrogant rich and honest but hard-working poor was true to life. Asked if he had encountered upper-class arrogance, he reported the following incident: while working at a gas station, a rich car owner once threw a tip at him. He protested, demanding the customer pick it up and respectfully hand it to him. Surprised, I remarked this is exactly what happens to Vijay as a shoe-shine boy in *Deewar*. Mukhtiar looked embarrassed, admitting remembering the scene immediately after narrating the episode. Mukhtiar's apparent identification with the young boy's experience in *Deewar* outweighs any consideration of the veracity of his narrative.

Star Victim

Deewar not only offers spectator identification of the kind described above, but is a particularly poignant text, even a master text, against which to read Amitabh Bachchan's career celebrated in publicity material felicitating 25 years in the industry and his sixtieth birthday (Somaaya 1999; Mohamed 2002). *Deewar* derives special iconicity as a text read against and in tension with the meta-text of Amitabh Bachchan's spectacular stardom achieved through the role of Vijay he performed in numerous films. Amitabh Bachchan's off-screen life, an actor briefly turned politician in the 1980s, resonates with Vijay's in *Deewar*, holding life and art together in strange tandem. Part of the aura surrounding the Bombay film industry is the wealth amassed by top stars like Bachchan. That these fortunes depend on tax evasion is public knowledge, and speculation in the 1980s abounded about Amitabh Bachchan's wealth. Yet his angry man image and urban proletariat voice, perfected in *Deewar*, was so powerful that when he turned to politics, ostensibly to help Rajiv Gandhi, in 1984 he was voted with an overwhelming majority to Parliament. Rajiv Gandhi, a signifier of hope, was named "Mr. Clean," referring to a record unblemished by corruption charges, a rarity in Indian politics. Many of his close associates, Amitabh Bachchan among them, were refreshing faces in the political scene, and hopes ran high for radical change in national politics.

However, in 1987 national politics was rocked by the Bofors scandal —an arms deal with a Swedish company in which top officials including Rajiv Gandhi, then prime minister, were accused of receiving kickbacks. Amitabh Bachchan's brother, Ajitabh Bachchan, allegedly pocketed a share he deposited in a Swiss bank. Amitabh Bachchan vociferously denied the accusation, claiming victimization by vindictive journalists. He resigned from Parliament in 1987, but in 1991 his victory in a London court vindi-cated the Bachchans, reclaiming the family's honor and loyal "nationalist" image.

These events in Bachchan's life, nearly a decade after *Deewar*, provide an ironic foil to the film's narrative. *Deewar* mobilizes melodrama, mak-ing the family the site of rhetorical "nationalist"/"anti-nationalist" conflict. The mother (read motherland) is torn between two sons—a contraband dealer, Vijay (the lawless anti-nationalist) and Ravi, a police officer (law-ful nationalist)—the kernel of state power. Smuggling, presumed com-plicit with the anti-national and anti-patriotic since colonial rule, signi-fied villainy in Hindi films of the 1970s and 1980s. In Amitabh Bachchan's off-screen life his brother stood accused of illegal paybacks, corruption charges, turning him and by association Amitabh Bachchan into anti-patriotic figures siphoning India's limited foreign exchange into secret Swiss accounts. That their father is Harivansh Rai Bachchan, associate of Nehru's government, and a leading national poet, placed a premium on "family honor," heightening the stakes of their relation to the Indian state. Amitabh Bachchan fought hard and, embittered by his foray into politics, blamed the media for smearing his family's name. It is no coincidence that the family is central to the drama in *Deewar* and other Hindi films: a common ploy is to "throw the domain of kinship morality into crisis" (Thomas 1989: 15).

Juxtaposing "plot points" in Amitabh Bachchan's life with his films and reading them intertextually, or parallel to the film text as Mishra first sug-gested, makes Bachchan's phenomenal stardom a compelling narrative. The publicity material surrounding Bachchan's over-three-decade career, reveals a fascinating star text, etching distinct phases: 1970–74 struggle in a film career; 1975–85 ascent, coupled with a life-threatening accident; 1984–87 foray into politics, dragged down by the Bofors scandal; resigna-tion from Parliament but victory in a libel lawsuit against *Dagens Nyheter* and *India Abroad* in 1991, a day after Rajiv Gandhi's assassination. This was followed by a "sabbatical" that ended in 1995 when he launched Am-itabh Bachchan Corporation Limited (ABCL), an effort to pioneer new corporate management practices in an unregulated industry, which in-stead brought him to the brink of bankruptcy. He turned the company's fortunes around by the new millennium, taking over its management, and cashing in his residual star value on television (hosting a *Who Wants to Be a Millionaire?* variant), grasping for advertising and film contracts to help repay his investors (Somaaya 1999: 237–74; Mohamed 2002: 172–76).

Stunningly, Amitabh Bachchan's own narrative of each segment of his trajectory is told as a story of victimization. During the initial struggle to break into the industry, he bore many slights while courting an already popular star, then Jaya Bhaduri, now his wife of 30-plus years. She claims in his ascendant years he "made it without the press," alluding to a decade-long standoff with the press, whose hostility Bachchan attributes to Indira Gandhi's 1975 Emergency and his own ties with her family (Mohamed 2002: 354). Bachchan's life-threatening accident on the sets in 1982 was followed by diagnosis of rare illness. His entry into politics, at Rajiv Gandhi's behest after Indira Gandhi's assassination, brought on the Bofors arms smear campaign, one he fought off valiantly to clear his family's name. *Dagens Nyehter* paid damages, although he was unsuccessful at making *India Abroad* pay the court's directed £110,000 (approximately $200,000), even after pursuing them in a New York court. Collectively this period conjures memories of battle on several fronts: "illness, politics, media" (2002: 354) and his resignation from Parliament, which Jaya Bachchan bluntly recalls as an admission of defeat (2002: 357). Remembering the same period, Yash Chopra recalls Bachchan's disillusionment with politics: "He withdraws when hurt. Then, he becomes closed and broods" (Somaaya 1999: 128). Chopra's description blurs the actor and his character roles.

In his "darkest days," swindled by his newly launched company's management, he verged on financial collapse. His liabilities, to the tune of $18–20 million, were turned around by taking the company's reins, seizing every job opportunity—hosting a television show that became wildly popular, endorsing products for advertisers, and reinventing himself in film until the success of *Mohabbatein/Many Kinds of Love* (Aditya Chopra, 1999) "resurrected" him financially (Mohamed 2002: 173). Meanwhile, he faced a national furor sparked by ABCL hosting the 1996 Miss World pageant—his vision for India's place in the sun—stepping up in the global entertainment industry, even as he stepped down onto the television small screen.

If the pageant ignited women's opposition from the political right and left in a cacophony of discourses on gender, sexuality, cultural nationalism, and global entrepreneurship, Bachchan emphasizes his own fight to negotiate an international contract showcasing local performance and talent, while dealing with the local state machinery, that in unprecedented fashion singled him out to pay for the police security (Hoad 2004: 56–81; Oza 2001: 1067–95; Parmeswaran 2004: 371–406). At odds with the media's name for him, "Big B," signifying the star, the corporate power, and capital associated with both, Bachchan's personal narrative is curiously one of a constantly picked on "Little b," heroic in the end, but only because he fights back spiritedly, rising phoenix-like to overcome his misfortunes.

A relatively modest but comfortable lifestyle of his childhood is remembered in images of poverty. This from a man whose father was supported by the Indian government through a Ph.D. in Cambridge, held an External Affairs Ministry position, while Amitabh Bachchan himself studied at a private boarding school, spent summers with Nehru's grandsons, Indira Gandhi's sons, Rajiv and Sanjay Gandhi, and counts as his close friends, Amar Singh, Subrata Roy, and Anil Ambani, leading Indian politicians and industrialists, who stood by him through his various trials. Yet this longstanding member of India's ruling class responds to queries about his indiscriminate choice of late 1990s films with candor: his haunting fear, "paranoia" about unemployment, and rejection by the audience and industry: "I don't have the courage to be with only one project at a time. I feel insecure and restless if I am not wanted" (Mohamed 2002: 192, 208).

No doubt the star's body, that combination of talent, skills, physiognomy, and voice, elements that shift with aging, had an unsettling effect on Bachchan's career. Star fortunes are known to be ephemeral, and changing audience tastes, desires, and industry trends can, at any time, make a star's carefully built niche redundant. In the late 1990s, after a five-year hiatus, Bachchan's return to the big screen, forced by desperate financial circumstances, occurred at a time when the industry had morphed —a younger star generation was emerging and romance, which Bachchan had eschewed, was replacing revenge narratives. Bachchan, an aging star playing opposite younger starlets, was savaged by critics and his films were box office hits only after several misses (Mishra 2002: 154). Raakhee, a co-star, astutely observes: "the image had become bigger than the actor," and that this was "his cross" to bear (Somaaya 1999: 91).

Not unlike the generic Vijay in *Deewar* and other films, Amitabh Bachchan himself looks back at his entire career as one of pain, victimization, reportedly with the brooding melancholy that seems as much part of his own persona as the characters he played—and possibly one explanation for his phenomenal success. *Deewar*, for instance, won awards in every category for that year, but Bachchan recalls being passed up for best actor award, called on instead to present the award to Sanjeev Kumar. He received a letter from B. K. Karanjia, editor of *Blitz*, for participating in the award ceremony, about which he says: "I've still kept the letter; it was sufficient consolation for me" (Mohamed 2002: 123–24).

It may be that publicity materials stage this narrative of slights, setbacks, and unjust treatment, just like the films, to create continuity between the person and the image. However, Bachchan's performance may have more than just the interpretation he brings to the characters, and it would take a considerable level of orchestration to have all family members, co-workers, and industry personnel synchronize their testimonies about his distinctive personality traits. Interviews with personnel surrounding him reveal a consistent narrative about his reaction to the extraordinarily publicized episodes of his life. His own reckoning is of a history of victimization, against which he fought each time with resilience and grit, uncannily matching the characters he played on screen.

His wife Jaya Bachchan testifies to his contradictory personality, both wanting and not wanting superstardom (the reason for presenting him *To Be or Not to Be Amitabh Bachchan* on his sixtieth birthday). More apropos perhaps to explaining his success, though, is the laconic comment from Rekha, co-star and long rumored other woman: "In many ways he's quite like the Vijay he plays on screen" (Somaaya 1999: 296).

Deewar, a vehicle launching Amitabh Bachchan to stardom, is quintessentially a 1970s film embodying the zeitgeist of a tumultuous post-independence period, capturing the pulse, unrest, and confusion of the time. Yet it can also be read as an open text, allowing audiences to "negotiate" multiple, competing meanings according to their own social location and cultural experience. *Deewar* effectively forced together ethical discourses about a troubled nation, simultaneously decrying and valorizing the state. Today the film serves as master text, offering uncanny insights into the meta-text of Amitabh Bachchan's stardom, his career in the film industry and politics, and his awkward position in the hyphen between nation and state.

BIBLIOGRAPHY

Brennan, T. 1990. "The National Longing for Form." In *Nation and Narration*, ed. K. Homi Bhabha, 44–70. London: Routledge.

Chakravarty, S. 1993. *National Identity in Indian Popular Cinema 1947–1987*. Austin: University of Texas Press.

Dwyer, R. 2000. *All You Want Is Money, All You Need Is Love: Sexuality and Romance in Modern India*. London: Cassell.

Dyer, R. 1995. *Heavenly Bodies: Film Stars and Society.* New York: St. Martin's Press.

Ellis, J. 1982. *Visible Fictions.* London: Routledge.

Fiske, J. 1987. "British Cultural Studies and Television." In *Channels of Discourse: Television and Contemporary Criticism*, ed. R. C. Allen, 254–89. Chapel Hill: University of North Carolina Press.

Gabriel, K. 2004. "The Importance of Being Gandhi: Gendering the National Subject in Bombay Cinema." In *South Asian Masculinities: Context of Change, Sites of Continuities*, ed. R. Chopra, C. Osella, and F. Osella, 264–304. New Delhi: Kali for Women & Women Unlimited.

Gledhill, C. 1988. "Pleasurable Negotiations." In *Female Spectators: Looking at Film and Television*, ed. D. E. Pribram, 64–89. London: Verso.

Hall, S. 1980. "Encoding/Decoding." In *Culture, Media, Language*, ed. S. Hall et al., 128–39. London: Unwin Hyman.

Hoad, N. 2004. "What the Miss World Pageant Can Teach about Globalization." *Cultural Critique* 58, pp. 56–81.

Kazmi, F. 1998. "How Angry Is the Angry Man? Rebellion in Conventional Hindi Films." In *The Secret Politics of Our Desires: Innocence, Culpability and Popular Indian Cinema*, ed. A. Nandy, 134–56. New Delhi: Oxford University Press.

Lal, V. 1998. "The Impossibility of the Outsider in Modern Hindi Film." In *The Secret Politics of Our Desires: Innocence, Culpability and Popular Indian Cinema*, ed. A. Nandy, 228–59. New Delhi: Oxford University Press.

Mazumdar, R. 2000. "From Subjectification to Schizophrenia: The 'Angry Man' and the 'Psychotic' Hero of Bombay Cinema." In *Making Meaning in Indian Cinema*, ed. R. Vasudevan, 238–66. New Delhi: Oxford University Press.

Mishra, V. 1989. "Actor as a Parallel Text." *Quarterly Review of Film and Video* 11 (3): 49–67.

———. 2002. *Bollywood Cinema: Temples of Desire.* New York: Routledge.

Mohamed, K. 2002. *To Be or Not to Be Amitabh Bachchan.* Mumbai: Saraswathi Creations.

Oza, R. 2001. "Showcasing India: Gender, Geography and Globalization." *Signs* 26 (4): 1067–95.

Parmeswaran, R. 2004. "Spectacle of Gender and Globalization: Mapping Miss World's Media Event Space in News." *Communication Review* 7 (4): 371–406.

Prasad, M. 1998. *Ideology of the Hindi Film: A Historical Construction.* New Delhi: Oxford University Press.

Sharma, A. 1993. "Blood, Sweat, and Tears: Amitabh Bachchan Urban Demi-God." In *You Tarzan: Masculinity, Movies, and Men*, ed. P. Kirkham and J. Thumin, 167–180. New York: St. Martin's Press.

Somaaya, B. 1999. *Amitabh Bachchan: The Legend.* Delhi: Macmillan.

Thomas, R. 1989. "Sanctity and Scandal: The Mythology of *Mother India*." *Quarterly Review of Film and Video* 11 (3): 11–30.

Chapter 13

The Indian Film Magazine, *Stardust*

Rachel Dwyer

Cinema reaches into almost every area of modern Indian urban culture, across every aspect of the media, from satellite and cable television, to the video industry, the popular music business, and magazine publishing.[1] These domains are mutually dependent and form dense networks of narratives and images which contribute to the viewing experience in the cinema hall. Some of these media are so recent (satellite and cable TV appeared in India only in 1992), it is not surprising that these key spin-offs of the cinema industry have been little researched.[2] One of these is film magazines, which date back to the 1930s, and form a long-established central feature of this culture.

Among the many types of Indian film magazines is a group that may also be described as star magazines, since their major preoccupation is verbal and visual images of stars in narratives, interviews, photos, etc. They have among the highest circulation of any Indian magazines, and some even have international editions. Perhaps they have been neglected because they seem too trivial, not about film at all, but consisting instead of stories of the exciting and scandalous lifestyles of the stars of the film world presented in a manner guaranteed to titillate bored, middle-class metropolitan housewives. I argue that it is these very assumptions which make these magazines so interesting. Although I question these assumptions, this study forms part of my analysis of these new middle classes and their culture.

Film magazines deserve serious study not only for their coverage of the star, their lively stories, and visual images, but also because they have created and developed a new variety of English, the language of many of the magazines, notwithstanding their exclusive concern with Hindi movies;

they provide a forum for the discussion of sexuality; and they link the commercial interests of this class with the semiotics and economics of advertising and its generation of lifestyle and consumption issues. Furthermore, these magazines are central to the history of the printed media in India, a major economic and cultural phenomenon in the current decade. The study of these English magazines sheds light on the role of the middle class, in particular, women and adolescents, as viewers and consumers not only of the cinema and its stars but also of a new urban lifestyle.

In this chapter I concentrate on one of the most popular of these film magazines, *Stardust*, a gossip magazine about the stars of the Bombay commercial cinema, which has been published in English in Mumbai since 1971. I discuss *Stardust's* major concerns, looking at how it has constituted an "imagined," interpretive community of readers, and the activities of this social group in creating and consuming the pleasures of the magazine (Hermes 1995; Radway 1991).

Approaches to Magazines, Popular Culture

In the Western context, the few studies of women's magazines can be seen as part of a feminist reappraisal of women's genres of popular culture (Winship 1987; McRobbie 1991; McCracken 1993; Hermes 1995). These include Janice Radway's pioneering work on the romance novel; Tania Modleski's analysis of women's fantasies through romance, Gothic novels, and TV soaps; and Ien Ang's discussion of soap operas (Radway 1987; Modleski 1982; Ang 1985). While not adopting any of their lines of enquiry, I have found many suggestive ideas in them. I have used caution in drawing on psychoanalytic approaches, which inform many of these works, trying to use them only for a general interpretation of pleasure. I have used a less abstract version of semiological analysis of the magazine than that of Angela McRobbie, following instead Christine Gledhill's model of negotiation, where meaning is constructed through the meeting of institutional and individual producers, texts, and audiences (Gledhill 1988). In this model, the socio-historical constitution of audiences, as well as the production process, become integral elements in the dispersion of textual meaning. My research is focused very deliberately on the magazines themselves. I drew on archives, and talked to magazine production teams and magazine readers on an informal basis. It became clear that the success of *Stardust*, whose origins are in the world of advertising, lies in the close connection between the advertisers and their target audience of readers, a relationship consolidated by solid market research for commercial reasons, and those who consume the magazines.

Since these magazines are one of the major media for the dissemination of narratives about Hindi film stars, I briefly consider theoretical work on the star. There are no tabloid newspapers in India equivalent to the British tabloids which narrate the lives of stars, although there is increasing coverage in the "serious press" in their lifestyle columns. The gossip and rumors generated by the media in India are largely undocumented. Little has been written about the star in Indian cinema, but Western film theory has proved useful in my analysis (Karanjia 1984; Kabir 1985; Mishra et al. 1989; Gandhy and Thomas 1991; Sharma 1993). I have drawn on Dyer's work on the star, which considers stars' images in social and historical contexts, arguing that stars matter beyond their films when they come to act as the focus for dominant discourses of their time.

I begin by giving a brief history of the film magazines, their origins, and their production. I then look at *Stardust*'s raison-d'être, namely, its adverts and the female bourgeoisie it targets, before examining narrative, theme, and language, to explore what they reveal to us about the readership and the nature of the magazines.

The earliest film criticism in India is found in newspaper columns, but film magazines in the vernacular languages and in English first appeared in the 1930s.[3] The first magazine devoted entirely to cinema coverage was the Gujarati *Mauj Majah*, published in 1924. One of the major magazines in English was the monthly *Filmindia*, which was published from 1935 to 1961. This expensive magazine, containing adverts catering to an elite market, was nearly all written by one person, Baburao Patel. The paper published reviews, responses to readers' letters, and so on, but editions from the final years contain lengthy polemics against Western medicine and pages on homeopathic and other indigenous medicines.

The postwar period saw the decline of the studio system of production and the rise of the independent producer and the growth of the star system. This required new forms of information that were supplied by trade publications in English, the first being a roughly produced weekly review sheet called *Kay Tee Reports*. It was supplanted by the better-produced magazine *Tradeguide* (1954–), which followed *Kay Tee Reports* by producing reviews of the week's films which journalists previewed on Thursday, in time for the Friday release. Such trade magazines are aimed at distributors and exhibitors, so their most important role is to predict the success or failure of particular films (rarely proved wrong) and to publish the box office statistics of recent movies. They contain no information about stars other than for commercial reasons.

Another type of magazine appeared in the 1950s, published by the major newspaper houses. The *Indian Express* newspaper group launched its in-house publication, *Screen,* in 1951. Its major concerns were films under production and recent events in the film industry. *Screen* can be situated somewhere between the trade and fan magazines, containing enough hard news for the industry and interviews with people in the business; it is read by both audiences. It also discussed Hollywood films, mostly in the context of distribution in India. The groundbreaking publication for the later wave of glossy English magazines was the launch of *Filmfare* in 1952 by Bombay's *Times of India* newspaper group. It was distributed throughout India by the newspaper's good distribution networks. Its first issue contained a manifesto:

> It is from [the] dual standpoint of the industry and its patrons, whom comprise the vast audience of movie fans, that "Filmfare" is primarily designed. This magazine represents the first serious effort in film journalism in India. It is a movie magazine—with a difference. The difference lies in our realisation that the film as a composite art medium calls for serious study and constructive criticism and appreciation from the industry as also from the public. (March 7, 1952: 3)

Filmfare combined serious film journalism with coverage of glamour, and included features about and interviews with the dominant figures in the industry. It was a sophisticated magazine, in keeping with the image of the *Times*, covering many cinema topics. It provided a forum for dialogue among the critics, the industry, and the audience while fulfilling the further function of being an upmarket family magazine with broad appeal to both the men and women's markets. It assured its place at the forefront of the film world in 1953 when it instituted the *Filmfare* awards. These were modeled on the Hollywood Academy Awards with the major difference that the magazine's readers cast their votes.

An important element of the magazine market is the vernacular magazines. These are quite different from the English monthly glossies (apart from the translated versions produced by *Magna* and *Chitralekha* publications). They tend to be weeklies, have low production values, and are printed on cheap paper. Photos are scarcer, mostly in black and white with a limited number of color pictures. Their downmarket advertising suggests they are aimed at a lower-class, male market.

The 1970s saw a whole new wave of magazines including the English-language glossies, which are the focus of this chapter. These introduced a new style of journalism in a new language, said to be invented by Shobha Rajadhyaksha (later Shobha Kilachand and subsequently Shobha Dé) (*Stardust*) and Devyani Chaubal (*Star 'n' Style*), although some claim that *Blitz* was first. I shall concentrate on *Stardust*, one of the first of these magazines, which undoubtedly has been the market leader.

Stardust may well have the largest circulation of any of the film magazines (in English 125,000; in Gujarati 1987—75,000; in Hindi 1985—30,000). The international English edition 1975–, sold in the United Kingdom, United States, Canada (specified on the cover), and South Africa and the Gulf, sells a further 40,000 copies; no figures are available for the English-language editions, 1996–, which cover the four southern regional cinemas. The only magazine with comparable sales is *Filmfare*, which is said by its journalists to have recently reached 200,000 per month, although much lower figures are published for 1994.

Stardust

Stardust is the flagship magazine of Magna Publications, a Mumbai-based publishing company owned by Nari Hira. Hira founded *Stardust* in 1971 as a marketing opportunity for his advertising business. The only major film magazine at the time was *Filmfare*, which ran film information and uncontroversial stories about the lives of the stars. His idea was to publish a magazine on the lines of the American *Photoplay* with celebrity gossip journalists like Hollywood's Hedda Hopper and Louella Parsons. Twenty-three-year-old Shobha Rajadhyaksha (later Dé), who had been working for Hira for 18 months as a trainee copywriter, was hired as the first editor. She had no interest in the movie world and had never worked as a journalist, but was given the job on the strength of an imaginary interview with Shashi Kapoor, whom she had never met. She and a paste-up man produced the first issue in October 1971 from unglamorous offices in South Mumbai. Later they were joined by a production staff of three, and a team of freelance reporters collected stories which she wrote up. Dé stubbornly refused to move in the film world, only meeting the stars if they came into the office. The style of the magazine was established during her time as editor and has been maintained under the succession of editors who followed.

The first issue of *Stardust* appeared in October 1971. A statement of intent was given underlining the magazine's purpose in its "Snippets" column:

> Very few movie magazines and gossip columns are either readable or reliable and hardly any are both. Most of them are inadequately researched and are the result of second and third hand reporting. One theory put forward has it that what often passes for news and fact is really much hearsay and gossip. Another claims that the people in the movie trade who are in a position to know are too busy to write or find it impolite to write down what they know. So, this column—largely as its reason for being—will be a reporter's column and not a mouthpiece of publicists and ballyhoos of the film trade. And here we go . . .

The magazine's manifesto is discussed throughout the whole issue, in particular in the Q&A page and letters page. The production features were much less glossy than they are today. Color was used only for the cover —an unflattering picture of the top box office star, Rajesh Khanna, and a series of photographs of the leading female star, Sharmila Tagore. The front page headlines were very suggestive—"Is Rajesh Khanna married?" and "Rehana Sultan: all about her nude scene"—but the stories were quite innocent. The main features were uncontroversial stories about Sharmila Tagore and her husband, the Nawab of Pataudi, the international cricketer. Along with the expected combination of photos, news, and gossip, some of the staple features of *Stardust* appeared in the first issue, including "Neeta's natter" written by "The Cat," the letters page, and the Q&A columns. The trademark Bombay English is not much in evidence, and there is little innuendo and few of the double entendres that became a central style in later issues. Several of the features were later dropped, including Hollywood coverage, "A day on the sets," "What's shooting," cartoons, and film criticism, features which brought it closer to *Filmfare*. Within a year, more of the staple features were established, including "Court Martial" (October 1972), and the special use of language is soon seen throughout the magazine.

The style of *Stardust* was firmly established in the first ten years and has remained largely the same to the present, even including the use of 1970s-style graphics. The style of production has also been constant. Editors, like most of the reporters, are college graduates from middle-class Mumbai families, without the glamorous social connections of Shobha Dé. The eight reporters and two freelancers (all under 30 years old) each has a set of stars to cover. Once the stories are collected, they are cross-checked with the stars to make sure they are happy about the stories. If there is something controversial which is a good story they may run it anyway, but gossip about a star's family is taboo and they never write anything on this topic without the star's permission. The stars usually collaborate with the magazines, but this does not always run smoothly. The ambivalent relationships between the stars and the magazines continue.

The stories cover 50 or more stars, concentrating on cover girls and glamorous figures who lead exciting lives or make controversial statements, rather than the top box office stars. *Stardust* also promotes stars by including glamorous photos and making romantic linkups with other stars. While few heroines have more than minor roles in the films, they are given great importance in the magazines, especially on the covers, since the editors believe that a woman on the front generates sales. Some actresses have had magazine careers that have outshone their screen roles, notably Rekha. This is part of the fairly fixed style of the magazine cover. In addition to the main picture, there is usually a woman or a star couple in an amorous pose, surrounded by up to four cutouts of stars with sensational headlines, at least one of which mentions sex. The headlines are usually far more salacious than the stories inside the magazines.

The magazine's regular features include the opening quasi-editorial "Neeta's Natter," short paragraphs of gossip, written as if by a celebrity about her social life in the film world, covering openings, films' jubilees, weddings, parties, etc. The stories praise those who are "in" and mock those who are "out." This is where the exaggerated language of the magazines is strongest, full of innuendo and puns. There is some photographic coverage of industry events, but the majority of photos are the session photos found elsewhere in the magazine. The other insider's gossip sections are "Star Track," which covers incidents in stars' lives, mostly stories from childhood, and events on the sets; "Snippets," which is more humorous, consisting mainly of jokes about star's gaffes in English, in etiquette, and then short puns and jokes; "Straight talk" covers other news items about the stars.

A number of regular formats for interviews include "Spot poll," a Q&A session with stars; "Court martial," where overtly hostile questions are asked of a controversial or fading star; "Favourite things," in which a star completes a cheesy questionnaire while the facing page features a signed glamour photo. Several interviews and articles about romances, quarrels, and gossip are interspersed with glamour shots of the stars. The major feature is "Scoop of the month," which is a big, gossipy story about an affair, a breakup of a relationship, or a special interview. Readers also have a chance to contribute to the magazine in two places: "Rumors and rejoinders," where they address queries to stars over gossip about unprofessional behavior or affairs and the star replies. Letters to the journalists are published in "International Mail Call," where readers seek information about their favorite stars; the stars' addresses are given for further correspondence.

Stardust has kept very much to the style established during its first decade, apart from the increase in the number of interviews by letter of the stars by the fans. Some of the graphics, such as those for "Neeta's Natter," have remained unchanged and look very dated with their "flower power" image, but these have provided the magazine with a recognizable identity. The general consensus is that, although the other glossies are of high quality and good reportage, in particular *Filmfare*, which many read in addition to *Stardust*, the latter still stands out from the other magazines because its gossip has more "bite."

Stardust: Adverts and the Consumer

There are no detailed surveys of *Stardust's* readership beyond the circulation figures given above. The best guide is to examine the magazine's other consumers, the advertising companies who provide the financing to produce the magazine. Market research gives the advertisers an idea of who forms a significant part of the readership and hence the important places to advertise, so some connection between the adverts and the readers is to be expected. However, it is likely that there is an additional readership, namely readers with less purchasing power who aspire to the consumption of these products and the corresponding lifestyle. A large proportion of this "Wannabe" readership is likely to come from among those who rent the magazines from their local "circulating libraries."

Stardust is heavily subsidized by its advertising: in 1996, a color page cost Rs80,000. This allows the magazine to have a cover price of Rs20, although each copy costs Rs50 to produce. Products advertised in recent Indian issues of *Stardust* range from household items to small luxuries, a wide spectrum of fashion, to expensive hi-fi goods, holidays, and scooters. There are also some surprising government promotions for jute and state tourist boards and more "non-family" items such as condoms, whisky, and cigarettes. Surprisingly, almost none of them feature the stars who one might expect to endorse glamour and beauty products such as soaps and shampoos.

The adverts do not show a strong gender bias toward products intended for consumption by women. The range of advertising allows a fairly clear idea of the magazine's purported readership. It is clearly aimed at an urban middle- or upper-middle-class readership, male and female, which has the purchasing power for these products. Although it is assumed the cinema audience largely consists of lower-class urban males, there is clearly a significant middle-class group, which has a deep enough interest in the Hindi film world to buy these magazines. The class emphasis here may explain the emergence of these new magazines in the 1970s as new class formations began to crystallize in urban India (Dwyer 2000).

The only difference between the domestic and international editions is the range of products advertised. The majority of the adverts in the latter are for the UK market, with several for the United States and one or two for Dubai. These give some impression of the NRI (Non-resident Indian) community reading the magazines for their "Wannabe" lifestyles, and as a way of imagining India as "home" and a world of glamour and style where the values they brought with them overseas can be fulfilled.

Issues of consumption reach beyond the adverts and are central to the magazines, since buying or renting the magazine is already an act of consumption. However, I wish to focus on consumption as part of the glamour of this public culture. Popular novels are often called "sex and shopping" novels because of their emphasis on an excess of consumption of mostly luxury goods. There are a whole set of overlapping perspectives on consumption presented in the magazines—in the photos and in the discussions. These include health and the body, which connects to discourses on sexuality, and consumption as a way of experiencing sexuality. The advertisements and their images are themselves sources of fantasies for pleasure (Winship 1987). Appeals are made to the aspirations to glamour of the target audience, with comments such as "If it's good enough for Kim Basinger, Tina Turner and Diana Ross, it's good enough for you!" (although the model for this hair treatment seems to be Asian). Fashion is a key issue here, since many women's interest in women stars is due to their display of conspicuous consumption (cosmetics, fashion, hairstyles, lifestyles) (Stacey 1993); in fact, throughout the magazines, stars are presented as idols of consumption, not of production. This address to women as consumers blends discourses on femininity and consumption as do women's magazines in the West, but in India there is further emphasis on class and modernity. The necessity of money to participate in this lifestyle is unquestioned, it being required even to read these magazines. Perhaps this focus on consumption has been part of the reason for disparaging the magazines by intellectuals.

Stardust: Language

The fact that the most popular magazines about the Hindi cinema are written in English is initially surprising. However, cinema features in these magazines as a source of glamour and a way of locating stars rather than as the object of the discussion. The major connection of the magazine is with the world of advertising, the aim clearly being to cater only to a small section of the movie-going (or video-watching) public—the section which has the highest purchasing power. This group of people may use English as their first language, or at least aspire to do so. The magazines use their own brand of language, a special variety of English. For example:

Mayday darlings. The heat is on again. Time for beaches, martini-on-ice, bikinis and cold-showers. Not that our cooler-than-*kakdi* stars can lose their sizzle with mere *thandai*. The higher their temperatures, the better to use their libidoes with, my dears. I'm jetting to Eskimo-land already. Phew! (May 1996)

This variety is called "Hinglish" or "Bombay English," a mixture of nonstandard varieties of English with the odd Hindi, Marathi, or Gujarati word or phrase inserted. The English used here refers to other English texts to show an insider's knowledge or to provide humor; it contains nonstandard varieties (one can't *use* one's libido; and the standard plural is libidos; note also the psychoanalytic term) and nonpolitically correct English. The use of Hindi is not because of a lack of ability in English; the star whose English is not up to scratch is scorned as a "vernac," a "vern" (user of a vernacular) or a "ghati" (a Mumbaikar's derogatory term for someone from nonmetropolitan Maharashtra, from the Ghats). Although most Mumbai English-speakers use a certain proportion of Hindi words in their everyday language, the use here is deliberately humorous ("cooler-than-*kakdi*" is a Hinglish slang which only makes sense if one knows the outdated English idiom "cool as a cucumber"). Hindi is used elsewhere to add spice, to show exasperation or, more often, simply to sound "cool." It is likely to be traced to the exaggerated form (which is not used by anyone in Mumbai) invented by these magazines, a code for insiders, knowing how to use it is part of the art of being cool. One has to know it to gain admission to the circle of the film world, a group imagined to speak the language. It is also a way of distancing oneself from one's everyday language with its overtones of region and social group. Being able to read it also shows one has competence in English and in Hindi. It is a fun language for modern, fashionable people; one can write letters to the magazines in this language, but any attempt to speak it out of context would result in loss of face. It also has the effect of providing a special language for the international editions. This delight in language and playing with it consciously for humor and effect is seen in the use of puns and word play found throughout the magazines.

The style of the writing is exaggerated from the breathless style of "Neeta's Natter," full of words of address ("pets, dahlings, darlings"), exclamations and an excess of punctuation (dashes, exclamation marks, inverted commas), to the purple prose of reports and descriptions of the stars. The stars' epithets (the "sexy [Jackie] Schroff," the "deadly [Sanjay] Dutt") and pet names (Dabboo, Chintu, and Chimpoo, the sons of Raj Kapoor) are used regularly and this causes confusion for the new reader. This is all part of the insider's knowledge, which has to be developed by continuous reading and accumulated knowledge.

The addressee is present in much of the writing. "Neeta's Natter" is always addressed directly to readers (forms of address as above, sign-offs such as "From one cat to another, meeow till next month!"[4]) This all adds to the feeling of a club, the close relationship of the fan to the magazine and the magazine to the stars. The readers have further opportunities to participate by sending in questions to the stars and writing letters for publication. The narratives provide the reader with a glimpse of a world of luxury and glamour, with events taking place in five-star hotels, deluxe restaurants, and expensive clubs.

This marked style of intimacy is also seen in the narratives, usually written in the first person, which gives a direct approach, a confessional mode, the feel of the eyewitness, often seeming to be in direct speech. The interviews with the stars themselves allow them to speak in the first person, furthering the effect of intimacy and revelation. The use of innuendo requires an audience, and it seems as if direct appeals are made to the reader to judge the lifestyle of the stars.

Stardust: Gossip

There are three major modes of narratives that may be presented in the form of interviews or told as narratives by the journalists. The three major forms of gossip outlined by Patricia Spacks (gossip as intimacy, gossip as idle talk, and gossip as malice) are found in the magazine (Spacks 1985).

The majority of the stories belong to the broad category of melodramas, tales of heartbreak, struggle, and survival. This is the gossip of intimacy. The tales of heartbreak may be caused by the ending of a relationship, but the most powerful are the stories of family tragedy. For example, the deaths of mothers of Juhi Chawla and Govinda in August 1996 were written from a personal and emotional position, concentrating on the grief of the bereaved stars and listing all those who supported them. The tales of struggle are usually stories of male stars who rose from ordinary backgrounds, who, through luck, hard work, and faith in their own abilities, have been able to triumph over life's difficulties. Their reliance on their moral qualities, their realization of the priority of home and family allow them to reach self-acceptance and maturity.

The backgrounds of female stars are rarely discussed; for them the central issues are those of morality and acceptability. Male stars often repeat that they would not marry a girl from the industry or let their daughters go into films, so women's backgrounds are given only when they are from star families or respectable middle-class homes. The stories are often about the star women who have reached a mid-life crisis, feeling they have sacrificed their education and are missing out on home and family. While the younger can say they are biding their time and intend to retire to family life, the senior stars have less room for maneuver. Women's struggle has to do with the lack of friendship and support in the industry; many interviews with women focus on rivalry between stars. These can be read as stories of outer happiness and inner sorrow, a typically melodramatic form. The moral of the women's stories is that success brings its own problems. The journalists put themselves in supporting roles here, while the reader is admitted to a world of emotion.

The second is the purely promotional treatment. This is usually reserved for newcomers, who are people like you and me but who often possess some "star quality," or the recently arrived crop of models. There is no gossip about these stars, just praise, flattery, and a set of glamorous photographs. In fact, all photographic material is of this nature—scandals are not corroborated by pictures from the paparazzi, nor are emotional photographs shown (except of a life event). All the photographs concentrate on the glamorous aspects of the stars, and there are usually plenty of studio photographs of the stars in the latest fashions or in theatrical costumes to accompany them.

The third category is concerned with malicious gossip and scandal. This is where the magazines derive their fame and notoriety. The gentler form is romantic gossip which exposes hidden love affairs, often between co-stars. A more malicious variety includes incidents of broken relationships, revenge, betrayal, and jealousy. This is based on the understanding that public figures lead public lives and can have no privacy. It is a refusal to allow the stars to have too simple a life, because all their transgressions will be found out. In "Neeta's Natter" and other snippets, the magazine makes fun of the stars who are no longer fashionable and laughs at their appearance and delusions of grandeur. Professional rivalry is a major topic, and stars are offered opportunities to attack each other and to respond to attacks on themselves by other people in the industry.

These three types of gossip have two main functions, namely, as a way of understanding oneself and the world, and for the creation of a sense of community, a feeling of belonging (Hermes 1995). I discuss the former, largely sexual gossip, below. The second function is of vital importance to the pleasure of these magazines. The depiction of the inside world of films is the main focus, establishing the credentials of the journalists and the magazine. This has the effect of providing intimacy, which stars shun in real life as they live often remote and sheltered lives, cocooned by security and air conditioning. The magazine allows its readers to feel that they are participating in this world, a feeling which is reinforced by highly personal forms of address, creating solidarity and connections. The effect is one of intimacy and distance: the stars are personalities like you or me, but they are different in kind, in that they have an excess or surplus of everything. The creation of intimacy with the stars makes them figures who are near and yet remote and so can function as unthreatening figures for the projection of readers' fantasies and discussions. The melodramatic mode of the narratives is central to this, depicting the stars as emotionally charged, quasi-family figures.

In summary, there is a dynamic of consumption. The magazine has an interest in creating a community of readers for its community of advertisers. The reader consumes these stories of the stars and the advertisements. This does not have to be in a passive way: she can read selectively, she can reinterpret the magazine in ways which are meaningful to her, and she has the ultimate power of refusal: not to buy or read the magazine.

Stardust: Sexuality

The major concern of such gossip has to do with sexuality, the major feature of all gossip in any society. This is probably due to the fact that it is now regarded as one of the most important and problematic areas of existence as well as one of the greatest sources of pleasure. A study of the issues raised in this context shows sources of anxiety and pleasure and, like all gossip, questions dominant values.

Sex without strings! The industry's orgy of immorality exposed![5]

The central concern of *Stardust* with sex and sexuality is emblazoned on every cover. The interest is not just with the sexual act itself, as is often assumed, but it discusses ideas, notions, feeling, images, attitudes, and assumptions about a whole range of topics pertaining to sexuality such as romance, marriage, feminism, masculinity, femininity, gay and lesbian issues, and the presentation of the body. This concern with sexuality is hardly surprising in Mumbai of the late 1990s where, along with lifestyle concerns, it is the dominant topic of conversation, especially among the young, upwardly mobile middle classes. These magazines are the sphere in which these major discourses on sexuality are sited outside of state locations such as education institutes, medical discourse, population control, and censorship.

India has a very limited and heavily censored pornography industry. There are only two widely available men's magazines, the soft-porn magazine *Chastity*, which has many pictures of naked women, and is entirely concerned with the discussion of sexual matters whether in narratives or "problem pages"; and *Debonair* (89,000), which belongs to the same proprietors as *Star 'n' Style*. However, the latter is also known for its coverage of the arts, in particular poetry. Its present editor, Randhir Khare, is also a recognized poet; formerly it has had two of India's best known poets, Adil Jussawalla and Imtiaz Dharker, working on its reviews and poetry pages. Its upmarket playboy image can be seen as part of its attempts to widen the discussion of sexuality, but the soft-porn photos have caused some controversy. Women have no equivalent, which is to be expected in view of women's lack of interest in viewing the male body displayed in magazines. There is some discussion of sexuality in the health pages of women's magazines like *Femina* (available in English, 113,000 and in Gujarati), and *Women's Era* (English, 101,000), but the majority of the writing is the usual female mixture of fashion, beauty, domestic tips, and romantic stories in the numerous women's magazines such as *Grhashobha* (Hindi, 315,000). In the last few years Indian editions of international magazines have begun to be published, including *Cosmopolitan*. The contrast remains between women's magazines (lifestyle, fashion, beauty, romance) and men's magazines, which tend to be sports, news, or business/financial.

The only magazine to give coverage to gay issues is *Bombay Dost*, mostly in English, with a few pages in Hindi and English. This is printed in black and white on low-grade paper and is mostly the work of one person, Ashok Row Kavi. Despite its struggle to acquire distributors and outlets, it has become an important publication for many gay activists in India. I know of no lesbian equivalent.

Apart from magazines, sexuality is discussed across a wide range of media. However, while the commercial films may provide visual displays of a sexually explicit nature, they pay lip service to a much more conservative view of sexuality than the magazines, leading to a complex and contradictory presentation of sexual desire (Kasbekar 2001). Film songs and their picturization provide greater opportunities for sexual display than dialogue and narrative sections of the films, with their specific images of clothes, body, and body language, while the song lyrics are largely focused on sexuality, ranging from romance to suggestive and overt lyrics. The films of the so-called parallel cinema, a term which covers films ranging from the middlebrow to the avant-garde, often deal with questions of sexuality in a more explicit way. Television, which has been seen as a threat to the film industry, is actually largely parasitic on the film industry. Much of the TV time of the new satellite and cable channels, which now number around 50 in Mumbai, is given to film, whether screening of films, programs about stars, music shows, and audience participation shows. TV's own unique genre, the soap operas, which are hugely popular in India, are melodramatic family romances rather than sexual romances.

Women's romantic fiction, whether Indian or imported, is more concerned with fantasies of love than of sex, although Shobha Dé has introduced a new form of popular, more sexually explicit writing in English, dealing with sadomasochism and lesbianism in a way not found elsewhere. In spite of a long tradition of erotic writing in India, I know of no academic study of its recent manifestations. Indian novels written in English, while not primarily erotic, contain frequent mentions of penises, masturbation, and early sexual encounters. These tend to be highly narcissistic and are treated on the same level of fascination as lavatorial matters. Gay writing has become more widespread, whether overtly as in the pioneering writing of Firdaus Kanga, or in more covert forms.

As one might expect, there is no single coherent discourse on sexuality. In the West, in particular in the United States, since the 1950s the major discourse has developed from psychoanalysis, but this has had a restricted circulation in India. However, one can identify two popular trends. One is that sexual permissiveness is one of the evils of westernization, and an Indian woman's major concern is her honor. The other is that there is a cover-up and deliberate obfuscation, a refusal to acknowledge the high number of prostitutes in Mumbai, the AIDS problem, extramarital affairs, and so on. Nevertheless, the abundance of discourses on virginity, the age of consent, the life of widows, Eve-teasing. etc., show the centrality of sexual discourses.

"I'm a virgin and I'm still at the top!" Mamta erupts![6]

This declaration by one of Hindi film's top sex symbols ("the *desi* sex symbol") that she is a virgin shows the high value placed on controlled female sexuality. This contrasts with the images of Kulkarni in magazines and films, where she features as the sexiest of all stars. The ideal woman is presented in the magazines as in the films, as a virgin, but often turned on by her own body in a narcissistic manner, eager for her sexual encounter with her life partner. In other words, the woman must be sexually available but only for the one, right man, a position that can be occupied easily by the male spectator/reader. But how does the female spectator/reader find pleasure in this position? If she is heterosexual, is she obliged to take a passive, masochistic position as suggested by Mulvey?

It seems that women readers are at least equally concerned with female stars as sources of identification as with male stars as figures of sexual fantasy. These women can be seen as providing role models for the new urban women. I argue that one of the reasons that women enjoy reading about female stars is because of the opportunities these features provide for questioning standard views of sexuality, by setting up opposites and negotiating new possibilities. The off-screen star is as vulnerable in her own life as the reader in hers, leading the reader to adopt attitudes of empathy and protectiveness. The star must face questions such as: Is it alright to sleep with someone without being married to him? Is it acceptable to live with someone without being married? What about having a child without being married? How should one deal with one's husband's infidelities? Are women always vulnerable?

From its beginnings, the cinema has been seen as unsuitable for respectable women. Famously, Phalke could not persuade even prostitutes to act in his films and the first female stars were from the Anglo-Indian community. This concern with respectability remains one of the major concerns for the female star. Early issues of *Filmfare* depicted female stars in traditional saris, in their homes, engaged in domestic light chores such as flower arranging, looking after a sister's children, or performing refined activities, such as painting or embroidery. Stars had to be presented as unmarried daughters or housewives with articles on how the stars liked to relax and spend their time at home. It seemed that any reference to labor was avoided, apart from the efforts the stars, who are always busy with their work, make to cope with their private lives. There is no direct reference in these magazines to women's domestic work or even the "servant problem." In fact, one of the major features that distinguishes these magazines from women's magazines is the silence about domestic life.

It may be surprising then that most of the female stars do not take an interest in any form of feminism. They mostly reject feminism with trite remarks such as, "Who wants to be equal to men? We're better!" A few women (Pooja Bedi, Pooja Bhatt, Anu Agrawal) step beyond the limits of female behavior, but this is reactive rather than suggesting meaningful alternatives to those on offer. The stories show a lack of female bonding and emphasize rivalry unless one group of women is ganging up on another woman. This is particularly disappointing in view of the fact that there has been numerical dominance of women among the magazine's reporters and editors.[7]

The photographs of the female stars can be interpreted by the female viewer as images of the inner person, following the widely held belief that the female body expresses the idea of female sexuality, where the inner life and sexuality fare the same. Women can also enjoy the fashion, the clothes, the makeup, and the hairstyles of the stars, which they may copy; they can also enjoy the pleasure of identifying with their beauty.

The photographs are always of the most glamorous women, who are not necessarily leading heroines. For example, many magazines carry photos of the actress Raveena Tandon, who has not had a big box office hit for a long time. The actresses are beautiful and elegant. The larger ideal has been marginalized, although not replaced, by taller, thinner women with smaller breasts and hips like Western models. The actress is heavily made up, wearing a particular type of Western costume which is more high street than high fashion. These often look cheap and vulgar and are not infrequently fetishistic outfits in black PVC. The actresses rarely wear Indian clothes for these shots, which is a sharp contrast from the early *Filmfares*, in which the women wore saris. The outfits tend to reveal rather than to conceal; camera angles are often invasive, with many cleavage shots, as well as some groin shots. However, nudity is not even considered. Close-ups usually emphasize eyelashes, lip liner, and heavy jewelry. There are frequently staged shots of a couple in passionate clinches —pre-orgasmic, orgasmic, and postcoital.

Hot! Are Industry Men Sex-Starved?[8]

While the images of the male stars are more complicated than those of female stars, the storylines are simpler. The male star can be the subject of scandal, which he can reject or enjoy, he can utter threats to would-be rivals, he can reveal himself as a sensitive soul or a survivor. These seem to approximate quite closely to the roles that the man takes on screen, unlike the woman's which is so different. Cinema provides mostly positive roles for male stars, the obvious exception being the villain. The villain is a lower category of star, even when hugely popular, for the male star is almost identical with the hero, or anti-hero.

One of the most interesting star texts is that of Akshay Kumar, a box office and magazine idol. He is described as a relentless womanizer and superstud; endless stories circulate about him and Raveena Tandon who may be secretly married, may be a couple, or may have ended their relationship, but he is also important as a gay icon. *Bombay Dost* ran an interview with "the new Eros of eroticism,"[9] accompanied by a review of Akshay's film "*Main khiladi tu anadi*" ("I am a player, you are innocent"), finding numerous homoerotic overtones and gay codes in this two-hero film. The picture accompanying a story in *Stardust* which referred directly to the *Bombay Dost* interview has Akshay dressed in uniform with arm around action hero Sunil Shetty. Akshay Kumar's statement in *Stardust* ("I feel nice about being a gay fantasy!"[10]) was reported with delight in *Bombay Dost*[11] showing an intertexual link between the two magazines. Akshay's status in the gay community may explain the numerous photographs of him in uniform, leather, and bondage gear.[12] Akshay himself is careful in all his interviews to offend neither his homosexual fans nor homophobes; his portrayal in film magazines is usually hypermasculine, as a body builder and a compulsive seducer of women, which is open to gay readings.

While many other photographs of male stars suggest gay readings, this is often inherent in the subject matter, photographs of the male body, rather than necessarily saying anything about the stars' sexuality. Codes of looking (men look, women are looked at) make it difficult to eroticize the male body for the female look or to allow for the voyeuristic female.[13] Dyer argues that images of the eroticized male body appear as gay images because the active gaze is thought to be male (Dyer 1982). This requires men in photographs to avert their eyes to deny the gaze, to appear as action types or to be hysterically male. Whether these rules apply in an Indian context is unclear. However, the direct look of the male star, the recent craze for body building, which on small men heightens the gay effect, as does the tight clothing required to display their muscles, and the use of soft textures and gentle lighting in the photographs certainly do not inhibit a gay interpretation of the images.

However, the magazines rarely speak directly about gay issues. There are infrequent suggestions that stars are gay, and, more rarely, coded references to their orientation, suggestions of a gay readership, and the occasional photograph, such as *Stardust*'s picture of two female stars, Farah and Khusboo, engaged in a passionate kiss.[14] The style of the magazines certainly lends itself to camp readings; camp interpretations are unpredictable. For example, the camp following of top female stars such as Sharmila Tagore and Meena Kumari, the preferred role models for drag artists, is likely to be because of the excess of femininity of the former and the tragic on- and off-screen images of the latter. There seems to be little similar to the Western prepubescent desire of girls for androgynous, nonthreatening males as typified by boy-groups such as Boyzone. However, the above interpretations show a Western interpretation that may not stand up to scrutiny in a serious analysis of Indian sexuality which is so far lacking.[15] The major stories are about heterosexual love and sex; the photographs of couples are almost all male and female.

The appearance of the hero indicates popular perceptions of beauty. He must be tall, and fair, usually north Indian and clean-shaven. His clothes are nearly always Western; a number of shots are designed to emphasize the physique; his clothes may be torn, or he may be topless; covered in sweat with his slicked back hair, or dressed as Western actors. In other words, the presentation of the male star is as hypermasculine or active. In addition to the male practice of body building mentioned above, two other major forms of body shaping have emerged in India in recent years. One is dieting, the other is plastic surgery. Stars are regularly criticized for putting on weight and praised for weight loss. Although this is seen in early issues of *Stardust*, it was clearly absent from early issues of *Filmfare*, where many of the stars were large by today's Western ideals. Anorexia and bulimia are not known as such in India and a tracing of these images of the body remains to be seen.

Far more drastic is the use of plastic surgery. Several stars have talked about it in public; several have clearly gone under the knife. However, a major feature on plastic surgery in *Stardust* was the most public and controversial discussion so far.[16] It begins by saying how common plastic surgery is in Hollywood and reports Dolly Parton's revelations about her own plastic surgery. There then follows an interview with two cosmetic surgeons, Dr. Narendra Pandya and Dr. Vijay Sharma. The magazine then gives its own list of male and female stars who seem to have had work done. The most frequent operation is breast implants for younger female stars, who often demand excessively large breasts with prominent nipples. Across the board the most popular operation is the nose job and more rarely liposuction, as well as breast augmentation, while many older stars have undergone face lifts. The often impossible demands of the stars reflect the beauty priorities, namely to be taller and to have lighter skin. Perhaps the most surprising part of the whole piece was Sharma's advice on which stars need what sort of plastic surgery, which seemed very close to British tabloid newspaper discussion.

Despite these forms of body improvement, health trends such as reasonable exercise, healthy eating, sensible drinking, and quitting smoking are discussed less frequently and stars are even featured smoking. The majority of the stories in the magazine are concerned with sex, love, and romance. These give different values to romance than the images portrayed on screen. On screen the focus is on the struggle with the ultimate happy ending, usually a wedding or at least the promise of one. In the magazines, the emphasis is on the problems of romance, its scarcity, its lack, the failures of the marriage, the infidelities, rather than on its success. This can be interpreted as a specialized form of reading romance:

> Romance reading, in this view, is escapist, cathartic and addictive, and serves the same gender-specific functions for women as does pornography for men. (Singh and Uberoi 1994: 94)

Although the terms "escapist, cathartic and addictive" raise more issues than they answer (escape from what to where and why? etc.), this remark raises an important issue avoided by Radway in her study of the romance, namely, the question of whether readers find the narratives of romance sexually arousing. It seems more likely that the pleasure in *Stardust* is found in the melodramatic mode in that the stars have everything —looks, money, fame—yet they still have to worry about romance and they still are not happy. The stories of stars are more heightened versions of romance along the lines of betrayal by one's partner with another desirable person, and the public knowledge of the situation. It also allows readers among whom dating is restricted, premarital sex is taboo, and arranged marriages—however loosely we use the term—are still the norm, to fantasize about such relationships and to learn about how they would behave in certain situations. They allow readers to be able to discuss issues of romance, love, and sexuality.

Despite the prominence given to romance and sexual liaisons, there is clear emphasis on the family and on controlled sexuality, especially in the case of women. There is an underlying theme about reconciling individuality with wider duties. The stories endlessly go over problems of romance and love in heterosexual monogamy.

Marriage is a key issue in the magazine and there is no questioning the respect given to marriage. Occasional discussions on "living in" always see it as a poor or unacceptable substitute for marriage. Marriage and a career in cinema are seen as irreconcilable for women. Women are expected to retire from the industry after marriage, partly because fans will not accept a married woman in romantic roles and also because her place is in the home. The only possibility is of a return to play mothers and character roles.

A regularly occurring feature is of the secret marriage between star couples. In 1995/96 a major story was published concerning the possible marriage of Akshay Kumar and Raveena Tandon. There were rumors of wedding photographs, although these were never seen. The issue of *souten* (co-wife) is usually silently acknowledged: an article about Dharmendra's (star) children Bobby and Sunny Deol will not mention Hema Malini, while an article about Dharmendra and Hema will not mention Bobby and Sunny. Divorce is seen as rather scandalous with even the divorce of star parents reported. The issue of whether to divorce or to take a second wife is frequently raised, for example Sri Devi (who was reported to be Mithun Chakraborty's second wife in 1990) is now pregnant and recently married the already-married Boney Kapoor.

All melodrama highlights the importance of the family. Even if characters in a melodrama are not relatives, they take on functions and roles of relatives to assume any importance (Brooks 1976: 4). Another melodramatic feature is that the families of stars take on the star's aura. The names of star partners are well known, stories are run about how wives of unfaithful husbands are forgiving, how the star has suffered due to the ill health of a partner, etc. Star children are a regular feature and are rarely mentioned without some reference to their parents, such as Sanjay Dutt (Nargis and Sunil Dutt), Karishma Kapoor (Babita and Randhir Kapoor, son of Raj Kapoor), Twinkle Khanna (Dimple and Rajesh Khanna). On the occasion of a marriage or the birth of children to stars, all enmities are dropped and congratulations, purple prose, and smoochy photos are in order. I conclude this chapter by looking at the pleasure of reading these magazines. Following Ang (1985), I argue that although readers would accept that they read the magazines for pleasure, no one can define what these pleasures actually are. Instead, I look at some of the mechanisms of pleasure.

The most obvious pleasure is often overlooked, which is the act of reading itself. Radway's study of the reading of romance fiction found that one of the central pleasures was in designating time for oneself, refusing the demands of one's family (Radway 1987). Hermes builds on this and finds that reading women's magazines is a secondary activity for filling time, the readers saying they read them instead of novels because they fill gaps in the day and yet are easy to put down (Hermes 1995). This can clearly apply to the consumption of magazines in India but there is no study of domestic reading practices. Personal experience suggests that magazines may be read while waiting for food to cook, during the afternoon rest or, in Mumbai, on the long commute to the office as a way of shutting out fellow commuters. In India, the magazine circulates among the household members, some of whom may just pick it up briefly and enjoy only the visual pleasure, such as the photographs of beautiful people, clothes, consumer items, and the like.

However, although Radway focused on reading in her research, she was unable to draw firm conclusions about the pleasures of reading. Most important, readers did not give enough information about whether they found the stories erotic or sexually exciting. The problems of eliciting such responses remains.

A second central pleasure is also extra-textual, namely the pleasure of an "imagined" community of readers, thus gaining an imaginary and temporary sense of identity and seeing the community as an extension of the family for the siting of melodramatic events (Hermes 1995). Gossip is circulated by the magazines through melodramatic stories, narratives in which the readers "get to know" the star, are addressed directly by the narratives, and share the consumption fantasies of the adverts. This is encouraged by the style of *Stardust*, which invites the reader to become part of the inner world, where the stars also read the magazine. The discussion of the stars and their lives, romances, marriages, reconciliations, become like interventions by other family members. The focus on sexuality is that the stars negotiate the concerns the readers face in their own lives (Dyer 1986). Although the concept of finding oneself through sexuality has prevailed in the West since the seventeenth century, the strength of this growing belief in India remains unclear (Foucault 1981: 6–7).

An examination of the stories raises the question: Why do the stories contradict all "normal expectations" of behavior and the roles associated with the star personae on screen? Clearly the audiences are not passive receivers of these messages, but they can interpret them in a wide variety of ways. The active role of audience in folk and other performances in India has been noted in that the audience uses texts as a way of dealing with inner dramas, not as models of behavior (Beck 1989; Kothari 1989). This has been noted also among viewers of soap operas in the West, where the emphasis is not on "escape" but on ways of dealing with one's everyday life (Ang 1985: 83). Dyer argues the lives of stars are places to discuss sexual morality, the role of the individual and of the family, the understanding of the body, consumer society (Dyer 1986). Gandhy and Thomas follow his approach in their study of three female stars of Hindi cinema, and draw attention to the fact that the star personae off screen "frequently encompass behaviors that are decidedly subversive of the strict social mores of Indian society and would be considered 'scandalous' in any other context, even by many of theirmost dedicated fans" (Gandhy and Thomas 1991). Of course, they do not simply transgress: stars are represented as finely balancing their transgressions with personifications of ideal behavior, especially in the domains of kinship and sexuality. Both the films and the subtext of gossip about stars are most usefully seen as debates around morality, in particular as negotiations about the role of "tradition" in a modernizing India (Gandhy and Thomas 1991: 108).

An undoubted source of pleasure lies in the creation and fulfillment of the desires of the readers in a new urban, consumer society. The links between cinema and desire, consumerism and capitalism and desire are highly complex (Laplace 1987). While mass media and popular culture embody and communicate society's dominant ideology, they also give grounds for resisting them. The magazines must seek and create their market, but the readers also choose what they prefer. The magazines can create desires and fulfill them, but the readers can subvert them so their own desires and needs are met. The content of the magazines must be relevant to the fantasies and anxieties that dominate the readers' concerns. Hermes identifies two dominant fantasies which can be fulfilled by such magazines, namely control through understanding other people's emotions; and the control of imagining difficult scenarios and how one would cope if faced with them in real life (Hermes 1995: 48).

We should be wary of thinking that the reader absorbs these magazines passively at face value. Readers may have their own ways of reading. They can choose which stories to read and which photos to look at; they can read with a sense of irony and humor, whether a camp style as identified by Hermes, or just as part of being a cool, urban person. The magazine sends itself up, notably in "Neeta's Natter," and the stars themselves point out they should not take it all too seriously: "*Stardust* proudly flaunts that it is a gossip and fun-seeking magazine, and that teaches us to have a sense of humour."[17]

The impact of the language of *Stardust* on South Asian writers in English was mentioned above, but the magazine's star stories are also appearing in the novels of Dé and Tharoor. India's daily papers are now publishing star stories as features, while new cable and satellite TV links are allowing more and more of such gossip to circulate to the new aspirants to this world of glamour and modernity. For example, Zee TV now offers a whole spectrum of film spin-offs in addition to the films themselves, including song shows, chart rundowns, and quizzes. The magazines have not stood still: *Stardust* along with other magazines now makes its own weekly TV show, using the language of "Neeta's Natter," and is already available on the Internet.

Taking these magazines seriously allows us to have a closer look at the concerns and aspirations of an emerging social group. A study of the consumption of these magazines by the diaspora would provide further rewards. Almost universally condemned as trash, an analysis of the magazines reveals the creation of an "imagined" community of readers and consumers of a new public culture. Unlike readers of women's magazines, who fantasize about perfect selves, the study of film magazines shows multiple points of identification and enunciation of fantasies.

In looking at the magazines, it is clear that the central underlying themes are the issues facing these new classes, at a time when values are shifting rapidly, and massive social changes are taking place in Mumbai. This can be seen in anxieties about class and respectability. For example, a recent issue of *Stardust* dealt with the issues of class, money, and "modern" views in one article.[18] Some film stars were hired by a diamond merchant to perform at his brother's wedding for large sums of money. In conservative terms, being hired to dance at a wedding has overtones of the *mujra* and hence associations with courtesans and prostitution. The magazine solicited the opinion of a number of stars. One admitted she had performed and taken money but claimed to feel degraded. Some stars denied any knowledge of the event, some said they had been tricked, while others said that it was shocking and degrading to the industry that any of its members should have behaved in this manner. A few of the younger female stars said that they thought a big fuss was being made over nothing and there was no problem in performing at such events. This presentation of a whole range of views allows the reader to consider this story of the breaking of a taboo from a number of perspectives. Since the magazine does not give an editorial line, the reader is allowed to draw her own conclusion on the issues raised.

Stardust does not stand apart from other cultural products, but it is a major source of pleasure among a whole range of forms. Its economy of pleasure centered around leisure, consumption, fantasy, and humor; its new language and modes of expression have reached the upwardly mobile middle classes in a national and international (diasporic) readership, tying together this class across the nation.

NOTES

1. An earlier version of this article appeared as "Shooting Stars: The Indian Film Magazine, *Stardust*" in Rachel Dwyer and Christopher Pinney (eds.), *Pleasure and the Nation: The History, Politics and Consumption of Public Culture in India* (New Delhi: Oxford University Press, 2001), pp. 247–285.

2. The exceptions include studies of billboards: Haggard (1988) and Srivatsan (1991); Manuel (1993) touches on concerns important to cinema in his wider discussion of the music cassette industry; and there has been some work on soap operas, including Mitra (1993) and Lutgendorf (1995).

3. Rajadhyaksha and Willemen (1995: 17–30) give details of mostly non-star magazines in their chronology of Indian cinema.

4. *Stardust*, August 1996.

5. *Stardust*, February 1995, cover.

6. *Stardust*, January 1994, cover.

7. See a feature on women reporters in *Filmfare*, April 23, 1996: 3.

8. *Stardust*, November 1994, cover.

9. *Bombay Dost*, 1995, 4 (1): 8–9.

10. Akshay Kumar, *Stardust*, June 1995: 82.

11. Volume 4 (2): 5.

12. A cover of *Filmfare* showed him dressed as the "patron saint" of gays, Saint Sebastian.

13. Theories of the gaze are mostly Eurocentric.

14. No datesee "Best of *Stardust*," Vol. III, 1981–1990: 16.

15. Kakar (1989) being the only study.

16. *Stardust* May 1996: 44–52.

17. Rekha, *Stardust*, August 1996: 46.

18. *Stardust*, May 1996: 60–66.

BIBLIOGRAPHY

Ang, I. 1985. *Watching Dallas: Soap Opera and the Melodramatic Imagination*. London: Routledge.

Babb, L. A. 1981. "Glancing: Visual Interaction in Hinduism." *Journal of Anthropological Research* 37 (4): 387–401.

Beck, B. E. F. 1989. "Core Triangles in the Folk Epics of India." In *Oral Epics in India*, ed. S. H. Blackburn et al., 155–75. Berkeley: University of California Press.

Brooks, P. 1976. *The Melodramatic Imagination: Balzac, Henry James, Melodrama and the Mode of Excess.* New Haven, Conn.: Yale University Press.

Dwyer, R. 1998. "'Starry Nights': The Novels of Shobha De." In *Unwriting Empire,* vol. 30, ed. Th. D'Haen, 117–33. Amsterdam and Atlanta: Rodopi.

———. 2000. *All You Want Is Money, All You Need Is Love: Sex and Romance in Modern India.* London: Cassell.

Dyer, R. 1977. "Entertainment and Utopia." *Movie #24* (Spring): 2–13.

———. 1979. *Stars.* London: British Film Institute.

———. 1982. "Don't Look Now: The Male Pin-up." *Screen* 23 (3–4): 61–73.

———. 1986. *Heavenly Bodies: Film Stars and Society.* London: British Film Institute.

———. 1993. *The Matter of Images: Essays on Representations.* London: Routledge.

Ellis, J. 1992. *Visible Fictions: Cinema, Television, Video.* London: Routledge.

Foucault, M. 1981. *A History of Sexuality.* Harmondworth, U.K.: Penguin.

Gandhy, B., and R. Thomas. 1991. "Three Indian Film Stars." In *Stardom: Industry of Desire,* ed. C. Gledhill, 107–31. London: Routledge.

Gledhill, C., ed. 1987. *Home Is Where the Heart Is: Studies in Melodrama and the Woman's Film.* London: BFI Books.

———. 1988. "Pleasurable Negotiations." In *Female Spectators: Looking at Film and Television,* ed. E. D. Pribham, 64–89. London: Verso.

———, ed. 1991. *Stardom: Industry of Desire.* London: Routledge.

Haggard, S. 1988. "Mass Media and the Visual Arts in Twentieth Century South Asia: Indian Film Posters, 1947–Present." *South Asia Research* 8 (2): 78–88.

Hermes, J. 1995. *Reading Women's Magazines: An Analysis of Everyday Media.* Cambridge, U.K.: Polity.

Kabir, N., ed. 1985. *Les Stars du Cinema Indien.* Paris: Centre Georges Pompidou/ Centre Nationale de la Cinematographie.

Kakar, S. 1989. *Intimate Relations: Exploring Indian Sexuality.* New Delhi: Viking.

Karanjia, B. K. 1984. "Le Star-Systeme." In *Les Cinema Indiens, CinemAction 30,* ed. A. Vasudev and P. Lenglet, 150–57. Paris: Editions du Cerf.

Kasbekar, A. 2001. "Hidden Pleasures: Negotiating the Myth of the Female Ideal in Popular Hindi Cinema." In *Pleasure and the Nation: The History, Politics and Consumption of Public Culture in India,* ed. Dwyer and Pinney, 286–308. New Delhi: Oxford University Press.

Kothari, K. 1989. "Performers, Gods, and Heroes in the Oral Epics of Rajasthan." In *Oral Epics in India,* ed. S. H. Blackburn et al., 102–17. Berkeley: University of California Press.

Laplace, M. 1987. "Producing and Consuming the Woman's Film: Struggle in *Now Voyager.*" In *Home Is Where the Heart Is: Studies in Melodrama and the Woman's Film,* ed. C. Gledhill, 138–66. London: BFI Books.

Lutgendorf, P. 1995. "All in the (Raghu) Family: A Video Epic in Cultural Context." In *Media and the Transformation of Religion in South Asia*, ed. L. A. Babb and S. S. Wadley, 217–53. Philadelphia: University of Pennsylvania Press.

Manuel, P. 1993. *Cassettte Culture: Popular Music and Technology in North India.* Chicago: University of Chicago Press.

McCracken, E. 1993. *Decoding Women's Magazines: From Mademoiselle to Ms.* New York: St. Martin's Press.

McRobbie, A. 1991. *Feminism and Youth Culture: From "Jackie" to "Just Seventeen."* London: Macmillan.

Mishra, V. 1985. "Towards a Theoretical Critique of Bombay Cinema." *Screen* 26 (3–4): 133–46.

Mishra V., P. Jefferey, and B. Shoesmith. 1989. "The Actor as Parallel Text in Bombay Cinema." *Quarterly Review of Film and Video* 11: 49–68.

Mitra, A. 1993. *Television and Popular Culture in India: A Study of the Mahabharat.* New Delhi: Sage.

Modleski, T. 1982. *Loving with a Vengeance: Mass-produced Fantasies for Women.* London: Routledge.

Mulvey, L. 1975. "Visual Pleasure and Narrative Cinema." *Screen* 16 (3): 6–18.

Radway, J. 1987. *Reading the Romance: Women, Patriarchy, and Popular Literature.* London: Verso.

———. 1991. "Interpretive Communities and Variable Literacies: The Function of Romance Reading." In *Rethinking Popular Culture: Contemporary Perspectives in Cultural Studies,* ed. C. Mukerji and M. Schudson. Berkeley: University of California Press.

Rajadhyaksha, A., and P. Willeman. 1995. *An Encyclopedia of Indian Cinema.* London: British Film Institute.

Sharma, A. 1993. "Blood, Sweat and Tears: Amitabh Bachchan, Urban Demi-God." In *You Tarzan: Masculinity, Movies and Men,* ed. P. Krikham and J. Thumim, 167–80. London: Lawrence and Wishart.

Singh, A. T., and P. Uberoi. 1994. "Learning to 'Adjust': Conjugal Relations in Indian Popular Fiction." *Indian Journal of Gender Studies* 1 (1): 91–120.

Spacks, P. M. 1985. *Gossip.* New York: Alfred A. Knopf.

Srivatsan, R. 1991. "Looking at Film Hoardings: Labor, Gender, Subjectivity, and Everyday Life." *Public Culture* 4 (1): 1–23.

Stacey, J. 1993. *Star Gazing: Hollywood Cinema and Female Spectatorship.* London: Routledge.

Vasudevan, R. 1989. "The Melodramatic Mode and Commercial Cinema." *Screen* 30 (3): 29–50.

Winship, J. 1987. *Inside Women's Magazines.* London: Pandora.

Chapter 14

IIIIIIIIIIIIIIIIIIIIIIIIIIIIIIIIIIIIIIIIIIIIIIIIIIIII

Bollyweb

Search for Bollywood
on the Web and See
What Happens!

Ananda Mitra

A casual search for the term "Bollywood" using two of the popular search engines produces quite staggering results. For instance, when done using Google, it produced nearly 36 million hits, whereas the term resulted in nearly 24 million hits when searched using Yahoo. While the number of hits is different, and the counts are dependent on a variety of factors such as the way a search engine operates, the exact time when the search is conducted, and several other technical issues, the fact remains that there are numerous digital discourses accessible on the Internet that have some connection with the Bombay film industry. Indeed, it would be safe to claim that the "real" Bollywood is encrusted by a significant "virtual" Bollywood on the Web, or Bollyweb.

The existence of Bollyweb is not only the product of a "supply-side economics" where many virtual discourses about Bollywood can be found on the Web, but is also a response to the "demand side" where many people are constantly seeking information about Bollywood on Bollyweb. Thus, while the search engines on the World Wide Web (Web) offer numerous places where Bollywood appears, on the other side of the coin it is also possible to report that some components of Bollywood also remain some of the most sought-after information on the Web. In other words, not only are there a lot of Web resources about Bollywood, there are also a lot of people who are accessing the Web to get information about Bollywood.

For instance, it was reported in 2005 that the ninth most popular search term used in the Indian site of Google was "Aishwarya Rai"—the name of one of the stars of Bollywood (Google 2006). There is thus a correspondence between the way the digital discourse about Bollywood has evolved with many resources about the industry as well as a large demand for information about the industry. This chapter considers some of the categories of resources that are available on the Web and then offers ways in which these resources play a role for the movie industry, its artisans, its artifacts, and its audiences.

Categories of Resources

A particularly interesting problem with the analysis of Web-based artifacts is finding a methodologically sound way of classifying a moving target. There are many reasons for this problem, including the sheer number of the artifacts as well as the fact that sometimes these Web pages represent a "moving target" where it is unclear when some of the discourses appear and others disappear. The number is also unstable because there are new Web pages and discourses that are constantly being added to the universe of Web-based resources about any phenomenon, just as some of the pages tend to disappear and are removed over time. Furthermore, the interconnection between Web resources, through copious hyperlinks, often produces a scale-free network whose beginning and end are difficult to identify, and it is only possible to find a set of more popular and less popular Web pages. Often popularity and inter-textuality have been considered to be a possible metric to begin to get a handle on Web analysis (Mitra 1999; Mitra and Cohen 1999). It is, however, possible to approach the analytical issue by developing a scheme to classify Web resources and then apply that model to a specific issue and elaborate on the way in which the map helps to understand a specific Web phenomenon. In other words, an a priori model can be proposed, and then it would be possible to see if there is evidence to support the model that classifies the vast amount of resources in manageable groups. This is the approach taken in this analysis.

In the case of Bollyweb, it is possible to identify a set of different kinds of Web resources which are often linked together to produce the larger discursive space. There are generally five different kinds of Web-based resources that can be identified.

Institutional Web Pages

Much like any other industry, Bollywood has a system of organizing itself as a commercial venture. As other chapters have pointed out, this system is arranged around stars, studios, producers, and directors who have attained international recognition. Bollywood movies have also transcended the geographic limitations and have now obtained a global reach—not only with Indians residing outside of India but also among a clientele of non-Indians who appear to enjoy the movies.

To be sure, this tendency has also required that Bollywood present itself in a sophisticated manner and be able to compete in a global market where presence is not only on the silver screen but also in the virtual electronic space. Thus, the different entities of Bollywood have created different kinds of Web presence. Consider, for instance, the official website of one of the superstars of Bollywood—Aishwarya Rai. This actress was judged to be one of the most beautiful women in the world, took the Bombay film industry by storm, and went on to be a player in the global film industry (CBS News 2005). Not unusually, there is an official website for this person located at http://www.aishwaryaworld.com/ which offers a myriad of information about the life of the actress and essentially serves to promote the actress. This celebrity official website is not unlike what is maintained by many other celebrities, where significant effort is put into creating a Web presence that helps to promote a person. Similarly, studios and conglomerates also offer institutional Web presence, as in the case of Yash Raj Films, which promotes itself and its movies at http://www1.yashrajfilms.com. Similar institutional websites are available for other segments of the institutions. Without a doubt, there are fewer institutional websites as compared to the next category of Web presence.

Personal Web Pages

This category is made up of Web pages that are maintained by individuals who are often disconnected from the film industry of India. These are the fan pages, and given the size of the resident and non-resident Indian population, the fan base is significant in size. A large portion of these fans also have easy access to the Internet and are thus able to create a presence for their film idols in virtual space. Often these could be pages dedicated to a specific actor or actress, or there may simply be a set of links to a set of Web-based resources about Bollywood.

Consider for instance the number of pages, official and personal, about the Indian movie icon Amitabh Bachchan. This actor appeared on the Bollywood screen in the 1970s, far before the advent of the Internet, and went on to become one of the most popular stars that Bollywood has ever produced; he developed a fan base that spans nearly two to three generations of people of Indian origin (Sharma 1993). A search on the term "Amitabh Bachchan" on a popular search engine yields nearly 1,760,000 hits, demonstrating that there are numerous Web pages that refer to the Indian film icon, and a significant portion of those pages are maintained by people who are not associated with the film industry in India. For instance, an individual fan, Debashish Chakrabarty, maintains a site that has the disclaimer, "This is a fan-site for non-commercial use and all material used has been taken from internet's free domain" (Chakrabarty 2006: n.p.). This site, like many other such personal sites, offers a series of resources about the actor, including downloadable pictures to serve as computer desktop images to specific dialogs from movies. This is a tendency that is common to most personal websites which often are about actors and actresses. In fact, the actresses often might receive a larger portion of the Web presence, as evidenced for Aishwarya Rai, whose name yields 3,120,000 hits on the same search engine as used for Bachchan. This larger presence can be attributed to the fact that there are many more Web pages produced by individuals about actresses than actors. Searching for other actresses would demonstrate this phenomenon. Most of these Web pages have a similar structure, with copious information about the person, filmography, dialogs, images, and videos. Indeed, these artifacts are often hyperlinked together, producing a network of Web pages which are also supplemented by people talking about Bollywood in the third category of Web resources—the Web log.

Blogs

An increasingly popular phenomenon in the early part of the twenty-first century is for people to maintain Web-based logs of their everyday life. These logs, also called "blogs," could cover a myriad of issues but have the common thread that they are maintained by individuals and are updated more frequently than Web pages. Blogs offer a digital equivalent to the traditional journal or diary with the important distinction that these journals can be made completely public, as they are placed in virtual space. Indeed, one of the purposes of maintaining blogs is to let the world know what a person does, feels, and believes.

Bollywood also has its presence through blogs, particularly in the form of people who would maintain a blog either solely about Bollywood and some of its components or a personal blog where Bollywood is mentioned frequently. The industry is also utilizing blogs by maintaining institutional journals and blogs that help to promote the industry and specific films. What is important to note is that it could be relatively difficult to find a specific personal blog that deals solely with Bollywood. On the other hand, for many Indians who maintain blogs, it is often the case that Bollywood features in their blog at some particular time and thus such blog postings contribute to the general popularity of Bollywood and add to the tapestry of Bollyweb. In the realm of the blog the distinction between the individual and the institution begins to blur, as there is an increasing tendency to use this particular Web phenomenon as another mechanism for creating a Web presence for the industry. Unlike the blog, the next resource represents an earlier use of the virtual to create a presence.

Usenet Groups

Far before the advent of the Web, there was a phenomenon that was popular on the Internet called "list serves." These were merely electronic bulletin boards where people would be able to send an e-mail, and that e-mail would be visible to all who subscribed to the bulletin board or who actively visited a specific virtual space to read "postings" to the group's electronic board. These groups came to be known as "Usenet" groups and continue as an active Internet phenomenon. The groups are often classified around specific interest areas and thus people with special interests can become attached to specific groups and begin to sense a feeling of community being built around the specific interest area.

Bollywood has been a theme in Usenet groups in two different ways. First, even though few dedicated groups deal only with Bollywood, there are numerous groups where Bollywood is a theme of discussion along with other themes. Thus, groups such as a "soc.culture.indian" or "rec.arts. movies.local.indian" have a significant focus on Bollywood, and members in these groups would often engage in a specific discussion thread that deals with the Indian movie industry. Sometimes, the individual posts are not specifically about Bollywood but are about issues that surround the movie industry in India. Consider for instance the following from a theme titled, "What happened to Hindustani culture in movies?":

Nowadays, all you get is synthetic songs like the ones in Bluffmaster, Ze-har etc where there is not a trace of Indian culture. Guess this is the way to go now with the Abhisheks and John Abrahams totally into the retro-sexual [sic] mood which reflects in the movies too like Taxi whatever, Bluffmaster etc. Even SRK is now toeing the line with modern pseudo-Western remakes of oldies like Don. Are there going to be movies like DDLJ, QSQT, HAHK with emotional Indian values going to ever be made again????? (Don, March 13, 2006 on rec.arts.movies.local.indian)

Posts such as this demonstrate that Bollywood remains a theme among many other similar topics in many of these Usenet groups. Indeed, the Indian movie industry is mentioned in many different Usenet groups, including ones such as "soc.culture.malaysia" where posters engage in discussions about issues about the Indian film industry.

The key to the Usenet groups is the fact that these are individuals who actively engage in a discussion in the virtual space of the Internet about a topic that is important to them, and many others can either follow the discussion or engage in the discussion itself. This is the tendency that can be traced in another Web resource that deals with Bollywood where similar discussions continue between people in "real time."

Chat Rooms

Simultaneously with blogs, chat rooms have also recently gained in popularity. Chat rooms represent a Web-based resource where many different people can have a discussion about specific issues, and the discussion is akin to a real group conversation since the people are assembled in real time in a virtual space. In other words, the chatters are all there together creating an energy that is quite distinct from reading someone else's Web page or responding to an e-mail. Indeed, the chat room is similar to the Usenet groups, but the emphasis here is on real time active participation as opposed to reading specific posts on Usenet groups. In most cases, these chat rooms are populated by individuals just as they are maintained and moderated by individuals, as opposed to spaces populated and controlled by institutions. The key to the use of the chat room remains in the fact that these are virtual spaces that can be occupied by people who could be separated by great geographic distances but are pulled together by thematic proximity. Also, chat rooms often require registration, where the chat room member must fill out some rudimentary forms and obtain an identity in the chat room to fully participate in the chatting process.

The key to the chat room is that the members must make a small effort to be a part of the group and take on the role of an agent who is willing to participate in a discussion. To be sure, there are those who only listen and are not active participants, but that behavior is not typically encouraged in chat rooms. This is particularly true about the chat rooms about Bollywood, where the participants often have specific ideas and thoughts about the movie industry. Much like the Usenet groups, there are numerous chat rooms that deal with India and many of them also deal with Bollywood. Unlike the thematic nature of Usenet groups or specific topic-related Web pages, chat rooms often evolve and discussions can revolve around many different topics, one of which could be the Indian movie industry.

These many resources all together play a role in creating the virtual presence of Bollywood on the Internet. Thus, the emergent Bollyweb is made up of a network of discourse which together has the potential to change the way in which Bollywood operated in the real cultural sphere, and it is useful to explore the ways in which Bollyweb could influence Bollywood.

Voices of Bollyweb

It has been argued that the Internet offers individuals an opportunity to find a place to voice their opinions (Mitra and Watts 2002). Indeed, one of the ways in which it is possible to understand the impact of the Internet is to consider it a space where individuals are able to speak with the hope that many people will listen to them. Unlike other means of mass communication, speaking in virtual space is a less resource-intensive project and anyone with some computer access and rudimentary knowledge of using the Internet is able to express themselves. This process has thus opened up the opportunity for individuals, who might have been traditionally powerless, to be able to gain a sense of power around the discourses and texts that they are able to produce and circulate on the Internet.

This is precisely what can be observed in the case of Bollyweb. Except for the institutional websites, nearly all the other manifestations of Bollyweb are individuals voicing their opinions and ideas. Similar trends can also be traced with other movie industries where a fan base constantly talks of the industry and its artifacts. In fact, this process has been around for a long time, far before the Internet came into being, where dedicated fans would discuss their favorite media programs and even have special celebrations about their favorite media formation. The Internet, however, adds a twist to the traditional "fan mail" because the voices that are heard in personal Web pages, blogs, chat rooms, and Usenet groups are able to transcend some of the traditional barriers that other fans would have experienced.

To begin with, these voices are unencumbered by institutional constraints. There is very little control on the way in which individuals are able to talk about the Bollywood industry when they do so in their Web pages. Indeed, not all of the discussion is complementary and there are many instances where the voices actually offer a strong critique of the industry. Consider for instance a review of a movie released in 2005, where one of the individuals posting on a Web-based discussion group critiqued the movie as a substandard movie made by a well-known production house in India. This particular review was certainly not complementary, but it found a space to be heard even though it was written by an individual unconnected with the film industry. It generated numerous responses as others read the review on the Web and either agreed or disagreed with the original poster (Prasidddha 2005). This is a process which mimics the informal discussions about movies that would take place in real life, but now provides many more with the opportunity to engage in these conversations, thus allowing many to have a voice about something.

Eventually, many such threads of discussion ranging from critiques of movies to lead songs from movies being digitized and distributed as ring tones for mobile phones make up a digital cacophony of voices, as many speak together to produce Bollyweb. Without a doubt this helps Bollywood because it allows the industry to have a Web presence that provides it with the exposure it needs to thrive in a global marketplace. As Fiske (1987) has pointed out, media texts are inherently intertextual and the primary text, such as a movie, is connected with the secondary and tertiary texts of reviews of the movies and the role and impact of the primary text is implicated by the secondary and tertiary texts. In the past, much of those secondary and tertiary texts were built around institutionally produced voices of movie critics and newspaper reviews, but the Internet has now been able to extend that voice to a larger community of individual speakers. Indeed, these voices are now becoming global, and can be produced anywhere in the world and can be heard anywhere in the world. This creates a condition where a localized phenomenon limited within a special interest group can take on a global potential where someone unconnected with the phenomenon stumbles upon a text about Bollywood on the Web and develops an interest in the industry.

Bollyweb Going Global

The fact that the voices can be heard globally is made possible by one of the key components of the Internet—it has made traditional boundaries disappear for a variety of human endeavors. Indeed, the entire notion of space has been transformed as it has become possible to access and connect texts and discourses from far-flung places into one seamless whole. The Web is one of the manifestations of this process. Eventually, the texts, which represent a multitude of voices, become connected in a global virtual space to create a unified voice. The process happens in the virtual but is able to bring together elements of the real in a way that has not been possible before, offering a new sense of power to people and institutions that were often powerless simply because of where they were located.

This globalization of voices has been felt in the case of Bollywood as well as its virtual counterpart—Bollyweb—as a global phenomenon. Traditionally, the Indian film industry had been geographically limited to India and perhaps some neighboring countries. The audience was primarily in India. However, with the increasing diasporic presence of Indians across the globe, there was a demand for Bollywood in other countries and the demand was met by bootlegged and inferior-quality copies of films. This began to change as the diaspora became more influential and demanded better quality products, and the Internet began to connect the diaspora such that they were able to make their demands heard and were also able to provide a global presence to the film industry.

With the various ways in which Bollyweb is manifest, it is no longer the case that the discussions about the industry are limited only to groups in India, as the chat rooms can be populated by people from anywhere in the world and the Usenet groups have subscriptions from a global audience. The latter becomes a particularly interesting illustration of the way in which Bollyweb has gone global, where Usenet groups that might have little to do with India could also have threads of discussions about Bollywood. Without a doubt, the industry has also done a better job of advertising itself globally and has been able to distribute its products in a global market, but the virtual voices about the industry have helped to supplement the efforts of the industry.

It is also important to note that while the industry is doing its part in the realm of the "real," it is individuals whose voices are globalizing Bollyweb. A large segment of the personal Web pages and blogs about Bollywood actually represent the voices of the diaspora. These are people who are not physically in India but have a fondness for Bollywood that has motivated them to produce some component of Bollyweb. Often the Web pages would make this explicit as the author claims that the process of putting together a page dedicated to some component of Bollywood is a very personal and private project which eventually has a very public effect. Consider for instance the home page of a person called "Jaydeep" who claims that he has lived in the United States for nearly 20 years and maintains a home page with numerous links about Bollywood (Jaydeep 2006). There are numerous such pages that come up when doing a search about Bollywood on the Web, and many such pages would either have information that the individual has gathered together about Bollywood or would provide links to institutional Web pages about Bollywood. Often these personal Web pages would also provide links to the Web pages of other individuals who might have interesting Bollywood pages. This interconnection between pages, mostly personal and some institutional, maintained and accessed by people across the globe makes Bollyweb global and provides an opportunity for the real life industry to find a way of leveraging its global virtual presence. The notion of presence becomes critical in this context because Bollyweb is increasingly globally present, and that not only transforms the way Bollywood might shape its future but it also impacts the way in which Bollywood would be remembered in the future.

Bollyweb as the Digital Memory of Bollywood

One of the outcomes of creating a global presence of voices on the Internet is that these voices could remain in the global Web space for a long time, and sometimes may become the digital memory that can be sustained for a long time. It has been argued that the idea of memory and how we remember our history is quickly being transformed by the Internet (Mitra 2005). History has typically been institutional as specific professionals have taken on the task of either discovering history or chronicling the present for the future. Such histories have been constructed around institutions, and the voices of many either are lost or were never heard. The Internet has the potential to change that.

Consider the way in which Bollyweb can begin to alter the way in which the industry might be remembered. There are some books, such as this, about the industry written by scholars, researchers, and historians who have been able to research and record the institution's history. On the other hand, a search for images of Madhuri Dixit, a Bollywood actress, yields 4,530 websites which in turn have multiple images of the actress. This is an alternative history that is being authored in the realm of the virtual, where the fans and the critics are creating a repertoire of texts, images, and sounds which could be preserved to create a networked digital history of Bollywood that would be much more textured than books and chronicles. This is a living biography, with its inaccuracies and factual gaps, but created from the authentic voices of those who look at the industry fondly. This process has been possible because of the technological changes that have made it possible to create and store large amounts of digital data that can also be made available globally.

Evidence of this process is quite visible in the Usenet groups which tend to maintain postings for a long time, so it is not unusual to stumble across discussions about movies that are not popular any more, but in those discussions a history of the movie has been preserved. Without a doubt the digital age has allowed for better preservation technologies, but it is not the technology only that matters. The digital memory remains once built around personal voices speaking about Bollywood that presents an alternative view of the industry. Consider for example the following quotation from such a personal voice:

> Hi, Welcome to my web site! There is lot for you here movies, downloads, favourite T.V. serials, Bollywood stuff and much more! Have fun guys and enjoy the site. (Anant 2006)

Then the author proceeds to provide the reader with a series of links and pictures of some of the key actors and actresses in Bollywood. Several links provide many more images and sounds and all together this and numerous such pages offer an ongoing chronicle of the industry, writing a non-institutional history of Bollywood.

Conclusion

As in the case of many different industries, the Internet has allowed for the creation of new cultural and social processes that simply did not exist before the Internet came into being. From commercial activities such as online shopping to interpersonal behavior such as communicating via e-mail, our everyday life practices have been irreversibly impacted by the Web. Specifically, two aspects have been most critically impacted. First, out notion of time has been changed, as there is a new urgency associated with much of what we do. Having to wait for things is increasingly unacceptable. For an industry like Bollywood, the tradition of having to wait for particular artifacts to be available for global consumption has now disappeared. Legal and illegal copies of movies, music, pictures, and other artifacts can be made available on the Web as soon as a movie might have theatrical release. Copies of movies, music, and images are freely circulated within the many different Web resources discussed here. Such movement of artifacts certainly raises important questions about ownership of copyright, but at the same time, it helps to quickly globalize the products of Bollywood. On another note, images that might have eroded with time have been resurrected and the contemporary products are being better preserved to withstand the vagaries of time, as the digital is supplementing analog products.

Second, the Internet has transformed the way we negotiate space. The boundaries that tended to divide and separate are disappearing, albeit new dividers constantly emerge. Yet, many restrictions produced by spatial separation are gone and many discourses, texts, and voices that were restricted to specific spaces have been able to transcend the distances. As demonstrated in the examples in this chapter, that has certainly been true for Bollywood, as the collection of voices—individual and institutional—originated in many different places and can be heard globally. Indeed, the origin of the voice becomes increasingly irrelevant as long as the speaker has something coherent to say about Bollywood and can thus contribute to the growth of the global Bollyweb.

Without a doubt, the blurring of the distinctions produced by space and time has had a significant and welcome effect on the commercial interests of Bollywood. While the film industry has attempted to gain a global presence by producing films that have achieved global recognition and by sending its stars abroad to gain exposure, particularly in the West, it has also always struggled to find a global audience. Perhaps Bollyweb is beginning to alter that, as people across the globe are beginning to "talk about" Bollywood and it is thus creating a cacophony of voices that together are able to offer Bollyweb a global space, thus paving the way for a global Bollywood. It is Bollyweb that can provide the catalyst to bring the large numbers of Indian, in India and outside, together while quickly globalizing the Indian movie industry.

It is also important to note that, much like many other things on the Internet, Bollyweb is not a static construct. The Web constantly morphs and new voices come into being while other voices might disappear. There are many factors that control the process of the transformation of the Internet, but there are some tendencies that can be noted about the Web in general. Most important among these is the way in which the traditional Web space, primarily composed of home pages, has been slowly colonized by institutional voices. Thus, what started in the 1980s as a space to put up one's personal Web page has now changed into a virtual space where the most noticeable pages are the ones maintained by institutions, corporations, and organizations who are using the Web as a marketing and publicity tool. This is true for Bollyweb as well. In fact, many of the most popular "hits" that are obtained when doing a search for Bollywood are commercial Web pages that have simply been put up to speak about the film industry. As pointed out earlier, these pages offer a different view of Bollywood from the personal home pages, which are often biased and slanted, but still speak for an individual who has a point of view and now has the opportunity to express it.

The increasing commercialization of the Web page phenomenon has thus produced a condition where the personal voices have found alternative spaces to reside in. Consequently, as seen in the case of Bollyweb, there is a plethora of blogs and Usenet groups where the individual can still find a safe virtual space in which to speak. This is particularly important because it offers a space where people who have felt powerless to speak can now find a space to express themselves and find others who are interested in speaking about the same issue. No doubt, such virtual groups help to promote Bollywood, but they also help to promote a global fraternity around Bollyweb which simultaneously serves the Indian industry and the people of India.

BIBLIOGRAPHY

Anant. 2006. "Anant rules!!!" Available at: http://anant_n.tripod.com/index.htm.

CBS News (February 17, 2005). "Introducing Aishwarya Rai." Available at: http://www.cbsnews.com/stories/2005/02/10/earlyshow/leisure/celebspot/6.shtml.

Chakrabarty, D. 2006. "Amitabh Bachchan: The King of Cinema." Available at: http://www.geocities.com/thisisamitabh.

Fiske, J. 1987. *Television Culture.* London: Methuen.

Google. 2006. "Zeitgeist: Search patterns, trends, and surprises." Retrieved on June 6, 2006, from: http://www.google.com/press/intl-zeitgeist.html#in.

Jaydeep. 2006. "Welcome to Jaydeep's personal homepage." Retrieved on August 25, 2006, from: http://www.geocities.com/Colosseum/Park/9801/JAYDEEP-25.html.

Mitra, A. 1999. "Characteristics of the WWW Text: Tracing Discursive Strategies." *Journal of Computer Mediated Communication* 5(1). Retrieved August 24, 2005, from: http://www.ascusc.org/jcmc/vol5/issue1/mitra.html.

Mitra, A. 2005. "Digital Memory." *Journal of Information, Communication & Ethics in Society* 3 (1): 3–13.

Mitra, A., and E. Cohen. 1999. "Analyzing the Web: Directions and Challenges." In *Doing Internet Research*, ed. S. Jones, 179–202. London: Sage.

Mitra, A., and E. Watts. 2002. "Theorizing Cyberspace: The Idea of Voice Applied to the Internet Discourse." *New Media & Society* 4 (4): 479–98.

Prasidddha, 2005. "Finally a Flop from Yash Chopra!!" Retrieved August 12, 2005, from: http://www.mouthshut.com/review/Neal_N_Nikki-88959-1.html.

Sharma, A. 1993. "Blood Sweat and Tears: Amitabh Bachchan, Urban Demi-God." In *You Tarzan: Masculinity, Movies and Men*, ed. P. Kirkham and J. Thumim. New York: St. Martin's Press.

lll

"We're Online, Not on the Streets"
Indian Cinema, New Media, and Participatory Culture

Aswin Punathambekar

On September 14, 2005, Tamil film star Vijaykant announced his entry into politics by converting his fan association into a political party.[1] The *Desiya Murpokku Dravida Kazhagam* (DMDK, National Progressive Dravidian Party) was launched at a conference organized by the Tamilnadu Vijaykant Fan Association, with the secretary of the fan association (Ramu Vasanthan) assuming the role of general secretary of the DMDK. The fan association's flag was adopted as the party flag as well. For several months preceding this conference, members of the fan association worked tirelessly to publicize and raise funds for the conference. Pointing to their preparedness for political activity, one magazine noted, "What stood him in good stead was the organization and structure of his fans' association, which is built in the form of a political party with units at the village, panchayat, town, district and State levels" (Subramanian 2005). In fact, in local body elections held in 2001, as many as 575 of Vijaykant's fans were elected to posts at various levels across the state of Tamilnadu (Subramanian 2005).

Around the same time in 2005, fans of renowned music director A. R. Rahman were hard at work organizing a concert in Bangalore. Fans managed everything from promotions and ticket sales to stage construction and crowd control on the day of the concert (October 8, 2005). As part of their effort to gain recognition as the "official" Rahman fan group, they also decided to present Rahman with a gift—a montage, composed of thumbnail images of all his album covers, which formed the contours of his face. Faced with the prospect of buying expensive software, a group of fans (who run a design company called 3xus.com) went on to develop their own software. After many sleepless nights of painstaking coding, they finally got to meet Rahman and present the gift. Acknowledging these fans' perseverance, technical and marketing savvy, and global network established through online activities, Rahman and his team have decided to collaborate with them to promote and organize concerts in different cities worldwide, evolve new modes of music distribution, and work together to tackle piracy. This story of fan activity went unreported in mainstream media. Referring to news stories of violent clashes between Vijaykant fans and activists of a political party who took offense at Vijaykant's remarks directed at their leader, the moderator of the Rahman fan community remarked, "We're online, not on the streets. We would never venture into street battles, and that does not attract media attention" (Interview, October 15, 2005).

Violent conflicts between fans of film stars and cadres of opposition political parties, cinema halls being vandalized, and film stars contemplating a career in politics by mobilizing their fan associations certainly make more sensational copy compared to a group of highly educated, technically skilled fans who discuss film music on the Internet. To those familiar with the history of cinema's links to politics in states like Tamilnadu and Andhra Pradesh, Vijaykant emerging as a political candidate is no great surprise. Indeed, when one raises the question of fan activity in Indian film culture, the standard response, among journalists and academics, is to point to Tamil and Telugu film cultures where fan associations devoted to former stars like M. G. Ramachandran and N. T. Rama Rao have played pivotal roles in their political careers (Pandian 1992; Srinivas 2000). As the editor of *Filmfare* remarked, "You'll find crowds outside Amitabh Bachchan or Shahrukh Khan's house. But never the level of passion you'd find in the south. There is no organized fan activity around Bollywood. No one asks Shahrukh Khan to float a political party or threatens to commit suicide just because his film flops!"

In this chapter, I argue against framing fan activity in Indian film culture in terms of devotional excess or in relation to political mobilization in south India. Detailing the formation and activities of the Rahman fan community, I suggest we shift our attention away from the cinema hall and heroes like Vijaykant to the realm of film music and the figure of the music director. This move will force us to take into account how cinema, as an experience and an object of study, is constituted in fundamental ways through convergence with other media. In other words, developing fan activity surrounding film music as an entry point entails rethinking the history of cinema's publicness as a history of media convergence, i.e., a history of cinema's intersections with various "new" media (radio, TV, Internet, and mobile phone).

Such a reconceptualization of cinema's public-ness will help us steer away from treating fan activity as mere epiphenomena of politics and transitions in the political sphere proper. This, in turn, compels consideration of fan practices surrounding Tamil or Telugu cinema that may have no connections to political parties and elections, and also to pose the question of fan activity in relation to Bollywood. Following this, I reassess the figure of the fan, arguing that we locate the "fan" along a more expansive continuum of participatory culture by dismantling the binary of *fan-as-rowdy* versus *fan-as-rasika*.[2] Finally, I situate fan practices in relation to the experience of cyberculture in India (Sundaram 2000) and suggest that fan communities constitute a privileged site for mapping, in historically grounded fashion, the emergence of the Internet as a vital new space of public culture in late twentieth and early twenty-first-century India.

Film Music and Fan Culture: The Case of A. R. Rahman

Among other distinguishing elements of popular Indian cinema, the presence of at least five or six songs with varied narrative functions is cited often. Choreographed into elaborate dance sequences, songs have been an integral part of Indian cinema ever since sound was introduced. As Majumdar explains, "Film songs and song sequences have their own circuit of distribution, both official, or industrial, and unofficial [. . .] they permeate the aural environment of India's public spaces, from markets and festivals to long-distance buses and trains" (Majumdar 2001: 161). The commercial value of film music has also meant that music directors and playback singers have occupied a key role in the industry from the very beginning.

Music directors have been central to developments and transformations in practically every aspect of the process—lyrics, expansion of orchestras and introduction of instruments from around the world, singing styles (transition from actor-singers to playback singers), and from the perspective of producers, responding to and shaping audience tastes (Arnold 1988). In fact, from the early 1940s, producers have been giving prominence to music directors. Film songs became a central component of pre-release publicity of films, and advertising began emphasizing the music director. Arnold points to a practice that continues to this day: major producers began to select commercially successful music directors to work on their new productions (1988: 206). Having their names displayed prominently on posters, billboards, and gramophone record sleeves, and radio shows such as the nationally popular *Binaca Geet Mala* (on Radio Ceylon), led to the construction of what Majumdar terms "aural stardom" (2001).[3] Over the years, songs came to be associated with music directors (and playback singers) just as much as with actors/actresses lip-synching on the screen.

Rahman started his musical career as an ad-jingles composer and emerged as a music director in the 1990s—first in Tamil cinema and post-1995, in the Bombay-based Hindi film industry. While translations of his work for Tamil-language films such as *Roja* (1992, Mani Ratnam) and *Bombay* (1995, Mani Ratnam) were highly successful, it is with *Rangeela* (1995, Ramgopal Varma) that Rahman made his mark as a "national" music director. Rahman's non-film projects have also been highly successful—for instance, his 1997 album *Vande Mataram*, released to coincide with the fiftieth year of Indian independence, sold millions of copies worldwide.

There are at least two things to keep in mind that set Rahman apart from other important music directors. First, projects such as *Vande Mataram* (1997) that involved Rahman in music videos, and promotions on cable and satellite TV channels like Channel [V] and ZEE, gave him a strong *visual* presence in addition to the aural stardom conventionally associated with music directors. In fact, Rahman figures prominently in posters advertising "Bollywood tours" worldwide—his performativity, in other words, extends beyond recorded sound. Second, his rise coincided with the Bombay film industry attracting mainstream attention in transnational arenas, in main part due to the Indian diaspora's close ties to cinema. This led not only to an expanded audience and fan base, but also to visibility generated in "world music" circles (Talvin Singh's music from the Asian Dub Foundation in London, for example), and composing music for international projects such as *Bombay Dreams* (2002) and the stage version of *Lord of the Rings: The Return of the King* (2006). The multiple boundaries that Rahman (and his music) traverses—linguistic (Tamil-Hindi-English), religious (Hindu converted to Islam), regional/national, diasporic, and global—are strongly reflected in the online fan community.

At a broader level, it is also important to locate Rahman's music as a defining element of films like *Roja* that inaugurated, as scholars like Niranjana have shown, a new Indian nationalism "premised on a detaching of the new middle class from the Nehruvian state of the post-Independence years" (Niranjana 2000: 138). *Roja* and *Bombay*, among other "patriotic love stories" during the mid- to late 1990s, tapped into and articulated a new and aggressive middle-class sensibility that acquired an unprecedented level of visibility "owing to a new configuration of forces which include[d] the rise of the Sangh Parivar and the liberalization of the Indian economy" (38).[4] Rahman's music, one might argue, was a critical aural dimension of this articulation of a new nationalism. Rahman's music served as a soundtrack for the new middle classes and for those outside this sphere, an aspirational sound. This is also reflected in the composition of the Rahman fan community—not only are India-based fans a part of this new middle class, their sense of being a "fan" is shaped strongly by the idea that Rahman's music represents a global-yet-Indian sound.

The Rahman fan community is an online forum that was formed on January 1, 1999 and today involves nearly 8,500 members from 26 different countries. This is a space that brings together, for instance, fourth-generation Tamil-Malaysians, second-generation Indian-Americans, Indians in Gulf countries like Dubai, youth in urban India, and a growing number of non-Indian fans.[5] Embedded as citizens in disparate ways, each fan brings her/his own linguistic/regional background, experiences of varying racial/ethnic politics, religious affiliations, different registers of knowledge and affiliation with India and "Indian" culture, to bear on her/his engagement with Rahman's music and Indian cinema in general.

Arrahmanfans.com, like most online fan groups that cohere around film, consists of a filmography, a member directory, a folder for creative works where fans post various clips of music, a music library where mp3 clips are stored, and a list of FAQs for new members. The group also maintains a large collection of photographs of Rahman from various occasions, and has recently developed a collection of Rahman-related videos hosted using YouTube. The "links" section contains URLs to a range of Rahman-related resources such as fan sites and blogs, newspaper and magazine articles, interviews, and websites about others in the film industry who work with Rahman.

Within the group, there is an emphasis on the need for all members to participate, and an acknowledgment of different competencies

—knowledge of Tamil and Hindi, for instance, in order to translate complex lyrics, or knowledge of technicalities of music that might be helpful in discussions. Rahman fans also monitor print publications, radio and television shows, and different websites for news and trivia about their star and, like other fan communities, perceive themselves as guardians of Rahman's image and attempt to control the circulation of negative coverage of Rahman's music or personal life. The community also includes people who work with Rahman on a professional basis, and these members have played a key role in getting this group recognized as Rahman's official fan group. Over the last two years, fans based in different cities around the world have also begun meeting offline to extend discussions conducted online, help organize concerts, and in some cases, to form bands and perform film songs.

Discussions are generally structured around the release of a film for which Rahman has composed music and revolve around lyrics, the use of different instruments and musical arrangement, songs' narrative functions, song picturization (and choreography), playback singers, and so on. Fans locate and post articles from various news sources and these become the basis for a discussion regarding previous collaborations between Rahman and film directors, lyricists, rumors about plotlines, and more generally, the "sound" of the music. Reviews in newspapers, magazines, and online portals such as *rediff.com* and *indiafm.com* are considered crucial, and fans make it a point to post feedback on these sites if they feel the reviews are exceedingly negative.

As soon as the music is released, discussion returns to the lyrics. Translations (from Tamil or Hindi into English) are posted and the poetic worth of the lyrics becomes an important component of evaluation. This is usually followed by talk about the instruments used—fans with formal knowledge of music, or who are musicians themselves, write about new instruments introduced, the amount of mixing involved, and what the instruments signify in terms of traditions and genres. These discussions also include the question of playback singers—why Rahman has used particular singers, the singers' track records, their performance in the song under question, whether their voice "fits" the song and the actor/actress in the film, and so on. Once the film is released, discussion shifts to the picturization of the song in the film and how the song works in relation to the overall narrative.

Enabled by the Internet, constituted by individuals from different parts of the world, and driven by interest in film music that reaches around the world, there is no doubt that the Rahman fan community is strikingly different when compared to fan associations such as those that form around stars like Vijaykant. We could begin by noting that the Rahman fan community is an elite space and one that is defined explicitly in opposition to "rowdy" fan associations. We could point out that compared to fan associations that meet at street corners, tea-shops, and in and around cinema halls in India, online fan communities are not dominated by men. It is also evident that the Rahman fan community is not invested in mobilizing around caste or linguistic identity. Given that it is first and foremost a community realized online, and that fans bring diverse stakes and affiliations to bear on their participation, mobilization along axes of caste or language is, at a basic level, rendered structurally impossible. For example, fans based in Malaysia, for whom participation in the Rahman fan community is part of a larger process of claiming a Tamil ethnic identity, share little in common with second-generation Indian-Americans for whom dancing to a remixed Rahman song at a club speaks to a very different set of concerns.

Therefore, while useful to start with, such comparisons only take us so far. It is not enough to merely point out that the "fan" in question here is a middle-class subject or a diasporic subject. We are still left with the problem of approaching and defining such new modes of participatory culture, an increasingly central aspect of Bollywood, in opposition to a specific and idealized mode of participation that is explicitly political. The pressing challenge, then, is to reconceptualize the relationship between cinema and public culture by looking beyond the cinema hall and its vicinity, and rethinking the figure of the "fan" before we begin examining the social dynamics of spaces like the Rahman fan community.

From Radio Ceylon to Arrfans.com: Participatory Culture beyond the Cinema Hall

Sivathamby provided what is perhaps the earliest articulation of cinema and the public sphere in India. He argued that "the cinema hall was the first performance centre in which all Tamils sat under the same roof. The basis of the seating is not on the hierarchic position of the patron but essentially on his purchasing power. If he cannot afford paying the higher rate, he has either to keep away from the performance or be with all and sundry" (1981: 18). As Srinivas observes, this "formulation can be read as pointing to the democratic possibilities of cinema" (2003a: n.p.). While there was a certain mode of policing this "democratic" space (e.g., seating codes, from the "gandhi class" all the way up to "dress circle"), this does "permit us to conceive of the cinema hall as a kind of public institution that had no precedence in India" (Srinivas 2003b: 20). Following this formulation, several scholars have grappled with how cinema relates in complex ways to the civic and the political, but fan practices have not been a focus of systematic research (Prasad 1998; Rajadhyaksha 2000; Virdi 2003). The two notable exceptions are Srinivas's pioneering work on fan associations in Andhra Pradesh (2000) and Dickey's analysis of audiences in Tamilnadu (1993).

Dickey locates fan activity at the intersection of the formal realm of politics and civil social activity (charity work, blood donation campaigns, and other "social services"). Building on work that examines relationships between the construction of stardom and the politics of mobilization (Pandian 1992), Dickey provides a very useful ethnographic account of this aspect of fan activity in Tamilnadu. However, she ignores the possibility of fan activity that might not necessarily be "public" in the sense of there being a neighborhood fan association that meets at street corners, at tea-shops, or outside cinema halls. Indeed, her analysis circumscribes fan activity in Tamilnadu as that defined by working-class (often lower caste) male youth in visible, public spaces.[6]

In his path-breaking work on the Telugu film industry, and viewing practices in the state of Andhra Pradesh more broadly, Srinivas theorizes fan activity as being structured by a dialectic of devotion and defiance (2000), as a struggle between fan expectations and the industry's careful management of the star persona to derive maximum mileage from fan activity. Focusing on "megastar" Chiranjeevi, Srinivas situates the formation of fan clubs in Andhra Pradesh in relation to a broader history of subaltern struggles (dalit movements, for instance) and considers fan practices as a domain of political activity that does not fit within classical liberal accounts of citizenship and political representation, but one that has clear links to linguistic/regional identity (Srinivas 2000). As Liang argues, "the history of early postcolonial cinematic space is also marked by sharp social conflict and anxiety. For Srinivas, it is this public space marked by its histories of exclusions that fans seek to occupy" (Liang 2005: 372). Thus, for Srinivas, the performative dimensions of fan practices, especially as they cohere in and around the cinema hall, lead to a conception of a cinematic public sphere where "the consumption of film becomes an occasion for a range of performances that are broadly *political* in nature" (Srinivas 2003a: n.p.), one manifestation being the links to party politics and election campaigns. Further, while he argues that we also need to understand the political nature of fan associations beyond their "linkages with the politics of linguistic/identity nationalism," he maintains that fan activity is political mainly because it "develops around the notion of spectatorial rights." He writes:

> The cinema exists because of my presence and for me. Further, the "I" at the cinema is always a member of a collective: *we make the film happen.* Anyone who has watched a Chiranjeevi or Rajnikanth film knows exactly what I am talking about. Not only do these stars address spectators in rather direct ways (including by looking at the camera) but seem to perform according to "our" demands. (2003a: n.p.; italics in original)

Even as he exhorts us to examine the various "webs of public transactions" involving cinema, and to rethink what constitutes the "political" beyond the narrow sense of the term, Srinivas's analyses remain bound by one particular, highly visible, mode of fan activity and the film industry's perception and management of such activity. He goes on to say: "Much work needs to be done across the spectrum of activities and organizations that fade into the cinema hall at one end and the political party at the other" (2003a: n.p.).

In the light of Indian cinema's flows worldwide, the question of who comprises the "we" in the cinema hall and what "our" demands might be complicates the notion of "spectatorial rights" (Rajadhyaksha 2000). For it would be difficult to maintain that third-generation Tamil-Malaysian fans of Rajnikanth are positioned as spectators in precisely the same way as fans in Tamilnadu or, for that matter, Japanese fans who watch subtitled prints. "Spectatorial rights" certainly does not help us explain the kind of activity that Rahman fans are involved in, as we saw earlier. While opening up an important line of inquiry, Srinivas's analysis needs to be extended in at least two directions.

The first question we need to address is: are the two poles of the spectrum—the cinema hall and the political party—useful analytic categories to begin with? If one were to consider film music, a component of films that circulates in the public realm much before and long after the film itself does, it forces us to consider the radio, television, the Internet, and mobile phones as sites constitutive of the publicness of cinema as much as the cinema hall itself, if not more. Considering audience activity surrounding film music also contributes to recent debates concerning the spatial dimensions of cinema. As Vasudevan writes:

> Let us consider the cinema as a more matter of fact everyday space: composed of the hall, its internal organization of foyer, auditorium, seating and the projected film, and its public presence, as in its facade, advertisements, marquees, hoardings. And let us see this space in relation to a broader space, in the market, near factories, schools, office blocks, in a mall, in residential areas. (2003: n.p.)

If we were to think more broadly about cultural geographies of Indian cinema, it becomes clear that accounts such as Vasudevan's would remain incomplete without a consideration of spaces formed by cinema's intersections with new media.

Consider, for instance, the story of Rameshwar Prasad Bharnwal, a resident of Jhumri Tilaiya in the northern state of Jharkhand (formerly a part of Bihar), who has mailed at least 10 cards a day to *Binaca Geet Mala* when the show was broadcast on Radio Ceylon (Krishnan 1991). Bharnwal, a member of a radio listener's club that discussed films and film music, recalls sending hundreds of requests for popular songs. Embedded in this vignette of participatory culture are traces of a larger narrative of struggles over defining a "new" medium's role in shaping postcolonial India's "national culture." I would argue that Bharnwal's story should not be read as mere fan obsession but rather, as a way to think through a moment of media transition that involved India's first Minister of Information and Broadcasting (B. V. Keskar), who deemed film music cheap, vulgar, and unfit for broadcast on All India Radio, millions of Indians who bought radio sets equipped to receive short-wave frequencies and tuned in to Radio Ceylon, and film producers and music directors who helped channel advertising money and licenses to the one-hour hit-parade *Binaca Geet Mala* (Awasthy 1965).

In other words, shows such as *Binaca Geet Mala* on radio, *Chitrahaar* and *Showtheme* on state-regulated Doordarshan, the popular game show *Antakshari* on ZEE TV, and other film-based shows on MTV-India and Channel [V], and websites like *wahindia.com* are all key sites of what we can term "participatory film culture" outside the cinema hall. Radio, television, Internet, and cell phone networks are spaces of public culture with intimate ties to the cinema hall, but with distinct institutional, cultural,

and political histories that have shaped our experience of cinema and indeed, cinema itself. I would argue, then, that a focus on fan practices that
emerge at and shape the intersection of cinema and "new" media opens
up the possibility of rewriting the history of Indian cinema's public-ness
as a history of media convergence, and as a history of participatory culture that does not necessarily originate in the cinema hall and culminate
in the sphere of political parties and electoral campaigns.

Between the Rowdy and the Rasika

The second question we have to grapple with concerns the image of the
fan that we derive from a focus on the cinema hall and its surroundings,
and fan associations of stars like Vijaykant: obsessive, male, working class,
and rowdy. The "excessive" behavior that marks viewers in front rows
of cinema halls, what Liang (2005: 371) calls the "protocols of collective
behavior"—whistling and commenting loudly, throwing flowers, coins,
or ribbons when the star first appears on the screen, singing along and
dancing in the aisles, etc.—is routinely cited as what distinguishes fans
from the rest of the audience. Further, the publicness of fan associations'
activities—celebrating a star's birthday or 100 days of a film, organizing
special pre-release functions, adorning street corners with giant cutouts of
the star, decorating theaters where the film has had a successful run, etc.
—and press coverage of such activities have further served to both mar-
ginalize and circumscribe fan activity as undesirable, vulgar, and at times,
dangerous. As Srinivas, drawing on Dhareshwar and Srivatsan's analysis of
rowdy-sheeters, writes:

> The fan is a rowdy not only because he breaks the law in the course of
> his assertion or his association with criminalized politics—the fan be-
> comes a rowdy by overstepping the line which demarcates the legitimate,
> "constructive," permissible excess, and the illegitimate [. . .] as far as the
> "citizen" is concerned, the fan is a blind hero-worshipper (devoid of rea-
> son) and a villain. The rowdy/fan is an agent of politics which is de-legit-
> imized. (Srinivas 2000: 314)

Fans, in this view, are imperfect citizens in aesthetic, sociocultural, and
political terms. Middle-class constructions of norms of excess are, without doubt, designed in part to maintain hierarchies of cultural production

and taste. In other words, it is clear that the *fan-as-rowdy* is constructed in semantic and social opposition to the idea of the *fan-as-rasika*—rowdy fans of the actor Rajnikanth as opposed to rasikas of Carnatic musician M. S. Subbulakshmi, for instance. Where, then, do we position film music fans, like members of the radio club in Jhumri Tilaiya, who wrote hundreds of letters to Ameen Sayani, the famous anchor of *Binaca Geet Mala*, and played a critical role in the consolidation of singers and music directors' aural stardom? In what terms do we describe the desires and attachments of thousands of "respectable" English-speaking middle- and upper-middle-class men and women who constitute the primary readership for magazines like *Filmfare*? How do we account for shows such as *Pepsi Ungal Choice* (SUN TV) that rely so centrally on fan participation? Finally, how do we understand online life-worlds of fans in diverse locations worldwide who come together as online and offline communities on the basis of shared attachments to film culture? I wish to argue that dismantling the *rowdy/rasika* binary will allow us to reframe participatory culture and broaden the arena of inquiry to include spaces such as the Rahman fan community.

First, academic interest in "rowdy" fan associations has resulted in a romanticization of fan associations as belonging to the realm of "political society." Political society is a term that Partha Chatterjee has proposed to conceptualize relationships between individuals or groups that are outside the rule-bound and legal framework of bourgeois civil society and the state in postcolonial societies such as India. He writes:

> Most of the inhabitants of India are only tenuously, and even then ambiguously and contextually, rights-bearing citizens in the sense imagined by the constitution. They are not, therefore, proper members of civil society and are not regarded as such by the institutions of the state. But it is not as though they are outside the reach of the state or even excluded from the domain of politics. As populations within the territorial jurisdiction of the state, they have to be both looked after and controlled by various governmental agencies. These activities bring these populations into a certain *political* relationship with the state. (2004: 38)

Chatterjee argues that the "sites and activities characteristic of . . . political society" have become particularly visible since the 1980s owing to changes in the techniques of governance and a "widening of the arena of political mobilization, prompted by electoral considerations and often only for electoral ends" (47). This is shaped, Chatterjee points out, not only by organized political parties but also by "loose and often transient mobilizations, building on communication structures that would not be ordinarily recognized as political" (47). Thus, political society, for Chatterjee, is the domain of the population, not citizens. Using the example of illegal settlements in the city of Calcutta, Chatterjee further argues that such individuals/groups are not completely outside the purview of the state. As individuals who reside within the territorial and juridical boundaries of the state, they have to be cared for and controlled by government agencies. Even if it is clear that such individuals/groups "transgress the strict lines of legality in struggling to live and work," the state cannot ignore them and is forced to enter into different kinds of negotiations.

Chatterjee's formulation can certainly be employed to understand relationships between fan associations and the democratic process, especially given that such extra-legal domains have typically been neglected in political theory. Using the term "political society" accords this domain of participation a certain visibility previously denied it. For example, the story of the Vijaykant fan association that I described in the opening section of this chapter is about participatory culture surrounding cinema serving as a staging ground for contests over regional and linguistic identity. Vijaykanth's decision to articulate a vision of a "Dravida Nadu" (Dravidian Nation), one in which there would be "no blind opposition to Hindi," was seen as a significant departure given the history of conflict over the imposition of Hindi as a national language and the resistance that this faced in states like Tamilnadu, where film stars-turned-politicians campaigned on a pro-Tamil platform (Subramanian 2005).

However, to bracket fans as a nonelite public and theorize "rowdy" fan practices as an expression of subaltern politics can also be misleading if it leads us to ignore the overlaps and intersections between different sites and modes of fan expression. Consider the issue of "illegal" networks of film and music piracy in a city like Bangalore and the Rahman fan community, a space of participation constituted by a large number of elite youth with access to new media. While the Internet remains the main site of interaction, it is crucial to recognize that in cities like Bangalore, Rahman fans also navigate and participate in the extra-legal world of pirated VCDs, DVDs, and mp3 collections. The extra-legal world is not an exclusive and closed-off subaltern space but rather, one that intersects with "elite" spaces like Internet fan communities and, in fact, informs the practices of Rahman fans online. It is critical also to recognize the ambivalence that marks

Rahman fans' attitudes and practices when it comes to the issue of being part of the "illegal city" (Liang 2005). While some Rahman fans create ftp sites and upload collections of Rahman's songs and pieces of background music ripped from DVDs, others police music stores (makeshift stores set up on pavements in busy shopping areas, in shopping complexes, and so on), threatening to call the police if pirated CDs of Rahman's music are not taken off the shelf.

Part of the work for scholars interested in fan practices, and participatory culture more broadly, thus involves shining a bright light on a range of sites and modes of fan expression around cinema that have so far been obscured by the sterile binary of rowdy/rasika. Doing so will allow us to rethink the figure of the fan: part rowdy, part rasika, part pirate, part copyright-enforcer, the "fan" is no longer a figure operating in the margins of public culture, defined in opposition to the subject position of the citizen (Liang 2005). The "fan" is in and of itself a subject position that is claimed and acted upon in myriad ways in Indian film culture.

Second, a more wide-ranging focus on fan activity would also recognize the many ways in which industry practices, modes of consumption, and social networks that criss-cross regional, national, and transnational boundaries, are being shaped by convergence between cinema and "new" media. Interrogating the rowdy/rasika binary cannot be an end in itself— we need to specify the contexts and conditions in which fan activity operates. We need to treat the "fan" not only as a fluid subject-position taken up by individuals in different locations, but also as a dynamic construct that is industrial, textual, and social. In other words, I am suggesting that we examine how the "fan" operates in a circuit of cultural production—in this case, the flow of film content across multiple "new" media platforms. How do media producers (dot-com journalists, for example) understand "fans," and how is this understanding translated into their practice of developing interactive content? In what ways do "new media" texts invite and structure fan activity? What does an examination of online spaces like the Rahman fan group tell us about the many new and complex relationships between cinema, new media technologies, and social lives? Such a shift toward examining the "fan" as a construct that is not eternal and essential, but rather, as shaped equally by industry practices, textual properties of film-based content that flow across multiple media, and social interactions in identifiable fan communities, is critical if we are to understand how the current phase of media convergence is altering the circulation and reception of Indian films and film music worldwide.

Conclusion

I have argued that thinking through cinema's public-ness in terms of its convergence with new media and opening up the category of the "fan" will be a first step toward radically revising our understanding of fan culture surrounding Indian cinema.[7] In this section, I wish to situate fan practices in relation to the experience of cyberculture in India, and make the case that fan communities can serve as ethnographic sites *par excellence* for mapping the emergence of "cinematic cyberpublics."

Let me begin with a sketch of how the Rahman fan community was formed. In 1998, a few months after the state-owned telecommunications provider VSNL offered dial-up connections to the Indian public, Channel [V] announced that votes for "best music director of the year" could be sent via the Internet. Gopal Srinivasan, a Rahman fan based in Bangalore, spent the next few months surfing websites and discussion forums, gathering email addresses and coordinating an online campaign that would ensure Rahman won the music award. Gopal came into contact with a large number of Rahman fans around the world, mostly students and young expatriate Indians in the United States, United Kingdom, and Singapore, participating in newsgroups such as *rec.arts.movies.local.indian*. Having developed a database of close to 100 Rahman fans, Gopal decided to launch a group focused on Rahman and his music. As he explained, "Initially the group was dominated by people outside India, mainly because Internet access here was expensive and connections were slow. But once private service providers entered the business, and with cybercafés at every street corner, more fans from India got involved." Many of the fans Gopal contacted in 1998 continue to participate in the group, and many have gone on to develop contacts with Rahman and his team in Chennai, India.

My goal in providing this brief description is to suggest that fans, as informants, offer the opportunity to carry out not only an ethnography of fans and online fandom—of the presentation of selves and a mode of sociality on the Internet—but also of the processes that shaped Indian cinema's convergence with the Internet. During the early years of the Internet, cinema-related content was entirely fan-produced. It was only in 1997–98 that dot-coms like IndiaFM.com and Indiatimes.com began offering film content on the Web, and it took until 2000–2001 for dot-com businesses to stabilize and begin forging relationships with the film industry to provide content that was previously unavailable on the Internet. As explained earlier, one of the primary activities of fans involves monitoring, collecting, and circulating content on Rahman and his music. However, fan discussions around these topics often spiral out to deal with issues concerning film music and the film industry more broadly. Browsing through the discussion archives yields valuable information on industry dynamics that gradually led to dot-com companies becoming an integral part of film industries. At the same time, the collective intelligence of fans can also be conceived of as an archive that can help us account for the role of grassroots cultural production in the emergence of a cinematic cyberpublic over the past decade, and remain attuned to the influence that fans continue to exert on the development of a vast, transnational network of Indian film culture.

NOTES

1. This is a significantly revised version of an essay published in Jonathan Gray et al. (eds.), *Fandom: Identities and Communities in a Mediated World* (New York: NYU Press, 2007).

2. The term "rasika," derived from an aesthetic theory (*rasa*) of performance, connotes a highly developed sense of appreciation of various "high art" forms. Rasika can be roughly translated as "connoisseur."

3. Majumdar argues for "an aural conception of stardom to account for the dual pleasures and recognitions in song sequences, a concept of stardom in which even the absence of glamour and the invisibility of playback singers can be regarded as defining features of their star personas" (2001: 171).

4. The term "Sangh Parivar" means the Sangh Family, and refers to a group of right-wing Hindu political and cultural organizations including the Rashtriya Swayamsevak Sangh (RSS), the Vishwa Hindu Parishad (VHP), the Bajrang Dal, and the Bharatiya Janata Party (BJP).

5. The moderator of the group informed me that over the last 2 years, over 50 percent of new subscribers have been non-Indians. A look at the conversations in the newsgroups indicates, however, that it is fans of Indian origin who participate the most and non-Indian fans are lurkers for the most part and have yet to assert their presence in the group.

6. A significant problem with this notion of a fan association as constituting a "public" relates to the question of gender. For instance, Dickey uncritically accepts responses from women who claim that they are not members of fan associations because it would not be looked upon kindly by their family members and would make their reputations questionable in the neighborhood (Dickey 1993: 153).

7. Indeed, this move might even be what is required for posing questions

concerning fan practices that cohere around texts and stars in television, where fan involvement can be traced back to the earliest soaps on *Doordarshan* (*Hum Log*) and has only intensified with the entry and establishment of cable and satellite television.

BIBLIOGRAPHY

Arnold, A. 1991. *Hindi Filmi Geet.* Unpublished dissertation, University of Illinois, Urbana-Champaign.

Arnold, A. 1988. "Popular Film Song in India: A Case of Mass-Market Musical Eclecticism." *Popular Music* 7 (2): 177–188.

Awasthy, G. C. 1965. *Broadcasting in India.* Bombay: Allied Press.

Chatterjee, P. 2004. *The Politics of the Governed: Considerations on Political Society in Most of the World.* New York: Columbia University Press.

Dickey, S. 1993. *Cinema and the Urban Poor in South India.* Cambridge: Cambridge University Press.

Ford, S. 2006. *Fanning the Flames: Ten Ways to Embrace and Cultivate Fan Communities.* White paper, Convergence Culture Consortium, MIT.

Hughes, S. 2003. "Pride of Place." *Seminar*, no. 525. Retrieved on February 23, 2004, from http://www.india-seminar.com/2003/525.htm.

Krishnan, M. 1991. "Jhumri Tilaiya: Abode of Audio Addicts." *Sunday Observer*, January 26.

Liang, L. 2005. "Cinematic Citizenship and the Illegal City." *Inter-Asia Cultural Studies* 6 (3): 366–85.

Majumdar, N. 2001. "The Embodied Voice: Song Sequences and Stardom in Popular Hindi Cinema." In *Soundtrack Available: Essays on Film and Popular Music*, ed. P. R. Wojcik and Arthur Knight, 161–85. Durham, N.C.: Duke University Press.

Niranjana, T. 2000. "Nationalism Refigured: Contemporary South Indian Cinema and the Subject of Feminism." In *Community, Gender and Violence: Subaltern Studies XI*, ed. Partha Chatterjee and Pradeep Jegannathan. New York: Columbia University Press.

Pandian, M. S. S. 1992. *The Image Trap: M. G. Ramachandran in Films and Politics.* New Delhi: Sage.

Prasad, M. 1998. *Ideology of the Hindi Film: A Historical Construction.* New Delhi: Oxford University Press.

Rajadhyaksha, A. 2000. "Viewership and Democracy in the Cinema." In *Making Meaning in Indian Cinema*, ed. Ravi Vasudevan, 267–96. New Delhi: Oxford University Press.

Sivathamby, Karthigesu. 1981. *Tamil Film as a Medium of Political Communication.* Madras: New Century Book House.

Srinivas, S. V. 2000. "Devotion and Defiance in Fan Activity." In *Making Meaning in Indian Cinema,* ed. Ravi Vasudevan, 297–317. New Delhi: Oxford University Press.

Srinivas, S. V. 2003a. "Film Culture: Politics and Industry." *Seminar,* no. 525. Retrieved on August 18, 2004, from http://www.india-seminar.com/2003/525.htm.

Srinivas, S. V. 2003b. "Hong Kong Action Film in the Indian B-Circuit." *Inter-Asia Cultural Studies* 4 (1).

Subramanian, T. S. 2005. "Another Actor in Politics." *Frontline,* October 7.

Sundaram, R. 2000. "Beyond the Nationalist Panopticon: The Experience of Cyberpublics in India." In *Electronic Media and Technoculture,* ed. John Caldwell, 270–94. New Brunswick, N.J.: Rutgers University Press.

Vasudevan, R. 2003. "Cinema in Urban Space." *Seminar,* no. 525. Retrieved on February 23, 2004, from http://www.india-seminar.com/2003/525.htm.

Virdi, J. 2003. *The Cinematic ImagiNation: Indian Popular Films as Social History.* New Brunswick, N.J.: Rutgers University Press.

Afterword

Fast-Forward into the Future, Haunted by the Past: Bollywood Today

Arvind Rajagopal

There is no easy conclusion that can follow this rich offering of essays. In its latest incarnation as "Bollywood," as several of the writers here show, Hindi cinema has indeed become accessorized as part of today's cosmopolitan *savoir-faire*, comfortably included in the swelling repository of "globalcult," the counterpart of what Dwight MacDonald in 1961 termed masscult.

It seems like only a few years ago that Hindi cinema was discovered by scholars to be a national medium, expressing a popular sense of an all-India collective before one could really be said to exist.[1] Until recently, after all, the developmental state seemed to stand for the nation, and its leaders spoke in words that were heard but seldom known to persuade or get repeated, and certainly were not sung. In contrast, Hindi cinema, scorned by the literati and denied the bounty of government subsidies, sought to anchor its appeal to a national market by creating a cinematic image of the state. In this shadow representation, which Javed Akhtar has described as a distinct entity, namely the state of Hindi cinema,[2] the policemen always arrived too late to sort out any trouble, but just in time to assert the authority to do so.[3] Meanwhile, it was the songs that most viewers identified with, often in extra-diegetic sequences whose ideological power lay more in their performance of a collective identity than in the construction of a classical Hollywood spectator as conceived in the pages of *Screen*, for example.[4]

Now it seems that, before Hindi cinema could move toward significantly more complex conceptions of the society, it has, or has been declared to be, globalized, as Bollywood. The center of gravity of the audience is therefore liable to be shifted by the weight of the NRI's stronger currencies. As a result, we find Bollywood focusing less on the growing pains of an emerging democracy and more on the lifestyle of a new Indian consuming class that appears literally to have taken off, making its location irrelevant.

This is not to say that its domestic impact is irrelevant. What we have witnessed as a result is a narrowing of themes and a greater social homogeneity across the characters. At the same time, the multiplex market has made niche market films possible, that are new and more varied in their combination of story and treatment. When the nation is an explicit theme, the political difficulties of appealing to a mass market appear to drive filmmakers toward either timidity or conservatism. What does it mean to be a good Indian today? Filmmakers may find it difficult to answer this question without negotiating the conundrums of caste, gender, sexuality, and religious politics.[5] For a film seeking to be nationalist, it is far easier to sidestep these issues and place the story in the colonial past, or in a foreign country, where the idea of India can safely be posed against non-native others.

To the extent that the nation is still a preoccupation of Hindi cinema, it is not always in the same exhortational mode. Films may instead adopt more tacit and interiorized forms of address, focusing on spatially and politically more limited themes that are harder to connect directly to the nation. One way in which this shift registers is in the disappearance of the traditional figure of a villain like Pran or Prem Chopra, who is committed to challenging basic social mores and requires punishment.[6] Instead, problems may be ceremonially resolved within lavishly rendered tableaux of the upper-caste Hindu undivided family, where everyone is redeemed, or aestheticized in gangster films where criminality permeates across state and civil society, and no one can be redeemed.[7]

For a period, call it the pre-Bollywood phase for the moment, Hindi cinema offered a pedagogical effort to define what the nation ought to stand for, whether as a project of upliftment requiring its citizens to sacrifice, an entity needing to thwart its internal enemies, e.g., smugglers and amoral women, or a plural society requiring communal harmony. In the cinema of the post-1994 era—to follow Ashish Rajadhyaksha's periodizing of Bollywood's emergence—there is a discernible expansion in the modes of pedagogy that is harder to characterize synthetically. On the one hand, there is a greater exclusivity in the imagined community being projected, more upmarket in its consumption habits, and more able to constitute a world of their own, without having to engage with members of different classes, or with villainous characters. A film like *Dil Chahta Hai* (dir. Farhan Akhtar, 2000) for example, altogether eliminates any People Like Them, or PLT, to use the appropriate marketing parlance. For the premium market, there is at the same time an increased range of films in the multiplexes, where departures from existing formulas are tested in limited-release ventures. On the other hand, the mass cinema market has its own downstream products, with more economical films with declining stars or aspiring ones being made for B and C class towns, which do not circulate in the metros. For example, Mithun Chakravorty has specialized in producing films that address this cultural hinterland for some years now. We observe a growing folk culture of VCD and DVD production, not only of pirated copies of big city cinema, but also produced by new entrepreneurs, morality tales as well as news events set to voiceover and folksongs, in regional languages like Bhojpuri and Haryanvi, pointing to the migration of cinematic forms across new media platforms.

Without properly reckoning with this diversity, we have moved quickly from ideas of a national cinema to a globalized Bollywood. However, the idea of the nation is itself only a place-holder, whose symbols and values represent a larger, shifting, and only partially known reality. There is a risk, in this categorial shift, of assuming that the nation is instead a determinate, homogeneous entity, whose many parts move in miraculous synchrony. Rather than necessarily assuming a theoretical unity to the audience as the national community, scholars have begun to investigate empirical viewers and their engagements with cinematic texts and the institution of cinema.

Thus, some of the essays in this volume gesture to the enigmatic plurality within the audience and in fan culture by invoking the distinction drawn by Partha Chatterjee, between civil society and political society.[8] For Chatterjee, the latter term stands for the *terra incognita* of not just the mofussil and the rural, but as well the urban hinterland, populated not by People Like Us but by People Like Them, whose lives tend to remain in discreet obscurity.

The importance of Chatterjee's argument hinges on its expansion of the domain of analysis legible to scholarly scrutiny, providing a framework within which otherwise theoretically aberrant characteristics of a country like India can be incorporated. Civil and political societies stand in a one-to-one relation with "formal" and "informal" realms respectively, in his conception; the informal realm has typically been treated as residual.[9] By naming it as political society, Chatterjee seeks to bring visibility to this below-the-radar domain, of which no ready archive exists, of the fugitive and often paralegal transactions by which the majority secures its livelihood.

"Political society" should be an invitation to further inquiry. If it is treated as a mere descriptor instead, it becomes a terminological cloak, one that requires to be lifted if we are to understand what the civil/political, formal/informal separation means and how it is actually performed. Those inhabiting the "formal" domain tend to perceive it as inevitable, while those in the "informal" domain see it as unjust. Thus, the distinction is hardly self-evident, but requires explanation in itself. Indeed, the cinema cuts across this divide and refashions it for consumption, in ways that would have to be inquired into.

So we can ask—what does Hindi cinema look like from the informal domain itself, for example from the side of the older and now neglected folk arts? Here is a view of the cinema expressed by a Kolhati, member of a Rajasthani nomadic community that has migrated to western Maharashtra, and engages in *tamasha* performances, dancing and singing by women before an audience of men. Practiced as a hereditary art, *tamasha* earns the women money but brands them amoral at the same time, effectively ostracizing them from respectable society.

> Dancing is our business and our art. But, these days all kinds of women indulge in blatant prostitution under the guise of dancing. If our *pallu* slips even a few inches off our chest it causes a commotion. But heroines in movies dance with bodies exposed, with a different hero each time and it is called art. They go to Delhi and win awards for it. It is all a joke played on us by shameless people. [10]

The statement is drawn from the autobiography of a Kolhati boy, Kishore Kale, whose aunt, Rambha *maushi*, is protesting the unjust treatment she receives as a kind of historic joke. The disparagement of Kolhatis is anachronistic when compared to the liberal sexual mores of the cinema, and yet there appears to be no ripple effect of change from the popularity of the cinema. Rather, the success of films and film stars looks to be in a self-enclosed world, in which membership is not open to all.

What is it about the cinema that apparently gives it a special status, able to be popular and celebrated while the same arts when performed off-screen can "cause a commotion"? When seen from the side of the cinema, this enchantment effect tends to be understood simply as an aspect of modernization and popular awakening. But the remark deserves to be taken seriously. We are accustomed to treating technology as instrumental to the ends it is meant to serve, but something more complex may be going on here, beyond the scope of this short afterword. By way of an answer, let us consider a different example, this time from the cinema itself.

A recent film, *Lage Raho Munnabhai* (2006, Rajkumar Hirani), both a popular and a critical success, offers some reflections on the topic of mediation in general. In this film, Mahatma Gandhi returns as a ghost; his charismatic presence is channeled through a radio talk show host, to a growing audience thirsting for ethical guidance. The ubiquitous statues and public portraits of Gandhi signify nothing to people any more, and a public library dedicated to preserving his memory stands empty and ignored. It is the magic of his spoken words, heard, remembered, and retold, that has the power to change people.

Here is a nation increasingly reliant on technologies of mediation and yet ever more distrustful of their artifice. The older technologies of stone, canvas, and paper have become hermetic and ineffective in their ability to communicate, perhaps not from any innate deficiency. For example, when the protagonist, Sanjay Dutt, spends three days and nights at the Mahatma Gandhi Library, the great man appears before him, moved by his prayerful attention when all else have forgotten his memory.

However, the newer technology of radio has a radiant energy, able to convey the force of Gandhi's wisdom through the obstacles not only of bricks, mortar, and physical distance, but of human obtuseness and moral turpitude as well, that obviously foil the simpler device of print. Here the specter of Gandhi inspires the nation to come together again, after decades of corrupt and divisive government.

Here is an apparent solution to the problem of visualizing the nation in an inclusive way today.[11] Is the radio here merely a tool, whose effects make people weep (as radio does in the film)? Can we separate the radio from the effects that apparently only it can achieve? Is the power of the cinema, discreetly omitted in the film's treatment, not analogous? Is the magic of electronic technology merely the indispensable accompaniment, or instead the real and durable basis of a vibrant national community today, bypassing the impersonal monuments and writings, the domes and tomes, that no longer serve as the focal points of identity? If the mystification and worship of technology is involved here, as I believe it is, does this not become a criterion of membership, a factor that decides who belongs and who does not, whom we can have "real" and honest intimacy with, and who is excluded? In Rambha maushi's comment to Kishore Kale, above, we notice someone whose tacit social exclusion is reflected vividly on the cinema screen. As this worship of technology proceeds unchecked, and technology itself develops rapidly, it will perhaps only be around the ghosts of the past that the nation can imagine itself as united, despite all the power of cinema.

NOTES

1. See, e.g., Sumita Chakravarty, *National Identity in Popular Cinema 1947–1987* (Austin: University of Texas Press, 1994); Jyotika Virdi, *The Cinematic Imagination: Indian Popular Films as Social History* (New Brunswick, N.J.: Rutgers University Press, 2003).

2. See Nasreen Munni Kabir, *Talking Films: Conversations on Hindi Cinema with Javed Akhtar* (New York: Oxford University Press, 1999).

3. See Madhava Prasad, *The Ideology of the Hindi Film: A Historical Construction* (New Delhi: Oxford University Press, 1999).

4. See Aniket Jaaware, "Who Is It That Is Singing? Shot-Music-Speech." Paper presented at Jadavpur University Seminar, November 17–20, 2005. Also the essay by Natalie Sarrazin in this volume, and Lalitha Gopalan, *Cinema of Interruptions: Action Genres in Contemporary Indian Cinema* (London: British Film Institute, 2002).

5. For insights on how they do negotiate some of these issues, see, e.g., the essays in this volume by Kalyani Chadha and Anandam Kavoori, and by Parmesh Shahani.

6. See Fareed Kazmi, *The Politics of India's Conventional Cinema* (New Delhi: Sage, 1999).

7. For an example of the former, see Patricia Uberoi, "Imagining the Family: An Ethnography of Viewing Hum Aapke Hain Koun," in *Pleasure and the Nation: The History, Politics and Consumption of Public Culture in India*, ed. Rachel Dwyer and Christopher Pinney (New Delhi: Oxford University Press, 2001). For an example of the latter, see Sandeep Pendse, "Bombay's Satya and Satya's Bombay," in *Bombay: Metaphor for Modern India*, ed. Sujata Patel and Alice Thorner (New Delhi: Oxford University Press).

8. See, e.g., the essay by Punathambekar.

9. See Partha Chatterjee, *The Politics of the Governed: Reflections on Popular*

Politics in Most of the World. University Seminars/Leonard Hastings Schoff Memorial Lectures. (New York: Columbia University Press, 2004).

10. Spoken by Rambha *maushi,* in *Against All Odds* [in Marathi, *Kolhatyache Por,* Kolhati Boy, Granthali Publishers, 1994] by Kishore Shantabai Kale. Tr. Sandhya Pandey. (New Delhi: Penguin, 2000), p. 152. Although the statement is not dated, it was probably made in the 1980s or in the early 1990s at the latest.

11. It bears mention in this context that Sanjay Dutt spent several months in jail as a co-accused in the Bombay blast case of 1993, and was, in November 2006, sentenced to three years of rigorous imprisonment for possessing illegally acquired weapons during the anti-Muslim riots that preceded the blast. As the son of a Muslim mother (the actress Nargis), Sanjay Dutt claimed he had acted with a view to self-defense. Dutt is appealing his sentence. For an account of the Bombay blasts and the investigations following it, see S. Hussain Zaidi, *Black Friday: The True Story of the Bombay Bomb Blasts* (New Delhi: Penguin, 2003).

About the Contributors

Kalyani Chadha is director of AASFE and The Media, Self and Society program at the Philip Merrill College of Journalism at the University of Maryland, College Park, Maryland.

Bisakha Dutta is the author of *And Who Will Make the Chapatis* and director of a documentary film entitled *In the Flesh*. She is also program director of Point of View, a Mumbai-based not-for-profit organization that aims to promote the points of view of women through creative and sustained use of media, arts, and culture.

Rachel Dwyer is Professor of Indian Cultures and Cinema at SOAS, University of London. She has published several books, including *All You Want Is Money, All You Need Is Love: Sex and Romance in Modern India*; *Pleasure and the Nation: The History and Politics of Public Culture in India* (co-edited with Christopher Pinney); and *Cinema India: The Visual Culture of the Hindi Film* (co-authored with Divia Patel).

Tejaswini Ganti is Assistant Professor of Anthropology at New York University. She is author of *Bollywood: A Guidebook to Popular Hindi Cinema*.

Padma Govindan resides in Chennai, where she is the founder of the Shakti Center for Women's Reproductive and Sexual Health.

Vamsee Juluri is Associate Professor of Media Studies at the University of San Francisco and the author of *Becoming a Global Audience: Longing and Belonging in Indian Music Television*.

Anandam Kavoori is Associate Professor of International Communication in the Grady College of Journalism and Mass Communication at the University of Georgia. He is author of *Thinking Television*, and a novel, *The Children of Shahida*.

Shanti Kumar is Associate Professor in the Department of Radio-Television-Film at the University of Texas, Austin. He is author of *Gandhi Meets Primetime: Television and the Politics of Nationalism in Postcolonial India,* and co-editor of *Planet TV.*

Ananda Mitra is Professor of Communication and Director of the Survey Research Center at Wake Forest University, Winston-Salem, North Carolina. He is the author of *Television and Popular Culture in India* and *India through the Western Lens.*

Atticus Narain received his Ph.D. in Anthropology from Goldsmiths College, University of London. His dissertation examined Hindi film consumption and identity politics amongst Indo-Guyanese.

M. Madhava Prasad is Professor at the Center for European Studies, Central Institute of English and Foreign Languages, Hyderabad, India. He is author of *Ideology of the Hindi Film: A Historical Construction.*

Aswin Punathambekar is Assistant Professor in the Department of Communication Studies at the University of Michigan–Ann Arbor.

Ashish Rajadhyaksha is co-editor of *The Encyclopedia of Indian Cinema,* author of *Ritwik Ghatak: A Return to the Epic, The Sad and Glad of Kishore Kumar,* and a senior fellow at the Centre for the Study of Culture and Society, Bangalore, India.

Arvind Rajagopal is Professor in the Department of Culture and Communication, New York University. He is the author of *Politics after Television: Hindu Nationalism and the Reshaping of the Indian Public* and co-author of *Mapping Hegemony: Television News and Industrial Conflict.*

Natalie Sarazzin is Assistant Professor of Music, State University of New York, Brockport.

Parmesh Shahani is presently based in Bombay, India. He is the author of *Gay Bombay: Globalization, Love and (Be)longing in Contemporary India,* and is a columnist for *Man's World* magazine, India.

Daya Kishan Thussu is Professor of International Communication at the University of Westminster, London. Among his key publications are: *News as Entertainment: The Rise of Global Infotainment* and *Media on the Move: Global Flow and Contra-Flow.* He is the founder and managing editor of the Sage journal *Global Media and Communication.*

Jyotika Virdi is Associate Professor at the University of Windsor in Windsor, Ontario. She is the author of *The Cinematic ImagiNation: Indian Popular Films as Social History*.

Index